M000114011

Lady in the Dark

© Al Hirschfeld/Margo Feiden Galleries Ltd., New York. www.alhirschfeld.com.
Courtesy and permission of Al Hirschfeld/Margo Feiden Galleries Ltd., New York.

Lady in the Dark

Biography of a Musical

bruce d. mcclung

OXFORD

UNIVERSITY PRESS

OXFORD
UNIVERSITY PRESS

Oxford University Press, Inc., publishes works that further
Oxford University's objective of excellence
in research, scholarship, and education.

Oxford   New York
Auckland   Cape Town   Dar es Salaam   Hong Kong   Karachi
Kuala Lumpur   Madrid   Melbourne   Mexico City   Nairobi
New Delhi   Shanghai   Taipei   Toronto

With offices in
Argentina   Austria   Brazil   Chile   Czech Republic   France   Greece
Guatemala   Hungary   Italy   Japan   Poland   Portugal   Singapore
South Korea   Switzerland   Thailand   Turkey   Ukraine   Vietnam

Copyright © 2007 by Oxford University Press, Inc.

Published by Oxford University Press, Inc.
198 Madison Avenue, New York, New York 10016

www.oup.com

First issued as an Oxford University Press paperback, 2009

Oxford is a registered trademark of Oxford University Press.

All rights reserved. No part of this publication may be reproduced,
stored in a retrieval system, or transmitted, in any form or by any means,
electronic, mechanical, photocopying, recording, or otherwise,
without the prior permission of Oxford University Press.

Library of Congress Cataloging-in-Publication Data
McClung, Bruce D., 1961–
Lady in the dark: biography of a musical / by bruce d. mcclung.
p. cm.
Includes bibliographical references and index.
ISBN 978-0-19-538508-3

1. Weill, Kurt, 1900–1950. Lady in the dark.   2. Musicals—History and criticism.   I. Title.
ML410.W395M35 2006
792.6'42—dc22   2006003132

3   5   7   9   8   6   4   2

Printed in the United States of America
on acid-free paper

for Jerry

Had I the heavens' embroidered cloths,
Enwrought with golden and silver light,
The blue and the dim and the dark cloths
Of night and light and the half-light,
I would spread the cloths under your feet:
But I, being poor, have only my dreams;
I have spread my dreams under your feet;
Tread softly because you tread on my dreams.

—*Yeats*

Acknowledgments

My interest in the music of Kurt Weill in general and *Lady in the Dark* in particular stems from the inspired teaching of Professor Kim H. Kowalke, who advised my doctoral dissertation on *Lady in the Dark*. His knowledge of musical theater and all matters Weill has helped to clarify my ideas at nearly every turn.

I am grateful for the generous financial assistance of the organizations that enabled me to research and write a dissertation on this topic: an American Musicological Society Alvin H. Johnson AMS 50 Dissertation Fellowship, a Kurt Weill Foundation for Music Dissertation Fellowship, and a University of Cincinnati Brodie Doctoral Award. A University of Rochester Robert L. and Mary L. Sproull Fellowship made it possible for me to complete graduate studies at the Eastman School of Music.

The following institutions and their archivists, librarians, and specialists proved invaluable for my research: Billy Rose Theatre Collection, New York Public Library for the Performing Arts; Library of Congress (Wayne D. Shirley); Museum of the City of New York (Kathy Mets and Marty Jacobs); New York Public Library General Research Division; The Rodgers and Hammerstein Theatre Library (Ted Chapin and Tom Briggs); State Historical Society of Wisconsin (Joanne Hohler); Weill/Lenya Archive, The Beinecke Rare Book Library (Kendall Crilly); Weill-Lenya Research Center (David Farneth and Dave Stein); and the Wisconsin Center for Film and Theater Research. Queries were answered by Leonore "Lee" Gershwin, Kitty Carlisle Hart, David Hummel, Sylvia Fine Kaye, Miles Kreuger, and Donald Mitchell.

The *New York Times Book Review* helped my research immeasurably by running an author's query for *Lady in the Dark*'s original cast members. Ten members of the company responded and graciously gave interviews: Rose

Marie Elliott (Brown), who played Ruthie on tour; Dan Harden, Ben for the tryout and first and second seasons; Fred Hearn, dance corps member for the tryout and first season; Manfred Hecht, Chorus member for the tryout and first season; Christine Horn (Perrone), dance corps member on tour; Ann Lee (Harris), Miss Stevens for the tryout and first and second seasons, and Alison Du Bois on tour; William Marel, Chorus member for the tryout and first and second seasons; Carl Nicholas, Chorus understudy for first season and Chorus member for the second season; Fred Perrone, Chorus member on tour, Baltimore to San Francisco; and Frank Spencer, second assistant stage manager, tryout and first and second seasons.

For musical insights, I am grateful to Maestro Maurice Abravanel, musical director and conductor for all of *Lady in the Dark*'s performances, whose interest in this study was a source of encouragement from the very beginning and who consented to several interviews. In addition, Lys Symonette, who began working as Weill's rehearsal pianist after *Lady in the Dark*, answered questions regarding the composer's working methods and the milieu of 1940s Broadway. Serving as a consultant for productions of *Lady in the Dark* for City Center's *Encores!* Series and the Royal National Theatre afforded me the experience of working in the theater. For such opportunities on both sides of the pond, I wish to thank Judith Daykin and Rob Fisher at City Center and Diane Benjamin, Kevin Lehman, and Mark Dorrell at the National Theatre.

I am happy to acknowledge the following individuals who assisted me in obtaining photographic reproductions and to the copyright holders that granted me permission to reprint them: Alfred Publishing Co. (Kathy Gutstein); The Beinecke Rare Book Library, Yale University (Karen Nangle); Center for Creative Photography, University of Arizona (Denise Gosé and Diane Nilsen); Culver Pictures (Eva C. Tucholka and Harriet Culver); Gallery 47, New York (Ken Leach); Ira and Leonore Gershwin Trusts (Mark Trent Goldberg); Irving S. Gilmore Music Library, Yale University (Suzanne Eggleston Lovejoy); Library of Congress (Susan Poxon); Margo Feiden Galleries (Daria Enrick); Museum of the City of New York (Marguerite Lavin); National Archives; National Museum of the Air Force (Brett Stolle); New York Public Library (Jeremy Megraw and Stephan Saks); *Time* magazine (Kelley Gately); Treadway Gallery (David Kalonick); Richard Tucker Estate (Julia Tucker); Carl Van Vechten Estate (Bruce Kellner); Warner Brothers (Jeremy Laws and Roni Lubliner); Warner Bros. Publications U.S. (Hope Chirino); Wisconsin Center for Film and Theater Research (Ben R. Brewster and Dorinda Hartmann); and the Kurt Weill Foundation for Music (Carolyn Weber). Grants from the University of

Cincinnati Research Council, College-Conservatory of Music (CCM) Dean Douglas Lowry, and Friends of CCM defrayed the expense for these reproductions and permissions.

For a biography of a musical about an editor who cannot make up her mind, I am thankful to my first editor at Oxford University Press, Maribeth Anderson Payne, who made up her mind to publish this book. In the interim, Kim Robinson shepherded it through various stages. Helpful with production have been assistant editors Soo Mee Kwon, Eve Bachrach, and Norman Hirschy, in addition to Jessica Ryan and Judith Hoover.

A sabbatical leave from the University of Cincinnati allowed me the time to draft six of the chapters. I am grateful to Kim Kowalke for commenting on early versions of all eight chapters, the three anonymous reviewers whose ideas and suggestions helped shape the final narrative, and Barbara McClung, Edward Nowacki, and Mary Watkins who proofed the completed manuscript. Finally, the critical eye and sunny disposition of my research assistant, Laura Eddleman, made the last year of revisions a pleasure. I wish to thank her for checking citations, assisting with permissions and reproductions, and preparing the book's index.

Jerry DeFilipps has been an understanding and supportive partner, patiently living with *Lady in the Dark* for the past nineteen years.

Contents

Illustrations appear after page 102

Credits

Front cover: photo "Gertrude Lawrence, *Lady in the Dark*, ca. 1940" by Louise Dahl-Wolfe, courtesy and permission of the Collection Center for Creative Photography, University of Arizona © 1989 Arizona Board of Regents; Endpaper illustrations: courtesy and permission of © Al Hirschfeld/ Margo Feiden Galleries Ltd., New York; Figures 1, 2, 5–7, 9–13, 15, 16, 19– 21, 23–25, 41, and 42: photos by Vandamm Studio, courtesy and permission of Billy Rose Theatre Collection, The New York Public Library for the Performing Arts, Astor, Lenox and Tilden Foundations; Figure 3: photo by Richard Tucker, courtesy of the Weill-Lenya Research Center, Kurt Weill Foundation for Music, New York, and permission of Julia Tucker; Figures 4, 14, and 22: courtesy and permission of Culver Pictures; Figure 8: photo by Vandamm Studio, courtesy of Wisconsin Center for Film and Theater Research and permission of Billy Rose Theatre Collection, The New York Public Library for the Performing Arts, Astor, Lenox and Tilden Foundations; Figure 17: photo by Vandamm Studio, courtesy of The Museum of the City of New York and permission of The Museum of the City of New York and Billy Rose Theatre Collection, The New York Public Library for the Performing Arts, Astor, Lenox and Tilden Foundations; Figures 18, 26, and 28: photos courtesy of The Kurt Weill and Lotte Lenya Papers, Irving S. Gilmore Music Library, Yale University and permission of the Kurt Weill Foundation for Music, New York; Figure 27: courtesy of the Library of Congress and permission of Leonore S. Gershwin 1987 Trust; Figures 29–36: courtesy of *Theatre Arts* and Billy Rose Theatre Collection, The New York Public Library for the Performing Arts, Astor, Lenox and Tilden Foundations; Figure 37: photos by Vandamm Studio and courtesy of *Look* magazine and David Kalonick; Figure 38: courtesy and permission of *Time* magazine

© 1941 Time Inc. Reprinted by permission; Figures 39 and 40: photos courtesy of the Weill-Lenya Research Center, Kurt Weill Foundation for Music, New York, and permission of Warner Bros. Publications U.S. Inc.; Figure 43: courtesy of the National Archives and Records Administration, Still Picture Branch; Figure 44: photo by David Kalonick and courtesy of Leach/Peters Collection, Gallery 47, New York; Figures 45 and 46: photos by Carl Van Vechten, courtesy of Carl Van Vechten Collection, Yale Collection of American Literature, The Beinecke Rare Book and Manuscript Library and permission of Van Vechten Trust; Figures 47–49: photos courtesy of the Weill-Lenya Research Center, Kurt Weill Foundation for Music, New York, and permission of Universal Studios Licensing LLLP; Figure 50: photo by David Kalonick; Back cover: photo by Vandamm Studio, courtesy and permission of Wisconsin Center for Film and Theater Research and Billy Rose Theatre Collection, The New York Public Library for the Performing Arts, Astor, Lenox and Tilden Foundations.

All lyrics courtesy and permission of *Lady in the Dark*, by Ira Gershwin and Kurt Weill © 1941 (Renewed) Ira Gershwin Music and Hampshire House Pub. Co. All Rights on Behalf of Ira Gershwin Music Administered by WB Music Corp. All Rights Reserved. Used by Permission. Warner Bros. Publications U.S. Inc., Miami, FL 33014.

Prologue

This is a biography of the legendary Broadway musical Lady in the Dark. Featuring an original script by Moss Hart, it dramatizes a woman undergoing psychoanalysis. The musical score, by Kurt Weill with lyrics by Ira Gershwin, comprises dream sequences, dreams that the psychiatrist in the play analyzes. In the hybrid form of a "musical play," spoken dialogue represents the heroine's consciousness, and the musical sequences her unconscious. The manner in which music signals the transition from her drab business life to her fantastic dream world is analogous to the juxtaposition of black-and-white with Technicolor® in The Wizard of Oz.

The production introduced a young nightclub entertainer named Danny Kaye and starred Gertrude Lawrence. Opening in 1941, Lady in the Dark played two seasons and then toured the country with a New York reengagement, for a total of 777 performances. The rush for seats helped to establish the practice of advance sales on Broadway, and the amount Paramount Pictures paid for film rights set a new record.

Lady in the Dark's subject matter was controversial and its form revolutionary. The therapeutic directive that Hart finish the play came from his own psychiatrist, and Hart dramatized one of the doctor's theories. In return, the psychiatrist promoted Lady in the Dark and even cited it in his published work. Hart based his plot on the Freudian allegory of a woman choosing among three men, representing the roles of father, lover, and husband. Music provided the key to the story: when the heroine is able to remember a childhood song and the events tied to it, her neuroses are brought to light and her tangled love life straightens itself out. That Lady in the Dark was conceived to be a didactic work, without any subplot or secondary love triangle, was also innovative. All aspects of the production reflected the topic of psychoanalysis: the plot, script, music, lyrics, and even the set, prop, and costume designs. In this way, *Lady in the Dark* foreshadowed the concept musical and such shows as *Company*, *A Chorus Line*, and *Chicago*.

So why don't we know more about *Lady in the Dark*? One reason is that its reassessment of the relationship between music and drama was unrepeatable. Even if it could have been imitated, the American musical theater took a very different turn while *Lady in the Dark* was on the boards. Another reason is that the work was so contemporary and specific to the times that much of its dialogue no longer packs the same punch. Additionally, *Lady in the Dark* is a difficult show to cast: the Herculean title role demands a legitimate actress who can carry dramatic scenes *and* stop the show cold with her singing and dancing. Finally, *Lady in the Dark* was a blockbuster musical: with a cast of fifty-five, a stage crew of forty-one, and five stage managers (plus an orchestra of twenty), the cost of producing it today on a similar scale would be prohibitive.

Although a few anecdotes about the show are part of Broadway lore, this book reconstructs *Lady in the Dark* through a variety of sources; miraculously, most have survived. Hart retained his typescripts for the play, Weill his sketches of the score, and Gershwin his worksheets for the libretto. The leading lady's scrapbooks contain more than twenty-three hundred articles, reviews, and features. Her business manager saved her contracts and script with much of the original blocking and costume changes. Some of the production scripts, designs for the sets and costumes, and original orchestral parts also survive. Helping to round out the picture are a complete run of the playbills, extensive correspondence, and memoirs. Nine of the original cast members, in addition to an assistant stage manager and the musical director, contributed interviews for this biography.

These interviews and sources enable us to relive opening night, not only what happened on stage, but what went on backstage, in the orchestra pit, and out front in the lobby. Production stills chronicle important scenes and enable us to see firsthand the actors, costumes, properties, and sets. With an integrated plot summary, we come to experience the importance of the occasion and the work itself. How such an experimental and daring show came to be comprises the story of its genesis, from the playwright's psychological demons to the process by which a European-trained composer and an American-bred lyricist reconciled their different working methods.

Lady in the Dark's musical score is certainly one of its outstanding features. Although confined to self-contained dream sequences, the score sprawled across more than two thousand measures. Weill described the sequences as "three little one-act operas," Hart called them "veritable *Traviatas*," and

Gershwin filled more pages with lyrics than he had for any previous show.[1] Weill came up with a number of musical analogies for Hart's drama, so that the score ingeniously resolves itself just as the lady escapes the darkness of her past. Small wonder the *New York Times* drama critic crowned Weill "the best writer of theatre music in the country."[2]

The production breathed life into *Lady in the Dark* in a way that the creators could not have imagined. From a tryout in Boston through the Broadway seasons to the tour, each period faced its own set of challenges, setbacks, and breakthroughs. In Boston, the show was saved at the eleventh hour by a series of events that would make theatrical history. On Broadway, the leading lady's British war-relief activities first threatened to close the show prematurely. However, after Pearl Harbor, the production played a seminal role in benefit activities. On tour, the production crisscrossed the country and, despite cutbacks and rationing, smashed attendance records.

That the United States changed so radically from *Lady in the Dark*'s genesis to its final performance brings into relief how forward-thinking the show had been. It came at the end of a difficult decade for Broadway: the Great Depression had diminished investors' capital for new shows, Hollywood lured away the most talented writing teams, the economy drove down ticket prices, and the talkies gave live entertainment a run for its money. Nevertheless, *Lady in the Dark*'s creators took bold risks. They sought to address such timely issues as the role of women in the workplace, the validity of psychoanalysis, and the problem of delayed marriage. By understanding *Lady in the Dark*'s original context, one comes to appreciate why it was so quickly overshadowed by *Oklahoma!* and how vividly social history can be read through the lens of the American musical theater.

Although a Broadway revival has eluded *Lady in the Dark*, the show has had a number of reincarnations outside the theater (the Paramount film starring Ginger Rogers, a radio play with Judy Garland, the television special featuring Ann Sothern, a benefit concert with Angela Lansbury, and Julie Andrews's film *Star!*). Though seldom produced in the usual stock and amateur venues, the musical play has shown remarkable longevity. In addition to recordings by Danny Kaye and Gertrude Lawrence, there is a studio album with Risë Stevens and a recent National Theatre (London) cast recording. Whether on shellac, vinyl, or compact disc, or on radio, film, or television, all have had to solve the problems of revival. Regardless of their individual success or failure, collectively they have kept the legend of *Lady in the Dark* alive.

This biography begins in a New York theater and ends in a Chicago train station. The theater is still standing and in 1983 was renamed the Neil Simon.

It had been the brainchild of producers Alex Aarons and Vinton Freedley, who teamed up to produce some of the memorable musicals of the 1920s, including George and Ira Gershwin's *Lady, Be Good!*, *Tip-Toes*, and *Oh, Kay!* In anticipation of producing their fourth Gershwin show, Aarons and Freedley decided to build their own theater in the middle of a block between Broadway and Eighth. They employed the Shubert's principal architect, Herbert J. Krapp, whose design featured a colonial revival facade finished in marble and terra cotta. Taking the first few letters of the producers' first names (ALex and VINton), the builders christened it the Alvin.

Past the outer lobby of black marble and the unadorned inner lobby, the theater's interior radiated pastel tones of blue, ivory, and gray, blended with old gold and studded with mulberry hangings. A delicately tinted mural graced the twenty-five-foot-high proscenium. The architect, who was known for being able to stuff the maximum number of people into the minimum amount of space, filled the Alvin with 1,376 seats. The stairway to the balcony ascended from the inner lobby rather than from the back of the theater so as to minimize disturbance to patrons in the expensive seats. Although the architect often had to skimp on amenities in favor of seating, the Alvin boasted an Old English lounge, "done in ivory and carved oak, with a great fireplace."[3]

The house was designed specifically for large musical entertainments and features an ample orchestra pit, a thirty-five-by-one-hundred-foot stage, a sixty-eight-foot-high gridiron, twenty dressing rooms, and a large rehearsal hall. Fred Astaire and his sister, Adele, opened the Alvin in 1927 with *Funny Face*. In the ensuing years, the theater saw its share of flops (*Treasure Girl* with Gertrude Lawrence) and hits (*Girl Crazy* with Ethel Merman). With the onset of the Depression, Aarons and Freedley lost the theater and dissolved their partnership.[4] Freedley continued to produce at the Alvin (under the ownership of its builders), scoring success again with Ethel Merman in Cole Porter's *Anything Goes*.

Tonight, however, is the opening of *Lady in the Dark*.

SAM H. HARRIS
presents

GERTRUDE LAWRENCE

in
A Musical Play

LADY IN THE DARK

by
MOSS HART

Lyrics by
IRA GERSHWIN

Music by
KURT WEILL

Production and Lighting by
HASSARD SHORT

Choreography by ALBERTINA RASCH   Musical Direction by MAURICE ABRAVANEL

Settings Designed by HARRY HORNER

Costumes Designed by IRENE SHARAFF   Gowns Designed by HATTIE CARNEGIE

Play Staged by Mr. HART

CAST

DR. BROOKS	DONALD RANDOLPH
MISS BOWERS	JEANNE SHELBY
LIZA ELLIOTT	GERTRUDE LAWRENCE
MISS FOSTER	EVELYN WYCKOFF
MISS STEVENS	ANN LEE
MAGGIE GRANT	MARGARET DALE
ALISON DU BOIS	NATALIE SCHAFER
RUSSELL PAXTON	DANNY KAYE
CHARLEY JOHNSON	MACDONALD CAREY
RANDY CURTIS	VICTOR MATURE
	Courtesy Hal Roach Studio Inc.
JOE, an office boy	WARD TALLMON
TOM, an office boy	NELSON BARCLIFT
KENDALL NESBITT	BERT LYTELL
HELEN, a model	VIRGINIA PEINE
RUTHIE, a model	GEDDA PETRY
CAROL, a model	PATRICIA DEERING
MARCIA, a model	MARGARET WESTBERG
BEN BUTLER	DAN HARDEN
BARBARA	ELEANOR EBERLE
JACK	DAVIS CUNNINGHAM

THE ALBERTINA RASCH GROUP DANCERS:
Dorothy Bird, Audrey Costello, Patricia Deering, June MacLaren, Beth Nichols, Wana Wenerholm, Margaret Westberg.
Jerome Andrews, Nelson Barclift, George Bockman, Andre Charise, Fred Hearn, Yaroslav Kirov, Parker Wilson.

THE SINGERS:
Catherine Conrad, Jean Cumming, Carol Deis, Hazel Edwards, Gedda Petry, June Rutherford, Florence Wyman.
Davis Cunningham, Max Edwards, Len Frank, Gordon Gifford, Manfred Hecht, William Marel, Larry Siegle, Harold Simmons.

THE CHILDREN:
Anne Bracken, Sally Ferguson, Ellie Lawes, Joan Lawes, Jacqueline Macmillan, Lois Volkman.
Kenneth Casey, Warren Mills, Robert Mills, Robert Lee, George Ward, William Welch.

THE SCENES

ACT I.

Scene 1—Dr. Brooks' Office.

Scene 2—Liza Elliott's Office. (The same day.)

Scene 3—Dr. Brooks' Office. (The next day.)

Scene 4—Liza Elliott's Office. (Late that afternoon.)

ACT II.

Scene 1—Liza Elliott's Office. (Late the following afternoon.)

Scene 2—Dr. Brooks' Office. (Later that evening.)

Scene 3—Liza Elliott's Office. (A week later.)

THE MUSIC

ACT I.

1. "Oh Fabulous One In Your Ivory Tower" . . . . Liza Elliott's Serenaders
2. "The World's Inamorata" . . . . Liza and her maid
3. "One Life to Live" . . . . Liza and her chauffeur
4. "Girl of the Moment" . . . . Ensemble
5. "It Looks Like Liza" . . . . Entire Company
6. Mapleton High Choral . . . . The High School Graduates
7. "This is New" . . . . Randy Curtis and Liza
8. "The Princess of Pure Delight" . . . . Liza and Children
9. "This Woman at the Altar" . . . . Entire Company

ACT II.

1. "The Greatest Show On Earth" . . . . Ringmaster and Ensemble
2. Dance of the Tumblers . . . . Albertina Rasch Dancers
3. "The Best Years Of His Life" . . . . Charley Johnson and Randy Curtis
4. "Tschaikowsky" . . . . Ringmaster and Ensemble
5. "The Saga of Jenny" . . . . Liza, Jury and Ensemble
6. "My Ship" . . . . Liza

All orchestrations and vocal arrangements by Mr. Weill.
All musical sequences staged by Mr. Short.

Lady in the Dark

1

Opening Night

Outside the theater on West Fifty-second, autograph seekers and the police guard are out in full force. The impressive opening-night audience includes theater and film personalities, as well as society matrons with their escorts. The top ticket price is $6.60, but some seats are reportedly selling on the street for $100 a pair.[1] The box office has notified all ticket holders to be in the theater by 8:30 P.M. and warned that there will be no seating during the important first scene.

Among those passing through the marbled lobby are the creative team and relatives of the cast: playwright Moss Hart (with psychiatrist in tow), lyricist Ira Gershwin, composer Kurt Weill, choreographer Albertina Rasch, and Gertrude Lawrence's husband and daughter. Drama critics for New York's nine dailies slip through the throng, while fashion reporters take note of the dresses, furs, and jewelry. There is costume designer Irene Sharaff in a strapless black taffeta gown with a big rose at the bosom, danseuse Tilly Losch with a long lynx coat and white gown, and socialite Mrs. Bill Hearst sporting a blazing diamond.[2] All of them cause heads to turn.

Down at the stage door, piles of telegrams stamped Thursday, January 23, 1941, await the nervous company. Those addressed to the composer have been sent by Russel Crouse, Vernon Duke, Rose Gershwin, Moss Hart, George S. Kaufman, Gertrude Lawrence, Vincente Minnelli, and Dorothy and Richard Rodgers. Hart's cable makes reference to the show's beginnings (CAN YOU HAVE LUNCH WITH ME AT THE HAPSBURG TO-MORROW?), Kaufman's to its central song (YOUR SHIP HAS SAILS THAT ARE MADE OF GOLD RELAX), and Lawrence's to the American pronunciation of the composer's name (BLESS YOU KURT MON

3

PETIT CHOUX LET'S STAY TOGETHER FOR A NICE LONG WEILL).

The longest greeting in the stack, however, is a letter from the playwright to his leading lady. In it Hart thanks Lawrence for her performance, without which the production would have been impossible, and for helping him "to recapture that sense of wonder and excitement [he] came into the theater with." It concludes, "Win, lose, or draw—I want you to know that a nervous author thinks you're wonderful."[3]

The Alvin, perfumed with its hallmark Prince Matchabelli's Royal Gardenia, is packed as the house lights dim on *Lady in the Dark*. The musical begins in silence to give the impression of a straight play—hence, no overture to cover the seating of latecomers.

Act I, Scene 1

The curtain rises to reveal a psychiatrist's office with bookshelves flanking a central doorway and a couple of side chairs. Floor-to-ceiling draperies frame a bank of windows stage left. Sunlight streams through these windows, reaching small potted plants resting on the sills and the analyst's couch. To the far stage right stands a door, by its plain appearance apparently a private entrance for the psychiatrist. Dr. Brooks (played by Donald Randolph) sits at a small desk signing letters.

After a brief exchange between the doctor and his secretary (Jeanne Shelby), the title character, Liza Elliott, makes a subdued entrance, stage center, dressed entirely in dark brown. The austere outfit, a business suit with shirt jacket, is a curious one for a glamorous star.[4] She wears no earrings or necklace, and brown gloves cover her hands. Remarkably, there is neither buildup nor an opening chorus to announce her arrival. Instead, the audience barely realizes that Gertrude Lawrence has taken the stage before she begins to speak (Figure 1).

Liza is the editor of a women's fashion magazine, *Allure*, and currently lives with an older married man, the publisher of her magazine. Her symptoms? Depression and anxiety. During a staff meeting the previous day, she had thrown a paperweight at her advertising manager, Charley Johnson, and then had broken down. Dr. Brooks convinces an apprehensive Liza to embark upon a trial period of analysis. He then seats himself at the head of the couch and asks her to speak whatever comes to mind (Figure 2).

Prompted by this exercise of free association, Liza is surprised when the vague memory of a childhood song surfaces. Dr. Brooks inquires as to when she last thought of it. She hesitates: "Last night. I knew I was coming here this morning—and it frightened me. The song kept running through my head. Over and over. Then I fell asleep—and the song was in the dream, too. Now that I think of it, the song is always there when I dream. It changes— but the music is always there."[5]

Although Liza cannot remember the words to the song, Dr. Brooks urges her to hum the melody. Two mournful notes on a clarinet initiate her recollection. (As Lawrence hums the first phrase of "My Ship," an electrician dims the lights, and by the end of the phrase, the stage is dark. Unbeknown to the audience, the set of the psychiatrist's office bridges two turntables. Before the turntables begin to move, stagehands behind the bookcases pull them backward, breaking the office in two. An assistant stage manager leads Lawrence safely off the stage-left turntable. Four stagehands working in pairs on opposite sides of that turntable mechanically turn it counterclockwise.) Meanwhile, the full orchestra has picked up the melody, played first by the 'cellos and saxophones, next by the flute and oboe, and finally by the trumpets, each in a new key and louder than the previous.

(Backstage, Lawrence has reached a portable dressing room stage left where she will have less than two minutes to change into a strapless evening gown designed by Hattie Carnegie, "America's First Lady of Fashion." The skirt of periwinkle blue is composed of small ostrich plumes, concealed by a lace coat fastened with a jeweled heart. Quickly a dresser helps her put on a red wig.)

The turntables have now rejoined and support a twenty-foot-high wall, composed of deep-blue accordion folds, which are frosted yet sparkly. Sliding portals have expanded the width of the stage. One of the small turntables set inside the large ones turns to reveal a lace- and glass-like confection suggesting an apartment entrance. The lights come up to bathe the stage in blue.[6] The scene change has occurred without a curtain and taken less than a minute (a ripple of marvels). Collectively, we have entered Liza's dream.

Eight men in royal blue suits enter in pairs and carry transparent lyres. They serenade Liza and compare their devotion to a famous pair of lovers:

Oh, Fabulous One in your ivory tower—
My heart and I, they both agree:
What Juliet was to Romeo
    Are you to me . . . .[7]

Liza's maid, Sutton (Evelyn Wyckoff), appears in the apartment doorway and informs the serenaders that Liza is resting. The men doff their hats and depart with a brief musical reprise. As the orchestra swells with the glamour theme, lights flash and Liza's boudoir appears.

(Meanwhile, the windows behind the couch in the psychiatrist's office open to give stagehands access to the small stage-left turntable. They bring a set of boudoir properties through this opening: a couch, mirror, and three perfume bottles. Designer Harry Horner has fashioned the props out of the latest wonder plastics.[8] Wyckoff also enters through this passage, to be whirled onto the stage as lights begin to flash again.)

The maid's entrance is nearly instantaneous. At each sound of a doorbell, a delivery boy brings gifts from Liza's admirers: first a coat of sable then a flower from His Royal Highness, the French Pretender. Beekman, the chauffeur (Danny Kaye), interrupts to sing a duet with Sutton in praise of Liza's clothes. In contrast to the pervasive blue, he is dressed in a yellow uniform with red gloves and matching boots, both with leopard trim. Sutton and Beekman wax poetic for an outrageous rhyme:

> When as in silks our Liza goes
> Then, then, methinks how sweetly flows
> The liquefaction of her clothes—
> The liquefaction of her clothes . . . .
>
> A delicate poem by Herrick—
> But, surely, heavier than a derrick
> Compared to our Miss Liza—she's so glamorous
> She makes all other women appear Hammacher Schlammorous[9]

(Lawrence, who has been waiting to enter behind the scenery, is going through one of her theatrical rituals: sucking on a red mint so that her tongue will match the color of her lips. Ready to go on, she sticks it on the back of the scenery.)[10] Beekman apologizes to Sutton: "A thousand pardons—I must quit the scene / I must be off to perfume the gasoline." The glamour theme prompts Liza's entrance; she is now dressed in brilliant blue—an appropriately lavish outfit for the star's entrance, albeit belated. In response to Liza's inquiry about messages, Sutton sings a number ("The World's Inamorata") that enumerates them all:

> Huxley wants to dedicate his book to you
>   And Stravinsky his latest sonata.
> Seven Thousand students say they look to you
>   To be at the Yale-Harvard Regatta.

Epstein says you simply have to pose for him.
   Here's the key to the Island of Tobago.
Du Pont wants you wearing the new hose for him.
   Can you christen a battleship in San Diego?

(Several audience members turn to acknowledge Igor Stravinsky, who is seated in the theater.)[11] Liza sings a reprise with Sutton, bids her good-bye, and as the lights dim, the orchestra plays a waltz version of "The World's In-amorata" fortissimo. Liza dances in a spotlight until she discovers Beekman.

He stands at attention, eyes forward. The music stops, he speaks: "I learned it would be blue tonight. So I'm driving the blue Duesenburg with the blue license plates and I've put the blue Picasso in the car." Both enter the vehicle, constructed from plastic, to motor to the Seventh Heaven, a nightclub. First a green light flashes, then a red one. (Meanwhile, the large turntables have been moved counterclockwise and the small ones moved one-sixth of a revolution in the opposite direction.) Beekman stops, and Liza gets out to make a speech on a blue soapbox. Her opening number ("One Life to Live") projects a carefree attitude:

I say to me ev'ry morning:
You've only one life to live,
   So why be done in?
   Let's let the sun in
And gloom can jump in the riv'!

After Liza and Beekman perform a short dance, they return to the car. Green lights flash, and suddenly the nightclub and its patrons appear. (Each of the two large turntables holds thirteen members of the combined Chorus and dance corps, outfitted in elegant evening wear. During the flashing lights, the car and its occupants had been whirled behind a blue wall via a small turntable while a fanciful gate with "7th Heaven" appeared. Back-stage, Lawrence is helped out of the coat to reveal the gown.)

After a foxtrot (performed by the Albertina Rasch Dancers), Liza makes her entrance stage center, accompanied by the glamour theme. The Chorus and dancers sing an ode to her beauty (Figure 3):

Oh, girl of the moment
With the smile of the day
And the charm of the week
And the grace of the month

And the looks of the year—
Oh, girl of the moment,
You're my moment
Ev'ry moment of the time.

During the number, Liza dances with the club's headwaiter, Pierre (Bert Lytell).

A bugle call interrupts, and a soldier, sailor, and marine enter upstage center in pastel uniforms (Dan Harden, Max Edwards, and Macdonald Carey, respectively). The marine announces that Liza's portrait is to be painted and her likeness used on the new two-cent stamp.[12] The soldier and sailor go offstage and return with an oversized postage-stamp canvas, a palette, and brushes. While the marine pantomimes painting, the Chorus sings "Girl of the Moment" in the style of a chorale (Figure 4).

The marine announces that the portrait is finished. The painting shocks and surprises: instead of depicting Liza attired in the gown she's wearing, it portrays her as she was in the psychiatrist's office: "austere, somewhat for-bidding, entirely without glamour." She recoils from the portrait, and an oboe and violin eerily play a snippet of the childhood song. Liza screams and runs through the crowd.

The Chorus mocks Liza, whose hands cover her face, by singing "Girl of the Moment" as a rumba. Offbeats displace the text and destroy its illusory meaning:

My dreams are torn asunder.
    Your image I drew.
I see you now and wonder
    What I saw in you.

The lights slowly dim, with one spot remaining on Liza crying. When the lights suddenly come up, she is miraculously back in the psychiatrist's office. The audience gasp is audible.

(Actually, Lawrence had kept running offstage, and a body double, Virginia Peine, wearing the same wig and ostrich-plume dress, had taken her place. During the rumba, Lawrence had changed back into her brown suit, removed the wig, and lay down on the couch with Randolph still seated in his chair. As the lights dimmed, the large turntables spun and the sliding portals reduced the size of the stage.)

Dr. Brooks remarks that in her dream, Liza appears to be the complete opposite of her waking self. In reality, he tells her, she is a woman who cares very little for "feminine adornments," but in her fantasy she is "the epitome of the glamorous woman." Dr. Brooks finds this ironic in that Liza has dedicated herself to telling *other* women how to be beautiful through her fashion magazine. Liza questions what all this means, but Dr. Brooks suggests that they will find out through psychoanalysis. Liza rises slowly from the couch and retrieves her hat and gloves, evidently still mulling over what he has said. She says good-bye and walks quickly through the central doorway. The lights dim.

Act I, Scene 2

(The large turntables unite once again to form the two halves of an office; instead of Dr. Brooks's, it is Liza's office at *Allure*.) When the lights come up, we see an office befitting the editor of a successful fashion magazine. Banded across the wall stage left are mock-up covers, and series of layouts hang from hooks. (All were borrowed from *Vogue*; the fashion police in the audience are scribbling notes.)[13] Liza's massive desk is accompanied by a large and heavy chair. There are two doors: a leather-bound public door off-center next to a couch and a plain private entrance downstage left. With the linoleum floor and oak paneling, the room is impressive—but cold.

Liza's secretary, Miss Foster, stands behind the desk. (Some in the audience recognize that she is Evelyn Wyckoff, the actress who played the maid in Liza's *Glamour Dream*.) Miss Foster tells the caller on the other end of the phone, Kendall Nesbitt (Bert Lytell), *Allure*'s publisher and Liza's live-in lover, that Liza is not in yet. We know that her late arrival is occasioned by her session with Dr. Brooks.

Miss Stevens (Ann Lee), *Allure*'s receptionist, rushes in to announce that Hollywood idol Randy Curtis has arrived for a photo shoot. Maggie Grant (Margaret Dale) interrupts the chatter. As the matronly member of *Allure*'s staff, she responds to Miss Stevens's palpitations about Randy Curtis, "Give up, dear. Even if you could have it, it's poison." Miss Stevens quips, "It's a lovely way to die, though."

Liza hurries through the stage-left door. After receiving her telephone messages from Miss Foster, Liza tells Maggie about her visit to the psychiatrist. Maggie is curious, but skeptical, referring to Dr. Brooks as the Wizard of Oz (Figure 5). Liza confides that he told her something staggering at the end of her session, but their conversation is cut short by the entrance of Alison Du Bois (Natalie Schafer), *Allure*'s madcap columnist. Alison's outfit is outrageous: string upon string of yellow necklaces, a red dress with matching hat, and a muff that looks, according to a wag in the press, like "the rump end of a Texas Holstein steer."[14] To those in the know, the necklaces and red dress are dead giveaways: the character is a send-up of Diana Vreeland, fashion editor for *Harper's Bazaar* (Figure 6).

Alison demands that Liza hear her idea of having the Easter issue "lay an egg" (by including a small insert). Liza is unimpressed. Alison's departure coincides with the arrival of Russell Paxton, *Allure*'s staff photographer. (It begins to dawn on the audience that Liza's coworkers inhabit her dreams, but in different roles. We recognize him as Beekman, the chauffeur.) Russell ceremoniously announces the arrival of Randy Curtis: "Girls, he's God-like! . . . I've taken pictures of beautiful men, but this one is the end—the *end!* . . . He's got a face that would melt in your mouth." (Danny Kaye's delivery of the campy lines elicits guffaws from the audience.)

On his heels comes advertising manager Charley Johnson (Macdonald Carey, the marine in Liza's dream). Although suffering a hangover, he is still a charmer in his herringbone suit. He makes an unwelcome and un-likely pass at Maggie: "Want a wet kiss?" Liza has no time for Charley, but before she can send him away, Russell returns with Randy Curtis in tow.

Nearly everyone on stage is in an uproar over the handsome movie star modeling a polo outfit. (In a case of shrewd typecasting, he is played by matinee idol Victor Mature.) Liza, however, is unfazed. She does not even remember the occasion when she had first met him. Randy persists, "At Mrs. Bracketts—about a year ago. I took you home, in fact. Don't you remember that? We sat in the car talking." Maggie deadpans, "Want to take *me* home some night, Mr. Curtis?—*I'll* remember!" Liza tries to save face by offering to have a drink with him that evening, but Randy is returning to the West Coast. Instead, they agree to have dinner next time he's in New York (Figure 7).

Charley, smarting from not being able to talk to Liza, takes advantage of the situation. He insincerely asks Randy for his autograph, much to the annoyance of Russell (Figure 8). Randy scribbles his signature before Russell escorts him to the photo shoot. After Maggie departs, Liza tries to apologize to Charley for yesterday's paperweight incident. He makes light of her gesture, and Liza explodes: "Look here, Johnson. I don't like you. I never have. Your so-called charm has always eluded me, and I am repelled by what you consider amusing, such as that little episode with Mr. Curtis just now. . . . Suppose in the future you confine your remarks to your work. If you don't think you can do that perhaps you can make a pleasanter ar-rangement elsewhere." Charley gets in the last word by whistling through his teeth, a habit known to irritate Liza.

As Charley exits, Kendall Nesbitt enters (played by Bert Lytell, the headwaiter in Liza's dream). Fiftyish, he dresses the part of a successful businessman; his face, however, has a soft, weak quality. Kendall is worried about Liza, but he brings important news. His wife has agreed to a divorce, which will clear the way for their engagement (Figure 9). Liza falters and appears almost to faint. Kendall tries to persuade her to go home, but she insists on staying. She agrees, however, to join him later for dinner. Miss Foster interrupts to announce "Mr. Randy Curtis." He has changed out of the polo outfit and now wears a suit. Travel plans have changed, and Randy offers to take Liza up on her dinner invitation. Although now unavailable, she accepts his invitation for the following night and nervously lights a cigarette.

After Randy leaves and Kendall excuses himself, Liza stands quite still and then crushes out her cigarette. The news of Kendall's impending divorce and his marriage proposal have thrown her for a loop. Walking slowly downstage, she flings herself onto the couch. Putting her arm across her face, she is still for a moment. Then the two familiar clarinet notes return: she begins to hum the first phrase of that childhood song. The lights dim, and we realize that another dream is beginning.

From the darkness, voices eerily sing the name "Liza" over a bolero beat. When the lights come up, we see the Chorus, framed by towering blue walls. The members walk downstage and form two semicircles, the men on the outside. They are dressed as high school graduates in gowns with bobbing mortarboards. The men sing, and the women hum a countermelody:

There's a girl—Liza Elliott.
We all knew her. We went to high school together.
We graduated with her.

After the graduates recall an incident from French class, they sing their alma mater, "Mapleton High Choral," in collegiate harmony:

Oh, Alma Mater, Mapleton High—
Your bounty is on every hand
And while we live we'll never deny
No finer school is in the land.

On the final phrase, the Chorus begins to move stage left to a raised platform on one of the small turntables.

The bolero rhythm resumes, and the Chorus proclaims, "And now a Mapleton High girl is to be married." Kendall Nesbitt appears upstage in formal attire and walks downstage right. Liza, the Mapleton High girl, enters upstage. (During the number's opening, Lawrence had quickly donned the red wig and a lavender chiffon gown.) The Chorus continues, "And now they are buying the ring." A jewelry salesman (actually Charley Johnson) shows the couple a tray of rings. Liza chooses, but instead of a wedding ring, the salesman produces a small gold dagger. (Few in the audience are so attuned to Freud's theories as to recognize the phallic symbol.) Liza recoils in horror and runs stage right.

The bolero rhythm ceases, and, after a pause, the strings play a chromatic ostinato. The Chorus intones, "Randy Curtis! Flame of the Celluloid!": he appears, spot-lit center in his polo outfit from the photo shoot. As the men in the Chorus describe his character—"A precious amalgam of Frank Merriwell, Anthony Eden and Lancelot"—Randy and Kendall walk stage right, and Kendall exits into the wings. The women in the Chorus continue, "Forty million women see him every week and forty million women love him. In Kansas, in Patagonia, in Hollywood itself he is a man every woman wants." On the word "Hollywood," Randy and Liza face each other and walk toward one another. They repeat their brief conversation from the office: Randy says, "I took you home, in fact. Don't you remember that? We sat in the car talking—." This time Liza responds positively, "Of course, I remember." Randy, taking her into his arms, exclaims, "Darling." Liza begins to sing a richly orchestrated ballad:

> This is new—
> I was merely existing.
> This is new
> And I'm living at last.
> Head to toe,
> You've got me so I'm spellbound.
> I don't know
> If I am heaven or hell-bound.

Chorus member Davis Cunningham sings the repeat of "This Is New" while Randy and Liza begin to dance. They are joined by six couples from the dance corps: the women dressed identically to Liza, the men in the same polo outfit as Randy (Figure 10). The Chorus, still in graduation gowns, completes the second refrain. "This Is New" builds into a full dance number with yet a third iteration sung by the Chorus.

The cadence is undercut by Liza eerily singing a fragment of "My Ship" as the dancers and Randy exit. The Chorus urges Liza to continue, but she can't remember any more. Instead, she recalls a school play she acted in as a child: "I was supposed to be the princess, but I wasn't. I can't remember why now." The Chorus sings, "We are listening." Liza says, "It was called 'The Princess of Pure Delight.'"

(The small turntables spin as the lights change. The one stage-left whisks the Chorus out of sight, while the one stage-right whirls on eight children garbed in Eastern-inspired turbans, tunics, and sashes [Figure 11]. The props include a small bench, a screen, a tree, and a castle tower.) Liza narrates the story of three princes in orange, in blue, and of lavender hue, each of whom desires the princess. Her father, the king, doesn't know which to choose, so his dean of sorcerers comes up with a riddle; the suitor who correctly solves it will win the hand of the princess. The sorcerer charges the king "twenty gulden." (The audience chuckles: "twenty gulden" is the going rate for psychoanalysis.)

"What word of five letters is always spelled wrong?" All three princes fail the test, but suddenly a minstrel appears:

"I'll answer that riddle," cried the singer of song.
"What's never spelled 'right' in five letters is 'wrong'
And it's right to spell 'wrong'—w-r-o-n-g!
Your Highness, the Princess belongeth to me!
    And I love her, anyway"

Despite the king's protestations, the minstrel is able to marry the princess through some clever machinations as a trumpeter begins to trumpet:

The Princess then quickly came out of her swoon
And she looked at her swain and her world was in tune.
And the castle soon rang with cheer and with laughter
And of course they lived happily ever after.

(As the lights dim, the children who pantomimed the story are whirled away on their small turntable.) The full orchestra swells and wedding bells chime.

Lights flash, and Liza crosses stage left, where she discovers her office desk. Confused and disoriented, she calls for her staff and ends up rehashing a confrontation with Charley Johnson. "May I keep the paperweight? Maybe I can tell the little ones what grandpa was doing during the last world war—or do you think you'll want to throw it at somebody else?" Liza crosses right and finds Alison and Maggie, who exclaim, "It's late, Liza. It's late! You must hurry. This is your wedding day."

As the bells continue to toll, Liza quickly hides among the columns behind the desk and is revolved off by a small turntable. (Gertrude Lawrence is led to the portable dressing room for her quickest change of the evening. Two dressers with lightning-fast hands have only fifty seconds to help her into a modern wedding gown.) The turntables spin on stage a fourteen-foot-high wedding cake with balustrades suggesting choir stalls (Figure 12). Dominating the center of the stage is a towering stained-glass window in three panels; 250 lights behind its border illuminate a nuptial scene.

Liza processes downstage as the choir sings, "And now Liza Elliott is going to be married." The May bride is then joined by her December groom. The dance corps completes the bridal party: men in starched tails, women in yellow bridesmaids' dresses (Figure 13). Randy, still in his polo outfit, impersonates a wedding soloist, while Charley officiates as the minister:

It's never too late to Mend-elssohn.
Two hearts are at Journey's End-elssohn.
Whate'er their future, they must share it.
I trust they Lohengrin and bear it.

(The audience groans.) The children circle Liza and Kendall, while the Chorus, still in their graduation gowns, form a church choir. The music builds and becomes more dissonant as various melodies combine in strenuous counterpoint. To this din another part is added; a sepulchral voice from the Chorus intones ominously:

This is no part of heaven's marriage plan.
This woman knows she does not love this man.[15]

Despite Liza's insistence that she *does* love Kendall, the *Wedding Dream* reaches its climax: a cacophonous musical nightmare over a throbbing bolero beat.

To applause, the lights are quickly extinguished. (Stagehands, many in black hoods, begin to move the turntables manually: eight men using four metal elbow rods press them into motion. Stage Manager Bernard Hart, brother of the playwright, sits at the prompt table but, because of the complicated machinery, cannot hear the actors. Instead, he gives instructions to the massive stage crew.)[16] As the turntables glide into position, the two halves of the psychiatrist's office are once again reunited. The orchestra plays a series of descending chords to cover the swift scene change.

Act I, Scene 3

The lights illuminate Dr. Brooks seated at his desk. Accompanying him is not Liza, whom we half expect, but Maggie Grant. In worried tones the fashion editor expresses concern for Liza (especially after the *Wedding Dream* of yesterday afternoon). She is skeptical about the newfangled practice of psychoanalysis. Dr. Brooks cautions that analysis takes time and patience, but reassures Maggie that he is inclined to be hopeful. Escorting her to the door stage right, the doctor buzzes his secretary to usher Liza in for her appointment.

Liza enters through the central doorway in a black dress with a pleated skirt. She exchanges crisp "good mornings" with the doctor, tosses her hat on a chair, and goes to the couch and lies down. (How differently the second session begins compared with the first!) The doctor takes his position in the chair at the head of the couch. After a moment he says, "I am listening." (The line draws smiles of recognition, because *Lady in the Dark* had been first announced with this title.)

Desperate, Liza wants to know how to respond to Kendall's marriage proposal, but Dr. Brooks cautions against making a rash decision. Instead, he points out that in her latest dream Liza was once again the glamorous woman, and the men the ones she sees every day. "All except Mr. Curtis," Liza corrects. Dr. Brooks inquires about her dinner engagement with him, but Liza informs him of her intention to break it. He questions why she wouldn't enjoy being seen with a handsome man. Liza bridles at his suggestion, and the doctor points out that in the dream Randy held her in his arms, but now she rejects him. Impatiently, Liza responds, "Yes, yes, what of it?"

Dr. Brooks notes that in the dream Liza found herself at the altar not with Randy, but with Kendall. He finds it ironic that the mocking voices of other women at the ceremony made it a nightmare, even though in real life Liza's position as editor of *Allure* is to make other women beautiful. She retorts, "We've been over that before, haven't we?" Undeterred, Dr. Brooks presses on: "I wonder if your scorn and hatred of other women is because you are afraid of them. You make them beautiful to appease them, but the more beautiful you make them the more they continue to rob you, and your hate and fear of them grows. Perhaps the reason for the way you dress is that it is a kind of protective armour—with it you are not forced to compete. You don't dare."

Liza rejects this and points out that he has forgotten Kendall. Dr. Brooks dismisses that relationship: "In a sense he is a man already taken—a man that you share. And the thought of having him alone sends you into a panic. You don't dare compete as a woman." Rising from the couch, Liza angrily quits the analysis and hastily exits (Figure 14).

(The large turntables pivot 90 degrees in opposite directions to complete Liza's office at *Allure*. Riding their way on the turntables are Danny Kaye, Natalie Schafer, and Margaret Dale.)

Act I, Scene 4

It is later that afternoon. The staff members are tired of waiting for Liza, and their tempers have grown short. Their banter has Alison reliving a fashionable party, while Russell interrogates Maggie about Liza seeing a "psychoanalyst." Harried, Liza arrives and dismisses Alison and Russell so she can talk to her confidante. Maggie is surprised and concerned to hear that Liza has terminated the analysis. Amid Maggie's protests that Liza should have given it more time, Miss Foster interrupts to announce Kendall's arrival. Maggie exits downstage left.

Kendall enters through the same door and demands to know what is happening: "You don't want to marry me. Is that right? Don't be polite. Is that true?" Liza admits that she doesn't, but is indecisive about the future. When Kendall accuses her of behaving like a child, Liza explodes, "Don't talk to me like that! I won't take it—not from you or anybody! I'm fighting as hard as I know how."

She pleads for more time, but their conversation is cut short by the arrival of Russell, stage center, bearing props and chiffon with two office boys. Four willowy models follow in tow dressed for a photo shoot. (No one seems to notice that the actress in the ski outfit also served as Gertrude Lawrence's body double.) Russell elaborately positions them around a suit of armor (Figure 15). Once Liza gives her approval, Russell and the models begin to leave.

Charley saunters in and pinches a model's behind. Although "Boss Lady," as he calls Liza, is in no mood to spar, Charley presses her for a decision about the Easter cover. Frustrated by Liza's indecision, he announces his resignation: "Better offer [from] *Town and Country*." Liza counters that she will match it, but Charley claims that it's not the salary: "I can get something there that I can never get here. (*He pauses slightly*) Your job. I'm afraid that's what I want." He accuses Liza of "marrying her desk" and "having magazines instead of babies." Such insubordination riles Liza. Feeling empowered, Charley continues, "Rage is a pretty good substitute for sex, isn't it?" Liza explodes and orders him out of her office. Charley delivers his parting shot: "Don't think it hasn't all been charming. And if we ever need a good man over there, I'll make you an offer. (*He strolls out, whistling*)" Liza crumples at her desk and begins to cry.

Miss Stevens appears in the doorway to announce Mr. Curtis's arrival. Preoccupied with Kendall's marriage proposal, Liza has let the dinner date slip. Bewildered, Liza asks, "Mr. Curtis?" In strolls Randy, dressed to the nines in white tie and tails. He playfully chides her for forgetting about him, but adds, "I wish you wouldn't go home and dress. Let's go out just as you are. I'll stop back at the hotel on the way and change—won't take me five minutes. Let's do that, huh? (*He hesitates*) I was so afraid I'd run into a glamour girl tonight instead of—"

"Instead of what?" Liza returns (Figure 16). Randy tries to recover. "You. As you are now. That's what I like so much about you, Miss Elliott. Just this." Liza grimly thanks him, but insists that she *is* going to dress for dinner.

She ushers him out and rips off her dress, revealing her slip. (The audience gasps, and some of the women stifle laughter. After all, what woman wears such fashionable undergarments under an office dress?)[17] Liza is crying again, half singing and sobbing her childhood song. Maggie enters, carrying a gown and evening wrap; Liza takes the gown, evidently intended for a mannequin, and puts it on. "Liza, what is this?" Maggie asks. The sleek lamé dress features gold and amethyst ornaments. Liza exclaims, "Advertisement! From *Allure*! Magazine of Beauty! Like the line? The most alluring women are wearing it!" She makes her exit, calling into the wings, "I'm ready, Mr. Curtis" (Figure 17). Maggie stands dumbfounded as the curtain rings down.

Intermission

For the glamorous in the aisles, intermission is a steady stream of "Isn't it wonderful? Isn't it divine?"[18] For the creators, the mood is less buoyant. No number brought down the house, and the seamless quality of the dream sequences obliterated the full stops, which would have signaled the audience to applaud. In addition, Harry Horner's whirling scene changes cinematically bled the office settings into the dream sequences and back again. But who claps during a film?

The swarm of drama critics artfully avoid saying too much to anyone or each other, lest their take on the show be scooped. *New York Post* columnist Alice Hughes tries to pull a quote out of Hart's psychiatrist on how similar *Lady in the Dark* is to his own procedures. Despite her lack of success, Hughes dishes in her column, "Although he and playwright Hart are friends, it violates the mumbo-jumbo of psychoanalysis for doctor and patient to meet socially, so they carefully avoid each other outside the office."[19] For most of the audience, however, intermission is an excuse to gape and gossip.

As the house lights dim, the orchestra strikes up the overture, which had been missing at the top of the evening (Figure 18). Served up is a chorus of "This Is New" (the romantic ballad from the *Wedding Dream*). After a preview of "The Saga of Jenny," "My Ship" is heard, lushly scored. Stragglers are seated, and the overture concludes with a rousing version of "Girl of the Moment" from the *Glamour Dream*. Musical director Maurice Abravanel takes his bow, and the curtain rises.

Act II, Scene 1

Liza is seated at her desk, intently studying a magazine layout. It is late the following afternoon: the dimness suggests the hour. Maggie breaks the solitude and exclaims, "Liza—you'll kill your eyes that way. (*She snaps on the lights*) It's as gloomy as a Willkie button in here. Can I buy you a cocktail on the way home?" Liza wears a purple wool suit with a handkerchief tucked in the breast pocket, Maggie a conservative dress with two strands of pearls. With fur, purse, and hat, Maggie is indeed headed home. Liza insists that she will stay and work.

Alison bursts in, all insecure. "Darlings, do I look too dreadful to bounce into '21'—just the bar, I mean. I wouldn't dream of going upstairs this way." (Her getup elicits the intended outburst of laughter; Figure 19.) Maggie offers to accompany her, but Alison crosses left to Liza's desk: "Liza, dear, you were the absolute sensation of The Stork Club last night—you and Randy Curtis. I didn't see you come in, you know, and somebody said, 'Guess who just walked in with Randy Curtis' and I said, 'Let me guess— twenty questions' and of course I never even came close to guess *you* darling. You looked divine and he's such a dreamboat that I almost couldn't believe it when I turned around. Nobody talked of anything else all night."

"Not even Hemingway?" Maggie deadpans. In a moment Maggie and Alison are gone. Liza stands up, goes to the window, then back to the desk and picks up two oversize covers, considering one, then the next. Wearily, she sinks into a chair.

A voice comes out of nowhere: "Can't make up your *mind*, can you?" Another, "Can't even decide on the cover!" And another, "You're not as efficient as you used to be."[20] Soon snatches of conversations from the men in her life return:

(*Kendall Nesbitt's voice*):	I won't stand aside while you proceed to destroy something very important to me. I'm going to fight, Liza. I can't help that.
(*Randy Curtis's voice*):	I was so afraid I was going to run into a glamour girl tonight. That's what I like so much about you, Miss Elliott. Just this.
(*Charley Johnson's voice*):	You married that desk years ago, and you're never going to get a divorce. I know your kind.

Then the disembodied voices return: "Decide on this cover. You've got to.... The Easter Cover or the Circus Cover. The Easter Cover or the Circus Cover...."[21] The lights have been dimming.

(When the stage is dark, Gertrude Lawrence walks off the turntables, turns her back to the audience, and unzips the jacket of her suit to reveal a sequined vest. The large turntables turn nearly 180 degrees in opposite directions; the towering blue accordion walls form an inverted V at the back of the stage. In the center is flown a gaudy flat: two big-top tents are bedecked with flags and emblazoned with LIZA'S CIRCUS. Trapeze swings, a giant wooden horse, and various circus props fill the stage.)

The lights come up, causing the props to flash and dazzle. Downstage with her back to the audience, Liza holds up the two covers. In a coup de théâtre, Liza has found herself in the very magazine cover she has been staring at (Figure 20). A calliope is heard in the distance, and a snare drum sets down a march beat. Who can resist "The Greatest Show on Earth"? The Chorus members march downstage right, singing "Ta ra ra, tszing, tszing, tszing—." While the ta ra ra's imitate a snare drum, the singers make cymbal movements with their hands on the tszings (both coordinated with the actual percussion in the pit). Their blue and pink costumes with accents of silver and gold are all variations on a clown theme—polka dots here, diamonds there, stripes every which way.

A group of midgets (actually children) enter downstage right. The girls are outfitted in miniature evening gowns with wiglets, the boys mustachioed, in multicolored top hats, canes, and capes. They bow and curtsy in a line downstage, while the Chorus, standing behind them, sings:

The Flower of Womankind
Who Can't Make Up Her Mind
Is A Feature You Will Always Recall!

On the repeat of "The Greatest Show on Earth," the clowns form a V at the back of the stage in two lines. The music comes to a full stop, and the audience applauds. (In the audience, the collaborators find themselves on terra firma.)

During the last refrain, the Ringmaster (played by Russell Paxton) entered. Dressed in white pants, pink vest, and light blue coat, he took Liza's hand and seated her in the swing and then proceeded downstage center. Very operatically he implores, "Ladies and Gentlemen, I Take Pride in Introducing The Greatest Show on Earth!" More arioso:

> Liza Elliott's Gargantuan Three-Ring Circus
> Featuring for the First Time
> The Captivating and Tantalizing Liza Elliott...
> The Woman Who Cannot Make up Her Mind!

Back to recitativo:

> In Addition, We Bring You an Assortment
> Of Other Scintillating Stars of the Tanbark Ring
> And a Galaxy of Clowns and Neuroses
> In a Modern Miracle of Melodramatic Buffoonery
> And Mental Tight-Rope Walking!
> The Greatest Show on Earth!

The clowns repeat their refrain while closing up the lines after the midgets have exited.

Ten members of the dance corps enter for "Dance of the Tumblers." Their costumes, consisting of beaded tops and flowing skirts for the women and tunics and harem pants for the men, create a vaguely Middle Eastern look (Figure 21). The energetic dancing could have come out of a Russian ballet, and the music, with its asymmetrical accents and rushing scales, contributes to that air.[22] The sheer spectacle and athleticism of the number brings another round of applause. After bowing, the dancers exit as the last phrase of music repeats.

A dancer playing a page (Parker Wilson) somersaults back on stage and presents the Ringmaster, seated next to the horse, with a parchment. "Ah! The charges against Liza Elliott." A bewildered Liza asks, "What is all this? Charges against me? What for? What is all this?" The Ringmaster stands with one foot at the base of the horse and the other planted on one of the circus drums. He reads in rapid parlando with choral interjections:

Whereas—

Liza Elliott cannot make up her mind about the Easter cover or the circus cover—Secundus—

Liza Elliott cannot make up her mind whether she is marrying Kendall Nesbitt or not—

Moreover—

Liza Elliott cannot make up her mind as to the kind of woman she wants to be—the executive or the enchantress—

And, inasmuchas—

In a world where tumult and turmoil reign, these indecisions of Liza Elliott add to the confusions of an already, as indicated, confused world—

Therefore, be it resolved—

That Liza Elliott be brought to trial and be made to make up her mind.

A cheer goes up from the clowns as they break into two groups, leaving upstage center open.

The Ringmaster qua Judge introduces "That Death-Defying Trapeze Artist and Prosecuting Attorney, Charley Johnson!" Next comes "That Thrilling Bareback Rider and Attorney for the Defense—Randy Curtis!" Both Charley and Randy wear circus capes over tights and gladiator boots. Charley stands downstage left next to the Ringmaster, and Randy plants himself next to Liza downstage right. The Ringmaster continues, "Introducing Those Merry Madcaps and Prankish Pantaloonatics—the Jury!" The clowns march downstage while making *Mikado*-like hand movements:

Our object all sublime
We shall achieve in time:
To let the melody fit the rhyme!—
The melody fit the rhyme.

Banging a gavel, the Ringmaster admonishes the jury:

This is *all* immaterial and irrelevant—
What do you think this is—Gilbert and Sellivant?

The jury shuffles forward and sings, "Ha ha ha ha ha ha ha ha! If this is just a sample / Then evidence is ample / You get your money's worth / At The Greatest Show on Earth." Back into position, the jury settles down, and the trial begins.

Charley Johnson: "Your Honor, Mr. Ringmaster! I would like to call That Peerless Witness and Lion Tamer, Kendall Nesbitt!" In a lion tamer's outfit with whip and plumed hat, Kendall enters upstage center. Positioning himself between Kendall and Liza, Charley begins, "Mr. Nesbitt,—you are divorcing your wife so you can be free to marry the defendant, isn't that so?" "Yes, sir." "You were led to believe the defendant *would* marry you, when, as and if." "Yes, sir." "But now she refuses to make up her mind." "Yes sir!" Climbing off the horse, the Ringmaster comes downstage to summarize the situation in waltz time (Ira Gershwin's lyrics go over big):

> He gave her the best years of his life.
> She was, shall we call it, his mistress?
> 'Twas only for her he's divorcing his wife
> And now the man's in *dis*tress.
>
> The mister who once was the master of two
> Would make of his mistress his Mrs.
> But he's missed out on Mrs. for the mistress is through—
> What a mess of a mish mash this is!

During the Chorus's repetition, a dejected Kendall exits.

The Ringmaster is back on the horse, and the defense attorney comes to his client's aid. Taking center stage, Randy sings to the same tune:

> She gave him her heart, but not her word—
> This case, therefore, is so much deadwood.
> Her promise to wed he never heard
> For she never promised she wed would.
>
> It's just that a change of heart occurred
> And although it may have dismayed him—
> When a maid gives her heart but does not give her word,
> How on earth can that maid have betrayed him?

Randy and the Chorus repeat this softly as Liza sings a descant. At the song's conclusion, Randy escorts Liza back to her seat on the swing.

The Ringmaster queries, "Charming, charming! Who wrote that music?" The jury responds as one, "Tschaikowsky!" He exclaims, "Tschaikowsky! I love Russian composers!" Trumpets in the pit play a short fanfare from a familiar symphony. The patter song that follows has nothing to do with the trial at hand, but holds the audience spellbound. (Danny Kaye, who will make a career of tongue-twisting gibberish, rattles off a slew of Russian composers' names in less than a minute; Figure 22.) The audience has been waiting for such a moment, and his rendition of "Tschaikowsky" stops the show cold. The applause is long, deafening, and rolls like thunder.

(Not to be outdone, Gertrude Lawrence shakes her head at the musical director, denying Danny his encore, and the trial proceeds.) As the dancers enter upstage left, the prosecuting attorney cross-examines Liza. "Miss Elliott, you've heard the charges against you. Have you made up your mind about any of these things?" "No I haven't." "Do you intend to?" "I don't know." Charley, exasperated, asks, "Can you give this court any reasonable explanation as to why you cannot make up your mind?" "Yes, I can."

Her defense is a morality tale about a girl named Jenny who makes up her mind at various points in her life to disastrous effects. (Lawrence, spurred on by Danny Kaye's number, bumps and grinds her way through "The Saga of Jenny" in a burlesque hall routine; see back cover.) The number is all the more titillating because the repressed Liza Elliott is now firmly in touch with her sexuality. She sings, "But I am sure the court'll / Find Jenny is immortal / And has a bearing on this case!" The Jury asks, "As, for instance?" and Liza begins, "Well, for instance—":

Jenny made her mind up when she was three
She, herself, was going to trim the Christmas tree.
Christmas Eve she lit the candles—tossed the taper away.
Little Jenny was an orphan on Christmas Day.

    Poor Jenny!
    Bright as a penny!
Her equal would be hard to find.
    She lost one dad and mother,
      A sister and a brother—
But she would make up her mind.

The subsequent stanzas catalogue Jenny's exploits, and a frisson pulses through the audience. (Lawrence has taken the handkerchief out of her pocket and is playing directly into the hand of the audience.) By now the jury agrees, "Jenny points a moral / With which we cannot quarrel. Makes a lot of common sense!" Liza finishes in a blaze of glory:

Don't make up—
You shouldn't make up—
You mustn't make up—
Oh, never make up—
Anyone with vision
Comes to this decision:
Don't make up your mind!

The audience claps and cheers wildly. (Lawrence's down-and-dirty routine has topped Danny Kaye's number.) The air is electric as waves of applause lap and roll over the stage.

Randy, the Ringmaster, and the Jury all congratulate Liza. She finally goes back to her seat and picks up the circus cover. Charley feigns appreciation, but continues his cross-examination: "A most excellent defense, Miss Elliott. May I ask what you have there?" "Why, the circus cover." "May I see it?" "Of course." "Thank you." Turning to the Jury, Charley says, "Gentlemen, look at this." The oboe sounds the two important notes that began the other dreams. Charley hands the circus cover to the Jury members, who pass it about and start to hum the melody. Liza protests violently, "No, no! Don't, don't! Don't sing that!" She rushes to them and snatches back the cover. Charley turns to the Jury. "You see?" And back to Liza: "You're afraid. You're hiding something. You're afraid of that music, aren't you? Just as you're afraid to compete as a woman—afraid to marry Kendall Nesbitt—afraid to be the woman you want to be—afraid—afraid—afraid!—afraid!!"

The music has been building in the orchestra, and the calliope music that began the dream returns. The ensemble turns on Liza and mocks her. In rhythm they whisper, "Make up your mind, make up your mind, make up your mind." The lights are dimming, and the Chorus hisses "afraid" on the revolve. (Lawrence has walked off the turntables and zips up her jacket. She steps back onto the turntables, which have returned the two halves of the psychiatrist's office. The sliding portals reduce the width of the stage, and the lights come up.)

Act II, Scene 2

It is later that evening, and Dr. Brooks sits at his desk. Having resumed her analysis, Liza points to the couch. "I—I don't think I can lie there anymore. Do you mind if I walk?" "Whatever is most comfortable for you." "Thank you. (*Silence again*)" Dr. Brooks: "What is it?" Liza: "That dream. I can't shake it off." Dr. Brooks asks Liza to analyze the *Circus Dream*, but all that she can recall is a feeling of remembered emotion: "In the dream, when they sang that song, I had that same feeling of humiliation and hurt that I used to have." "When?" inquires Dr. Brooks. Liza replies that it was the same "bad feeling" that she had as a little girl. "Can you possibly remember when you first felt it?" Liza responds that it was when she was very little—

three or four years old. Muted brass play a series of descending chords as the lights dim.

(The two large turntables revolve to bring back into view the towering blue walls. Gertrude Lawrence is still standing stage left, but the psychiatrist and his office are gone.) The lights come up stage right on two couples in formal wear: it is the year 1904. Liza's father carries a little girl in his arms. Next to him stands a woman with red hair. It is Liza's mother (in a turn of triple casting, she is played by Virginia Peine). Another dream sequence must be beginning, yet there is no music. Instead, the actors speak, which at first is jarring (Figure 23).

Liza's father: "Here she is! To say good night and sing her little song, and off to bed with her!" The guest couple fusses over the little girl, but her father protests, "Now, now! We're reconciled to Liza's looks. In fact, I'm rather pleased at having a plain child. (*He pats his wife's cheek tenderly*) One beauty in the family is enough, I can tell you! I couldn't stand two!" After a brief exchange, Liza's mother turns to her and scolds, "I'm afraid you're never going to be able to wear blue, my darling, and we must be careful how we do your hair, but we shall make the most of your good points, Liza, won't we?" (No wonder Liza dreams in blue!) Liza's father interrupts, "She'll never be a beauty, Helen, no matter what you do, and I'm glad of it!" The adults laugh (a short gasp from the audience).

Suddenly the adult Liza exclaims, "I wanted to cry out: 'It's not true! It's not true! I'm like my mother!' I wanted to shout and make them stop!" Liza's father cajoles the little girl into performing for the guests. "Daddy's little ugly duckling, isn't she! Come, Liza! Sing us your song, and then a good-night kiss. (*The child buries her head in his shoulder*) Why, Liza! Is this our smart little girl? Come now. That song we sing together. (*He sets her down*)" She seems to be about to cry, but instead falteringly begins to sing "My Ship." After a few notes, she breaks into sobs and runs from the group. The lights dim. (The small stage-right turntable wheels the actors out of view.) In the spotlight, Liza recalls, "I ran to the nursery and looked in the mirror. I felt ugly and ashamed. When my mother came in I hated her because she was so beautiful!"

On the opposite side of the stage, a small turntable has brought a group of schoolchildren and their teacher. Blowing on a small pitch pipe, the teacher asks her students to rehearse the end of a play. They sing, "And of course they lived happily ev-er a-fter" ("The Princess of Pure Delight" from the *Wedding Dream*!). "That was fine, children. Now! For the Prince, I have chosen David Reed—and for the Princess, Liza Elliott." Little Liza jumps for joy, but David Reed throws a tantrum. "Why can't we have a pretty

Princess—like Barbara? A Princess ought to be beautiful, oughtn't she? Liza will spoil everything! I don't want to be the Prince if she's the Princess."

The Liza of today relives the feeling. "I couldn't bear it. I wanted to hide. I wanted to crawl away and hide." Although the teacher reprimands David, the damage has been done. The child Liza sobs, "I don't want it!" and bolts from the room. (The lights dim as a small turntable wheels the flashback away.) In the spotlight, Liza admits, "I wanted it more than anything else in the world! For the first time, I felt alone—alone. I stayed alone, by myself."

The lights come up stage right to reveal ten-year-old Liza sprawled on the floor, reading a book and eating an apple. The housekeeper enters to tell her that her mother has died. The adult Liza recalls, "I wanted to cry. Yet, somehow, I couldn't. I knew I loved my Mother. But I could feel no grief. The tears wouldn't come." Ten-year-old Liza returns wearing her mother's evening cloak; turning around, she admires herself in a mirror she carries. Softly, she begins to sing "My Ship." Her father enters and exclaims, "Liza! Liza, what are you doing! (*He rips the cloak from her shoulders and tears the mirror from her hand*) Go to your room at once." The lights fade, and the adult Liza reveals, "But that—feeling was gone. I don't know why. It was gone. Until—one night—the night of our High School Graduation dance."

A turntable has brought out Chorus members dressed in period attire, the women in matching white starched dresses, the men in blue serge suits with boutonnieres. Behind them is a fanciful tree festooned with Chinese lanterns. A boy announces, "The Graduating Class of Mapleton High School votes Homer Adams the Boy Most Likely to Succeed, Henry Conrad the Best Athlete, Barbara Joyce [the girl David Reed wanted to be princess] the Most Beautiful Girl, Ben Butler the Handsomest Boy, and Liza Elliott the Best Student." After each, applause goes up.

As the other students begin dancing, Liza approaches Ben to congratulate him. Ben extends an invitation to Liza for dinner. (Ben is played by Dan Harden, the teenage Liza by Gertrude Lawrence, still in her purple suit.) Liza asks Ben why he isn't having dinner with Barbara and learns they are on the outs. Ben and Liza detach themselves from the group and walk to a bench on the opposite side of the stage. (As the lights on that side come up, the other side dims, and gradually the dancers disappear.)

Liza and Ben chat about his disagreement with Barbara. Evidently seeing Liza in a new light, Ben asks her to accompany him on the boat ride. After a few fumbled attempts, they express interest in one another, and Ben impulsively kisses her. Love is blossoming, and without realizing it, Liza begins to hum. Ben stops her. "What's that song, Liza?" "Why, I—I didn't even know I was singing." Ben urges her to continue. Liza falters, "I don't know whether I can remember it—I haven't thought of it in years." Ben wraps his arm around her waist and she leans her head against his shoulder. She sings the entire song, the orchestration is rich and full:

My ship has sails that are made of silk—
The decks are trimmed with gold—
   And of jam and spice
   There's a paradise
    In the hold.

After the applause dies down, Liza admits that the song is one she has always known, but she has never been able to remember all the words before. Their romantic idyll is broken by a beautiful blonde's entrance. Barbara has come back to retrieve Ben. Following a brief interchange, Ben excuses himself. It is obvious that he will not be back. This soon dawns on Liza, and she plunges her head into her hands, crying uncontrollably. She then haltingly sings the last half of the song again. The irony is palpable: Liza has indeed waited years for the ship to arrive that will bring her true love. But in a moment he has been stolen away by a woman as beautiful as her own mother—the beauty who prevented Liza from obtaining her father's love.

When the lights come up, Liza is safely back in the confines of the psychiatrist's office. Dr. Brooks stands up and crosses right to his desk. He offers to postpone his analysis, but Liza urges him to continue. He lays it out with blunt precision: "A little girl, convinced of her own ugliness, rejects herself as not as good as other little girls, and then is rejected by the world." After her mother dies, the "bad feeling" disappears, because "that constant reminder of beauty—of all that you were not and longed to be—was no longer there." Once in high school, "Then you blossomed as yourself—until once again, and at a most crucial moment—a beautiful girl robs you. I think, then, that you withdrew as a woman. That you would no longer risk being hurt as a woman competing with other women. But the longing remained—and so did the rage and that deep sense of injustice. And what you are facing now is rebellion—rebellion at your unfulfillment as a woman."

The last line stings. "But that's not true! I did love Kendall. And I know he loves me. How can you answer that?" Dr. Brooks suggests that there may be an answer for that, too. He rises from his seat. "Tomorrow at the usual time?" Liza, her mind elsewhere, responds, "Yes. Good-day. (*She goes quickly out*)"

Act II, Scene 3

The lights come up on Liza's office a week later. Maggie sits at Liza's desk, Charley on the couch. Four models, dressed in evening wear, are in various stages of waiting. Russell storms in. "That bitch! That stinking blinking ruddy bloody bitch!" Charley cracks, "I always thought you were fond of your mother, Russell." (The line gets a big laugh. From the seriousness of psychoanalysis, we are plunged into the brittle repartee of *Allure*.) Evidently Alison, the ditsy columnist, has loaned Russell's color plates to a friend. Despite the seriousness of the offense, Russell's exit line draws laughter: "Maggie, you of all people know that I've put up with Alison in an absolutely God-like fashion. Now, either she goes or I do. And just before I leave I may tear out her entrails and photograph them in color."

Tired of waiting, Maggie excuses the models to go for ice cream. With the room emptied, Maggie reminds Charley of his promise to apologize to Liza. Satisfied that he'll comply, she eases up and asks him why he can be such a heel. He replies that six years with the magazine "is a long time to be irritated by a woman." Maggie retorts, "You furnish your own share of irritation, my boy. And on purpose. I've watched you do it." "Know why?" Charley asks. "No, I don't." Maggie sits in the chair by the couch.

> Because I like her and admire her. I've always admired her—as a person. As a woman she makes me sick. (*Crossing to Maggie*) Let me tell you something, Maggie. It's not what I say or the way I behave sometimes that gets under her skin. It's because I see through the pose. The big executive pose. She can't stand that. It frightens her. She needs that authority she wears like a thick enamel—she's afraid without it, God knows why! (*Crossing left*) I knew that from the first day I walked into this office—but I could never resist chipping bits of it off and seeing what was underneath. Because underneath it, she's a helluva girl.

Maggie is taken aback by his candor, but before their conversation can go much further, Alison bustles in looking for Liza.

In reply to Maggie's inquiry about Russell's plates, Alison quips, "Oh, *that*! Darling, I didn't loan them. I dropped them and broke them—I haven't told him yet." Alison instead is enamored with her latest idea, to have "a Bonwit-Teller window-dummy, male, to fall in love with a Saks dummy, female, and carry out the love affair in the two store windows." Maggie is unimpressed, but Alison is undeterred. "Saks is *so* conservative—I think they sometimes mix themselves up with St. Patrick's, they've been next to each other for so long!" Soon Liza's office is empty. Miss Foster comes in to put a new batch of papers on her desk. As she starts out, Liza arrives with Randy Curtis in tow. She wears a beige silk blouse with a pleated skirt—a far cry from her dark suits that began the evening. Randy wears a suit, but his shirt is open and without a tie. Their relaxed demeanor speaks volumes.

Miss Foster informs Liza about an appointment, and soon Liza and Randy are alone. They have enjoyed a leisurely lunch, and Randy is clearly infatuated. Liza, however, insists that she *has* to get to work. Randy starts to leave, but seeks assurance that she really enjoys his company and not just his Hollywood persona. "I didn't want it to be that way—with us." Quietly Liza replies, "It isn't, Randy" (Figure 24). He appears tongue-tied but then pops the question. The Question! Although Liza appears surprised, it is not unexpected. (After all, it is late, and the leading lady always ends up with the handsome man.) Randy suggests that Liza wouldn't have to give up the magazine on his account. Liza says that she would give it all up for him. He breathlessly asks, "Liza—does that mean—'yes'?" She nods and he sinks into a chair.

Maggie enters and the spell is broken. With a call waiting, Randy elects to take it outside. Overcome with emotion, Liza embraces Maggie, who starts, "Now, don't tell me boy meets girl—." Liza informs her about Randy's marriage proposal and assures Maggie that this is what *she* wants: "My whole relationship with Kendall was a flight from something I didn't dare face. Only now I know the reason—and now I want and need Randy to lean on—to take care of me—I want to be as other women are. Be happy for me, Maggie—I think I've found the answer!"

Maggie assures her, "Oh, Liza, dear, I am. It's what I've always hoped for you." Her next line breaks the mood again. "And I want a big picture of Freud right in my office." She exits downstage left and Randy enters right center.

The telephone call has brought great news from his studio: "They want me to form my own producing unit—set up a whole separate corporation—I'd be in complete control—stories—production—profits—everything!" Things appear to be heading for the final curtain, but they take a detour when Randy confesses that he needs Liza to be in charge: "I guess the truth is I'm a pretty frightened guy inside. Anyway, what'll I tell the Coast, Liza? Shall we take it on? Or let's talk it all over tonight, huh? I shouldn't have barged in like this anyway. But I just had to run to somebody—and you're the one I'll be running to the rest of my life—you might as well get used to it."

Soon he is gone. Liza stands looking after him, stunned. Before she has time to digest what has happened, Russell bursts into her office demanding an immediate showdown with Alison. Liza: "Please Russell, not now!" He throws a fit. "Not now! Not now! What am I supposed to do to get some attention—bleed in front of you?" Russell exits in a huff as Charley arrives.

Looking all business in a three-piece suit, Charley surveys Liza for a moment and then launches into his rehearsed apology:

> I'm supposed to apologize for what I said the other day—promised Maggie I would. But I've been thinking it over quietly in the Men's Room and I've decided I'm not going to. I'm sorry—I can't help it. It's just that—I'm a man and you're a woman and *you've* had to be the boss—always—and something in me deeply resents that. I can't help it. I know I've been pretty rotten to you—and I've kicked myself for it afterwards. But there's always been that secret battle between us—from the very beginning—and I've always had to win—because, well, because I'm *me*, I guess. Anyhow, I want you to know—now that I'm leaving—that for all your goddam shenanigans I think you're fine. (*He turns away and eases up center*) I've turned in the Hattie Carnegie layout to Paxton, so I guess that washes me up. Anything else?

(The mention of Hattie Carnegie brings smiles: nothing like writing the designer right into the play.)

During Charley's speech Liza has been gazing at him in an entirely new light. Suddenly animated, she urges him to return the paperweight and stay. She blurts out, "It appears that I'm slowly getting a divorce—from myself. I think you ought to stick around and see the fun. What do you say?" Charley is hesitant and points out that it wouldn't work with two bosses. Liza counters that they could run the magazine together. "I might even drop out after a while if you didn't get too drunk with power." Now it is Charley's turn to be energized. After a slight pause, he tosses the paper-weight back to her, signaling his decision to stay.

Soon Charley and Liza are side by side pouring over the upcoming issue. Liza is excited by his ideas for the magazine's format (Figure 25). Maggie's entrance goes unnoticed and she stares at them with growing disbelief. Without looking up, Liza asks Maggie to "be an angel and ask Miss Foster to call Mr. Curtis at the Waldorf and tell him that I'm going to have to work tonight." Liza's doubt that the redesign can be accomplished by July is put to rest by Charley, who has a mock-up in his office. On his way out to fetch it, he says to Maggie, "Be nice to me, Wonderful. I'm your Boss now." Maggie slowly turns to Liza. "Would you mind telling me, Miss Elliott, exactly what the hell goes on here?" Liza admits to Maggie that she almost made the same mistake by agreeing to marry Randy: "He's another Kendall. Frightened and insecure—seeing in me what Kendall saw—needing what Kendall needed. A mother—not a wife! I almost did the same thing all over again. And I'll tell you something else—I've suddenly seen Charley Johnson for the first time—and suddenly I know the reason *why* for a great many things. (*Gaily*) Don't worry about me, Maggie! I'm going to be all right!"

Before Maggie has time to respond, Charley is back with an armful of papers. He spreads them out on Liza's desk and soon their heads are back together. Intently studying the mock-up, Liza absentmindedly begins to hum. Charley adds the words to the next phrase, "And of jam and spice, there's a paradise in the hold." Liza, astonished: "Why—do *you* know that song too?" "Yeah—haven't heard it since I was a kid, though. Go ahead—do you know it all?" Liza, slowly: "Yes...I know all the words—now." As Liza sings, Charley softly joins in. Maggie wryly looks at one, then the other. She sinks into a chair and folds her hands in her lap. The reprise of "My Ship" is earnest, without irony. The ship has indeed brought Liza her own true love. As the curtain slowly descends, they look into each other's eyes.

The ending has taken some in the audience by surprise. The leading lady has not only rejected her live-in lover (played by Bert Lytell, president of Actors' Equity) and the young dashing movie star (played by Hollywood heartthrob Victor Mature), but has ended up with her advertising manager (played by an unknown actor from Iowa). The curtain is now back up, and troupes of children, Chorus members, and dancers are taking their bows. The surprise ending will be sorted out later. Soon the principals are taking their turns, with the largest ovation reserved for Gertie Lawrence.

The audience has risen to its feet for the actress who has carried the burden of the evening on her shoulders. Rarely has she been off the stage. Her face is flush with excitement, and although she continues to take her fellow actors' hands for company bows, the audience refuses to let her leave. After countless curtain calls (one reporter estimates them in the teens), the ovation forces her to make a small curtain speech. Thanking the audience, she apologizes for her illness that had postponed opening night and kept "the lady waiting in the dark so long."

Because of the hour and to make their deadlines, drama critics have already vacated their seats on the aisle—some even before the critical last scene. The playwright, worried that missing the surprise ending might affect reviews, had gone to the extraordinary effort of flying several of them to Boston to see the tryout.[23]

Backstage, the dressing rooms are packed full of well-wishers and relatives. Out on West Fifty-second, a blind concertina player serenades first-
nighters leaving the theater with "My Ship." The evening is topped off with
a large party at the Waldorf Astoria thrown by William Paley of CBS for
Lawrence and everyone connected with the production. The star, whose
bout with the flu had postponed the opening, is shuttled back to Doctor's
Hospital. Propped up in bed and wearing flannel pajamas, she recalls, "I was
only semi-conscious, I think. I don't remember anything, except that my
knees felt like cotton wool and all those spotlights and revolving stages made
me light-headed."[24]

Despite Gertie's fuzzy state, metropolitan newspapers the next morning
praise her razor-sharp performance.[25] Writing for the *Post*, John Mason
Brown reports that if her voice "still showed the effects of the grippe when
she started off last night, it was entirely liberated before the evening was
over." Lawrence's dramatic abilities cause the critics to trip over one another:
"She is as believable in the doctor's office scenes of mental anguish, as she
is captivating in the dream stories, and she emerges triumphantly" (John
Anderson, *Journal-American*); "Her versatility is put to a tremendous test,
and meets it without a quaver" (Richard Lockridge, *Sun*); "Miss Lawrence
who, by the dazzling excitement of her presence and the radiant versatility
of her talent, makes the new work her personal triumph" (Richard Watts Jr.,
Herald Tribune). The *Times* critic, Brooks Atkinson, tops them: "As for
Gertrude Lawrence, she is a goddess: that's all."

In contrast, about half the critics express reservations over the drama.
Watts feels that the play's "emotional power is by no means overwhelming,
and its propaganda for the soul-curing virtues of psycho-analysis is rather on
the primitive side." Although Brown claimed that the dialogue had been
"vigorously pruned" since the Boston tryout, Anderson still found the play
"wearisomely long." The most pointed objections are by Sidney Whipple
and Louis Kronenberger, the former charging that "the story of Mr. Hart
[which] is telling at times becomes repetitive and dull," and the latter
damning the play as "superficial, somewhat clumsily written, and utterly
uninspired in plot." Despite these criticisms, all agree that the production's
spectacle more than makes up for the drama's shortcomings. Even Kronenberger qualifies his objections: "But it's not meant to be taken all by itself;
and with the lady's dreams set lightly to music and blown up into a gorgeous
spectacle . . . *Lady in the Dark* becomes very good theater."

Weill and Gershwin's contributions are roundly praised. Many believe
that *Lady in the Dark* represents the composer's best score: Atkinson de-

scribes it as "a homogeneous piece of work, breaking out into song numbers over a mood of dark evocation—nostalgic at times, bursting also into humor and swing." Gershwin's lyrics are similarly praised; according to Watts, "He has come through with great success, keeping handsomely to the mood of fantasy and remaining bright and witty."

Among the actors, Danny Kaye is singled out for special honors. Burns Mantle describes him as one "who steps forth confidently to justify his admirers in the belief that he is started on a fine career." Another newcomer, Macdonald Carey, is also heralded, with Watts predicting that he is "in great danger of being snapped up by the screen at any moment." All of the critics praise the production and design team for their efforts. Whipple goes so far as to conclude that *Lady in the Dark* is "the most lavish and beautiful entertainment to reach Broadway in many seasons."

With the ink barely dry on the newsprint, one of Broadway's most innovative shows was launched. It provided Gertrude Lawrence the greatest vehicle of her career, one that melded her abilities as a dramatic actress and music hall comedienne. For fellow actors Danny Kaye and Macdonald Carey, *Lady in the Dark* gave them the big break for their respective careers. After just the first season, Paramount Pictures signed Carey (fulfilling Watts's prediction), and Kaye snagged the lead part in a new Cole Porter musical (catapulting him from nightclub entertainer to Broadway headliner in less than a year).

The celebrity *Lady in the Dark* lent to its stars outshone the personal, but no less significant, breakthroughs for each of it creators. For Moss Hart, it signaled his creative independence from his longtime collaborator, George S. Kaufman; for Ira Gershwin, his successful return to the stage after his brother George's death; and for Kurt Weill, a mainstream Broadway show and his first box-office success in the United States.

Each took his percentage of the profits and pursued the American dream of owning a home. For Gershwin, it helped pay for a large house at 1021 North Roxbury Drive in Beverly Hills, next door to where he and George had rented when they went to work for RKO. Because of the estate's size and luxury, Harold Arlen dubbed it the "Gershwin Plantation."[26] For Weill, it meant purchasing his first and only house in the United States. The nine-room farmhouse in New City, New York, was called "Brook House" by virtue of a little stream that still runs through the property.[27] For Hart, plans were more grandiose and included building an addition to his farm in Bucks County, Pennsylvania. Containing a forty-by-thirty-foot playroom, study, and four double guest rooms, the addition was christened "the Gertrude Lawrence Memorial Wing."[28]

As similar as their responses were after opening night, their varying careers prior to collaborating made them strange bedfellows. The five-year odyssey of how Hart, Gershwin, and Weill came to conceive *Lady in the Dark* is another story—one that begins again at the Alvin.

Illustrations

Figure 1. Act I, Scene 1: Dr. Brooks's office. Dr. Brooks (Donald Randolph), Miss Bowers (Jeanne Shelby), and Liza Elliott (Gertrude Lawrence). Photo by Vandamm Studio, courtesy and permission of Billy Rose Theatre Collection, The New York Public Library for the Performing Arts, Astor, Lenox and Tilden Foundations.

Figure 2. Act I, Scene 1: Donald Randolph and Gertrude Lawrence. Photo by Vandamm Studio, courtesy and permission of Billy Rose Theatre Collection, The New York Public Library for the Performing Arts, Astor, Lenox and Tilden Foundations.

Figure 3. Act I, Scene 1: *Glamour Dream*, "Girl of the Moment." Photo by Richard Tucker, courtesy of the Weill-Lenya Research Center, Kurt Weill Foundation for Music, New York, and permission of Julia Tucker.

Figure 4. Act I, Scene 1: *Glamour Dream*. Courtesy and permission of Culver Pictures.

Figure 5. Act I, Scene 2: Maggie Grant (Margaret Dale) and Liza Elliott (Gertrude Lawrence). Photo by Vandamm Studio, courtesy and permission of Billy Rose Theatre Collection, The New York Public Library for the Performing Arts, Astor, Lenox and Tilden Foundations.

Figure 6. Act I, Scene 2: Maggie Grant (Margaret Dale) and Alison Du Bois (Natalie Schafer). Photo by Vandamm Studio, courtesy and permission of Billy Rose Theatre Collection, The New York Public Library for the Performing Arts, Astor, Lenox and Tilden Foundations.

Figure 7. Act I, Scene 2: Liza's Office. Maggie Grant (Margaret Dale), Russell Paxton (Danny Kaye), Miss Foster (Evelyn Wyckoff), Charley Johnson (Macdonald Carey), Randy Curtis (Victor Mature), and Liza Elliott (Gertrude Lawrence). Photo by Vandamm Studio, courtesy and permission of Billy Rose Theatre Collection, The New York Public Library for the Performing Arts, Astor, Lenox and Tilden Foundations.

Figure 8. Act I, Scene 2: Danny Kaye, Macdonald Carey, and Victor Mature. Photo by Vandamm Studio, courtesy of Wisconsin Center for Film and Theater Research and permission of Billy Rose Theatre Collection, The New York Public Library for the Performing Arts, Astor, Lenox and Tilden Foundations.

Figure 9. Act I, Scene 2: Liza Elliott (Gertrude Lawrence) and Kendall Nesbitt (Bert Lytell). Photo by Vandamm Studio, courtesy and permission of Billy Rose Theatre Collection, The New York Public Library for the Performing Arts, Astor, Lenox and Tilden Foundations.

Figure 10. Act I, Scene 2: *Wedding Dream*, "This Is New." Photo by Vandamm Studio, courtesy and permission of Billy Rose Theatre Collection, The New York Public Library for the Performing Arts, Astor, Lenox and Tilden Foundations.

Figure 11. Act I, Scene 2: *Wedding Dream*, "The Princess of Pure Delight." Photo by Vandamm Studio, courtesy and permission of Billy Rose Theatre Collection, The New York Public Library for the Performing Arts, Astor, Lenox and Tilden Foundations.

Figure 12. Act I, Scene 2: *Wedding Dream*, Gertrude Lawrence. Photo by Vandamm Studio, courtesy and permission of Billy Rose Theatre Collection, The New York Public Library for the Performing Arts, Astor, Lenox and Tilden Foundations.

Figure 13. Act I, Scene 2: *Wedding Dream*, "This Woman at the Altar." Photo by Vandamm Studio, courtesy and permission of Billy Rose Theatre Collection, The New York Public Library for the Performing Arts, Astor, Lenox and Tilden Foundations.

Figure 14. Act I, Scene 3:
Donald Randolph and
Gertrude Lawrence.
Courtesy and permission
of Culver Pictures.

Figure 15. Act I, Scene 4: Danny Kaye (Russell Paxton) and four models: Carol (Patricia Deering), Marcia (Margaret Westberg), Ruthie (Gedda Petry), and Helen (Virginia Peine). Photo by Vandamm Studio, courtesy and permission of Billy Rose Theatre Collection, The New York Public Library for the Performing Arts, Astor, Lenox and Tilden Foundations.

Figure 16. Act I, Scene 4: Victor Mature and Gertrude Lawrence. Photo by Vandamm Studio, courtesy and permission of Billy Rose Theatre Collection, The New York Public Library for the Performing Arts, Astor, Lenox and Tilden Foundations.

Figure 17. Act I, Scene 4:
Gertrude Lawrence. Photo by
Vandamm Studio, courtesy of
The Museum of the City of
New York and permission of
The Museum of the City of
New York and Billy Rose
Theatre Collection, The New
York Public Library for the
Performing Arts, Astor, Lenox
and Tilden Foundations.

Figure 18. Intermission:
Overture (before Act II).
Photo courtesy of The Kurt
Weill and Lotte Lenya Papers,
Irving S. Gilmore Music
Library, Yale University
and permission of the
Kurt Weill Foundation
for Music, New York.

Figure 19. Act II, Scene 1: Margaret Dale,
Natalie Schafer, and Gertrude Lawrence. Photo
by Vandamm Studio, courtesy and permission of
Billy Rose Theatre Collection, The New York
Public Library for the Performing Arts, Astor,
Lenox and Tilden Foundations.

Figure 20. Act II, Scene 1: *Circus Dream*, "The Greatest Show on Earth." Photo by Vandamm Studio, courtesy and permission of Billy Rose Theatre Collection, The New York Public Library for the Performing Arts, Astor, Lenox and Tilden Foundations.

Figure 21. Act II, Scene 1:
Circus Dream, "Dance of the
Tumblers." Photo by Vandamm
Studio, courtesy and permission
of Billy Rose Theatre Collection,
The New York Public Library
for the Performing Arts, Astor,
Lenox and Tilden Foundations.

Figure 22. Act II, Scene 1:
Circus Dream, "Tschaikowsky,"
Danny Kaye. Courtesy and
pemission of Culver Pictures.

Figure 23. Act II, Scene 2: Childhood flashback, Gertrude Lawrence. Photo by Vandamm Studio, courtesy and permission of Billy Rose Theatre Collection, The New York Public Library for the Performing Arts, Astor, Lenox and Tilden Foundations.

Figure 24. Act II, Scene 3: Gertrude Lawrence and Victor Mature. Photo by Vandamm Studio, courtesy and permission of Billy Rose Theatre Collection, The New York Public Library for the Performing Arts, Astor, Lenox and Tilden Foundations.

Figure 25. Act II, Scene 3: Macdonald Carey and Gertrude Lawrence. Photo by Vandamm Studio, courtesy and permission of Billy Rose Theatre Collection, The New York Public Library for the Performing Arts, Astor, Lenox and Tilden Foundations.

2

Genesis

In the theater a rehearsal of a new show was under way. A young African American actress sang about a sultry summer day in Charleston. Because of the bright lights, the Chorus accompanying her could not have seen the two people standing at the back of the Alvin. Otherwise, they certainly would have recognized the heavier of the two, a quiet, bespectacled man who had written many of the words they were singing. None of them, however, would have known the lyricist's guest, a balding man who also wore glasses but looked much older than thirty-five. If they could have heard him speak, they would have detected his thick accent, for he had been in the United States less than a month, having arrived from Europe on the SS *Majestic*. The visitor leaned over and whispered into his host's ear, "It's a great country where music like that can be written . . . and played."[1] The lyricist must have smiled in agreement.

This rehearsal was probably the first time Kurt Weill ever stepped into a Broadway theater. Shortly after arriving in the country on September 10, 1935, he and his ex-wife, Lotte Lenya, had attended a party at George Gershwin's duplex on East Seventy-second. Weill and Ira Gershwin had not exchanged more than a few words when Weill expressed a desire to collaborate with him.[2] Although taken aback, Gershwin invited him to attend a run-through of *Porgy and Bess*. Weill must have suddenly felt like a Broadway insider at being allowed to watch a closed rehearsal. He had first met George during the Gershwins' European trip in 1928. Now, seven and a half years later, Weill found himself previewing their masterpiece. This exposure to one of Broadway's most unusual offerings exerted a profound influence on Weill—perhaps the most profound of his nearly fifteen years in the United States.

35

The work that had brought Weill to New York for what was supposed to be a four-month visit was quite different, but equally daring. *The Eternal Road* told the story of the Jews in a biblical pageant. It was intended to be a parable for what was happening in Germany under the Nazis. Planned in Europe, *The Eternal Road* was scheduled to open in December 1935, two months after *Porgy and Bess*. After several delays, *The Eternal Road* was indefinitely postponed in February with a debt of a quarter of a million dollars. Weill and Lenya, who had been living out of suitcases at the Hotel St. Moritz on Central Park South, were now faced with finding work or returning to Europe.

The options for an émigré opera and theater composer stranded in the United States in 1936 were limited if he hoped to earn a living as a professional. A composer with credentials could pursue a teaching appointment, which would enable artistic pursuits on the side. Or he could travel to Hollywood and join the émigré community there. Yet another option would be to try to break into the commercial theater, then confined almost exclusively to New York, where a street had become synonymous with a style and mode of production, if not also a genre: Broadway.

Weill's options were more limited than most. His meager credentials gave him little hope for a teaching position. In any case, based on his brief experience in Berlin, he appears to have had little interest in teaching. As far as opera was concerned, Weill's friend and former student Maurice Abravanel was conducting at the Met and tried interesting the management in producing one of Weill's works, but to no avail.[3] The League of Composers presented Weill in a concert devoted entirely to his works, but by intermission much of the audience had left. To conserve dwindling finances, Weill and Lenya gathered up their belongings and moved to cheaper lodgings at the Hotel Park Crescent at Riverside and Eighty-seventh.

Weill must have known the tremendous odds against a Broadway success. Even his European hit, *Die Dreigroschenoper* (*The Threepenny Opera*), had flopped in New York after just twelve performances in 1933.[4] As it turned out, Weill was recruited by the Group Theatre for his first U.S. stage work. Founded by Harold Clurman, Cheryl Crawford, and Lee Strasberg, the Group was known for its leftist leanings and politically oriented productions.[5] In his notes for a lecture presented to the Group, Weill summed up his assessment of music-theater in the United States and where he saw his future: "Situation of musical theatre in this country: Metropolitan, worst example of old fashioned opera (museum) on the one side, musical comedy, which tries to be sophisticated and low brow at the same time, on the other side. Nothing between. Enormous field for musical theater."[6]

Clurman and Crawford brought Weill and playwright Paul Green together for the first musical ever undertaken by the Group, which was ill-
equipped to mount such a large-scale production. The reviews were better
than anticipated, but the pacifist-themed *Johnny Johnson* failed to find an
audience and closed after sixty-eight performances. Near the end of its run,
The Eternal Road, with a reassembled company, reached its destination. With
a cast of over two hundred and total cost of around $500,000, the mammoth
pageant was generally well received. Although lasting 153 performances, the
show ran up a huge deficit from weekly running costs and provided no income
for Weill. Nearly broke, he traveled to Hollywood.

His assignment was to compose a score for a picture to be cast primarily
with members of the Group. Clifford Odets and Lewis Milestone's screenplay concerned the recent Spanish Civil War. Weill began composing, but
producer Walter Wanger had a falling out with Milestone (also signed to be
the director) and commissioned a new script. Knowing that his score would
never be used, Weill nevertheless had to finish it to be paid his $10,000 fee.[7]
He bitterly recorded his feelings about the studio system in a letter to Cheryl
Crawford: "A whore never loves the man who pays her. She wants to get rid
of him as soon as she has rendered her services. That is my relation to
Hollywood (I am the whore)."[8]

Disillusioned but undaunted, Weill accepted another commission, this
one for a film entitled *You and Me*. Norman Krasna's story concerned a
convict working on parole in a department store who falls in love with a
fellow employee, not realizing that she, too, is a former convict. As part of
the score, Weill composed a "Knocking Song" for the department store's
other parolees, who plan a robbery and recall tapping on prison walls to
communicate with one another. Scored for pitched and unpitched percussion
instruments, the piece echoes *Porgy and Bess*'s "Occupational Humoresque"
played on everyday objects by members of Catfish Row.

During 1937 Weill and Lenya made a commitment to stay together,
remarry, and settle permanently in the United States. Reflecting patriotism
for his new homeland, Weill's next five projects all drew on American
history. With the Group Theatre in disarry, he turned to New York's other
alternative subsidized theater, the Federal Theatre Project.[9] He and his
collaborator from *Johnny Johnson* began a pageant about colonial America.
Although they decided to build it around Samuel Adams, the project missed
its deadline and was shelved.[10] Weill then began another show with playwright Hoffman R. Hays called "The Ballad of Davy Crockett." When it
was nearly finished and Henry Fonda was lined up to play Davy, financial

backers could not be found.[11] By the spring of 1938 Weill had lost patience with alternative theater.

That year Maxwell Anderson, S. N. Behrman, Sidney Howard, Elmer Rice, and Robert E. Sherwood broke ranks with the Theatre Guild and founded the Playwrights' Producing Company.[12] Weill convinced Anderson, one of America's foremost dramatists of the 1930s, to collaborate on an adaptation of Washington Irving's *The History of New York by Diedrich Knickerbocker*. Anderson's script combined the political foibles of the Dutch settlers of Manhattan in 1647 with a central love story. A thinly disguised satire of FDR's New Deal, *Knickerbocker Holiday* starred Walter Huston and opened as the Playwrights' second offering.[13] Despite a run of 168 performances and a meager budget, *Knickerbocker Holiday* was neither a financial nor a critical success.

With their budding friendship, Weill and Anderson embarked on an adaptation of Harry Stillwell Edward's novella *Aeneas Africanus*. Its improbable story concerned an African slave, separated from his owners during the Civil War, who spends Reconstruction wandering through the South trying to return his master's silver. In its idyllic depiction of plantation life, the novella recalls Stephen Foster's plantation songs. Not coincidentally, Weill and Anderson planned to include a minstrel show for the protagonist to join. It is no wonder that Paul Robeson refused the part, and, with Bill "Bojangles" Robinson currently engaged in *The Hot Mikado*, the project was abandoned.[14]

During this period Weill was commissioned to provide the music for one of the New York World's Fair exhibits focused on transportation. The Eastern Presidents' Conference, an organization of twenty-seven railroad companies, sponsored *Railroads on Parade*. Edward Hungerford's script traced the history of U.S. rail transport from 1825, through the advent of steam locomotives, to the modern Pullman car. Showcasing events in U.S. history, the pageant featured actors, singers, an ensemble of one hundred, and even functioning locomotives. Staged near the Corona Gate, *Railroads on Parade* proved to be immensely popular.[15]

Nevertheless by the fall of 1939, Weill's options had virtually dried up. Congress, after a heated debate, had abolished the Federal Theatre Project. The Group Theatre had ceased mounting productions and would soon disband. Weill's feelings about Hollywood had further soured, as little of his score for *You and Me* survived the final editing. Although he and Maxwell Anderson planned to write a radio cantata, he had no other prospects for the 1939–1940 season. To bide his time, he composed some incidental music for Sidney Howard's *Madame, Will You Walk?* and Elmer Rice's *Two on an Island*. With only the avenue of Broadway before him and a major show still not in sight, he recalled the operatic aspirations of *Porgy and Bess*: "We can and will develop a musical-dramatic form in this country, but I don't think it will be called 'opera'.... It will develop from and remain a part of the American theater—'Broadway' theater, if you like. More than anything else, I want to have a part in that development."[16] What Weill could not have realized is that his part in the development had already begun.

That fall at a fashionable restaurant on East Fifty-fifth, he had met with Moss Hart, one of the pillars of 1930s theater, whose numerous comedies with George S. Kaufman had made him a household name. The luncheon had lasted well into the evening, as the two discussed the type of show each wanted to do.[17] For Weill, it was not the regulation musical comedy that tried to be, as he had lectured, both sophisticated and lowbrow. For Hart, it was not a musical that would shackle his creative aspirations. Instead, they decided, it was a show in which music carried forward the essential story. Because Hart had another play on the horizon and limited experience drafting a libretto, he suggested a lyricist who he and Weill agreed would be perfect: Ira Gershwin.

Since George's death in 1937, Ira had virtually retired. He dabbled with Jerome Kern on a series of single songs, the titles of which seem to document the depth of Ira's grief at losing both a brother and collaborator: "Something's Wrong," "Once There Were Two of Us," and "Now That We Are One." Ira recalled that it was George's music that finally brought him comfort: "One afternoon I got to the record player and somehow found myself putting on the Fred Astaire–Johnny Green recordings of the *Shall We Dance* score, most of which had been written in that very room less than a year before. In a few moments the room was filled with gaiety and rhythm, and I felt that George, smiling and approving, was there listening with me— and grief vanished."[18] Ira memorialized this event in another song with Kern, "I've Turned the Corner."

Although he dipped into George's unpublished melodies for the World's Fair theme song, Ira did not return to writing full time until joining *Lady in the Dark*. As he remembered it, the call came in early 1940: "Moss Hart on the wire in New York. He was writing a new show about a brilliant editor of a fashion magazine, a woman admired and envied yet unhappy and alone. The action would revolve around her psychoanalysis. Kurt Weill had agreed to do the score. They both wanted him for the lyrics. Would he consider it?"[19] Without pausing, Ira said yes and hung up.

Given his string of comedies, Moss Hart was an unlikely collaborator for a new musical, although the topic of psychoanalysis was a natural. His meteoric rise to success is one of the great rags-to-riches stories.[20] Teaming with George S. Kaufman in 1929 to help him rewrite his play *Once in a Lifetime*, Hart achieved overnight success. The extended run of 406 performances allowed him to move his parents and brother from their run-down Brooklyn apartment to a fashionable Manhattan address. Hart insisted that they leave everything behind: furniture, clothes—even kitchen utensils.[21] After twenty-six years of poverty, Hart was suddenly the toast of the town. The rapid change was difficult on his psyche, and around 1933 he began seeing a psychiatrist.

Hart worked on several projects before he and Kaufman settled into a steady collaboration. First there was *Face the Music*, for which Hart provided the book and Irving Berlin wrote the music. Hart and Berlin followed that with a musical revue entitled *As Thousands Cheer*; its sketches were cleverly derived from headlines of an imaginary newspaper. Hart's next project was the book for a biographical operetta about the Johann Strausses, father and son, entitled *The Great Waltz*. Hart and Kaufman reunited for *Merrily We Roll Along*, which examined in reverse chronological order the career of a disillusioned playwright. Hart's last endeavor before he and Kaufman solidified their partnership was written during a four-and-a-half-month cruise around the world with Cole Porter. Opening two nights after *Porgy and Bess*, *Jubilee* recounted the lighthearted story of a royal family celebrating its Silver Jubilee.

Hart's sessions with the psychiatrist were paying off, as Kaufman noted in a letter to his wife: "Moss . . . is well again—that's all I can say. I asked him in detail, and didn't get a lot—he says he is back where he was two years ago. Others who have been around him say they never see any signs of unhappiness. He looks marvelous, and to me that's that."[22] Together Kaufman and Hart penned *You Can't Take It With You*, about the eccentric Sycamore household, a loony but lovable menagerie with a snake tank in the living room, a fireworks assembly plant in the cellar, and mottos from Trotsky above the front door. Coming at the depth of the Depression, *You Can't Take It With You* was the perfect escape and racked up 837 performances. Not only did it win the Pulitzer Prize for drama, but the following year's film version also won Academy Awards for best picture and best director (Frank Capra). Its critical success was matched by its commercial draw: *Variety* estimated the Broadway income at $1,250,000, the film rights were sold to Columbia Pictures for $200,000, and numerous touring companies made it the playwrights' most valuable property.

Hart took his share of the royalties and purchased a farmhouse on eighty-seven acres in New Hope, Pennsylvania. As much joy as the country retreat gave him, it also served as a refuge during his depressions, which typically followed his successes. With his creative counterpart nearby at his own farm in Bucks County, weekends assumed a predictable pattern: Friday evening at the Kaufmans' Barley Sheaf Farm, Saturday evening at Hart's Fairview Farm, and lots of time spent shuttling between the two for cards and croquet.[23] Kaufman and Hart's collaborations assumed the rhythm of writing a play or two in the spring for production the following season. After *You Can't Take It With You*, they wrote six more together.

Drawing on his personal experience, Hart suggested psychoanalysis, and specifically the Freudian technique of free association, as a topic for their fourth play. He explained the process in a *New York Times* interview: "You lie down on a sofa and let your mind drift and you come through with everything that flashes across your consciousness." Kaufman and Hart in-tended Marlene Dietrich to star (her box-office decline in Hollywood meant that she might be available). After a couple of weeks' work, they had drafted the first act: "Dietrich was the central figure and she was taken over the hurdles, the hot sands, the loops, and what have you. It was six times as fantastic as a Marx Brothers film and crazier than an opium smoker's dream. It was so completely ga-ga that it was torn into small pieces at the end of two weeks and burned."[24] In those ashes, the seeds for what would become *Lady in the Dark* had been planted.

Kaufman and Hart instead penned a satire about FDR entitled *I'd Rather Be Right*, with a score by Richard Rodgers and Lorenz Hart (no relation to Moss). Coming on the heals of *You Can't Take It with You, I'd Rather Be Right* fused the partnership of Kaufman-and-Hart in the minds of many Americans. Although the marriage of their two names into a single entity gave their shows brand recognition (along the lines of Harrigan and Hart and Gilbert and Sullivan), Hart eventually grew restless.

His correspondence with Dore Schary offers glimpses into his depressions during this period.[25] Hart and Schary's friendship extended back to 1929, when Hart had been social director of Camp Flagler in the Catskills and Schary was his assistant. Schary had also been part of the playwright's theater troupe when Hart first mounted a reading of *Once in a Lifetime*. Schary had convinced the aspiring playwright to show his play to a producer, which eventually led to his partnership with Kaufman. After Schary's Broadway debut in *The Last Mile* in 1930, he left for Hollywood, where he began a long career as a film writer, producer, and, in 1941, MGM executive.

From the Waldorf-Astoria, Hart wrote Schary about a recent suicide attempt: "Last week I came very close to what is called putting an end to it all—but I threw the stuff away, and I don't think I'll ever come that close again." A short note sometime later, again from the Waldorf, shows Hart hanging in there: "Please forgive my silence—I've been very low the last few weeks.... The only news I can report is that I'm still here and not completely cracked-up—and that at least is a victory." By early January 1938 things were again looking up: "I spent Christmas down here at the Farm, trimmed my first Christmas Tree with these two hot little hands, and as I write I am suffused with a kind of contentment and serenity that is completely alien to me—but oh, how nice it is to have a kind of peace in one's flesh at last!"[26]

Despite the upbeat tone of Hart's correspondence, by the time he and Kaufman returned from Hollywood in March, his mood was bleak. Rehearsing a new revue, *Sing Out the News*, casting *The Fabulous Invalid*, writing a new work about the Nazis, and planning a project with Irving Berlin seem only to have intensified Hart's troubles. He wrote to Schary in mid-August, "As a kind of medicine, I have filled my days with work to the point of exhaustion on the basis that the less time I have to think the better. It doesn't help very much but it fills in the days."[27] To make matters worse, both of his collaborations with Kaufman that fall flopped.

Kaufman and Hart's next undertaking was to be a pageant with a cast of no fewer than 260 in Rockefeller Center's thirty-eight-hundred-seat Center Theatre. Before *The American Way* went into rehearsal for its January 1938 opening, Hart gave Schary an update on his condition: "The best news is that I'm making progress with the Doctor—painful and oh so slow, but I'm much better than I've been in months. At least that awful mania to destroy myself doesn't sweep over me every other night. I'm beginning to breathe again."[28] *The American Way*, a thinly disguised parable about rising fascism in Europe, opened to favorable reviews despite Hart's fear that it would go down like the SS *Titanic*.

After Hart visited Schary in California, he and Kaufman sat down in late February to write a play for and about their friend Alexander Woollcott and a weekend experience at Fairview Farm. After tryouts in Hartford and Boston, *The Man Who Came to Dinner* began a long and profitable run of 739 performances. During the Boston tryout, one of the seeds for *Lady in the Dark* sprouted. Hart had long admired Katharine Cornell, who was also in Boston opening a new show. He had first seen her in the 1924 revival of Shaw's *Candida*. After that performance, he had waited outside the stage door for a glimpse of the star:

Finally, when it seemed that I must perish with the cold, the stage-door opened, and, silhouetted against that magic and wonderful background of light that only stage-doors glimpsed down an alley on a Winter's night possess, stood Candida herself.

Though she has since denied any recollection of it, I could have sworn Katharine Cornell smiled directly at me, and if she didn't whisper "You must write a play for me some day" as she brushed by, you have only my word against hers.

Now, fifteen years later, Hart again waited outside a Boston stage door to see Cornell, this time after her performance in S. N. Behrman's *No Time for Comedy*. At this meeting he promised to write a play for her, adding, "I'll catch you in Philadelphia—end of March—and read you the first act."[29] After his next comedy with Kaufman, he intended to write a serious drama by himself.

That fall Hart typed a long letter to Schary describing the first snow of the season and his happiness at being in the country. He also outlined his plans to be in Chicago Christmas evening and Los Angeles in February for the opening of those cities' productions of *The Man Who Came to Dinner*. During this period Hart met Weill for the first time at a party given by Walter Huston. The meeting was uneventful. Hart recalled their introduction, dished up with theatrical relish:

> "How do you do, Mr. Weill. I'm a great admirer of your music."
> "Thank you, Mr. Hart. I have no alternative but to say that I admire your plays. But I really do."
> "Lovely party, isn't it?"
> "It was. Getting late, though. I'd better be going. Nice to have met you."
> "Good-night, Mr. Weill."[30]

Hart's name, however, came up when Weill and stage designer Hassard "Bobby" Short were discussing a script entitled "The Funnies," based on the drawings of John Held Jr. Little is known about the project, but the subject matter probably prompted Short to think of Hart, who had provided the sketches for the newspaper-inspired *As Thousands Cheer*, which Short had directed. He advised Weill to arrange a meeting with Hart regarding the script: if anyone was in a position to evaluate a comedy, it was Moss Hart.

Weill sent the script to Hart, who read it and then telephoned Short to set up a luncheon date. As Hart recalled, he and Weill ultimately decided they were uninterested in working on the project:

> One rainy afternoon . . . Kurt Weill and myself sat at a table in a little midtown restaurant and told each other vehemently why we would not write a musical comedy. . . .

> We parted in complete agreement though it was a far cry from the purpose of the meeting. We had arranged to meet to see if we could not do a show together and had thoroughly succeeded in discovering that we couldn't. That is, we were both completely disinterested in doing a show for the sake of doing a show, in Broadway parlance, and the tight little formula of the musical comedy stage held no interest for either of us.[31]

After lunch Hart must have realized that in articulating what he was *not* interested in doing, he had indeed outlined the type of work that *would* interest him. As he was attempting to free himself from Kaufman, Hart confessed to Weill that he had little motivation to collaborate on someone else's script.

The next week Hart and Weill met again for lunch, this time for Hungarian Viennese cuisine at the Hapsburg House on East Fifty-fifth. There Hart revealed to Weill what he believed would be, in his words, a perfect amalgam of their talents: "Why not show someone in the process of being psychoanalyzed and dramatize the dreams? And what more natural than that the dreams be conveyed by music and lyrics so that the plane of reality and that of the dreams would be distinct?"[32] Weill must have been impressed that Hart already had a scenario, although the topic had been entertained by Hart and Kaufman nearly three years prior. Additionally, the composer must have been reassured that Hart had already promised Katharine Cornell the central role. Weill was acutely aware that on Broadway a star could either make a show (what Walter Huston had done for *Knickerbocker Holiday*) or break it (what Bill "Bojangles" Robinson had done to the adaptation of *Aeneas Africanus*).

After Hart's telephone call to Ira Gershwin, the *New York Times* caught wind of their project and ran the headline "Hart Writes Play; Has No Co-Author: Serious Drama Being Written by Him Independently for a Fall Premiere; Sam H. Harris to Produce." The reporter did not have many details, but he did know that "its presentation would come after the new play on which Messrs. Hart and Kaufman expect to start writing on June 1 at their summer homes in Bucks County, Pa."[33] Hart worked out the particulars of the collaboration with Gershwin when he traveled to Hollywood to confer on the movie version of *The Man Who Came to Dinner*. On February 18, the *Times*'s Rialto Gossip column revealed that the "full outline" of Hart's play was finished and that he was "speaking the dialogue into a dictaphone."[34] Both the *Daily Mirror* and *Herald Tribune* learned of Gershwin's involvement and speculated that he might be checking in soon.

Hart returned to New York on Friday, February 23. He wasted no time in contacting the *Times*, which ran a story the following day, headlined

"Moss Hart Play Will Have Songs." It mentions Weill and Gershwin for the "incidental music," but cautions that the work, a "romantic story of a woman's failure," is, in Hart's words, "definitely . . . not a musical comedy."[35] On Sunday he spoke to a reporter to clarify the extent of Weill's involvement. On Monday the *Times* printed a retraction: "Moss Hart, author of 'I Am Listening,' explained yesterday that Kurt Weill's score for his new play could not be classified as 'incidental music.' His contribution and Mr. Weill's are of equal importance to the production."[36] With the play properly announced, Hart retired to Fairview Farm on March 1 to begin writing.

Hart's idea for the project had originated with psychiatrist Lawrence S. Kubie, who saw Hart as a patient from about 1937 until he retired from private practice in 1959. As Hart liked to tell it, he had been going to Kubie's office so long that when he first went up Fifth Avenue "the Indians were still shooting arrows from behind the trees."[37] Hart and Kubie's relationship eventually transcended the clinical to include personal correspondence and attending lectures and dinner engagements together. In an interview, Hart revealed his reasons for writing the play: "Over the last few years I've literally sabotaged every serious idea I've had for a play. And so my psychoanalyst made me resolve that the next idea I had, whether it was good or lousy, I'd carry through. This was my next idea, and it was about the toughest one I've ever had to realize."[38]

Lawrence Kubie received his MD from Johns Hopkins University in 1921. Like Freud, his early study focused on neurohistology. He received his psychoanalytic training at the London Institute for Psycho-Analysis from 1928 to 1930. During this time he was analyzed by Edward Glover and, later, Herman Nunberg. Upon returning to the United States, he joined the faculty of the New York Psychoanalytic Institute and established a private practice. During his illustrious career, he was on the faculties of Yale and Columbia Universities, the staff of Sheppard and Enoch Pratt Hospital, and finally the faculties of the University of Maryland and Johns Hopkins University.[39]

During the 1930s a debate had raged about the role of lay psychologists. In the foreword to his first book, *Practical Aspects of Psychoanalysis: A Handbook for Prospective Patients and Their Advisors*, Kubie outlined his position:

This book is written to help people recognize sound psychoanalytical procedure when they meet it, and to introduce them to those institutes for the training of psychoanalysts which at present constitute their best protection against charlatans in this field.

This is a fighting book, in that one of its purposes in clarifying the meaning of psychoanalysis is to exterminate pseudo-analysis by inadequately trained or irresponsible analysts, whether these are found within or without the official psychoanalytic fold.[40]

Kubie's belief that psychoanalysts should have graduated from medical school was a hotly contested issue between Freud and his American colleagues. After Freud's publication of *The Question of Lay Analysis* in 1926, in which he defended the practice, the *New York Times* quoted him as saying, "A medical man cannot practice psychoanalysis because he always has medicine in his mind, which is not necessary in cases where my treatment can effect good."[41] In a 1927 international symposium on the topic, Kubie's mentors, Glover and Nunberg, had supported lay analysis, whereas American psychiatrists, such as Kubie, opposed the practice. This debate subsequently played a role in Hart's play.

Hart based the premise of "I Am Listening" on Freud's 1913 essay "The Theme of the Three Caskets."[42] Freud begins by examining a scene from Shakespeare's *The Merchant of Venice* involving three caskets made of gold, silver, and lead. Portia's father has stipulated that she will take as her husband whichever suitor chooses the casket containing her portrait. After the first two suitors have unsuccessfully picked gold and silver, the third, Bassanio, chooses lead and wins Portia's hand. Shakespeare borrowed this scenario from the medieval *Gesta Romanorum*, in which a girl must make a similar choice. Freud in his essay emphasizes that the tale of a girl or boy choosing between three suitors is an ancient one: variants can be found in the Estonian folk-epic Kalewipoeg, the Greek myth of the shepherd Paris, and the fairy tale of Cinderella.

For Freud, the theme of the three caskets or suitors is not so much about the choice per se, but uncovering the hidden forces within the person who must choose. He analyzes the three possibilities as a type of unconscious wish fulfillment with love standing in for the necessity of death (represented by the lead casket). Freud reads the choice between three caskets (for him, symbolically representing women) as archetypal of the three relations that a man has with a woman: the woman who bore him (his mother), the woman who is his mate (his wife), and the woman who destroys him and in which he is buried (Mother Earth).

For "I Am Listening," Hart adapted some version of the *Gesta Romanarum* story. In the medieval tale, the gold casket bears the inscription that whoever chooses it shall find what she deserves. Out of humility, the girl rejects the casket, and it turns out to contain a dead man's bones. The silver casket promises that choosing it will provide what her nature craves. The girl passes over it, saying, "My nature craves for fleshly delights."[43] Finally, the leaden casket's inscription reads that whoever chooses it will discover what God has ordained for her, and it proves to contain precious jewels. By making a wise choice, the girl wins the hand of the emperor's son. In Hart's play, Kendall Nesbitt, an older, wealthy businessman, represents the gold casket. Randy Curtis, a Hollywood heartthrob, stands in for the silver casket. And Charley Johnson, an ordinary advertising manager, represents the lead casket. Liza Elliott's suitors thus symbolize the three relationships that she has or will have with men in her life, standing in for the roles of father, lover, and husband.

Hart initially structured "I Am Listening" in two acts of four scenes each, alternating between Liza's office and Dr. Brooks's, with a detour in the second act for a scene at a restaurant called Le Coq d'Or:

Act I

Scene 1—Dr. Brooks's Office
Scene 2—Liza Elliott's Office
Scene 3—Dr. Brooks's Office (the same afternoon)
Scene 4—Liza Elliott's Office (late the next afternoon)

Act II

Scene 1—Liza Elliott's Office (late the following afternoon)
Scene 2—Dr. Brooks's Office (later that evening)
Scene 3—Le Coq d'Or
Scene 4—Liza Elliott's Office (the next afternoon)[44]

Each of the acts took Hart approximately two and a half months to write, the first from March to mid-May and the second from mid-May until August 1940. About two-thirds of "I Am Listening" was drafted at Fairview Farm, during a process that Hart described as "pure torture."[45]

After sequestering himself, Hart did not give any more reports to the press. He may have been worried about losing his story because of so many psychoanalytic projects in the news, occasioned by Freud's death the previous fall. On March 22 a notice appeared that Martin J. Lewis, an importer of foreign films, intended to produce "Doctor Freud." Written by psychiatrist Luis Perelman, the play promised to document Freud's entire career. Two days later the *Times* announced that Murdock Pemberton, a member of Norman Bel Geddes's staff, and Walter Casey, a radio writer, had collaborated on a play called "Cradle and All." Its subject matter revolved around "young people who get tangled up with Freud." In addition, several times during February and March, Guy Endore's screenplay "The Life of Freud" was mentioned as an upcoming vehicle for Edward G. Robinson.[46]

On March 18 Ira Gershwin typed a letter to Weill about their upcoming project. He wrote that he was planning to arrive in New York at the end of April and expressed delight that Katharine Cornell's husband, Guthrie McClintic, was also interested in the project. In the letter, he devotes equal space to "The Funnies" and "I Am Listening," although admitting that his enthusiasm for the former had been dulled by "I Am Listening": "Now that Moss feels (and I agree) that our Gary Cooper character [Randy Curtis] should be in a Western scene that he dominates [Liza's daydream] I have unconsciously been comparing that scene with the scenes in 'Funnies' that Red Ryder would have had." Gershwin discouraged Weill from pursuing both projects, because "the treatment of the dream fantasies would be somewhat similar."[47]

The greatest problem for Gershwin and Weill was getting started. Weill was accustomed to producing a musical score once a libretto had been fashioned according to a carefully planned scenario. With the exception of *The Eternal Road*, he had taken part in this process, helping to shape the libretto according to his musical designs and making specific plans based on it. In contrast, Gershwin was accustomed to "fitting words mosaically to music already composed."[48] He had provided witty lyrics for his brother's memorable melodies, which had often been improvised at the piano. Although many of the Gershwins' songs were incorporated into revues, musicals, and film scores, Ira was rarely responsible for the sketches, book, or screenplay. The conundrum in which Weill and Gershwin found themselves was that each wanted the other to make the first move.

Gershwin's letter was a response to a telephone call from Weill requesting lyrics that he could set. Gershwin went to great lengths to explain the working method of Broadway lyricists:

> I don't think I have any stray lyrics you can be fooling around with—much as I'd like to send you a batch. In nine cases out of ten I have written to music, or just have given a title and a couple of possible first lines. In the case of "Listening" as in *Of Thee I Sing* and *Let 'Em Eat Cake* which were not song shows in the usual sense but combined song with recitative and patter there should of course be some lyric matter written first—but until we know pretty definitely how we are going to treat each musical scene and until I get some sort of outline of the whole I really think the best thing is for you to continue jotting down musical notions, whether they be in complete song form or only starts in 4 or 8 bars.[49]

Weill, who was expanding *Railroads on Parade* for the 1940 World's Fair, filled fourteen pages of a spiral sketchbook with musical ideas. Although most of these never found their way into the score, the composer was able to notate initial ideas for what became "One Life to Live," "This Is New," and "My Ship."

To prepare himself fully for the project, Weill examined his own psyche for possible inspiration. Sitting down at his typewriter, he brainstormed about dreams in general, wrote out one of his own dreams from the previous night, and listed several ideas for the project (Figure 26).[50] Weill's dream is particularly revealing. The setting—a party of people representing leaders of music in different countries—could have been inspired by his ongoing involvement in the World's Fair (by nature, a global cultural exchange). Given his recent projects with American themes, it is no surprise that the German émigré dreamed of being appointed a musical representative for a new country.

The dream shifts to a personal situation involving literary agent Harold Freedman. The masculine demeanor of Freedman's daughter mirrors Liza Elliott, who dresses in severely tailored business suits. Weill's relationship to the mannish girl (who resembles Freedman and, once Weill agrees to marry her, actually becomes Freedman) resonates with his on-again, off-again relationship with Lenya ("living in sin" versus marriage). Weill's own interpretation of this dream—"Mixture of emotion and business (a business acquaintance suddenly in the place of a lover)"—anticipates Liza's *Wedding Dream* where Randy Curtis becomes a romantic interest.

Weill's typescript concludes with a list of ideas for the show. The idea for a film studio setting was originally part of the *Wedding Dream*. "Coq d'Or" refers to the setting of Act II, Scene 3, which Hart described in the script as "a fashionable luncheon place in the East Fifties." One wonders if Hart and Weill were memorializing their two important luncheon meetings by setting this scene in the same locale.[51] *Le Coq d'Or* is also the name by which an opera of Rimsky-Korsakov's is known in the West. Based on a fairy tale by Pushkin, it was staged by Sergey Diaghilev in Paris and London, with the singers sitting on the sides of the stage and the action pantomimed by dancers.[52] *Le Coq d'Or*'s fairy-tale story and pantomimed action may have been the inspiration for "The Princess of Pure Delight."

Another idea of Weill's was "a musical scene on the basis of 'Strange Interlude,'" which invites comparisons between that 1928 play and the project at hand. Both are based on the same allegory of a woman with three suitors. A four-and-a-half-hour play in nine acts, Eugene O'Neill's *Strange Interlude* was noteworthy for a new theatrical device, the interior monologue. Each of the characters verbalizes his or her thoughts, allowing the audience to be privy to the inner self—a situation not so different from *Lady in the Dark*'s dream sequences. Weill probably knew *Strange Interlude* in the 1932 Metro-Gold-wyn-Mayer adaptation starring Clark Gable and Norma Shearer, from which director Robert Z. Leonard handled the interior monologues as voice-overs. Weill's suggestion of "a chorus singing the real meaning of what people are saying" could be compared to a voice-over technique.

Those ideas that did not directly find their way into the musical play suggest other influences. *The Women*, a 1939 black-and-white film with an extended color fashion show, may have inspired the proposed beauty contest in which Liza is mistaken for her mother. Although the European allusions of the final typewritten idea were not incorporated, *Allure* was modeled on *Vogue*. After removing the paper from the typewriter, Weill scribbled down one last idea: "Mirror [underlined]: Hot song, she sings in place of him when she comes back to town/Paris, but has changed into big Jewel of America." It is not clear whether the "hot song" here is the same one mentioned in the last typewritten idea or a different piece. In either case, Weill already intended for Liza to sing a big number to close the show.

Down at Fairview Farm, Hart was battling artistic as well as personal demons. A series of deadlines were closing in: he had promised to read the first act for Katharine Cornell in less than a month, he and Kaufman had agreed to get together around the first of June to write a new play, and he was under contract for *The Man Who Came to Dinner*'s screenplay. The parallels between what Hart began writing and Kubie's *Practical Aspects of Psychoanalysis* suggest that the desperate author turned to it for guidance.

Psychoanalyst Alexander Brooks is a medical doctor, as Kubie firmly believed he should be. Liza's general physician referred her to him, as recommended in Kubie's handbook. Dr. Brooks and Liza show no signs of familiarity in their first meeting—an important prerequisite for what Kubie termed "analytic incognito." Liza comes to Dr. Brooks and discusses the desirability of analysis rather than asking to be analyzed, another piece of Kubie's advice. Her nervousness and halting delivery correspond to Kubie's description of patients approaching analysis with hesitation and misgiving. When Liza finally breaks down and asks Dr. Brooks for his help, he advises her to "embark upon a trial analysis—for a month," just as Kubie suggested.

With Liza now prepared to undergo analysis, she wants to delay scheduling her first session until the following week. Dr. Brooks's insistence that she begin immediately follows Kubie's admonition that "treatment be instituted just as early as the patient can be brought to realize his need of help."[53]

Dr. Brooks convinces Liza to begin and engages her in the basic analytic tool of free association. Kubie had adopted the British Medical Association's limitation on the term "psychoanalysis" to only "the method evolved by Freud and to the theories derived from the use of this method."[54] In Hart's first draft, Liza inquires, "Is this strictly according to Freud?" At the end of the session, Liza schedules her next appointment for the following day. This adheres to Kubie's dictum regarding the necessity of a daily session.

Liza's analysis also follows the trajectory Kubie outlined in his handbook. In his fifth chapter, Kubie describes the two roles the analyst must play: "In one he maps out for the patient a hitherto unknown psychic territory. He describes in a quiet, friendly, but impersonal manner the significant connections which he sees between the various components of the patient's free thoughts." This is the role Dr. Brooks assumes at the first session: he notes that in Liza's dream of celebrity, she appears to be the opposite of her real self. The dispassionate behavior of the analyst in this first role contrasts with the second: "The patient soon discovers, however, that this work cannot proceed in an emotional vacuum; and that no matter how quietly encouraging and impersonal the psychoanalyst remains, . . . [he] soon becomes the storm-center of highly charged emotions. . . . This is what is known technically as 'the analysis of the transference-situation.'"[55] At the end of Liza's second session such transference occurs.

Kubie recommends, "When a patient gets into a state of obsessional indecision, . . . the analysis tries to defer all impulsive pseudo-solutions of the problem." At the session Liza is distraught over what to do with Kendall's proposal, but Dr. Brooks recommends that she do nothing. Instead, his persistent questioning about her austere dress and her indifference to Randy precipitates the transference. In Kubie's words, such questioning should be "as tactful and judicious as possible in the administration of pain, but in the end he [the psychiatrist] must be merciless in hounding the neurosis out of every false cover." Dr. Brooks's indictment is so disturbing to Liza that she directs her anger at him, rejects his diagnosis, and terminates the analysis. Kubie believed that only through such transference would it be possible "for the psychoanalyst to make clear to the patient how feelings of which he has been unconscious may warp his relationships to other human beings." The stage is now set for the third session, where, by "unearthing the sources of these feelings in early childhood, the analysis makes it possible to lessen their intensity."[56]

Kubie may have initially recommended his handbook to Hart when he began his analysis, as its subtitle suggests: *A Handbook for Prospective Patients and Their Advisors*. Or he may have suggested the book as a resource for Hart's project. In either case, one of Kubie's colleagues remembered, "He numbered many creative and well-known people among his friends and patients and was intensely interested in the portrayal of human nature in drama and story."[57] When Hart revealed his desire to write a play about psychoanalysis, Kubie may have realized that such a dramatic venture could accomplish one of the underlying goals of his book: "That anyone who contemplates an analysis should have some inkling of the differences between that which is truly psychoanalytic and those many abuses which masquerade under its banner."[58] Hart's play was scrupulous in its depiction of Kubie's brand of Freudian psychoanalysis.

Gershwin boarded *The City of Los Angeles* train on May 3, 1940. As he recalled, the trip was a somber one because Germany had recently invaded France. He arrived in New York and checked into a suite at the Essex House. The week was a busy one, with the Allied Relief Ball at the Hotel Astor on May 10 (both Hart and Kaufman participated, along with Noël Coward) and the opening of the World's Fair the next day (which included the new edition of Weill's pageant). The three collaborators then began an intensive creative period, which lasted until mid-August. Gershwin described it as one of "twelve-to-sixteen[-hour]" days during "one of the hottest summers New York had ever known."[59] Weill and Gershwin's workweek spanned Monday through Saturday. Gershwin described a typical day: "Kurt would arrive from his country home [a rented farmhouse in Suffern, New York] shortly after noon and we would work until dinner time. Frequently we were at the piano after dinner until 11 or 12, when he would leave for the country while I then would go on working until 4 or 5 in the morning on the lyrics for the tunes he had left me. And then I would try to get ideas for the next day's collaborations."[60]

Near the middle of May, Hart put the finishing touches on the first act. Relieved that it was finished, he dashed off a letter to Schary: "I've finished the first act of the play. . . . I've got only two weeks and a half to do the rest of it, because I start work on June first with George on a play for which we haven't got even the remotest idea at the moment. We just arbitrarily said we'd meet June first and do a play. I'm down here alone for that two and one half weeks, and pray for me. How the hell I'm going to write two plays, get them on, take the lecture tour, write the movie script of T.M.W.C.T.D. [*The Man Who Came to Dinner*] and arrive in Hollywood on February 15th alive, I don't know."[61]

Weill and Gershwin began with the only music specified in Hart's script: the childhood song. Its composition was crucial for the drama and the establishment of a working relationship between composer and lyricist.

Several versions of "My Ship" testify to the various dramatic and personal agendas at work. Beyond this song, there appear to have been conflicting ideas as to the extent and style of music the dreams would contain. It is clear from the length of Hart's script that, despite his retraction in the *Times*, he must have considered the music incidental. For Gershwin the model appears to have been his and George's political operettas. Weill, on the other hand, tended to think of the score in operatic terms. Given the divergent models and ideas about the music, it is no wonder that the sequences presented a host of problems.

The *Glamour Dream*, which Weill and Gershwin composed next, sprawled to 778 measures. It is the longest sequence and was the only one to have a consistent title during composition (the spelling was Anglicized from "Glamor" to "Glamour" to seem even more glamorous). Although Hart's scenario for the sequence has not survived, it appears from Gershwin and Weill's drafts that there was never any question as to the sequence of events. In this regard, it is the most integrally conceived of the dreams because the action relates most directly to the drama itself.

The sequence depicts Liza's alter ego in four scenes, which alternate outdoor and indoor locales: first an outdoor serenade ("Oh Fabulous One in Your Ivory Tower"), then indoors for celebrity salutations ("The World's Inamorata"), back outdoors for a speech at Columbus Circle ("One Life to Live"), and finally indoors at the nightclub ("Girl of the Moment"). Each scene leads into the next to create a compelling story, like chapters in a novel. The *Glamour Dream* revolves around two songs that function as nodal points for the sequence: Liza's opening number and the paean to her beauty. These depict a carefree and glamorous Liza from the first and third person, respectively. In contrast to the patter sections, Weill and Gershwin labored over the composition of these two numbers.

Once the songs were finished, Weill and Gershwin drafted each of the four scenes. To glue the scenes together, Weill composed a "glamour theme." He drafted the *Glamour Dream* on the first twenty-one pages of a bound manuscript book. The instrumental prelude that begins the dream sequence and covers the scene change appears to have been composed last and was greatly expanded from the initial draft. Probably because of the sequence's strong narrative, no songs or substantial sections were ever dropped, cut, or added. The principal revision, an expansion of "Girl of the Moment," addressed production demands.

The *Glamour Dream* dashes the audience's expectations based on musical comedy norms of the late 1930s. For example, the opening male chorus replaces the standard female chorus line. The ensuing scene in Liza's boudoir delays her opening number, which, when it finally occurs, fulfills the "I Am" convention of musical comedy (where an actor sings a song to sum up his or her character).[62] There is no parallel number for a male lead, because at this point in the drama, there is none. Liza's suitors subsequently present musical numbers in the *other* sequences, with her true love not singing until the final moments of the play. The first sequence is solely about Liza's glamorous persona.

After the *Glamour Dream* was nearly finished, Weill and Gershwin spent one of two working weekends at Fairview Farm. Gershwin ecstatically remembered the visits: "The food was excellent, the guestrooms cozy; there were a large swimming pool and thousands of trees and any amount of huge and overwhelmingly friendly, woolly dogs; there was even that rarity for those days (1940), a TV set."[63] Weill and Gershwin probably did not spend more time there because it was functioning as the creative headquarters for Kaufman and Hart's last comedy about a city couple who attempt to restore a dilapidated country house in Bucks County. Kaufman's country retreat was, in turn, the scene of another collaborative endeavor: his wife, Beatrice, was working with Charles Martin on a play called *The White-Haired Boy*.[64]

During the first working weekend, Hart, Gershwin, and Weill spent several hours discussing the outlines of the second and third dream sequences. When they gathered, the first portion of "The Second Dream" (as the *Wedding Dream* was then known) had been drafted, including "This Is New" and a song entitled "Unforgettable." After discussing possible conclusions to the dream, Hart retreated to his library. In an hour he returned with two typed outlines. One, headed "Dream Two," documents his ideas of how that sequence should end, beginning with an interpolated movie-set scene and "Unforgettable." Hart's outline for "Dream Three" reveals that it was the least developed at that time.[65]

The *Wedding Dream* is episodic in character. At 356 measures it is the shortest of the three completed sequences and can be likened to an anthology of short stories that share many of the same characters. Originally, five stories alternated and combined recollections from Liza's childhood and adolescence with projections from the future. In the first, Liza's high school classmates reminisce as she and Kendall choose a wedding ring ("It Looks Like Liza" and "Mapleton High Choral"). This mixture of past and future is interrupted by Liza and Randy's love duet ("This Is New"). The third replays a scene from childhood when Liza and her classmates enacted a fairy tale ("The Princess of Pure Delight"). The projected fourth story transported Liza's staff onto Randy's turf: Russell impersonates a movie director, with Liza and Randy assuming the romantic leads ("Unforgettable").[66] The jumbled nightmare concludes with Liza and Kendall's wedding ("This Woman at the Altar").

Weill and Gershwin appear to have begun the *Wedding Dream* without a clear sense of where it would end. They composed and drafted several of the stories before Hart outlined the finale. Gershwin's recollection of composing "The Princess of Pure Delight" underscores just how open-ended the process was: "When Kurt and I were on the Second Dream Sequence we came to a spot where Liza and some children were alone on the stage. I suggested—and Kurt liked the notion—that here a sung fairy tale might be incorporated. So next day I got hold of some Andersen and Brothers Grimm, and leafed through for something not too well known to base a narrative on."[67] As the collaborators added various stories, the sequence's lack of a title or concept gave Weill fits on how to fuse it together. Part of the problem with its conception may be attributed to Hart's completion of the second act as the score for the first was being composed. That is, certain requirements referred to at the end of the drama, such as the children's play, had to be retroactively added to the sequence. Weill turned to a dance idiom to provide structural coherence. The composer's choice of a bolero does not appear arbitrary given the romantic tenor of the stories.

After the first half of the sequence had been drafted, the collaborators decided to axe "Unforgettable" and the soundstage. Two ballads, both of which included Liza and Randy, seemed redundant, so Weill and Gershwin composed "It's Never Too Late to Mendelssohn" for the wedding scene. Because the song is not described in Hart's outline, Weill and Gershwin must have decided to give Russell a comic song to help enliven the sequence, which Weill described as a "little slow, dragging and humorless."[68]

As he did with the *Glamour Dream*'s prelude, Weill composed the introduction to the *Wedding Dream* late in the process and did not include it in his preliminary draft. Had a continuity draft of the entire sequence survived, it might have shed light on how it was assembled (there are only a few surviving sections in the bound sketchbook). Weill and Gershwin labored on the composition of "It's Never Too Late to Mendelssohn" and even composed two different versions; however, the song eventually had to be dropped. In his outline of the sequence's conclusion, Hart called for several events to happen simultaneously:

As Johnson begins to read the marriage service, Randy begins to sing "THIS IS NEW" in the manner of 'O, Promise Me.' As Johnson comes to the part in the service: "Does anyone know of any reason why this man should not take this woman in marriage? Speak now or forever hold your peace!" The Choral again speaks: "Yes.! This woman does not love Kendall Nesbitt. She does not want to marry him."...Now the Choral rises to a musical denunciation of the fact that this marriage is a lie, against which Randy and the guests are singing "This Is New." Liza stands with her face buried in her hands.

The 813-measure *Circus Dream* had the most checkered composition. It went through three versions: a trial minstrel show ("Minstrel Dream"), a circus trial with recess ("Circus Dream"), and a one-part circus trial (*Circus Dream*). Hart's scenario, drafted during the first working weekend, reveals that the two pivotal songs were to be Liza's testimony, "A Woman Has a Right to Change Her Mind," and Randy's defense speech, an astrology song. Given his experience with adapting *Aeneas Africanus*, Weill may have suggested a minstrel show setting. Gershwin cast Dr. Brooks as the interlocutor and judge ("Your vices get paralysis / When into them I pry— / For in the last analysis / An analyst am I"),[69] Charley as an end man and prosecuting attorney, and Randy as the other end man and defense attorney. Gershwin's draft of the "Minstrel Dream" is incomplete, but after the introductions, the end men— "Mr. Bones" and "Mr. Tambo"—pose riddles.

The composer's draft of the sequence, titled "No. 3 Minstrel Dream," includes the Chorus's entrance, the arrival of the interlocutor, and the end men's introductions. At two points Weill left gaps for the riddles; presumably they would have been spoken. Gershwin remembered that despite their progress, "One day, Hassard Short, in charge of the physical production (scenery, costumes, turn tables, etc.), felt this sequence would be more spectacular if the trial proceedings took place in a circus rather than a minstrel show."[70] Short may have figured out that a circus setting could be motivated by the play itself (the circus cover under consideration at *Allure*). Gershwin attempted to go through the typescript draft and change references to the minstrel show. Both he and Weill must have soon realized that the sequence needed to be rethought. Although some of the rhymes and speeches could be salvaged, what was needed was a new beginning.

Gershwin rewrote the interlocutor's opening for a barker ("Ladies and gentlemen, I take pride in introducing / The Greatest Show on Earth"), although he never specified *who* was to play the part. Instead of Dr. Brooks as the interlocutor and Judge, Kendall substituted as the Ringmaster and Judge. Perhaps Hart felt that introducing Dr. Brooks into one of Liza's dreams would complicate matters and might reinforce the perception that patients always fall in love with their analyst. Gershwin retained the introductions of Randy and Charley as the respective defense and prosecuting attorneys. However, Charley asks Kendall (the Judge!) to take the witness stand and explain to the jury how Liza refused to marry him.

To summarize the situation, the barker sings "The Best Years of His Life." Liza's response to this accusation is a gloss on the barker's song, with a new lyric to the effect that she gave him her heart, but not her word. Because Kendall is hungry, a recess in the trial is called. The second portion of the trial features two additional witnesses: Maggie Grant as a lion tamer and Alison Du Bois as a snake charmer.[71] Alison's explanation that consulting an astrologer could have averted Liza's problems prompts Liza's "No Matter Under What Star You're Born." The trial concludes with an exhibit of each of the zodiac signs, while Randy convinces the jury that his client's fate is in the stars ("Song of the Zodiac"). Convinced that they had completed the sequence, Weill and Gershwin turned their attention to the next one.

As no documentation of the second working weekend at Fairview Farm survives, one can only speculate that Hart must have drafted the outline for the remaining sequence at that time. Although a Western scene was planned for Randy, the "Hollywood Dream," or "Day Dream" as it was variously known, was never completed. This sequence was intended for the scene at Le Coq d'Or. It takes place the day after Liza's session with Dr. Brooks when they explore events from her childhood.

In the original Act II, Scene 3, Liza makes a lunch date with Randy. She arrives at the restaurant and runs into Kendall, who is drowning his troubles at the bar. Maggie is also there waiting for Charley, who arrives inebriated. He compliments Liza for dating such a "butch" man. Kendall pleads with Liza not to leave, as she tries to explain that she is terminating their relationship because of her self-discovery. With the arrival of Randy and as her relationships converge, Liza is no longer sure she can eat lunch. Following Kendall's and Charley's lead, she orders a drink and, after two more, feels a bit calmer. As she and Randy talk, she begins to daydream about what life would be like as his wife.

Liza imagines the staff of Randy's southern California ranch preparing the estate for her: filling the swimming pool, air-conditioning the house, installing additional tennis courts, and tending the gardens. A crowd of Hollywood celebrities gathers to welcome Randy and his new bride. Liza, unaccustomed to such a party, eavesdrops and hears the guests discussing a film preview the previous evening, troubles with servants, and remodeling of palatial homes. When the guests bid Randy and his new bride farewell, he assures her that the gathering has been a very good Hollywood party.

The dream survives only as separate scenes, which were never fused into a sequence. From what remains, it appears that the daydream was not intended to be as long as the previous sequences. The surviving three vignettes suggest a narrative thread. First there is the frenetic preparation by Randy's staff for their arrival ("The Boss Is Bringing Home the Bride"), then Randy's presentation of his West Coast estate to Liza ("In Our Little House in the San Fernando Valley"), and finally a lavish party ("Hollywood Party" or "Party Parlando"), which is interrupted by a flood and a fire. Hart outlined the never-realized conclusion: "Liza goes to Randy's arms for a reprise of the San Fernando Valley song, but this time with new lyric covering lapse of years. The stage is growing darker as they sing, and blends into the trick of Christmas tree and children at the end."[72] The central song for the daydream appears to have been "In Our Little House in the San Fernando Valley"; as in the previous sequences, more compositional material survives for it than the sections for the Chorus. Gershwin's lampoon of the lavish southern California lifestyle and its wealthy inhabitants (which he was a part of) served as West Coast counterpart to the East Coast setting of the *Glamour Dream*.

Because of the sweltering heat, the collaborators called a break in mid-August. Gershwin returned to California, and Hart and Weill escaped to New England. Hart went to Woollcott's artistic colony in Lake Bomoseen, Vermont, while Weill journeyed to the Owl's Head Inn in Maine. While at Woollcott's island retreat, Hart jotted off a note to Schary: "I'll try and send you a script of my play. It's completely experimental—not a comic line in it—and I may go right on my ass. But it's a very adventurous thing to have done, and I don't care much if it's an absolute failure. It's a play with music running through it, you know, and Kurt Weill has done what seems to me to be a magnificent job. And Ira's lyrics are enchanting. It's a most difficult play to do and quite likely to be a mess unless we have a bit of luck, but I look forward to all the difficulties with a good deal of eagerness."[73] Hart was joined on Neshobe Island by a cast of theatrical associates: Noël Coward, Laurence Olivier, Vivien Leigh, Ruth Gordon, Thornton Wilder, and Alfred Lunt and Lynn Fontanne.

At the Owl's Head, Weill ran into Benjamin Britten and Peter Pears. Britten recounted their meeting in a letter written on the inn's stationery: "We came in to dinner the other evening & heard some pretty sophisticated talk going on & recognised Kurt Weill! He was spending a few days here with Mr. & Mrs. Maxwell Anderson.... We saw quite alot of him & he really was awfully nice & sympathetic, and it was remarkable how many friends we had in common, both in Europe & here."[74]

Once back in New York, Hart and Weill began attending production meetings. At one of them, it was suggested that the title needed changing. "I

Am Listening" was Kubie's stock phrase once his patients were lying on the couch. The germ for the new title can be found in Act I, Scene 3, when Dr. Brooks tells Liza, "I don't think you ought to make a decision in the dark, do you?" and in the Coq d'Or scene where Kendall refers to himself as "a child in the dark." In Gershwin's first letter to Weill after returning to Beverly Hills, he comments on the change, "Think the new title is just what Dr. Brooks prescribed—it has lots of vitamins and is easy to swallow. I like it."[75]

At another production meeting on August 28 at Hart's house, Short suggested to Weill that the restaurant scene and the "Hollywood Dream" be dropped. Weill quickly saw that cutting from the childhood flashbacks to the final scene would tighten the drama. The cut would also reduce the book scenes to two locales, the offices of Dr. Brooks and Liza, which would simplify the stage design. Such a cut, however, threw off the symmetry of two dream sequences per act. To balance the relationship of music and drama in Act II, Weill suggested to Gershwin that they write a song for the flashback to Liza's high school dance.

At the same meeting, Short expressed concern over Liza's defense number. He felt that what was lacking was a "really funny song" or, as Weill explained it to Gershwin, "a show-stopping song with laugh lines." Short and Hart agreed that "No Matter Under What Star You're Born" and "Song of the Zodiac" were too much on the contemplative side. Stung by their criticism, Weill was reluctant to give up either number, and in his next letter to Gershwin suggested simply adding another song for Liza, either in the trial's recess or at some point during the proceedings. Gershwin, who was recovering from a cold, failed to respond. Weill wrote again proposing additional solutions. These included turning "Song of the Zodiac" into a duet for Randy and Liza (Figure 27) and writing an additional number for Liza, a triumphant song about "a woman's ability to win battles." With the piling up of numbers, the circus trial was growing to elephantine proportions. Weill suggested that the recess needed to be cut and the sequence done "in one big crescendo up to the climax."[76]

In October Gershwin again boarded the train for New York, and he and Weill began to rethink the third sequence. Instead of a barker, the opening was rewritten for a Ringmaster to be played by Russell, who would double as the trial's judge. This simplified matters and allowed Kendall to assume the singular role of witness. With the recess gone, "The Best Years of His Life" had to be scaled back, and the choral arrangement already prepared in rehearsal score dropped. Both astrological numbers were tossed out and a number for the loquacious Russell and a show-stopping number for Liza added instead. Despite the popular success of these numbers, structurally the *Circus Dream* breaks down into a succession of songs with tenuous connections. Under pressure to complete the sequence, Weill gave up employing his sketchbook for continuity drafts and used it instead for hasty sketching. Weill and Gershwin wrote "Bats about You" for the flashback scene to Mapleton High School as a duet for Liza and Ben.

Reflecting the *Circus Dream*'s troubled genesis, Weill borrowed a waltz from his unfinished operetta "Der Kuhhandel" for "The Best Years of His Life," and the "Battle of the Alamo" from "The Ballad of Davy Crockett" for "Dance of the Tumblers." A factor that further complicated matters was that as the second sequence was shortened and the fourth sequence was cut altogether, the demands on the *Circus Dream* kept increasing. Weill probably cobbled together "Tschaikowsky" because Russell's song from the first act had been discarded ("Unforgettable").[77] Weill added the "Dance of the Tumblers" because the second act lacked any production number. As in the crafting of a crossword puzzle, the collaborators juggled the clues and words to seek a workable solution.

Weill and Gershwin knew that once rehearsals for *George Washington Slept Here* began, Hart would have limited time for *Lady in the Dark*. When Kaufman and Hart's play was in tryout, Weill turned his attention to orchestrating the musical score (some 350 pages) and beginning work on the piano-vocal score. Although he would be photographed for his subsequent Broadway productions busily orchestrating while the show rehearsed, here he managed to complete the bulk of it before the scheduled start of rehearsals on November 15. With *Lady in the Dark* becoming ever more lavish, Hart remarked to Weill, "You see, we had a nice little lunch at the Hapsburg last fall—and here is the result." To which Weill replied tongue-in-cheek, "We should have had lunch at Child's."[78]

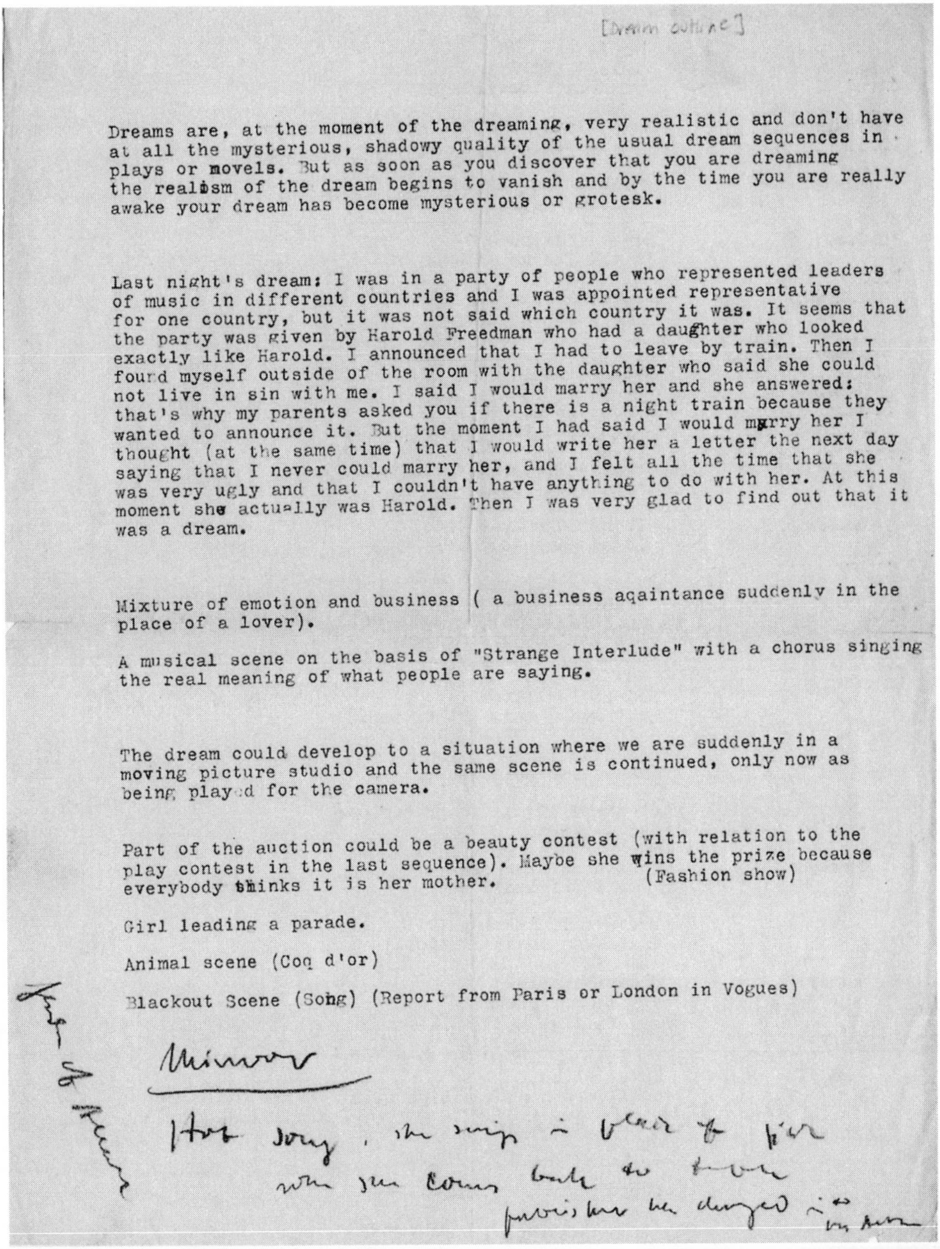

Dreams are, at the moment of the dreaming, very realistic and don't have
at all the mysterious, shadowy quality of the usual dream sequences in
plays or novels. But as soon as you discover that you are dreaming
the realism of the dream begins to vanish and by the time you are really
awake your dream has become mysterious or grotesk.

Last night's dream: I was in a party of people who represented leaders
of music in different countries and I was appointed representative
for one country, but it was not said which country it was. It seems that
the party was given by Harold Freedman who had a daughter who looked
exactly like Harold. I announced that I had to leave by train. Then I
found myself outside of the room with the daughter who said she could
not live in sin with me. I said I would marry her and she answered:
that's why my parents asked you if there is a night train because they
wanted to announce it. But the moment I had said I would marry her I
thought (at the same time) that I would write her a letter the next day
saying that I never could marry her, and I felt all the time that she
was very ugly and that I couldn't have anything to do with her. At this
moment she actually was Harold. Then I was very glad to find out that it
was a dream.

Mixture of emotion and business (a business aqaintance suddenly in the
place of a lover).

A musical scene on the basis of "Strange Interlude" with a chorus singing
the real meaning of what people are saying.

The dream could develop to a situation where we are suddenly in a
moving picture studio and the same scene is continued, only now as
being played for the camera.

Part of the auction could be a beauty contest (with relation to the
play contest in the last sequence). Maybe she wins the prize because
everybody thinks it is her mother.   (Fashion show)

Girl leading a parade.

Animal scene (Coq d'or)

Blackout Scene (Song) (Report from Paris or London in Vogues)

Mirror

Hot song, she sings in place of fire when she comes back to ... publisher her changed in ...

Figure 26. Kurt Weill's typescript page of ideas. Photo courtesy of The Kurt Weill and Lotte Lenya
Papers, Irving S. Gilmore Music Library, Yale University and permission of the Kurt Weill Foundation
for Music, New York.

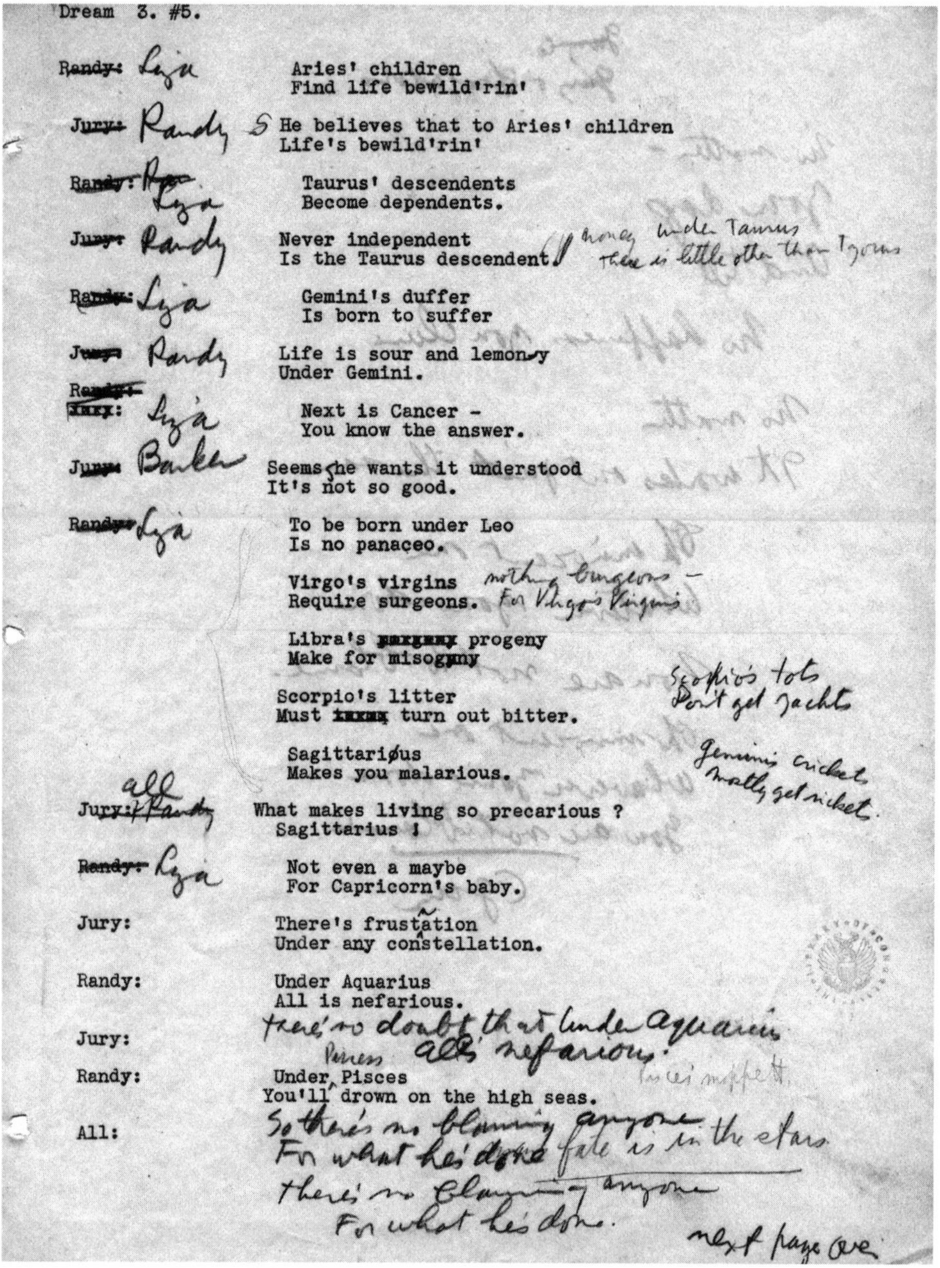

Randy: *Liza*

Aries' children
Find life bewild'rin'

Jury: *Randy* 5 He believes that to Aries' children
Life's bewild'rin'

Randy: *Liza*

Taurus' descendents
Become dependents.

Jury: *Randy*

Never independent
Is the Taurus descendent. *money under Taurus*
there is little other than Tgorus

Randy: *Liza*

Gemini's duffer
Is born to suffer

Jury: *Randy*

Life is sour and lemony
Under Gemini.

Randy: *Liza*

Next is Cancer –
You know the answer.

Jury: *Barker*

Seems she wants it understood
It's not so good.

Randy: *Liza*

To be born under Leo
Is no panaceo.

Virgo's virgins
Require surgeons. *nothing dangerous –*
For Virgo's Virgins

Libra's progeny
Make for misogyny

Scorpio's litter
Must turn out bitter. *Scorpio's tots*
Don't get Jachts

Sagittarigus
Makes you malarious. *Gemini's cricket*
mostly get nickel.

Jury: *all* *Randy* What makes living so precarious ?
Sagittarius !

Randy: *Liza*

Not even a maybe
For Capricorn's baby.

Jury:

There's frustation
Under any constellation.

Randy:

Under Aquarius
All is nefarious.
there's no doubt that under aquarius

Jury:

Pisces *all's nefarious.*
Pisces moffett.

Randy:

Under, Pisces
You'll drown on the high seas.

All:

So there's no blaming anyone
For what he's done fate is in the stars
there's no blaming anyone
For what he's done.
next page over

Figure 27. Ira Gershwin's draft for the "Song of the Zodiac." Courtesy of the Library of Congress, and permission of Leonore S. Gershwin 1987 Trust.

Figure 28. Kurt Weill's third version of "My Ship." Photo courtesy of The Kurt Weill and Lotte Lenya Papers, Irving S. Gilmore Music Library, Yale University and permission of the Kurt Weill Foundation for Music, New York.

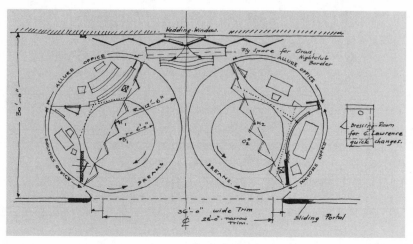

Figure 29. Harry Horner's ground plan sketch. Courtesy of *Theatre Arts* and Billy Rose Theatre Collection, The New York Public Library for the Performing Arts, Astor, Lenox and Tilden Foundations.

Figure 30. Harry Horner's sketch for Dr. Brooks's office. Courtesy of *Theatre Arts* and Billy Rose Theatre Collection, The New York Public Library for the Performing Arts, Astor, Lenox and Tilden Foundations.

Figure 31. Harry Horner's model for Dr. Brooks's office. Courtesy of *Theatre Arts* and Billy Rose Theatre Collection, The New York Public Library for the Performing Arts, Astor, Lenox and Tilden Foundations.

Figure 32. Harry Horner's prop sketches. Courtesy of *Theatre Arts* and Billy Rose Theatre Collection, The New York Public Library for the Performing Arts, Astor, Lenox and Tilden Foundations.

Figure 33. Harry Horner's sketch for *Glamour Dream*, "Oh Fabulous One in Your Ivory Tower." Courtesy of *Theatre Arts* and Billy Rose Theatre Collection, The New York Public Library for the Performing Arts, Astor, Lenox and Tilden Foundations.

Figure 34. Harry Horner's sketch for *Wedding Dream*, "This Woman at the Altar." Courtesy of *Theatre Arts* and Billy Rose Theatre Collection, The New York Public Library for the Performing Arts, Astor, Lenox and Tilden Foundations.

Figure 35. Irene Sharaff's costume designs for "The Princess of Pure Delight." Courtesy of *Theatre Arts* and Billy Rose Theatre Collection, The New York Public Library for the Performing Arts, Astor, Lenox and Tilden Foundations.

Figure 36. Will Anderson's cartoon of backstage. Courtesy of *Theatre Arts* and Billy Rose Theatre Collection, The New York Public Library for the Performing Arts, Astor, Lenox and Tilden Foundations.

Figure 37. Photo essay of Gertrude Lawrence performing "The Saga of Jenny." Photos by Vandamm Studio, courtesy of *Look* magazine and David Kalonick.

GERTRUDE LAWRENCE AND DREAM FIGURES
A psychoanalytical circus with four revolving rings.
(Theatre)

Figure 38. *Time*, February 3, 1941. Courtesy and permission of *Time* magazine © 1941 Time Inc. Reprinted by permission.

Radio Version

JENNY

From Production "LADY IN THE DARK"

Lyrics by IRA GERSHWIN   Music by KURT WEILL

VERSE

There once was a girl named Jenny
Whose hist'ry was held up to many
Because she was always inclined
Promptly to make up her mind
And Jenny points a moral with which you cannot quarrel
As you will find

CHORUSES

(1)

Jenny made her mind up when she was three
She, herself, was going to trim the Christmas tree
Christmas Eve she lit the candles, tossed the tapers away
Little Jenny was an orphan on Christmas Day

Poor Jenny! Bright as a penny
Her equal would be hard to find
She lost one dad and mother
A sister and a brother
But she would make up her mind

(2)

Jenny made her mind up when she was twelve
That into ancient literature she would delve
And at seventeen she finished every book that she could
But the knowledge didn't help her and it did her no good

Poor Jenny! Bright as a penny
Her equal would be hard to find
To Jenny I'm beholden
Her heart was big and golden
But she would make up her mind

(3)

Jenny made her mind up at twenty-two
To get herself a husband was the thing to do
So she picked herself a number and she nearly went daft
When the honeymoon was over he was gone with the draft

Poor Jenny! Bright as a penny
Her equal would be hard to find
Deserved a bed of roses
But history discloses
That she would make up her mind

(4)

Jenny made her mind up at thirty-nine
She would take a trip to the Argentine
Now in Washington the Congress and the Senate agree.
Jenny was the one who started the good neighbor policy

Poor Jenny! Bright as a penny
Her equal would be hard to find
She let her heart go Latin
Forgot about Manhattan
But she would make up her mind

(5)

Jenny made her mind up at fifty-one
She would write her memoirs before she was done
By the time her golden hair was silver
Hist'ry relates, she had left a trail of broken hearts
    in forty-eight states

Poor Jenny! Bright as a penny
Her equal would be hard to find
She could give cards and spades
To many other ladies
But she would make up her mind

(6)

Jenny made her mind up at seventy-five
She would live to be the oldest woman alive
But life and love and destiny play funny tricks
And poor Jenny kicked the bucket at seventy-six

Jenny points a moral, With which you cannot quarrel
Makes a lot of common sense
Jenny and her saga, Prove that you are gaga
If you don't keep sitting on the fence
Jenny and her story, Point the way to glory
To all men and womankind
Anyone with vision, Comes to this decision
Don't make up, you shouldn't make up
You mustn't make up, oh never make up
Anyone with vision, Comes to this decision
Don't make up your mind

Copyright MCMXLI by CHAPPELL & CO. Inc., New York

Figure 39. Expurgated radio version of "The Saga of Jenny." Photo courtesy of the Weill-Lenya Research Center, Kurt Weill Foundation for Music, New York, and permission of Warner Bros. Publications U.S. Inc.

One rainy afternoon a year ago Kurt Weill and myself sat at a table in a little midtown restaurant and told each other vehemently why we would not write a musical comedy. Kurt Weill because he would not write the music for the regulation musical comedy book, and myself because I would not write the book for the regulation musical comedy music.

We parted in complete agreement though it was a far cry from the purpose of the meeting. We had arranged to meet to see if we could not do a show together and had thoroughly succeeded in discovering that we couldn't. That is, we were both completely disinterested in doing a show for the sake of doing a show, in Broadway parlance, and the tight little formula of the musical comedy stage held no interest for either of us.

We met again the following week and after another luncheon, that lasted well into the evening, we discovered the kind of show we both definitely *did* want to do.

It was, we decided, a show in which the music carried forward the essential story and was not imposed on the architecture of the play as a rather melodious but useless addenda.

This is an easy phrase to write but to achieve that end it was necessary to create both a new technique and a new musical form. I say this at the risk of sounding a little pompous, but it seems to me that in "Lady in the Dark" this has in some measure been successfully accomplished.

I cannot in all modesty discuss my own contribution, but I can with enormous enthusiasm discuss the contributions of Kurt Weill and Ira Gershwin. They have, it seems to me, created a new musical and lyrical pattern in the American Theatre. I think for the first time—at least so far as my memory serves,—the music and lyrics of a musical "show" are part and parcel of the basic structure of the play. One cannot separate the play from the music or vice versa. More than that, the music and lyrics carry the story forward dramatically and psychologically.

All this, it seems to me, has been done with enormous resource, musicianship and skill. As a dramatist interested in new forms in the theatre it seems to me that Kurt Weill has made a contribution to our present day theatre of inestimable value.

MOSS HART

March 18, 1941

Figure 40. Moss Hart's foreword to the piano-vocal score. Photo courtesy of the Weill-Lenya Research Center, Kurt Weill Foundation for Music, New York, and permission of Warner Bros. Publications U.S. Inc.

Figure 41. Hattie Carnegie's redesigned wedding gown for second season and tour (Gertrude Lawrence). Photo by Vandamm Studio, courtesy and permission of Billy Rose Theatre Collection, The New York Public Library for the Performing Arts, Astor, Lenox and Tilden Foundations.

Figure 42. Hattie Carnegie's redesigned opening outfit for second season and tour (Richard Hale and Gertrude Lawrence). Photo by Vandamm Studio, courtesy and permission of Billy Rose Theatre Collection, The New York Public Library for the Performing Arts, Astor, Lenox and Tilden Foundations.

Figure 43. Northrop P-61 Black Widow "Lady in the Dark," parked on airstrip at Iwo Jima, Bonin Islands, March 1945. Courtesy of the National Archives and Records Administration, Still Picture Branch.

Figure 44. Dorothy Gray's Lady in the Dark perfume ($15 an ounce). Photo by David Kalonick and courtesy of Leach/Peters Collection, Gallery 47, New York.

Figure 45. *This Is the Army*: Private Alan Manson impersonating Jane Cowl. Photo by Carl Van Vechten, courtesy of Carl Van Vechten Collection, Yale Collection of American Literature, The Beinecke Rare Book and Manuscript Library and permission of Van Vechten Trust.

Figure 46. *This Is the Army*: Corporal Nelson Barclift in the "Russian Winter" sequence. Photo by Carl Van Vechten, courtesy of Carl Van Vechten Collection, Yale Collection of American Literature, The Beinecke Rare Book and Manuscript Library and permission of Van Vechten Trust.

Figure 47. 1944 Paramount Film *Lady in the Dark*, interpolated nightclub scene. Ray Milland (Charley Johnson), Frances Robinson (Girl with Randy), Jon Hall (Randy Curtis), and Ginger Rogers (Liza Elliott). Photo courtesy of the Weill-Lenya Research Center, Kurt Weill Foundation for Music, New York, and permission of Universal Studios Licensing LLLP.

Figure 48. 1944 Paramount Film *Lady in the Dark*, *Circus Dream*. Photo courtesy of the Weill-Lenya Research Center, Kurt Weill Foundation for Music, New York, and permission of Universal Studios Licensing LLLP.

Figure 49. 1944 Paramount Film *Lady in the Dark*, *Wedding Dream*, "Suddenly It's Spring." Ginger Rogers and Don Loper. Photo courtesy of the Weill-Lenya Research Center, Kurt Weill Foundation for Music, New York, and permission of Universal Studios Licensing LLLP.

Figure 50. Advertisement for 1944 Paramount Film *Lady in the Dark*. Photo by David Kalonick.

3

Musical Score

When Weill joked with Hart about their restaurant choice, he implied that the score to *Lady in the Dark* was no longer a group of musical numbers akin to an à la carte menu at a bar like Child's. Instead, the score had grown to be three full courses, comparable to the fare at a gourmet restaurant such as the Hapsburg. Years later, Weill admitted that he thought of his score for *Lady in the Dark* as "three little one-act operas."[1] Like opera, each sequence is self-contained, individually titled, and a mixture of aria and recitative. This being Broadway, the arias are songs, and the recitative patter. Despite the sequences' different subject matter, Weill unified them in at least three ways: each is based on a dance idiom, each includes snippets of "My Ship," and each lampoons different styles of operetta. In addition, the composer came up with several musical analogies for the drama's denouement. With Weill's own artful orchestrations, the musical score turned out to be one of his finest.

Composing *Lady in the Dark* took Weill back to his twenties, when he began his theatrical career in Germany with three one-act operas: *Der Protagonist* (an expressionist-inspired drama), *Der Zar lässt sich photographieren* (*The Czar Has His Photograph Taken*, a comic episode involving a camera and an assassination plot), and *Royal Palace* (a surrealist work set at an Italian resort). There are parallels between these works and the structure and plot of *Lady in the Dark*. In *The Protagonist*, the actor and his theater company twice rehearse a pantomime. For these episodes Weill composed sequences to represent the different levels of reality, similar in function to *Lady in the Dark*'s dream sequences. *The Czar* uses the dance idiom of the tango as a metaphor for the dangerous game that is being played with a revolver-laden camera. In a similar vein, Weill employs dances to mirror the tensions between Liza and the men in her life.

Lady in the Dark's closest relative, however, is *Royal Palace*. The central premise is the same: a woman choosing among three men. In modernist fashion, the names of the characters in *Royal Palace* reveal only their role: Yesterday's Love, Tomorrow's Enamored One, and the Husband. The setting of the Italian resort foreshadows the Seventh Heaven nightclub. In *Royal Palace*, fawning bellboys perform a ballet around the heroine; for Liza, it is tuxedoed admirers who serenade. The section in *Royal Palace* where the suitors take turns offering the heroine lavish gifts parallels the series of deliveries to Liza's boudoir. Because Weill actively collaborated with Gershwin and Hart to create the dream sequences, these parallels are most likely instances of modeling.

Another way that Weill revived his musical past was by invoking dance idioms. Whereas in the 1920s and early 1930s it had been the foxtrot, tango, and Boston (waltz), for *Lady in the Dark* he employed the rumba, bolero, and circus march. Each dream sequence was conceived with a specific dance that would define the atmosphere and relationship between the characters. For Weill and Bertolt Brecht in the late 1920s, this concept was referred to as *gestus*. An almost impossible term to translate, *gestus* was described by Brecht as the attitude adopted by characters toward one another.[2] In the *Glamour Dream*, the Afro-Cuban rumba, with its quick-quick-slow dance step, creates rhythmic displacement as the patrons at the Seventh Heaven mock and ridicule Liza. Although they had originally sung her praises, they are now literally and figuratively out of step with her.

For the *Wedding Dream*, Weill chose the bolero. This Spanish dance, popularized by Maurice Ravel, serves as a metaphor for the romantic pairings in which Liza finds herself: first buying a wedding ring with Kendall, then in amorous duet with Randy, and finally at the altar back with Kendall. The promenade quality of the Spanish bolero, a couple's dance, parallels the dramatic procession up the aisle for the sequence's climax. Gershwin goes so far as to invoke the two traditional wedding promenades by Wagner and Mendelssohn ("It's never too late to Mendelssohn....I trust they Lohengrin and bear it!").[3]

For the *Circus Dream*, Weill employed a circus march in traditional 2/4 time. When Liza finds herself in the magazine cover she is considering, a dance idiom summarizes the situation. Here, it is the three-ring world of a lion tamer (Kendall), bareback rider (Randy), and trapeze artist (Charley) with which Liza (a mental acrobat) must compete. Weill included the familiar "triumphal entries" to introduce the various acts, and fanfares and drumrolls to build tension and excitement.[4] On the broadest level, then, the musical score for *Lady in the Dark* can be thought of as a dance suite, with each movement serving a *gestic* function to define the relationship between Liza and those around her.[5]

Within each sequence, Weill included other dances that do not serve a *gestic* function but are used to accompany small scenes. For example, after Liza has put on her glamorous gown in the first sequence, she dances an impromptu waltz while waiting for Beekman to get the car. Once she and Beekman reach the nightclub, she and the patrons perform a brief foxtrot. There are also individual songs that use a particular dance rhythm; again, these serve only a local function. Kendall's testimony in the *Circus Dream*, "The Best Years of His Life," uses waltz rhythm, and Liza's defense speech, "The Saga of Jenny," features a boogie-woogie accompaniment.

On Broadway, audiences expect that characters in a book musical will dance, either for dance breaks or evolutions, or in an extended ballet. *Lady in the Dark* offers both. "This Is New" was choreographed from a simple duet into a full-blown production number. The "Dance of the Tumblers" displayed the athleticism of the dance corps and fulfilled the audience's expectation for such a number at the beginning of Act II. What *was* new with *Lady in the Dark* was the use of dance idioms that served as the organizing principle for the musical score. A sign of how fundamental these were to the work's conception is that both Weill and Gershwin actually used "Bolero" as a working title for the *Wedding Dream*.[6]

With the dance suite operating on the largest level, Weill employed other musical styles *within* the sequences for the patter. There is actual speaking over music: Beekman delivers his entrance lines ("I learned it would be blue tonight") over a sustained chord and rhythmic ostinato. Weill mimicked recitative for the marine's opening speech in the *Glamour Dream*: rhythmically declaimed dialogue on a single pitch ("I bring a message for Miss Liza Elliott"). There are instances of *Sprechstimme* where Weill specified notes for speech-song: Sutton's replies of "Come in!" are to be intoned on a and e-flat.[7] And finally, he composed arioso, where speech is given a melody, such as in Liza and Sutton's initial exchange (Liza: "Are there any messages?" Sutton: "Quite a number"). This variety of musical declamation enabled Weill to fashion sequences in which characters speak, recite on single tones, speaksing on pitch, and sing short melodies, all interspersed with songs. The end result gives the sequences a continuous quality, adding to their operatic flavor.

Augmenting the basic patter/song framework are places where Weill invoked instrumental forms for dramatic effect. An example is theme and variation. In the opening sequence, the glamour theme is repeated seven times. The original theme is heard when Sutton addresses Liza's suitors.

When it returns as the suitors are leaving, the triplet accompaniment is replaced by sixteenth-note figuration and the melody is extended. Its appearance for Liza's entrance is nearly twice the length and features arpeggios. When the nightclub appears, the theme returns, but the accompaniment is intensified with quivering tremolos. The theme also serves as the melody for the ensuing foxtrot. The Chorus adds words to its final phrase, "Darling! How nice of you to come! Darling! How are you?" The glamour theme makes its final two appearances before and after the marine paints Liza's portrait. Weill also employed variation technique for "Girl of the Moment." First sung in unison as a foxtrot, it is repeated in choral harmony with chain suspensions, and finally modified with offbeat accents for the rumba.

Compared to Weill's facility with European musical forms, the songs gave him the most trouble. American popular song form was, in essence, an industry standard for Tin Pan Alley and Broadway composers during this period: a short verse, which functions as an introduction, and a thirty-two-measure refrain. The refrain consists of four phrases, each eight measures long. The first, second, and fourth are nearly identical, but the third is different and results in an AABA form where A is referred to as the main strain or hook, B the bridge or release. Weill had experimented with this form only a few times prior to *Lady in the Dark*.

Weill's exposure to American popular song form occurred while working in Hollywood in 1937.[8] He first employed it for the title song of a never realized film called "The River Is Blue." The A strains are sixteen measures long rather than eight and were adapted from the "Tango Habanera," part of a work he had composed in France called *Marie Galante*. The second time he used it was for "The Right Guy for Me" from *You and Me*. It includes a twenty-six-measure verse and a standard thirty-two-measure refrain. In the film, "The Right Guy for Me" is sung by a torch singer, played by Carol Paige. The song had a modest success when Lenya sang it for a three-week engagement at the New York nightclub Le Ruban Bleu during the spring of 1938.

Weill's third crack at American popular song form became a standard: "September Song" from *Knickerbocker Holiday*. The song, composed at the eleventh hour for Walter Huston, includes a fourteen-measure verse, which sets the mood. The refrain has a bridge similar to that in "The Right Guy for Me," which consisted of sequential material. However, in "September Song," the repetitiveness perfectly matches Maxwell Anderson's lyric: "Oh, the days dwindle down to a precious few, September, November!" Here an aging codger desires a May-December relationship but mourns his fleeting days while in the September of his life. The bridge's dramatic pauses and thwarted melody beautifully capture his dilemma.

For *Lady in the Dark*, Weill composed no fewer than nine songs in American popular song form; six ended up in the final score: "Oh Fabulous One in Your Ivory Tower," "The World's Inamorata," "One Life to Live," "Girl of the Moment," "Mapleton High Choral," and "My Ship." The three that did not are "Unforgettable," "It's Never Too Late to Mendelssohn," and "No Matter Under What Star You're Born." Because all but "My Ship" were intended for dream sequences, Weill rarely bothered to compose a verse to set the scene for the refrain. As it turned out, he was relatively facile at composing the mainstrain material, but the bridges caused him fits.

Part of the problem was that his first two A phrases tended to be in antecedent-consequent phrase structure, by nature a complete musical thought. With such a firm cadence at the end of the second phrase, the melody did not lead naturally into a bridge. Weill soon realized the problem and began modifying the melody of the second phrase so that it was less conclusive. Another issue was that Weill did not tend to sketch the bridge at the time of his initial inspiration. Going back later and trying to find a contrasting phrase that would fit with the original idea complicated matters. As a result, the sketches for over half of *Lady in the Dark*'s songs in American popular song form document discarded bridges.

Those songs not in American popular song form are either in AA' form or specialty numbers. Because Weill tended to sketch in musical periods, the songs in AA' form presented many fewer problems than those in American popular song form. Three numbers in this form are "This Is New," "The Best Years of His Life," and "Bats about You." The three specialty numbers in *Lady in the Dark*'s score were composed in response to particular situations, and each is in a different form. The function for each song seems to have dictated its own form, and, unusual for *Lady in the Dark*'s musical score, all are in minor keys.

"The Princess of Pure Delight" alternates two musical ideas with a contrasting central section in a rondo-like arrangement: ABABCABA. Richard Rodgers, who was a dinner guest at Fairview Farm during the first working weekend, provided Gershwin with a riddle ("What word of five letters is always spelled wrong? . . . W-r-o-n-g"). Weeks later, when Gershwin and Weill were putting the *Wedding Dream* together, Gershwin decided on a fairy tale with Rodgers's riddle being the test for the suitors of the king's daughter. (The princess and her three suitors mirror Liza and the men in her life.) Gershwin described the process:

> I had a rough idea of what I wanted to say, but none about the number of lines it would take. I finally decided on a title and came up with an opening stanza, which I gave to Kurt for tentative setting. Tentative

because I was prepared to change the approach if he felt that a longish lyric with regular, confining stanzas might make for musical monotony. Soon after, he played me a setting I liked; then said there'd be no problem—that, no matter how many stanzas were required, the musical end would be reasonably cohesive. With this assurance I kept furthering and tickling up the narrative, with Kurt never more than a stanza behind me; and in a few days this section of the dream was completed.[9]

The second specialty number was a catalogue piece to show off Danny Kaye's talents. Gershwin returned to a poem called "The Music Hour," which he had published in 1924 in *Life* magazine under the pseudonym "Arthur Francis."[10] The budding lyricist had compiled the names of forty-seven Russian composers from the back covers of George's piano and orchestral scores. Because the relationship between this tongue-twisting list and *Lady in the Dark* was tenuous at best, Weill sketched a quotation from the third movement of Tchaikovsky's Sixth Symphony (one of the forty-seven composers) to introduce the song. Ira reworked "The Music Hour" list, adding seven new names and omitting five others. When Weill needed another composer's name for the coda, Ira added "Rumshinsky" (a Yiddish playwright), increasing the total number of Russian names to fifty.[11]

Liza's defense, "The Saga of Jenny," became the third specialty number. Weill and Gershwin had originally composed the now lost "Song of the Zodiac" for this climactic spot.[12] In response to Short's request for a funny song, Weill drafted a melody tinged with blue notes. Gershwin let his imagination run wild and sketched thirteen stanzas about the fictitious Jenny; six of these were incorporated into the final version of the song. This piece is a close relative to the famous "Moritat vom Mackie Messer" ("Mack the Knife") from *The Threepenny Opera*: each was composed at the last minute, both have a sixteen-measure refrain repeated six times, each chronicles the exploits of a notorious protagonist, and both eventually became their respective work's most famous number.

The three songs from the never completed "Hollywood Dream" survive only in preliminary drafts. "In Our Little House in the San Fernando Valley" is in AA' form, like "This Is New." "The Boss Is Bringing Home the Bride" and "Hollywood Party" are similar in form to "The Princess of Pure Delight." It appears that Gershwin was "tickling up the narrative," and Weill was one step behind him setting the text as it was completed. "The Boss Is Bringing Home the Bride" repeats two musical ideas with a contrasting section (AABBCBA), and "Hollywood Party" alternates two ideas (ABABA) before breaking into recitative sections.

Weill's sketches for the "Hollywood Dream" and the specialty numbers reveal an ease of composition. He was most comfortable setting text, and these numbers appear to have been completed in record time. Given how happy he was with his usual method of composition, one wonders why he worked so hard to master American popular song form. One might speculate that after the success of "September Song," Weill was trying to capitalize on it. A more probable reason was his collaborator. For Ira and his brother George, American popular song form had been their preferred form. Despite his difficulties mastering it, Weill eventually promoted American popular song form: "It seems to me that the American popular song, growing out of the American folk-music, is the basis of an American musical theatre (just as the Italian song was the basis of Italian opera), and that in this early state of the development, and considering the audiences we are writing for, it is quite legitimate to use the form of the popular song and gradually fill it with new content."[13]

One bit of Weill's content is a motive that permeates his works. If one hums the first three notes of "Mack the Knife" ("Oh, the shark"), the combination of tones is a minor third (m3) followed by a Major second (M2). Weill was also fond of the reverse of this motive: a Major second followed by a minor third. He was consciously aware of this reciprocal quality of the motives when he combined two numbers from *The Threepenny Opera* for an instrumental suite. That is, he juxtaposed "Mack the Knife" (m3/M2) with the "Lied von der Un-zulänglichkeit menschlichen Strebens" ("Useless Song," M2/m3) in the same tempo for the second movement of the *Kleine Dreigroschenmusik*. With the numbers side by side, the motivic connection is unmistakable.[14] The composer himself hinted at such a musical thumbprint when he was interviewed shortly after arriving in the United States: "My style is melodious. People say they can recognize my music when they hear only three measures of it. I believe in the simplification of music. If someone has something to say, it is not important what means he uses so long as he knows how to use them."[15]

Five songs for *Lady in the Dark* employ Weill's motive in either its prime (m3/M2) or retrograde (M2/m3) form: "My Ship," "One Life to Live," "This Is New," "It's Never Too Late to Mendelssohn," and "In Our Little House in the San Fernando Valley." A special case is "One Life to Live" whose verse begins with the retrograde form, but whose refrain starts with its prime. Weill included even more of these motives in the score. The retrograde form is employed for all of the choral interjections at the beginning of the *Wedding Dream* ("There's a girl"; "We all knew her"; "And now a Mapleton High girl"; "Liza Elliott is marrying"; "Randy Curtis!" Flame of the Celluloid!"). The prime form is used for the wedding chimes in the sequence's finale. Although not every song with this motive made it into the final score, many that did are heard numerous times (e.g., "My Ship"), creating a motivically saturated score.

One of the most musically sophisticated aspects of *Lady in the Dark* is its tonal organization. In simplest terms, the drama is about a woman's journey from depression (darkness) to mental health (lightness). Liza discovers that the root of her problem is represented by a song from childhood tied to emotionally abusive events concerning her father. A snippet, or leitmotif, of this song is heard at critical junctures in all three sequences. Each time the leitmotif appears, it provides a clue to her past. The gradual decoding of what "My Ship" signifies sustains the drama, a process like the "Rosebud" cipher in Orson Welles's *Citizen Kane* from the same year.

The musical demands placed on "My Ship" are enumerated in the play's initial scene. First, it must have the character of a childhood song. Second, because Liza is able to remember only a few measures, its melody should be memorable. Most important is Liza's description of the song in her dreams: "It changes—but the music is always there." If the song's melody were to change, this might imply some type of thematic transformation. This technique would have been too musically sophisticated for a simple children's song. A second possibility would be that the harmony changes, but the melody remains constant. Weill chose this latter route. It is unclear whether Hart or Gershwin came up with the topic, but the song's predecessor is certainly the following nursery rhyme:

I saw a ship a-sailing,
   A-sailing on the sea,
And oh, but it was laden
   With pretty things for thee!

There were comfits in the cabin,
   And apples in the hold;
The sails were made of silk,
   And the masts were all of gold.

The four-and-twenty sailors,
   That stood between the decks,
Were four-and-twenty white mice
   With chains about their necks.

The captain was a duck
   With a packet on his back,
And when the ship began to move
   The captain said, Quack! Quack![16]

Whereas the original ship carried mice and a duck, Liza's ship carries her own true love. The melding of nursery rhyme imagery with the drama's conclusion (Liza *does* find her true love) enabled "My Ship" to be both a recollection and a premonition.

Composing "My Ship" presented challenges for Weill and Gershwin because of their different working methods. To intensify matters, the dramatic demands of the song were considerable. Small wonder, then, that three different versions of "My Ship" survive.[17] The first, a slow waltz in D-flat Major, sounds vaguely European; the music may have originally been composed for an aborted 1937 project about a European theatrical troupe forced to flee Nazi Germany. Nothing about "My Ship has sails that are made of silk" suggests 3/4 time, and the awkward text setting suggests that Weill and Gershwin were attempting to marry a preexistent melody with a new lyric. The second version, in E-flat Major, corrects the rhythmic problem with a meter of 4/4. The issue with this version seems to have been its chromatic melody, which again would not have been in keeping with the style of a children's song.

The third version, in F Major, became the one that we know today. Weill worked into the melody some tonal ambiguity by consciously avoiding the tonic note f. Instead, the melody emphasizes d, and many of those fall on downbeats. The song's opening melodic motive (c-d-f) includes Weill's musical thumbprint (M2/m3), but stresses the note d with the word "Ship" on the downbeat. The pitch center of d for an F-Major melody gave Weill a musical riddle that could be worked out over the course of the drama. The minor mode, with its melancholic associations, would gradually give way to the Major mode to parallel Liza's journey from depression to mental health.

The beginning of "My Ship" is composed of only five pitches: c, d, f, g, and a. Pentatonicism such as this is common in folk music and children's songs, so the melody captures a childhood affect. In addition, the gapped scale makes it a memorable tune. The d minor/F Major orientation enabled it to change harmonically, and the music—or melody—to be always present. Typical for Weill's musical ideas, the main strain of "My Ship" is seven measures long, so the last note (sung on the word "hold") had to be sustained for two measures to create an eight-measure phrase.

What complicated the completion of "My Ship" was its bridge. In his first attempt, Weill adapted the bridge from Harold Arlen's "Over the Rainbow." The rocking motion of "Some day I'll wish upon a star and wake up where the clouds are far behind me" did not work so well for "I can wait for years till it appears on a fine day one fine spring." Furthermore, the singsong quality of Arlen's melody sounded glib for the arrival of a ship bringing one's own true love. Weill composed a new bridge, the one we know today, whose stepwise motion and sequence contrasts nicely with A material. He had the final note of the bridge land squarely on d, creating a melodic parallel with the beginning. Although completed through a tortuous process, "My Ship" fulfilled all of the dramatic requirements and could now provide a musical solution to the heroine's problems.

The leitmotif from "My Ship" makes its first appearance in the opening scene of *Lady in the Dark* and is accompanied by a sustained d played by a clarinet. This pedal tone emphasizes the d-minor quality of the melody. Harmonically, the misterioso motive (Gershwin's term) suggests that Liza is indeed in the dark, and the rather hollow timbre of the clarinet adds to the tune's plaintive quality. It makes its second appearance at the climax of the sequence. When Liza views her portrait, the tune is transposed to the key of D Major and is accompanied by a drone consisting of a Major second (a and b). The oboe, which has a warm and rich timbre, plays the leitmotif, but the dissonant pedal tone makes it sound menacing. Upon hearing it, Liza screams in horror at her portrait. Here the leitmotif symbolizes the tension between fantasy and reality.

The leitmotif also initiates the *Wedding Dream*, accompanied again by a d pedal tone played by a clarinet. It makes two further appearances within the sequence. The first occurs at the end of her duet with Randy. The Chorus holds an octave c pedal (the dominant of the tune's true key of F Major) while Liza vocalizes the melody. The leitmotif concludes on a d, which produces a Major second with the pedal. Such a dissonant clash depicts the conflict between Liza's indecision over her groom and the sentiments of the wedding guests. The leitmotif recurs at the conclusion of "The Princess of Pure Delight." The trumpets play it in F accompanied by an ostinato of ninth chords. The first trumpet then repeats it in C Major (the dominant of the "correct" key), but harmonized by the "incorrect" one (a dyad of d-a). With this appearance, the tune is moving toward its true tonal orientation.

Before Liza is prepared to recall "My Ship," the leitmotif makes a final appearance at the climax of the *Circus Dream*. The jury of prankish pantaloonatics mocks Liza's inability to make up her mind by humming the tune. For the first time, the pedal tone accompanying the motive is in the tonic key of F Major. Despite Liza's protests ("No, no! Don't, don't! Don't sing that!"), Charley persists with his closing argument. Liza realizes the basis of her problems just as the harmonic implications of "My Ship" make themselves heard. What had been a childhood song with presumably a simple tonic-dominant relationship became a melodic nightmare, musically portrayed by various "incorrect" harmonizations and tonal clashes.

Weill duplicated the trajectory of d minor to F Major within the harmonization of "My Ship" itself. That is, he substituted a first inversion d-minor triad where one would normally expect to find a tonic F-Major harmony. He made this substitution nine times: at the beginning, in the middle, and near the end of each A phrase. The first time we hear an unadulterated F-Major triad on a downbeat is in the bridge ("I can wait the years / Till it appears / One fine day one spring"). With the arrival of the ship bringing Liza's own true love, the harmonic veil is lifted. Thus, building tonal ambiguity between F Major and d minor provided a musical riddle that Weill worked out on the micro level within the harmonization of the song itself and on the macro level over the course of Liza's psychoanalysis.

Although the combination of F Major and d minor creates what is commonly referred to as an added-sixth sonority (F^{+6}), Weill treated them as constituent parts of a "double tonic" complex.[18] The grafting of the two triads can be seen most clearly in the final chord of "My Ship": Weill stemmed a d-minor triad in one direction and the F-Major triad in the other (Figure 28). The constituent triads had different meanings for the drama (d minor = darkness, F Major = lightness), and Weill consistently separated them, suggesting that the same melody and tonic complex could embody both a dark and a light side.

Some music critics faulted Weill for using "commercial" sonorities, such as the one that concludes "My Ship." When a critic wrote Weill a letter complaining about his adoption of the same sonority for *Down in the Valley*, Weill vigorously defended its use: "I am sorry that I offended your ear with the sixth in the last chord. But you can see in the piano score that I arrive at the sixth entirely out of 'Stimmführung' (development of voices), so it is not used as an 'effect.' But here again, it offends your ears because it is being used a great deal in popular music today."[19] Weill's choice of the German *Stimmführung* reveals a structural connection between the tonic and the sixth (or submediant) beyond a simple color chord. The musical score for *Lady in the Dark* demonstrates how he composed out the harmonies of d minor and F major in a contrapuntal fashion.

Weill took the three important keys for the harmonization of "My Ship" (d minor, C Major, and F Major) and extended them to the tonal organization of the dream sequences and ultimately to the resolution of the drama itself. The *Glamour Dream* begins in the key of d minor, but concludes in the key of D Major. With the key of d minor representing darkness, Liza's overblown and unrealistic dream about herself demonstrates just how out of touch with reality she is. Weill's observation that "dreams are, at the moment of the dreaming, very realistic and don't have at all the mysterious, shadowy quality of the usual dream sequences in plays or novels" may have convinced him to use the Major mode for all four songs in this sequence.

Conversely, the *Wedding Dream* is in the key of c minor. The sequence is unified by the various appearances of the bolero music, which is virtually always in this key. Here Liza is better grounded in reality than in her first dream. First she imagines what it would be like to marry Kendall. Dr. Brooks's probing as to why she has rebuffed Randy's advances then prompts her to fantasize what it might be like to be involved with him. Compared to the impossibility of the *Glamour Dream*, the *Wedding Dream* is about possibilities: accepting Kendall's proposal, going out with Randy, and mulling over what experiences in grade school and high school meant.

The *Circus Dream* begins in D Major but inconclusively ends on a half cadence of F. Like the *Glamour Dream*, it depicts an improbable situation: Liza imagines herself on trial for not being able to make up her mind. The circus music is primarily in the key of D: "The Greatest Show on Earth" (D Major) and "Dance of the Tumblers" (d minor). Having quit her analysis with Dr. Brooks, Liza's dream shows her back in the clutches of the past, incapable of making even a simple decision about a magazine cover and stuck in the key of darkness. The hallucination convinces her to return to Dr. Brooks, and she is now poised to probe deeper into her past to discover the root of her problems.

At Liza's final session, Dr. Brooks analyzes a whole series of events from her childhood. These flashbacks are sometimes referred to as the *Childhood Dream*.[20] Although not a full-fledged sequence, the scenes include brief passages of music. Liza as a little girl attempts to perform "My Ship" for her parents' dinner guests. In elementary school, she and her classmates sing the conclusion of "The Princess of Pure Delight." Finally, at her high school graduation dance, she hums "My Ship" for Ben, a classmate and sudden romantic interest. He urges her to sing the song, and Liza happily complies. All of the *Childhood Dream*'s musical passages are in the key of F Major.

Thus, Liza's journey begins with d minor, which presents itself as the false personality, or dark side of the tonic. When Liza is grounded in her true identity, C Major (the dominant of F Major) points a path to therapeutic catharsis. This battle between d and C is finally resolved with "My Ship" in the key of her authentic self: F Major. Weill not only composed out the motive that begins "My Ship" (c-d-f) in a linear fashion with the various appearances of the leitmotif, but also employed it in a horizontal fashion to organize the sequences. With such a tightly constructed musical score operating tonally in two dimensions, it is not surprising that he did not transpose any of the numbers of *Lady in the Dark* to fit the vocal ranges of the actors cast to play the roles.[21]

Weill extended the associative use of tonality (d minor = darkness or depression; F Major = lightness or mental health) to depict the characters and their relationships. Liza sings in the key of F Major/minor for actual life events: the school play is in f minor, her childhood song in F Major. Even when Russell sings about Kendall and her relationship ("The Best Years of His Life"), he sings in F Major. This key is associated with the real Liza and her biography. When she represents herself in a distorted fashion, Weill employed the key of E-flat Major. She sings "One Life to Live," which could not be further from the truth, in this key. Liza repeats "The Best Years of His Life" also in this false key, faking a fluttery descant about giving her heart but not her word.

Those numbers where Liza fantasizes about the woman she wants to be are all in the key of C Major/minor. The suitors serenade her with "Oh Fabulous One in Your Ivory Tower" and the Seventh Heaven patrons welcome her with "Girl of the Moment," both in C Major. Liza's high school classmates recall her time at Mapleton High as she wishes it had been, in c minor. When Liza delivers her climactic defense as part of the circus trial, the fictitious Jenny serves to illustrate what would happen if Liza (who in real life has difficulty making decisions) were to be decisive. Jenny operates as Liza's wish fulfillment. The key for "The Saga of Jenny" is again c minor. To summarize, when Liza buys into her negative core beliefs (that she is unattractive, inferior to other women, etc.), her flights of fancy take the key of C.

Liza's relationships with the three men in her life revolve in this same tonal orbit. The romantic duet with Randy, which she dreams about, is in A-flat Major. Associated with the minor mode of her fantasy-life key (c minor), ultimately Randy is not meant for Liza. Kendall's key is E Major when he impersonates Pierre, the maitre d' at the Seventh Heaven. Like A-flat Major, E Major is tonally distant from Liza's authentic self. Only Charley sings in keys that are compatible with her true self. As the marine who paints her portrait, Charley addresses the patrons and Liza in her authentic key of F Major. When he introduces himself in the *Circus Dream*, he sings in the key of B-flat Major, a closely related key. Finally, when he sings the second phrase of "My Ship" in the final scene, he is in her key of F Major. The associative use of tonality defines which of the three men Liza should choose.

Lady in the Dark thus operates on two different tonal axes, analogous to the two levels of reality in the show (spoken dialogue representing Liza's consciousness, musical sequences her unconscious). The first axis is that of F Major/d minor. These keys represent the light and dark sides of Liza's personality. She begins her sessions with Dr. Brooks in the key of depression and anxiety (d minor), but concludes her analysis firmly in the key of mental well-being (F Major). The second axis is that of c minor/E-flat Major. These keys represent the two sides of her psyche (or unconscious dream state). When her fantasies are tethered to actual events, the key is c minor; when they are deceptions, the key is E-flat Major. Because this axis is the inversion of her waking self, the Major/minor relationship is reversed: it is the minor mode, instead of the Major, that points Liza out of the dark.

In terms of style, *Lady in the Dark* invokes many varieties of operetta, using its conventions as a send-up. This may have been Ira's idea, given that he and George had turned out three satirical operettas and that the duo had been referred to in the late 1920s as "the Jazz Gilbert and Sullivan." Musically these shows appear to have been the models for *Lady in the Dark*. In his earliest letter to Weill, Gershwin mentioned both *Of Thee I Sing* and *Let 'Em Eat Cake* as prototypes for how patter could be combined with songs. Likewise, when Moss Hart drafted the conclusion for the "Hollywood Dream," he cited *Of Thee I Sing* and *Strike Up the Band*. By choosing operetta conventions, Weill and Gershwin were able to set up expectations that could then be either dashed or fulfilled with a twist.

The *Glamour Dream* is patterned after the opening of an early twentieth-century American operetta. Victor Herbert, Rudolf Friml, and Sigmund Romberg often began their operettas with a male Chorus singing one or two rousing numbers, often of marching or drinking variety, before the men accompany the leading lady's entrance song.[22] Representative examples include "Tramp! Tramp! Tramp!" sung by Captain Dick and his rangers in Herbert's *Naughty Marietta*, the song of "The Mounties" for Sergeant Malone and his officers in Friml's *Rose-Marie*, or the "Riff Song" for the Red Shadow and his men in Romberg's *The Desert Song*. Probably the most famous example is Romberg's *The Student Prince*, whose original Broadway production included a thirty-six-member male Chorus who sang the "Students' Marching Song" and "Drinking Song," after which the prima donna entered and sang "Come Boys."

The *Glamour Dream* begins with just such a male Chorus who come to serenade in TTBB harmony. As the music swells with the first appearance of the glamour theme, we are led to expect the entrance of the leading lady, who would then sing a number with her admirers. Instead, her maid appears and tells them Liza is resting! After a short reprise of "Oh Fabulous One in Your Ivory Tower," the men depart, and we see Liza in her boudoir getting ready for a night on the town. Her entrance number is thus delayed until she steps out at Columbus Circle to sing "One Life to Live." Her admirers long gone, she sings the number only to her chauffeur.

The rumba that concludes the *Glamour Dream* resembles Jacques Offenbach's first-act finale to *Barbe-Bleue* (*Bluebeard*). The German-born French composer is regarded as the father of operetta. He combined spoken dialogue, songs, and dances to form a full-length entertainment, which was originally called opéra bouffe.[23] *Barbe-Bleue* (1866), a satire of the medieval story (the wives have not been killed but been given sleeping potions), features a South American dance to end Act I. Weill's use of the rumba to conclude the *Glamour Dream* and the gradual speeding up of the tempo of "Girl of the Moment" create an exciting Offenbach-type climax.[24]

The *Wedding Dream* employs another operetta convention for "This Is New." This romantic ballad describes an exotic locale: "With you I used to roam/Through the Pleasure Dome of Kubla Khan,/I held you tight, my love,/In the gardens of Old Babylon." Irene Sharaff's costume for Randy was a polo outfit, which resembled a safari suit. The number recalls the North African locale and title song of Romberg's *The Desert Song*. Both were intended for the romantic baritone to sing to the heroine, who then repeats a chorus of the song herself.[25] But "This Is New" is parody and not mere imitation: the setting is not an exotic locale but a Hollywood sound stage, and Randy Curtis is no Red Shadow but merely a "flame of the celluloid."

The sequence concludes with a traditional Act I operetta finale. Such an ensemble brings together all the primary characters. This occasion shows off the genius of the composer, with his ability to combine different melodies in athletic counterpoint, the ability of the singers to harmonize their parts, and the skill of the librettist to find an excuse to bring all the principals on stage. For the climax of the *Wedding Dream*, Weill wove together five different melodies, sung by Randy Curtis, the Chorus, the children, and Charley Johnson. He began by joining "This Is New" with two Chorus melodies ("What a Lovely Day for a Wedding" and "This Woman at the Altar") in two different sections separated by the sepulchral voice in the Chorus. He then combined all three melodies and finally added the fourth ("It's Never Too Late to Mendelssohn," reduced to chanting) and fifth ("The Princess of Pure Delight").

Unlike the first two sequences, which use French and American operetta as their models, the *Circus Dream* is indebted to Gilbert and Sullivan, in particular their *Trial by Jury*.[26] It was Gilbert and Sullivan's first success, performed in the United States already in 1875 and an evergreen on Broadway (revived many times, most recently a year before *Lady in the Dark* opened). *Trial by Jury* concerns a case brought by Plaintiff Angelina and tried under the "Breach of Promise" clause. The Defendant, Edwin, is summoned before the jury, and his defense claims that because of his fickle nature he will wed one girl today and another the next. The Counsel for the Plaintiff reminds him that such a practice has been a crime in England since James II. The dilemma appears to be insolvable until the Judge agrees to marry Angelina himself. Perhaps because of the work's brevity and lack of dialogue, Sullivan titled it a "dramatic cantata in one act," although today it is considered Britain's best operetta up to that time.[27]

Young Ira had first heard Sullivan's verse over his father's Victrola and as a teenager had read *Trial by Jury*. The link between *Trial by Jury* and *Lady in the Dark* is preserved in his first draft of the *Circus Dream*. The Chorus begins the minstrel show with the following patter:

> Hello, hello, hello.
> We're ready to start the show.
> We're ready to start the minstrel show—
> Hello, hello, hello.
> The name of the show is "A Breach of Promise."

Gershwin and Weill turned the plot inside out so that instead of the spurned woman (Angelina) bringing suit against her unfaithful fiancé (Edwin), here the forsaken man (Kendall) files a charge against his mistress (Liza). Gershwin modeled the defendant's introduction directly on Sullivan's, even going so far as to preserve his central metaphor of a "star in the ascendant."

Both Angelina's and Kendall's testimonies concern passing time. Angelina sings, "O'er the season vernal,/Time may cast a shade;/Sunshine, if eternal,/Makes the roses fade!" and Kendall's situation is summarized in "The Best Years of His Life." To provide the other side of the story, both Edwin and Liza defend their actions on account of a change of heart. Edwin sings, "You cannot eat breakfast all day,/Nor is it the act of a sinner,/When breakfast is taken away,/To turn your attention to dinner." Liza sings, "Tra la—I loved him at the start/And then I had a change of heart./Tra la—The rights of womankind/Tra la—permit a change of mind." Weill and Gershwin also borrowed the title character's entrance music from *The Mikado* for the jury's introduction.

Despite the *Circus Dream*'s close association with Gilbert and Sullivan, "The Best Years of His Life" recalls Viennese operetta, which often used the waltz to unite the romantic leads. An example is the third-act waltz "Lippen schwei-gen" from Franz Lehár's *Die lustige Witwe* (*The Merry Widow*). The soprano typically sings a descant above a full-choral statement to express her joy, such as Hanna's "la la la" in "Das hat Rrrrass'! So" from *The Merry Widow*'s second-act finale. For "The Best Years of His Life," Weill includes just such a treatment, including a descant for Liza. But in this waltz finale, Liza *refuses* to marry Kendall, so the number becomes an inversion of the model.

Collectively, Weill and Gershwin were familiar with the full range of operetta repertory. Gershwin knew his Gilbert and Sullivan and the Broad-way operettas of the 1920s, which had run opposite his and George's shows. As a young man Weill conducted all of the continental varieties when he worked for the municipal theater in Lüdenscheid. In 1930s America, operetta was very much current, with MGM adapting the works of Herbert, Friml, and Rom-berg as vehicles for Jeanette MacDonald and Nelson Eddy. In addition, for a brief time in 1939 *The Swing Mikado* and *The Hot Mikado* had both played concurrently on Broadway, before the latter transferred to the World's Fair.

Operetta created a style not only for the individual sequences, but for the entire show. *Lady in the Dark* was billed as "a musical play," which on Broadway had long been a euphemism for operetta. Friml's *Katinka* and *The Vagabond King* and Romberg's *Maytime* and *The Desert Song* had each been designated a musical play. Given Weill's occasional unidiomatic translations, it is even possible that when he described *Lady in the Dark*'s dream sequences as "three little one-act operas," what he meant by "little opera" was, in fact, his translation of "operetta."

The last stage in the compositional process was the orchestration, which Weill did himself. Although not unprecedented (George Gershwin orches-trated *Porgy and Bess* as did Victor Herbert for most of his operettas), the prevailing norm on Broadway is to hire a professional arranger to orches-trate the composer's score. Many professional arrangers cultivate their own signature sound, but Weill created a particular sound world for each of his works through differing instrumentation. On his preliminary sketch for *Lady*'s overture, he jotted down the disposition of instruments and number of players: "Fl., 3 Cl., 3 Trp, 1 Trb, Org., Piano, Drums, 6 Viol., 2 Vc., Bass."

By omitting violas from the string section, Weill created a texture that emphasized treble and bass, reminiscent of dance orchestras. This type of ensemble is in keeping with the overall form of *Lady in the Dark* as a suite with three dance idioms. The inner harmony usually provided by the violas was taken over by the reed players and keyboards. *Lady in the Dark*'s percussion part is very large and requires two players. Such instruments as rumba drums, door chime, automobile horns, sirens, telephone bell, church chimes, and wood (gavel) provide special effects, in addition to mallet instruments (vibraphone, glockenspiel, xylophone) and the usual battery of drums and cymbals. Typical of Broadway practice, the woodwinds are grouped into "reed books" in which the player is expected to play various instruments. Morris Stonzek, who contracted *Lady in the Dark*'s orchestra, remembers that Weill was excited by the possibilities of reed books, even though he referred to them as clarinet parts.[28]

The inclusion of a Hammond organ is typical of Weill's works from this period. American engineers Laurens Hammond and John M. Hanert had developed the instrument in 1933–1934. It was first demonstrated in April 1935, and about eighteen months later Weill first wrote for it.[29] The different timbres on the Hammond are made available by adding overtones to the basic pitch with a system of drawbars.[30] For *Lady in the Dark*, Weill indicated when the Hammond organ should sound like a harp, bells, church organ, and even a French horn, suggesting that he thought of it as a modern synthesizer. He added a footnote to the score about its use: "The Hammond organ is used mostly as a 'fill-in.' It should be used very sparingly and never be noticeable." In the original production, the pianist played both the piano and the Hammond organ.

Although Weill orchestrated virtually all of *Lady in the Dark* himself, he did contract arranger Ted Royal for two sections: "Bats about You" and a thirty-six-measure dance break to "One Life to Live." "Bats about You" was intended to be in an early Irving Berlin style, with which Weill was unfamiliar, to evoke the era of Liza's high school graduation. Throughout his American career, Weill tended to entrust arrangers with unusual assignments or hot dance arrangements.

In his orchestrations, Weill went so far as to describe a particular attitude he desired from a player. For Charley's introduction in the *Circus Dream*, he wrote "mocking" above the first clarinet's interjections. Similarly, to emphasize the absurdity of Russell's summary of the situation, he wrote "like [a] hammer" in the piano part. This indicated that the dance rhythm was to be played with no rubato and none of the lilt of a true Viennese waltz. In other spots, the orchestration gives the listener a mental picture. When the minstrel reappears in "The Princess of Pure Delight," Gershwin tells us that he is "quite out of breath." As the minstrel recites the answer to the riddle, Weill composed frenetic chromatic scales between each phrase played by the flute and clarinets to depict his gasping breath.

Another of Weill's gifts as an orchestrator was his ability to set a scene in a short introduction. At the beginning of the *Circus Dream*, he not only instructed that the Hammond organ should sound like a calliope but captured the sound of one through his choice of piccolo, keyboards, cymbal, and snare and bass drums. This combination replicates the sound of a calliope, with its shrieking pipes and rhythm section, and gives a sonic image of a circus and the type of mechanical instruments that accompany its rides. For "Oh Fabulous One in Your Ivory Tower," he recreated with strings, piano, and Hammond organ the type of "giant guitar" accompaniment of early nineteenth-century Italian opera. Taking his cue from Gershwin's lyrics that mention famous operatic lovers ("What Brünnhilde was to Siegfried... What Butterfly was to Pinkerton...What Carmen was to Don José"), Weill imitated a type of operatic accompaniment. With pizzicato playing in the strings and rolled chords in the Hammond organ and piano, the orchestration links "Oh Fabulous One in Your Ivory Tower" with a long tradition of serenades sung to the allure of the eternal feminine.

In a few spots, Weill even had the orchestra join in the drama. As Liza is mocked at the end of the *Glamour Dream*, the first violins' and piccolo's ascending runs and trills create a type of distorted hilarity. It is as if the orchestra is giddy and itself laughing at Liza. The orchestra also contributes to the action onstage when Liza asks Sutton if there are any messages. During the following recitativo passage, the maid attempts quickly to sort out the letters, cables, and telegrams. A solo clarinet imitates her flurry of activity and hurries her along. For the verse to "One Life to Live," there is a syrupy violin countermelody when Liza sings, "And I want to make the most of it." The oversentimentality undercuts what Liza is claiming to be.

Weill's imaginative orchestrations were often created out of practical limitations. During this period, the Alvin Theatre had a house minimum of twenty players for the orchestra. Weill scored *Lady in the Dark* exactly to that number, no doubt because of the budget. He regarded such restrictions, however, as opportunities: "The important concessions to Broadway are of a practical nature: limitation in the size of orchestra and chorus, and limitation in the size of leading singing parts. But in the history of the arts, such limitations have often brought very excellent results because they represent a challenge to the imagination and the skill of the creative artist."[31]

Out of such limitations, Weill was often able to say much with very little. Maurice Abravanel loved to rehearse the story of when Aaron Copland first heard *Lady in the Dark*. The next day, when the two sat down to lunch, Copland questioned him about the orchestration: "It is very interesting how Kurt goes from the realistic scenes to psychoanalysis to the dreams. What's the orchestration there?" Abravanel, "Clarinet." Copland, "Yes, clarinet and what?" Abravanel, "Clarinet." Copland was incredulous. "What do you mean? Clarinet. Just clarinet?" Abravanel, "Just clarinet...two notes."

Copland, "Damn it! Those are things that we work months to get. Kurt gets them with two notes."[32]

The pride Weill must have felt for his musical score is reflected in the care that he took with it. His handwriting is uncharacteristically neat; he fastidiously notated expression marks, dynamics, and phrasing; and he went to the trouble of recopying the first page, which had been a little messy. A small herd of union copyists prepared the orchestral parts directly from his score. After they were finished, Weill had it finely bound. On its spine in gold lettering is the show's title and the names of Hart and Gershwin and his own. On a blank title page, the composer wrote, using his German spelling, "Kurt Weill, 'Lady in the Dark' Complete Orchesterscore (Original Manuscript of the composer)." With the musical score to *Lady in the Dark*, Weill had realized his artistic credo:

> The special brand of musical entertainment in which I have been interested from the start is a sort of "dramatic musical," a simple, strong story told in musical terms. . . . This form of theatre has its special attraction for the composer, because it allows him to use a great variety of musical idioms, to write music that is both serious and light, operatic and popular, emotional and sophisticated, orchestral and vocal. Each show of this type has to create its own style, its own texture, its own relationship between words and music, because music becomes a truly integral part of the play—it helps to deepen the emotions and clarify the structure.[33]

4

Tryout

As Moss Hart was feverishly writing *Lady in the Dark*, another drama began to play itself out. When he traveled to Philadelphia at the end of March 1940 to share his progress with Katharine Cornell, he downplayed the musical component. He remembered feeling on the way home "torn between an honest desire to tell her exactly what she was letting herself in for . . . and a grave doubt as to whether she could do it."[1] Cornell, five feet seven inches tall with a dark complexion and slightly exotic features, had built her reputation as a dramatic actress on Shakespeare and Shaw. Her husband, Guthrie McClintic, had co-produced and directed all of her plays beginning in 1931. Both McClintic and Cornell were considered for *Lady in the Dark*.[2]

The Sunday after Hart returned, he attended a rehearsal for a British War Relief Party for which he and Kaufman were contributing an act. As he watched Gertrude Lawrence perform, he realized that she was better suited than Cornell for the leading role. After the rehearsal, Hart invited Lawrence to the Plaza Hotel, where, over beer and a snack in the Oak Room, he outlined the play.[3] The two agreed to meet the next day so that she could hear some of its dialogue. As Lawrence's play *Skylark* was preparing to leave for its tour and Cornell's tour of *No Time for Comedy* was winding down, both actresses were searching for vehicles for the next season. Having now essentially offered the role to both of them, Hart had a difficult time sleeping that night.

Lawrence's career had its beginnings in revue and musical comedy. Born in Britain in 1898, she got her first taste of the stage at a seaside party at the age of six. It was in Gerhart Hauptmann's 1913 dream play *Hannele* where she met another child actor, Noël Coward, who would become a lifelong friend.

She cut her theatrical teeth on a series of small touring companies but received her big break in André Charlot's revue *Tabs*. After several more revues, Lawrence teamed up with Walter Williams and toured music halls in London and the provinces. It was this training that would later surface during *Lady in the Dark*'s tryout.

Lawrence came to the United States with *André Charlot's London Revue of 1924*. It took the critics by storm and ran for fifteen months in New York and on tour. The actors reunited for *Charlot's Revue of 1926*. After another successful run and tour, Lawrence starred in the Gershwins' musical *Oh, Kay!*, which racked up 256 performances in New York before transferring to London, where it played another 214. This gave Gertie the distinction of being the first British actress to originate a role on Broadway before playing it in the West End. The Gershwins and Lawrence tried to repeat their success with *Treasure Girl*, but it flopped. The actress tried film with *The Battle of Paris*, which also flopped, despite two songs from Cole Porter.

Lawrence then made a transition to spoken theater, first appearing in 1929 in a Viennese comedy adapted for New York entitled *Candle-Light*. She returned to London and briefly to musical revue before Coward sent her the script for *Private Lives*. Arguably the best British comedy since Oscar Wilde's *The Importance of Being Earnest*, *Private Lives* played for three months in the West End before transferring to Broadway, where it cemented the partnership of Noël and Gertie. By the time of *Lady in the Dark*, American theatergoers thought of Lawrence primarily as a straight theater, romantic comedienne.

Following *Private Lives*, she returned to England, where her professional career took a mild dip; however, Coward's *Tonight at 8:30*, a series of nine one-act plays performed in alternating triple bills, revived her career. Rachel Crother's play *Susan and God* gave Lawrence her greatest success in a straight play. After its New York run, she embarked on a tour of twenty-seven cities. By the time the tour reached Chicago, she had become a U.S. resident. She subsequently starred in Samson Raphaelson's *Skylark*, a slight comedy about the neglected wife of a money-crazy advertising man. During this period, romance blossomed between the actress and Richard Aldrich, a Boston Brahmin. He was managing the Cape Playhouse, where *Skylark* had its summer stock tryout.

Beginning on January 22, 1940, *Skylark* substituted a Thursday afternoon matinee for its Monday evening performance. This odd arrangement of three matinees and five performances gave Lawrence extra rest over the weekend. After the Sunday British Relief rehearsal and tête-à-tête with Hart, she was free on Monday to sample *Lady in the Dark*'s dialogue. Hart called that afternoon at her West Fifty-fourth penthouse, which was decorated in Arabian Nights décor with satin curtains and chairs of various colors. Lawrence recalled, "I invited him to my apartment to read the play and, as I had just had the thing done over, I knew I could set the stage. I love to act offstage even better than on, so when Mr. Hart arrived I was at the end of a long living room gracefully posed with a throw over my knees, knitting."[4] Despite the atmosphere, which she described as pure Cecil Beaton, Hart drew up a chair and began reading the first scene of *Lady in the Dark*. "I knew he was distracted so I just kept on knitting," Lawrence teased. "Finally I was so intrigued I had to put the sweater away."

Afterward they chatted over tea. Hart was buoyed by her reaction: "She had liked the play. I could tell that. And she literally *was* the part as she walked about the room talking about it. It was more than exciting, she kept repeating. It was an adventure in the theatre and something she's always hoped for as an actress."[5] Hart basked in the glow of her enthusiasm and was poised to clinch the deal. Lawrence demurred, however, because her astrologer had advised her not to make any important decisions until after May 7. Dejected, Hart returned to Fairview Farm and took out his frustration by writing laugh lines about astrology into the play, which in turn inspired Weill and Gershwin's astrological numbers.

Lawrence may have been reticent to commit to the project because of her personal life. She and Richard Aldrich were dining out three or four nights a week at a small French restaurant in the East Fifties, and their relationship had turned serious. Unlike most Americans' reaction to the "phony war," Lawrence had thrown herself headlong into war relief efforts that winter. Her desire to serve her homeland was so strong that she vowed to cancel her tour of *Skylark* and return to Britain.[6] Realizing that he might lose her, Aldrich, with the help of the British ambassador, convinced Lawrence to stay in the United States and work against America's isolationism.

Hart continued writing until the appointed time, when he telephoned Lawrence. She was in a jovial mood. "It's all working out beautifully, because I've just had a cable from Noël and he arrives tomorrow morning. Isn't that wonderful?" Hart wondered what Coward had to do with it when Gertie replied, "But don't you see, darling . . . it all works out! My astrologer said to do nothing until April [*recte* May] 7th and I never do anything without Noël's advice, and here he is arriving on the very day. You must read the play to Noël and if he says 'yes' I'll do it."[7] Before Hart could meet with Coward, the Sunday *Times* announced Katharine Cornell's involvement in *Lady in the Dark*. The article reported McClintic saying that his wife "could sing, although she never had 'publicly.'"[8]

After a trip to Washington, DC, where he dined with President and Mrs. Roosevelt, Coward met with Hart on May 8. Following lunch at the Farm, Hart read the first act. When he finished and looked up, Coward beamed, "Gertie ought to pay you to play it."[9] Thrilled, Hart and Coward drove into the city before Lawrence's matinee let out. Her reaction seemed positive: "Bless you, darlings." As Hart was dropping Coward at his hotel, Noël confided, "Uncle Moss...*now* your troubles are really beginning." Hart protested, "But Gertie said 'yes,' didn't she?" "That's just my point, my boy," Coward replied. "Gertie said 'yes'!" Before Hart could stop him, Coward dashed into the hotel.[10]

A few days later Coward took Lawrence to lunch: "[I] wagged an authoritative finger in her face as I had so often done in the past. She shilly-shallied a bit, took refuge in irrelevancies, giggled and finally gave in."[11] Or so Coward thought. Hart waited a couple of days before telephoning her for a confirmation. Lawrence postponed making a definite decision until the first act could be read for Fanny Holtzmann, her lawyer and business manager. "I never do anything without her, darling. We'll be at your house tomorrow for lunch at two. Bless you, darling!"[12] Soon after Hart put the phone down, Katharine Cornell called wanting to hear how work was progressing. Hart put her off in the hope that things could quickly be wrapped up with Gertie.

At the luncheon, Hart, Weill, and Gershwin all pitched the show to Lawrence and her manager. Holtzmann liked it and assured them, "We'll have it all settled by the end of the week." Hart and Weill then paid a visit to Cornell to explain the musical demands that would prevent her from taking the role. To their astonishment, she was unfazed: "Not at all, it sounds fine. As a matter of fact I love to sing and sing much better than anyone suspects. Why don't you both come back here next Tuesday and let me sing for you?" Hart and Weill sheepishly agreed and left. Hart admitted, "It was as awful a half-hour as I have ever spent and I think Kurt agreed with me."[13]

Cornell ended up going to Martha's Vineyard, which postponed her singing audition for some three weeks. However, negotiations with Holtzmann dragged on. With Lawrence soon to depart on her *Skylark* tour, Aldrich proposed marriage and she accepted. They held a moonlit ceremony on July 4, her forty-second birthday. Hart was losing patience and demanded a signed contract or the whole thing would be off. He even entertained offering the part to Irene Dunne instead. A telegram arrived from Lawrence explaining that the delay was because of her marriage the night before. Hart cabled back to Aldrich, CONGRATULATIONS AND ARE YOU SURE GERTIE SAID 'YES'?

After tracking her down, Hart demanded that Lawrence make up her mind (perhaps he was inspired while writing the second act to give Liza precisely the same problem). Lawrence voiced surprise: "But darling, I said 'yes' months ago, didn't I? Whatever are you troubling your little head about? I am coming into town on Monday—let's have lunch at Voisin and I will bring the contract with me all properly signed. Bless you, darling."[14]

After cocktails at Voisin, Hart was primed to receive the contract, but instead Lawrence blurted out, "Darling, the most awful thing has happened, I left it in Cape Cod and Fanny is drawing another one [up] this very minute. We will have it for you the day after tomorrow. . . ." Hart tensely replied, "But you are leaving for the tour of *Skylark* day after tomorrow. . . . Are you sure about this?" Lawrence replied, "Of course I am, darling. . . . It has all worked out beautifully, hasn't it?" With that she left for her appointment at Elizabeth Arden's. Hart fiendishly wrote that he "would have given anything to have been the masseur and pommeled the hell out of her."[15]

Two days later Holtzmann called and requested that Hart meet her at producer Sam H. Harris's office in the Music Box Theatre, where she would deliver the contract at 2:00. When she ceremoniously presented it, Hart's heart sank. Lawrence had neglected to sign the rider, and in one hour she was leaving for Los Angeles to begin *Skylark*'s tour. Although she was in her final rehearsal, it was agreed that Jack Potter, her personal manager, would sneak into the theater, snag her as she exited, and have her sign the rider.

Hart and Weill joined Gershwin at the Essex House to wait for the contract. All three paced about Gershwin's suite waiting for the telephone to ring. Finally the call came: it was Holtzmann. There was one important detail that Lawrence wanted to add to the contract: *Lady in the Dark* must open at the Music Box Theatre or the whole thing was off. Hart lost it, screaming into the receiver, "The whole thing is off. I will be here for fifteen minutes longer and if that contract is not here by then, just tear it up."[16] Gershwin, known for his mild demeanor, thought Hart had been rash, and all three worried that after nearly three months of negotiations, they had lost their leading lady. After fifteen very tense minutes, the contract arrived signed in all the right places, and the drama had come to an end.[17] (Or at least an intermission.)

The standard Actors' Equity contract drawn up by Sam Harris back on June 21 promised Lawrence $2,000 a week and included both the 1940–1941 and 1941–1942 seasons, with a planned opening on December 23. The rider assured Lawrence the right of a vacation without pay between June 1 and September 15, 1941, and, beyond the $2,000 minimum, additional compensation each week at 10 percent of the first $10,000 of the gross box-office receipts and 15 percent of all weekly gross receipts exceeding $10,000.[18] For negotiating such a generous contract, Hart described Holtzmann "as helpless as the Bethlehem Steel Company and as delicate as 'Jack the Ripper.'"[19]

With Lawrence finally aboard, Hart wrote an apologetic, and not entirely truthful, letter to Cornell: "To state it quickly: the music went 'round and 'round. I mean by that that the play fairly reeks of music now—if there were great musical stretches before there are veritable 'Traviatas' now. There was some doubt in both our minds you know, about there being too much music for you, and as Weill and Gershwin went on with their part of it, it became more and more apparent that we ought to have someone almost musical comedy to handle it." He closed the letter with the irony that "the way this whole bloody thing" began was a "dream of writing a play for Katharine Cornell."[20]

The only other actor signed by then was Danny Kaye. Born David Daniel Kaminsky, he had gotten his start in 1929 in Jewish summer resort hotels in the Catskills. There the tall, lanky red-haired comic honed his shtick, which involved verbal slapstick, double-talk, and outrageous foreign accents. He had begun as a *tummler* (Yiddish: someone who keeps things lively, a jester) at White Roe Lake House in Livingston Manor, New York.[21] His summer employment had eventually blossomed into an act in a vaudeville show, which traveled to Japan and the Far East in 1933–1934.

He moved up the ranks as a Borscht Belt comic to the President Hotel in Swan Lake, New York, in 1936 and Camp Tamiment in Stroudsburg, Pennsylvania, in 1939. At Tamiment a talented pianist named Sylvia Fine crafted numbers for him that often included fey humor to exploit his boyish manner. Specialty numbers she wrote for him included "Stanislavsky" (done in a faux Russian accent about the director's acting methods) and "Pavlowa" about a Russian danseuse (Kaye performed it *en tutu*). The entertainment from Camp Tamiment became the basis for a Broadway revue that opened in 1939. *The Straw Hat Revue*, with songs by Sylvia Fine and James Shelton, featured, in addition to Kaye, the young Imogene Coca, Alfred Drake, and Jerome Robbins. Kaye and Fine soon fused their respective talents into a single artistic persona: he, the consummate performer and comic, she, the creator of all of his numbers and accompanist. Kaye liked to pun, "Sylvia has a Fine head on my shoulders."

After their marriage in early 1940, Kaye's debut came in the form of a one-week stint at Dario's La Martinique. The basement nightclub at 57 West Fifty-seventh paid him a staggering $250 for the brief engagement. Kaye's first late show made him the talk of the town. His twelve-minute act included signature numbers, such as "Stanislavsky" and "Pavlowa," as well as new pieces, such as a take-off on a Russian tenor called "Otchi Tchorniya." After a standing ovation, Kaye sang virtually every number he knew for encores, and the show finally closed with him leading an impromptu conga line gibbering away in Spanish-accented double-talk. Kaye's one-week engagement stretched out to thirteen, and his pay doubled and then tripled.[22]

One of Hart's associates dragged him to see Kaye's act. Hart recalled, "I was really taken with this young man. And he came to the table afterward, and I said to him, 'I'm writing a show now for next fall and I'm going to write a part in it for you.' " Hart admitted, "I had never thought of writing a part originally, but I broke the first act open, which I had partly completed, and put a part in."[23] No doubt Kaye's number "Anatole of Paris," about a misogynist fashion designer who "shrieks with chic," inspired the role of Russell Paxton. Kaye signed for $250 a week with the distinction of being the first actor cast for *Lady in the Dark*.

Once Lawrence had signed, production duties were divvied up. The team split directorial duties, with Hart in charge of the dramatic scenes and Hassard Short the musical sequences. Although unusual today, two directors had become almost a tradition with Hart's plays with music. Short had worked on producer Sam Harris's *Music Box Revues* (1921, 1922, 1923), as well as Hart's *As Thousands Cheer*, *The Great Waltz*, and *Jubilee*. He was known for his innovative use of moving stages, mirrors, and colored lights. He is even occasionally credited with replacing footlights with lights hung from the gridiron.

In contrast to Hart's familiarity with Short, he had never worked with designer Harry Horner. Born in Vienna, Horner had come to the United States in 1936 as a technical assistant with *The Eternal Road*. When the show was postponed, he found work on Broadway doing stage designs. One of the shows he worked on, *All the Living*, was about an insane asylum. Hart saw the play, and the presence of a psychiatrist in that show made him think of Horner for *Lady in the Dark*. The script Horner received was "terribly complicated and read like a film, with 'dissolves' and 'fade-ins.' " "There were so many scenes; and a careful reading of the script convinced me that a curtain between each scene would slow or completely dam the flow of the story."[24] To produce the needed transformations, he imagined a kaleidoscope and decided to employ turntables.

Horner's ground plan featured two large turntables (each with a radius of 12.5 feet), half of which would be used for the dream sequences and half for the offices of *Allure* and Dr. Brooks. Sliding portals reduced the proscenium to twenty-eight feet for the two office settings but increased it to thirty-six feet for the dream sequences. This ingeniously suited the relatively few actors in the office scenes but accommodated the singers, dancers, and children for the musical sequences. Because of the changing locales within the sequences, Horner placed two small turntables within the primary ones. These six-foot-radius turntables did not share the same axes as their larger counterparts, but were placed primarily in the dream sequence half of those turntables. With this arrangement, the realistic office scenes did not have to be reset (Figure 29).

Horner carefully researched both the floor plans and décor of a fashion editor's office and a psychiatrist's office. He did part of his research at *Vogue*, whose editors lent him mock-up covers on which he attached the name *Allure*. One wonders if Horner did the remainder of his research at Kubie's office. Hart had provided a detailed description of Dr. Brooks's office in the opening scene of the play, but Horner admitted, "There are always typical details which a photograph or description might fail to reveal, a lamp in a certain position always used by a psychoanalyst, certain books, minor details which give a touch of life."[25]

One such detail was the placement of the psychiatrist's chair, which Hart never described in the script. However, Kubie recommended in his hand-book that the analyst sit just behind the head of the couch so that he could observe the patient's facial expressions. Horner's sketch of Dr. Brooks's office shows the placement of the couch and chair precisely as Kubie advocated (Figure 30). That placement remained constant in Horner's scaled model, as well as in the actual set (Figures 31 and 2).

Horner created a few props to suggest different locales within the dream sequences. These furnishings were all based on a central fashion motif of a ribbon and an "L" for Liza. According to the designer, "The chairs, the automobile, the couches, all were designed to look like fantastically arranged lace ribbons" (Figure 32).[26] These could be quickly set up on the small turntables and whirled into place. Movable accordion walls divided the turntables in half and hid both the turntables' axes and the back of the offices. They provided a neutral blue backdrop for the dream sequences and can be seen in Horner's sketches (Figures 33 and 34).

On August 27, Horner presented his design to Harris, Hart, Short, and Weill at Harris's office. Using the model, Horner demonstrated that with turntables the stage crew would be able to change scenes swiftly without the use of curtains. The rough cost estimate for the production, however, was $125,000. Harris threw his support behind the design but urged all concerned to keep the show within its $100,000 budget.

That evening Hart read the script for the men at Harris's office, a tradition that began when Harris became the primary producer of Kaufman and Hart's work. It was then that Harris and his staff questioned the necessity of the Coq d'Or scene and the "Hollywood Dream." Hart, Short, and Horner met later that week to confer about the budget. Even with the cuts, the estimate for the production had come in at $130,000. Worse, the machinery for the turntables was deemed so complicated that it would be impossible for the show to tour. Horner left the meeting despondent: "For nights and days I tried out methods of designing *Lady in the Dark* without turntables and with the ability to tour. I was more of a whirling dervish at that point than those turntables will ever be."[27]

Horner and Short eventually returned to his initial plan but set out to solve the portability problem. The design originally had a series of intricate gears that enabled a single stagehand to operate the turntables by means of a winch. "The trouble was that the gears alone would have cost $8,000," Horner admitted, and "would have required far too much time for setting up and taking down."[28]

Instead, manual labor would be employed: the two large turntables would each be turned by two teams of two men, and the two small ones by a single man with a crank (for a total of ten men). Horner designed a series of holes on the outer rim of the large turntables so that metal elbow rods could be lifted out by the stagehands and put in different spots for the rotations. He designed each section of the large turntables in subsections no larger than six feet wide in order for them to fit through the door of a railway boxcar. With the portability problem solved, the T. B. MacDonald Construction Company was contracted to build the stage machinery.

Horner then turned his attention to the materials for the dream sequences. Like Weill, he tried to examine his own dreams for inspiration, but with less success:

> For the life of me I could not conjure up visions of the physical backgrounds of any of my own dreams. The more I tried to remember what my dreams looked like the more I dreamt and the more I couldn't remember what I had dreamt when I awakened in the mornings. The vague feeling I had about dreams led me to decide that the texture of the dream scenery should be of a different quality than those of the realistic sets in the two offices. My first thought was glass. My second Lucite. But the former didn't seem right, and the latter material entailed prohibitive costs.

Instead, he chose cellulose acetate, which was being marketed under the name Marolin: It "could be molded into any desired shape or form. It could be fireproofed. It could 'take' paint. It could be backed by any kind of material and could be tinted any color."[29] The ability of Marolin to be translucent, but not transparent, enabled the audience to see the properties and gave Short the ability to create special effects by using colored lights. For the towering accordion walls, Horner covered the screens with Marolin in a liquid form. In certain areas, he rubbed off the acetate before it had dried to allow the brilliant blue foil on the screen to show through. Props constructed from Marolin included trees, lanterns, the apartment entrance, dressing table, chairs, sofa, letters, telegraphs, an automobile, portals, chandeliers, bottles, glasses, and a five-by-six-foot postage stamp. Horner did employ methyl methacrylate (Lucite®) for the lyres of Liza's admirers, the key to the island of Tobago, and the artist's palette.[30]

The producers chose Irene Sharaff to design the costumes. She had previously designed Hart's *As Thousands Cheer*, *The Great Waltz*, *Jubilee*, *I'd Rather Be Right*, and *The American Way*. Boston-born Sharaff had the distinction of being the first American to design for the Ballet Russe and was known for her use of color.[31] For the "Princess of Pure Delight," she concocted costumes of orange, blue, and a lavender hue (as specified in Gershwin's lyrics), with gold paillettes. She accessorized them with striped turbans in metallic colors and added sashes to emphasize the torso (Figure 35). The *Circus Dream* featured what was the most spectacular ensemble costuming: pink and blue outfits with accents of silver and gold.

Hattie Carnegie created wardrobes for the female staff members of *Allure*. She designed Liza's tailored business suits as well as her dream gowns. For Alison Du Bois, Carnegie created two outfits that showed fashion gone awry. Alison's opening lines in the play about a column entitled "Why Not" parody Diana Vreeland's column "Why Don't You" from *Harper's Bazaar*.[32] When the actress who originated the role expressed difficulty finding her character, Carnegie invited her to meet Vreeland: "[She] came in with her head draped in a brilliant cerise turban caught with a huge sparkling pin. She wore at least a dozen necklaces and clips and brooches, most of them junk jewelry. She walked through Miss Carnegie's home with her lower body slung forward, saying as she entered each room, 'It's divine! SIMP-ly divine!' in a half-British half-dead-end accent."[33]

Carnegie also designed the girls' evening dresses for the dance break of "This Is New" and chose Vinylite® for the women's shoes. The importance of this synthetic material and the influence that *Lady in the Dark* exerted on fashion trends caused one fashion editor to report, "All the fashion magazine 'girls' are in love with Vinylite shoes."[34] In contrast to the opulence of the women's fashions, the men's were credited to "Willhouse," an East Forty-seventh Street tailor, with Randy's formal wear to Dunhill.

The other members of the production team included choreographer Albertina Rasch and musical director Maurice Abravanel. During the 1930s Rasch was one of Broadway's leading choreographers and had worked with Hart on *Face the Music*, *The Great Waltz*, and *Jubilee*. Abravanel was a relative newcomer, but his association with Weill went all the way back to 1922. Weill's and Abravanel's careers had been made simultaneously, with Abravanel conducting several of the composer's works in Germany. In the United States, Abravanel left the Met to conduct *Knickerbocker Holiday*. Weill implicitly trusted him: he was the only collaborator who bridged all periods of the composer's career. Abravanel described himself in Wagnerian terms as Kurwenal to Weill's Tristan.

Once *George Washington Slept Here* went into rehearsals on August 28, Hart was able to turn his attention to completing *Lady in the Dark*'s casting. Weill reported to Gershwin, "Moss wanted for Maggie and Alsion two very good actresses and has found and signed them (Margaret Dale and Virginia [*recte* Natalie] Schafer)....I have found (through Cheryl Crawford)...a young actor whom we all like very much for Charley Johnson. His name is Macdonald Carey. We also found an actor called Randolph for the doctor."[35] Margaret Dale had previously appeared in three of Sam Harris's productions, including Kaufman and Ferber's *Dinner at Eight*, and Natalie Schafer had most recently been seen with Lawrence in *Susan and God*. Donald Randolph had appeared in Maurice Evan's cycle of *Richard II, Hamlet*, and *Henry IV, Part I* on Broadway in 1937, 1938, and 1939. Macdonald Carey had performed Shakespeare at the Dallas Globe Theatre (a spin-off from the Chicago World's Fair). He had moved to New York in 1938 and was a regular on the radio soap operas *Stella Dallas, Young Widder Brown*, and later *Second Husband*. Carey read for the whole team at the Music Box Theatre. Sam Harris thought he was too young to play Charley Johnson. However, a week later, while walking by the Shubert Theatre, Carey heard Hart calling behind him saying that he had landed the part.[36]

Weill kept Lawrence, on tour with *Skylark*, abreast of the show's progress. On August 24, he wrote her that 90 percent of the score was finished and that after completing the rehearsal score he would begin orchestrating. He enclosed two of the songs that she would be singing: "My Ship" and "One Life to Live." After receiving the letter in San Francisco, Lawrence wrote back on September 14 from Kansas City:

I do wish we had more time—this tour is long and arduous and I shall be very tired by the end of it—also I am dreadfully upset over the goings on in England, which makes sleep very difficult, and there is so much to do for War Relief. There is no time to relax for an instant.

Frankly I do not feel that it is humanly possible or wise for any woman in normal times to go from one long run of one play into another play with music the size of Moss's—and these are not normal times by any means.[37]

With both her tour scheduled to close and rehearsals for *Lady in the Dark* set to begin on November 15, there was no time to relax! Weill briefed Harris and Hart about the conflict. In his next letter to Lawrence, he wrote that he had begun orchestrating, despite the fact that Gershwin had yet to return to fix the conclusion of the *Circus Dream*: "We all had hoped that you could quit this road tour a little earlier, but since that does not seem possible we all agreed that we should make it possible for you to get a two weeks' rest, and we decided therefore to postpone rehearsals, for your sake, until December 2nd, although you can imagine how tough that is for us."[38]

To make matters worse, Lawrence was getting cold feet about her singing. Arrangements for lessons had been made in San Francisco, but she admitted in a letter to Weill that after leaving the Bay Area, "There have been no more lessons and Heaven alone knows where there will be!" Weill responded with caution to her request for a vocal coach: "I am always somewhat afraid of singing teachers because I have seen them spoil the individual qualities of natural voices in many cases (and I think you have a wonderful natural voice). I think what you want is somebody who would help you to relax your voice after the hardships of this road tour."[39]

The roles of Kendall and Randy were the last ones cast. For Kendall, several actors read for the part, but ultimately the producers chose Bert Lytell. The most difficult assignment was finding a Randy, whom Hart describes as a "rugged, powerful" Hollywood star with "none of the movie 'pretty-boy' about him." On September 2 Weill wrote to Gershwin, "We still haven't found anybody for Randy. Isn't there anybody in Hollywood?" Twelve days later Weill added, "We have seen a number of people, but they are either too operatic or they cannot sing." Although the names of Leif Erickson, Ronald Graham, George Houston, and Vincent Price were floated, the casting was not completed until Gershwin returned in late October:

A friend of mine, Gene Solow, just in from California, popped in to see me at the Essex House. When I told him of our casting problem, he said that a likely prospect, Victor Mature, had been on the plane with him, but he didn't know where Victor was to stay. I was busy shaving and asked: "Would you mind calling the Hotel Pierre? Maybe he's just registered there." No Mature. "Try the Algonquin." No Mature. "21" was phoned, with the same result. "It's probably crazy—but try the hotel desk here." "Crazy, eh?" said Gene a few seconds later—"He's registering right now."[40]

Mature, who had made *1,000,000 B.C.*, *Captain Caution*, and the film version of *No, No, Nanette*, signed for his Broadway debut. Principal casting was now complete.

Chorus auditions took place at the Lyceum Theatre on November 9. Although the *Post* reported that the auditions would be for Short and Weill, the composer called on his friend Lehman Engel to assist: "Kurt asked me to audition the singers for the show as he felt that I had more experience with American singers than Maurice [Abravanel]."[41] Because Short wanted "sixteen boys and girls who *looked* no more than twenty-one, had very good figures, and attractive faces," Engel was forced to eliminate them by type: "The two stage managers lined up the females, then males, ten at a time. The people in each line stood breathless as I tried to assess possibilities. It was embarrassing for all of us: like selecting animals. . . . This selecting-and-rejecting process took an entire morning, then the singing began."[42]

The cattle call was not entirely satisfactory because on November 11, the *Post* ran an additional casting call for boys. Notices appeared one last time for both sexes the following Monday. All told, Engel estimated that three thousand hopefuls auditioned for the sixteen spots. Manfred Hecht, one of the lucky ones, remembers being offered the union minimum of $40 a week.[43] Rasch held an audition for specialty dancers (one boy and one girl) at the Alvin on November 29. The specialty probably involved gymnastics for "Dance of the Tumblers." Costume fittings occurred during the last week of November, before rehearsals were slated to begin on Monday, December 2. And that is when production plans stalled.

Lawrence's understanding was that her *Skylark* contract had expired on November 15, but the producer, John Golden, maintained that her contract extended three weeks past that date. Hart's sleepless nights resumed. If Golden was correct, Hart tallied, "$60,000 of scenery already built and $40,000 worth of costumes already at work, would have to be discarded and the cast dismissed with two weeks' salary because, that three weeks' postponement plus the two weeks' vacation for Gertie which it was vital for her to have, would mean that the play could not open [in New York] until the end of February, and, with as expensive a venture as this, that was quite impossible."[44] Desperate, Hart wrote

Golden a letter and, with Harris's permission, offered him a financial piece of *Lady*'s pie and even the possibility of having his name on the program. Golden refused, work halted on *Lady in the Dark*, and the dispute went before the Equity Council. Hart, Weill, and Gershwin, with their dreams at stake, awaited the outcome in isolation, the playwright down at Fairview Farm, the composer at the house in Suffern, and the lyricist back in Beverly Hills.

Hart took a "long cold walk" in the country and then began a series of "long cold drinks" waiting for the results. When the telephone rang, he hesitated "for a split second before I lifted the receiver—I almost did not want to know—here was a whole year's work and the hardest part of it still ahead and it was to be tossed into the ash can by the simple 'yes' or 'no' over the telephone." Morris Jacobs, Harris's general manager, relayed the news: "We've lost." Hart hung up and put in a long-distance call to California to advise Gershwin not to leave for rehearsals. The next call was to Weill. "Kurt took the news bravely and tried to console me as best he could—suddenly the operator broke in on the call—'New York was frantically trying to reach me—would I take the call?'"[45] It was Jacobs back on the wire. The first report had been false: the Equity Council had indeed voted in their favor. *Lady in the Dark* had been saved at the eleventh hour.

The next morning, three weeks of rehearsals began. Hart recalled:

> All plays sound frightful at the first reading.... The stars or the principals mumble through their parts in a hopeless monotone, and if one of the minor players...reads his one or two speeches with a semblance of performance peeping through, he is stared at and contemptuously dismissed as a "good reader" or "radio actor," and the mumbling goes agonizingly on.
>
> Gertrude Lawrence, at the first reading of *Lady in the Dark* ... plunged into [her] part with an electric excitement, from the first line onward, that was contagious enough to make [her] own excitement spread through the rest of the cast like a forest fire; it made this usually dispiriting experience a thing to be set apart and remembered with gratitude.[46]

Because of the work's unusual form, the cast rehearsed in three locations. At the Alvin, the dance corps went through its paces. At the Lyceum, Weill, Abravanel, and a rehearsal pianist taught the music to the Chorus, and Short staged the dream sequences. At the Music Box, Hart blocked the actors in the book scenes of the play. After dinner, the actors would rehearse their singing and dancing. In addition, twelve children had to be taught their parts. "It was the first play I was to direct myself," Hart remembered, "and it was rather a frightening task." To his surprise, however, "Gertie was the very antithesis of her contract-signing self. A brilliant and intelligent actress I knew her to be, but what I did not know was that she was a perfect angel. Sensitive and kind and completely conscientious, I would have to drive her out of the theatre at night."[47]

The production team debated how to advertise *Lady in the Dark*. Neither "musical comedy" nor "play with incidental music" fit the bill. After deliberations, it was announced that *Lady in the Dark* would be subtitled "a musical play." Not only did this description have operetta associations, but it also captured *Lady*'s hybrid form (half spoken, half sung).

Hart's "perfect angel," meanwhile, was having reservations about the acting abilities of Danny Kaye. Harris also realized that, without an audience, Kaye was having problems. During the second week of rehearsals, Harris and Lawrence both asked Hart to replace him. Hart tried to explain, "Sometimes nightclub comedians disappear when the footlights light up."[48] Although Hart prevailed in keeping Kaye in the show, the tensions between Lawrence and the young comedian continued to simmer.

Surviving scripts document how production personnel tightened the drama. For the opening scene, many of Liza's long speeches were pared down and whole sections left out. Lawrence remembered, "When it came to cuts, what Moss Hart left out were his own lines, not the lyrics."[49] Hassard Short cut the dream sequences to a lesser extent. However, Russell's number "It's Never Too Late to Mendelssohn" had to be dropped. Weill was able to salvage the lyric and gave it instead to Charley. Abravanel remembered Danny Kaye collapsing in his arms and saying, " 'They cut that, there is nothing left of my part.' And I told him, 'There is still Tschaikowsky.' He laughed, 'thirty-seconds—Tschaikowsky.' "[50]

Over at the Alvin, rehearsals hit a snag. Albertina Rasch was ill, and the dancers had to devise much of the choreography themselves. Luckily, Nelson Barclift and Dorothy Bird, who had danced with Martha Graham, took charge.[51] At the Music Box, it became clear that the actress originally chosen for Miss Foster was not working out. Under the five-day clause, under which actors worked without compensation, the producers let her go and picked an unknown actress fresh out of Northwestern University, Ann Lee, to replace her.

Back at the Music Box, Lawrence was creating more problems. Upon hearing "The Saga of Jenny" she complained, "This is not a song for me; this is for Ethel Merman. And it's not very funny anyway."[52] Because her heart was not in it, she tried to kill the number by walking through it during rehearsals. Hart insisted that she keep rehearsing "Jenny," but promised her that if it did not go over in Boston, it would be cut. (It did not assuage

Lawrence's growing jealousy that Kaye's number for the *Circus Dream* had been fashioned expressly for his talents.)[53]

Various painters, seamstresses, and technicians were realizing Horner's, Sharaff's, and Carnegie's designs. At this point there does not appear to have been much fiscal restraint. Carnegie was quoted as saying, "Don't spare the horses on cost."[54] For Liza's office, Horner chose real oak paneling. In addition to the lamps and books he picked out for Dr. Brooks's office, Horner even found a signed photograph of Freud to hang in the vestibule.

Frank Spencer remembers that the night General Manager Jack Kennedy hired him to be an assistant stage manager, he helped lay out the turntables on the stage of the Alvin. Spencer recalled, "I stood up, and somebody from behind reached around and embraced me from the rear with her arms around my neck. It was Gertrude Lawrence, whom I had never met before. She had been out to dinner and had enjoyed a little wine." Short was sitting out in the theater, and Lawrence said, "This is exactly the color I want to have, Bobby," As Spencer remembered, "She was a brunette at that time. So her maid came out and took a clipping off the left back portion of my hair. She went to Helena Rubinstein the next day and emerged as an ash blonde for *Lady in the Dark*."[55]

At the beginning of the third week of rehearsals, the technical crew planned to leave for Boston. This would give them a week to assemble the set before the cast arrived the following week for a series of five dress rehearsals. As the date drew near, Horner became nervous: "One could still have observed the designer and property man chasing through department stores selecting desk sets, ashtrays, books, and so forth."[56]

Lady in the Dark's stage crew and the set and properties rolled out of New York by train on December 16. Once in Boston, the crew transferred them to the Colonial Theatre. By midweek the press reported that carpenters and set builders were working overtime to extend the stage over the orchestra pit to provide enough room for the turntables. Faced with so much scenery, Short realized, Lawrence would have difficulty making her costume changes. So Horner designed a small dressing room for her near the stage-left turntable. In a fit of whimsy, he draped the walls with material and lined the closets and shoe racks with velour.[57]

As marvelous as everything appeared, the crew ran into a couple of problems: First, because of their size and weight, the turntables made too much noise when put in motion. General stage manager John Kennedy had the builders go back and grease every wheel to make them turn easily and quietly. Second, the turntables did not properly synchronize because they were being turned by hand. This was critical for the two halves of Liza's and

Dr. Brooks's offices, which needed to realign themselves perfectly. Kennedy spent the remainder of the week "rehearsing the stagehands as if they were actors, each one of them doing his bit over and over until he knew his part."[58]

With the turntables now spinning like clockwork, the company boarded the train for Boston on December 24. With 165 people aboard, the costumes, baggage, and equipment filled seven regular-size boxcars. (No seventy-footers were available because of the Post Office holiday rush.) News in the passenger cars created a positive buzz: the Colonial Theatre box office had opened the day before, and advance mail orders had already shattered a previous record. One of the Chorus members remembers Lawrence spreading holiday cheer: "Each cast member received a letter personally signed from her, in which she wrote about how she had made a contribution to Bundles for Britain in the name of that person."[59]

After Christmas, cast and crew buckled down for four days of dress rehearsals before opening on Monday, the 30th. Problems had to be ironed out again with the turntables. At first the revolving motion disoriented the actors. Then Lawrence found herself literally in the dark during the shifts from reality to fantasy and was unable to find her portable dressing room. One of the office boys, "Joe" played by Ward Tallmon, was drafted as third assistant stage manager. His sole duty when not on stage was to escort Lawrence to and from the turntables with a blue flashlight. The stage crew also discovered that Lawrence's humming at the beginning of the *Glamour* and *Wedding Dreams* could not be heard. To compensate, they devised an elaborate cue: general stage manager Kennedy stood in the wings and sang into a microphone along with Lawrence. At a certain point, an electrician began moving a switch one notch per measure. After four measures the stage was completely dark, and the men at the turntables began to push (Figure 36).[60]

With the play up and running, but running much too long, Hart called in George S. Kaufman, renowned for play doctoring. He trimmed some of the banter among the *Allure* staff, and Natalie Schafer saw her role as Alison Du Bois substantially shortened. Sitting in the orchestra section of the theater, she was near tears as Kaufman attempted to explain why the cuts were necessary. To ease her pain, she asked him to fetch her an ice-cream soda. Kaufman acquiesced and the gentle act began a romance that blossomed two years later.[61]

Lawrence was scarcely happier than Schafer. Two days before the opening, her husband joined her and did not like what he saw: "Gertrude's role was eclipsed by the material furnished to a young, and at that time unknown, featured player—Danny Kaye. Danny had what to my mind was the only show-stopping song in the score, a specialty number called

'Tschaikowsky.' Since his role in *Lady in the Dark* was distinctly a minor one, this struck me as a serious imbalance." That evening over dinner, Aldrich suggested that Gertie should have "Tschaikowsky" cut. Lawrence disagreed. "Danny is a talented performer and he's entitled to his chance. As for my not being able to top his song—don't worry about me....I can take care of myself."[62] Unaware of her resolve, Short took Weill aside and gave him some advice to share with Gershwin: "You boys had better get two new numbers ready in a hurry. You'll find that 'Jenny' and the Russian number won't make it."[63]

The final dress rehearsals were not without lighter moments. For the playwright, all of the details were seriously contributing to his insomnia and made him resent anybody who was getting sleep: "One morning I came down the elevator and I said, 'I didn't sleep last night. Did you?' And Weill said, very tenderly, 'Yes I did...but I had bad dreams!'"[64] The day before the opening, Victor Mature made a stir when he and other members of the cast attended Mass at Our Lady of Victory Church. Reportedly, the choirboys ignored their musical duties while pointing out the hero of *Captain Caution*. In the afternoon, a press conference was held at the Ritz Carlton. Approximately a quarter of the cast attended, posed for photographs, and held interviews with the press. Lawrence gushed, "It's the most exciting thing that's ever happened to me."[65]

With the tryout opening set for 8:30 on December 30, ticket holders began gathering in the Colonial Theatre lobby forty-five minutes early to catch a glimpse of celebrity attendees. The curtain rose to a sold-out house with twenty standees. The first act went without a technical hitch. By intermission, however, the team doubted whether they had a hit. Lawrence, apparently to compensate for such an unusual entrance only thirty seconds into the show, had played the first scene at hysterical pitch. The audience, accustomed to her usual comedic roles, laughed at much of her dialogue with the psychiatrist. Abravanel remembers Gershwin's wife, Lee, coming to him at intermission and saying, "Boy, I am nervous...we are not making it."[66]

Backstage nerves were just as edgy, as Macdonald Carey reported: "Danny and I hear yelling in the big dressing room next door. It is Vic. He is a very emotional Italian and we find him jumping up and down on the tights he has to wear in the upcoming circus scene. The zipper on the back of his tights is broken. Danny and I get him back into them and safety-pin him together."[67]

After intermission, Kaye, dressed in white pants, pink vest, and a light blue coat, rattled off the list of fifty Russian composers in less than a minute. The effect on the audience was electric. Standing at the back of the theater,

Hart was initially thrilled by the response, but then panicked as it reached a deafening roar: "I was saying 'Sh . . . sh!' trying to quiet them, knowing that the more they applauded the more likely the song was to be cut. And Danny kept bowing to Gertie as if to indicate she would sing next. And, of course, the more he bowed generously, the more they applauded."[68] A member of Sam Harriss's staff, who was also in the back standing next to Gershwin, clutched his arm and muttered, "Christ, we've lost our star!" and headed for the lobby.[69] Abravanel, from his unique position on the podium, thought fast:

> So I motioned to the trumpets after awhile who were . . . on my right. They were not great instrumentalists, but they were show people and used to improvising. And so I made a sign cutting my throat. I raised my right hand to them, and they nodded understanding that I would omit the recitative and go to . . . the introduction of "Jenny."
>
> I extended my arms—big, big hand of applause from the audience for doing the encore. They all stopped applauding thinking that it would be the encore they wanted. In that split second, Gertrude leapt—jumped— from that swing.
>
> And she understood right away because she knew that she could not go during the applause [because] they would have booed her. But she jumped and improvised a totally different "Jenny." The "Jenny" we had rehearsed was in good taste for 1940—but she went for the throat. Her life was there [at stake]. . . . And so she improvised a "Jenny" with bumps and grinds.[70]

With a shocking and aggressive performance borrowed from her music hall days, Lawrence took Liza's destiny into her own hands. She produced a conclusion to *Lady in the Dark* removed from the intentions of the male creators and directors. A photo essay from *Look* magazine gives an idea of what that first Boston audience saw (Figure 37). "The Saga of Jenny" received thunderous applause, and the experimental musical play was saved (again). At a few minutes shy of midnight, the curtain rang down.

The next morning, six reviews appeared, unanimous in their praise.[71] Elinor Hughes of the *Boston Herald* claimed, "No one present at the Colonial Theatre last night is likely to forget *Lady in the Dark*, for so remarkable a production and so astonishing a performance are not met with except the proverbial once in a lifetime." Lawrence was extolled for her "Hamlet of a part," and John K. Hutchens of the *Boston Evening Transcript* noted, the "long and arduous role she plays, a sort of reprise of her career, calling upon her talents as a dramatic artist, a comedienne and the musical comedy singer that she was when the American theater first knew her."

Elliot Norton of the *Boston Post* singled out Danny Kaye, "a bright young comedian with a grip of earthy things and the capacity, too, for riding a moonbeam in the interest of antic foolery, [who] took a lot of the playing honors last night." Concerning *Lady in the Dark*'s score, the reviewer from the *Boston Globe* pointed out that it is "far from incidental. At times there is a symphonic weight in the orchestra." L. A. Sloper of the *Christian Science Monitor* observed, "Mr. Hart is resourceful in putting to use his experiences and observations of the human comedy" in a work about the methods of psychoanalysis. Concerning *Lady in the Dark*'s visual magic, Helen Eager of the *Boston Traveler* raved, "As for Harry Horner's settings, nothing like them ever has been seen before."

Despite its overwhelmingly positive reception, *Lady in the Dark* was not without flaws. Most agreed that, at three and a half hours, it was too long. Several reviewers gave Victor Mature a lukewarm response, noting that he "gives an excellent impersonation of himself" in a performance that was only "acceptable."[72] His duet with Lawrence in "This Is New" was, according to the *Globe*, "in urgent need of alteration." Both Sloper and Norton (in an expanded Sunday feature) criticized Lawrence for "overdoing the emotional scenes" and urged her to tone down the earlier ones. She agreed: "I never played anything that commenced in such a low mood—and without the least help beforehand from anybody else's lines....If you are too intense in the beginning, you have nowhere to go in the later emotional scenes. And if you underplay, the audience doesn't get any hint of the woman's mental distress."[73]

At rehearsals the next day, the directors shortened *Lady in the Dark* by thirty minutes. One of the cuts was the song "Bats about You." Dan Harden, the actor playing Ben Butler, recalled, "It was a disadvantage to me because it was the only tune I did separately with another lady in the show. Barbara [played by Eleanor Eberle] and I did it together, including a bit of a soft-shoe dance with it. It was a disappointment to me as a young man."[74] Another casualty was the verse to "This Is New," which had the twin benefit of saving time and eliminating Mature's painful rendition. As Gershwin put it, "When handsome 'hunk of man' Mature sang, his heart and the correct key weren't in it."[75]

The second performance of the show concluded with Lawrence giving a curtain speech. In wishing everyone a happy new year, she reminded the audience that she was an Englishwoman and that the situation in Europe was worsening. This became a hallmark of her performances in *Lady in the Dark* during most of 1941: on stage she played the distressed Liza, offstage she worked to end American isolationism. Three days later,

Lawrence showed her support by attending the Greek War Relief Ball at the Mechanics Building after the Friday performance. During the week she received a letter from Great Britain's Queen Mary, which was printed in the *Boston Post* the following week. The letter thanked the actress for her work with the American Theatre Wing for Allied War Relief and Bundles for Britain, and concluded with a call for action.[76]

In Boston *Lady in the Dark* played a standard eight performances per week, with a 2:30 matinee on Wednesdays and Saturdays. Ticket prices ranged from $1.10 to $2.75 for the afternoon performances, with a top cost of $3.30 for the evening. For the first week, *Variety* gave the gross earnings as $26,000, with the theater "limited only by standee regulations."[77]

The struggle between Lawrence and Kaye had not quite resolved itself. During "Tschaikowsky," Kaye could not hear the orchestral accompaniment very well beneath the stage extension, but he was able to gauge the audience's reaction. With his rubber-faced antics, each new face brought a bigger laugh from the audience. One night he noticed that his routine was not producing the expected results. The same thing happened the following evening as well. Out of the corner of his eye, he noticed that Lawrence was copying his faces, causing the audience's attention to be focused on her. Unable to complain for fear that Lawrence would have him fired, Danny gave Gertie a dose of her own medicine. During a matinee he mimicked "The Saga of Jenny." Without a word exchanged, Lawrence ceased stealing Kaye's applause, and they reached a truce.[78]

One of the more fantastic stories that circulated in Boston had to do with *Lady in the Dark*'s backers. It first broke in New York's *Daily News*: "Moss Hart had his favorite psychiatrist read and approve the script. But backer Marshall Field wasn't satisfied until he had his favorite Chicago psychiatrist read and pass on it too. The Chicago doctor disagreed on certain details, so Hart's mental medico had to fly to Chicago for a medical consultation and come to an agreement with his rival before financial aid was forthcoming."[79] Marshall Field was not one of the show's backers, but this yarn was widely reprinted. The musical play's backers included Harris and Hart (for a total of $71,000), Paramount Pictures ($35,000), and a number of investors who contributed small amounts: George S. Kaufman, Max Gordon, Jules Brulatour, Bernard Hart, and Joseph M. Hyman.[80]

On January 11, *Lady in the Dark* completed its sixteen-performance tryout with gross earnings of $27,000 for the second week.[81] The entire production packed up and traveled back to New York for the anticipated opening on Thursday, January 16, with a single preview the night before, a benefit for the Manhattan School of Music's scholarship fund. Because the Alvin's management considered *Lady in the Dark* a homecoming for Lawrence, three dressing rooms were dismantled to make a suite for its returning star. Gertie mused, "It has just about everything except a southern exposure."[82]

The company held a dress rehearsal in its new home on Tuesday, January 14. Because of the excitement for the opening—the papers had all run preview articles, photographs, and drawings the previous Sunday—no one was allowed to watch. The *Daily News* reported that even Dr. Kubie was unable to get in. Lawrence, suffering from flu she caught in Boston, got progressively sicker as the rehearsal wore on. Because of her health, the benefit was moved to Sunday. Still hoping to open on Thursday, Hart rehearsed the cast without her on Wednesday night. As Lawrence had no understudy, Hart himself played the role of Liza Elliott. After his initial foray in Dr. Brooks's office, the stage darkened and the turntables began to spin. Although Ward Tallmon led Hart to safety, he reportedly shrieked, "God!, who'd be crazy enough to write something like this?"[83]

Lawrence's condition worsened, and the official opening had to be pushed back a week. She checked into Doctor's Hospital, and her physician expressed doubts whether she would be well enough by Sunday. To get the cast back in shape, it was announced that there would be three benefit performances prior to the opening: Monday for the Manhattan School of Music, Tuesday for the New Yorkers' League for Volunteer Relief, and Wednesday for the United Neighborhood Houses of New York. The postponement cost the producers about $6,000 with the Chorus, orchestra, and stage crew paid, but principals forgoing payment because the contracted fifth week of rehearsals had not been used.

The delay only increased anticipation for opening night. By the weekend Lawrence's physician agreed to allow her to perform, provided she would return to the hospital after each performance. With a hypodermic of strychnine, sunlamp treatments on her chest and back ("fore and aft," she quipped), and intravenous vitamin B, insulin, and glucose, the star rallied for the three benefit performances.[84] And with that, the stage was set for the long-awaited *Lady.*

Broadway Run

After opening on January 23, 1941, *Lady in the Dark* settled in for a long and popular run. Despite a snowstorm, there were eighty-five standees at the second performance on Friday evening. On Saturday, there were a hundred standees at both performances. The gross for these three performances alone was $12,509, with a top ticket price of $4.40. In the first week, advance ticket orders skyrocketed from $50,000 to $120,000.[1] Out-of-town critics warned their readers that even ticket brokers did not have tickets for days to come. As a sign of *Lady in the Dark*'s popularity, Gertrude Lawrence graced the cover of *Time* magazine (Figure 38). Despite its runaway success and the fact that a full house could take in $32,100, the show had a substantial weekly running expense of $18,000 (of which approximately $4,000 was paid to Gertrude Lawrence).[2] Consequently, *Lady in the Dark* did not pay back its $127,715 investment until November.[3]

Although lines of ticket buyers snaked out the doors of the Alvin Theatre, Lawrence was not yet out of the woods. She did not miss any performances but remained at Doctor's Hospital between performances. Forced to decline any benefit appearances, she spent her time there knitting seaman's socks. After recovering fully, she vowed to "begin raising money for concert tours in the British Isles…to entertain the soldiers."[4] After the third week of performances, she was discharged from the hospital. Society watchers spotted her and Aldrich celebrating that evening at Fefe's Monte Carlo.

Lawrence's hospitalization had worried producer Sam Harris, who knew that, without an understudy, she was indispensable to the production. The day after the opening, newspapers reported that an insurance policy with Lloyds of London was in the works. Once Lawrence was released from the hospital, *Variety* outlined the terms of the policy. Harris was to receive $1,500 for any performance that she missed because of illness; however, four consecutive performances had to be missed before payment would become due. Should the show be forced to close for that reason, Lloyds would ante up $100,000. For such coverage, the premium was dear: $6,000 initially with a $1,400 monthly payment.[5] As it turned out, Harris need not have worried: Gertie was a trooper and missed only three performances that first season.

With *Lady in the Dark*'s ship successfully launched and its golden sails beckoning, Hollywood expressed interest in getting aboard. Jack Cohn, vice president of Columbia Pictures, reportedly elbowed himself backstage on opening night and offered Hart $200,000 on the spot.[6] Despite Paramount Pictures' investment in the production, the Dramatists Guild agreement stipulated that the film rights had to be thrown onto the open market. Warner Brothers bid the current record that had ever been paid for a literary or dramatic property, $275,000.[7] Not to be outdone, Paramount bid $285,000.[8] The amount took both Hollywood and Broadway by surprise. The bidding had not been expected to go much over $200,000 because of the collapsing foreign market.

Weill and Gershwin had wanted to sell the rights on a cash basis; however, the sale amount was paid in installments because of restrictions regarding the film's release date. Paramount agreed to withhold release until September 1, 1942, so as not to compete with the Broadway production. Moreover, the film could not play in "such cities included in such tour or contemplated tour until after the play has completed its run therein."[9] There would be no further restrictions after June 1, 1943. After the 3.5 percent negotiator's fee ($9,975) had been deducted, the contract yielded the traditional 40 percent for the producer ($110,010) and 60 percent for the authors ($82,507.50 for Hart and $41,253.75 each for Weill and Gershwin).

Hollywood was not alone in trying to cash in on *Lady in the Dark*'s success. In an early example of an industry tie-in, three of Hattie Carnegie's designs for *Lady in the Dark* were sold in her showroom at 42 East Forty-ninth. They included Liza's lavender chiffon dress, purple wool suit, and seashell beige silk frock. In addition, *Women's Wear Daily* announced a promotion of Gertrude Lawrence hats designed by Alice May Hats. The designer featured the color purple, inspired by Lawrence's outfit for the *Circus Dream*. The following week a Sandcheck fabric in sage green was named in honor of Lawrence, and Celanese Fabrics held a party at which the company's president presented her with a $500 check for British war relief. A fashion show in the form of a skit based on *Lady in the Dark* followed the presentation.[10] Always one to top an act, Lawrence introduced her own line of dresses from the Bloomsburg Silk Mill of American Enka Rayon. *Lady in the Dark*'s playbills advertised these dresses, and the advertisement in *Vogue* featured Lawrence modeling the fashions in her Alvin dressing room. The proceeds benefited the British War Relief Society, Bundles for Britain, and the British American Ambulance Corps.[11]

One might have thought that Hart's psychiatrist would have begged anonymity after a newspaper reporter identified him on opening night, but Kubie actively promoted the show. "Dr. K." attended a performance with Sidney Whipple, drama critic of the *World-Telegram*. Afterward Whipple bluntly asked him, "Well, what was the matter with her?" Kubie replied:

> The patient is suffering from mixed neuroses. It is a combination. This would fall, I think, in the classification of anxiety hysteria with a marked depressive element, one symptom of which was her inability to make decisions. . . .
>
> . . . It appears Liza's strong Oedipus complex was aggravated by unconscious jealousy of her mother's beauty, which, she was cruelly told, she completely lacked; narcissism played its part; and there was bi-sexual predisposition that worked itself out, so to speak, in editing a magazine devoted to feminine beauty; while she herself remained in a plain, unadorned state.[12]

Kubie also wrote a letter to Lawrence, which she stashed in her dressing room. When giving interviews, she would let the reporter quote from the letter signed by "Lawrence S. Kubie, M.D., a New York psychiatrist." The letter read:

> I am sure that you have received many an enthusiastic word of congratulation for your *Lady in the Dark*. It is possible, however, that just as the reviewers have been too dazzled by the glitter of the play to see its essence, so many of your writers of fan letters may miss the extraordinary sensitivity and integrity of your picture of Liza. For strange and perverse reasons, human beings tend to sneer at the age-old human tragedy in the face of plenty. Apparently we have to protect ourselves by jeering at the neurotic misery that is all around us. You have done an inestimable service by giving such dignity to this portrayal of a woman in pain. I think it will be remembered as one of the great creations of the stage.[13]

One wonders if Kubie began to take some heat from his colleagues. A subsequent Associated Press interview began, "Out of playwright Moss Hart's visits to a psychoanalyst, who asked that his name not be used, helped him with the play and in this interview tells about the psychoanalytic factors involved."[14] As a postscript to Kubie's interviews and analyses of Liza's condition, Lawrence got in her own two cents by way of a Valentine greeting published in the *World-Telegram*:

> In dreams you are my Valentine,
>   My very dear psychosis.
> Even more than a pal o' mine—
>   You're the object of my neurosis.[15]

There had been reports during opening week that Lawrence would cut an album, but she postponed the recording because of her hospitalization. Once discharged, she was still hesitant to commit her performance to disk. What finally got her into the studio was Hildegarde's recording of songs from *Lady in the Dark*. Lawrence's five-hour recording session for RCA Victor took place on Sunday, February 23. Even though this was just before the advent of Broadway cast recordings, a male quartet from the Chorus (Gordon Gifford, Davis Cunningham, Len Frank, and William Marel) joined her. They cut a total of six selections: an abbreviated *Glamour Dream* medley of "Oh Fabulous One," "Huxley" (formerly "The World's Inamorata"), and "Girl of the Moment," as well as "One Life to Live," "This Is New," "The Princess of Pure Delight," "The Saga of Jenny," and "My Ship."

A smattering of press was on hand to document the evening session. They photographed Lawrence munching on oranges and discussing the score with conductor Leonard Joy.[16] The selections required a total of twenty takes, and RCA Victor subsequently released them on three ten-inch records. Vocally, Lawrence's performances were no competition for Hildegarde's, as Weill wrote to Gershwin: "The Lawrence album is musically very good, but her voice sounds a little shaky. . . . I like very much the way Hildegarde sings the songs. She takes them very relaxed and that is good for the lyrics and the music."[17] In a follow-up letter, Weill complained, "If she would only stop singing those high notes!"[18] Not only did Gertie hit the high f at the end of "My Ship," but she even threw some high c's into "The Saga of Jenny."

Danny Kaye recorded six numbers for Columbia. On February 28 he cut "The Princess of Pure Delight," "My Ship," "Jenny," and "The Trial of Liza Elliott/Tschaikowsky," which included some bits of the trial scene, including "The Best Years of His Life." Unlike Lawrence's recordings, which stick close to how the numbers were performed on stage, Kaye's swing with vocal improvisation. The March 3 playbill advertised his nightclub engagement back at La Martinique. Each night after *Lady in the Dark*, Kaye gave two shows accompanied by his wife. He usually sang "Tschaikowsky" twice: first slowly and then as fast as possible in hopes of bettering his previous time. This stunt became a signature part of his act for the rest of his career. The next month, he teamed up again with Abravanel to record "One Life to Live" and "It's Never Too Late to Mendelssohn."

Despite the number of recordings, few were heard on the air. In defiance of ASCAP's increased fees for radio performance, radio owners and executives banned ASCAP's catalogue and founded a new performing-rights organization, Broadcast Music Incorporated (BMI). The situation had come to a head on December 26, 1940, when the Justice Department announced it was adding the National Association of Broadcasters, BMI, NBC, and CBS to the defendants in a criminal antitrust action.[19] The ban by radio stations of ASCAP repertoire was detrimental for Weill and Gershwin, whose music could now be played only on independent radio stations.

Gershwin recalled his frustration in a commentary called "What Happened; or, 'Jeanie' Displaces 'Jenny'": "Soon one could hear only public domain music plus a few new songs BMI was sponsoring. And 'Jeanie with the Light Brown Hair' received so overwhelmingly a number of performances daily and nightly that I imagine some members of the many Stephen Foster Societies began hoping their eponymous composer had never existed. So during most of 1941, and until ASCAP and radio finally came to terms, none of the many songs in the enormous ASCAP catalog was heard on the air."[20] Jack Mason, an arranger, informed Weill that the important big bands had their arrangements of songs from *Lady in the Dark* ready to go. Weill and Gershwin kept hoping that the ban would be lifted, but that did not happen until late October 1941—too late to make a significant impact for a show then in its second season.

During the ban, some independent radio stations balked at programming "The Saga of Jenny." As a result, Gershwin drafted an expurgated "radio version," which replaced the risqué portions of the verse and four of the stanzas (Figure 39). Despite "Jenny's" limited airplay, two months later it was outselling not only the rest of the sheet music from *Lady in the Dark*, but that of other Broadway shows as well. Weill reported to Gershwin, "Max Dreyfus [of Chappell Music Company] showed me a weekly statement about the sale of sheet music. . . . 'Jenny' was at the top of the list, with 350 copies (which is, according to Max, equivalent to about 4000 copies if we would be on the air)."[21]

Chappell initially brought out five songs from *Lady in the Dark*: "Girl of the Moment," "This Is New," "My Ship," "One Life to Live," and "The Princess of Pure Delight." All featured the same violet-colored cover whose center appeared to have been ripped away to reveal a publicity photograph of

Gertrude Lawrence. (The same photograph also adorned *Lady in the Dark*'s poster and weekly playbills.) The keys of the songs are identical to those in the show, but Weill composed instrumental introductions for "Girl of the Moment," "My Ship," and "This Is New," as well as first and second endings.

Chappell later brought out "The Saga of Jenny" and "Tschaikowsky." For the former, the Chorus section was removed ("Who's Jenny? Never heard of Jenny!, Jenny is out of place," etc.), as the sheet music was intended for solo voice. Not satisfied with the fifth stanza about Jenny's memoirs, Gershwin revised "So she wrote 'em and she published all her loves and her hates/And had libel suits in forty of the forty-eight States" to "The very day her book was published, hist'ry relates/There were wives who shot their husbands in some thirty-three states."

"Tschaikowsky" differs most widely from how it was done in the show. Chappell appended a subtitle, "And Other Russians," perhaps to avoid the potential confusion for music stores stocking a piece by one composer whose title was the name of another. Weill and Gershwin wrote a nine-measure verse to give the song a context:

> Without the least excuse
> Or the slightest provocation,
> May I fondly introduce,
> For your mental delectation,
> The names that always give me brain concussion,
> The names of those composers known as Russian.[22]

Compared to the recordings and sheet music, *Lady in the Dark*'s piano-vocal score was much slower in coming. The composer reported in late February, "The piano score is progressing slowly but steadily."[23] After Chappell prepared the first dream around March 7 or 8, Weill sent it to Gershwin for proofing. Various drafts flew between the coasts, and Weill read the final proofs on April 10. Gershwin wanted to check the third proof of the *Circus Dream*, but the score's editor, Albert Sirmay, and Weill felt that the corrections had been made. Gershwin then wrote a special letter to Sirmay to make sure that the lyric "This is all immaterial and irrevelant" was corrected to "irrelevant."[24] Despite the request, the typo ended up in the published score. Weill elected to have Hart write the foreword which re-counted the genesis of the show (Figure 40).

The piano-vocal score by and large presented the dream sequences as they were performed on stage. The orchestral sections that Weill considered particular to the production were omitted (Act II "Overture" and the "Music for Light Cues and Flashbacks"). Weill also did not include some of the music for the production numbers, such as "This Is New." However, Weill and Gershwin reinstated the verse to "This Is New," which Victor Mature had been unable to sing and other cut sections. Sirmay gave "My Ship" the designation *Childhood Dream* to match the other sequences, although the bits of music accompanying the other flashbacks were not included.

Weill's preparation of the piano-vocal score came during two of the most scathing critiques he had ever received. On February 23 Virgil Thomson, music critic for the *Herald Tribune*, wrote, "Mr. Weill seems to have a great facility for writing banal music and the shamelessness to emphasize its banality with the most emphatically banal instrumentation." Another modernist composer, Samuel L. M. Barlow, lamented in his column for *Modern Music*, "Something first-rate has gone third-rate, which is a loss for everyone who cares deeply for an art, beyond any prejudice or timeliness or mode."[25] Taken aback, Weill wrote to Gershwin, "Virgil Thomson wrote a violent attack against me. It was all very personal and his main point was that I am no good any more since I stopped working with Brecht."[26] Weill chalked up such criticisms to the petty jealousy of other composers. By the end of April, the attacks had ceased and the piano-vocal score was published without incident.

Random House had planned a deluxe edition of the piano-vocal score in full-leather binding for $12.50. The details of the project included a limited print run of three hundred numbered copies, of which only 250 would be offered to the public. Lawrence, Hart, Weill, and Gershwin agreed to personally sign each copy. Gershwin remembered spending hours signing the insert sheets, but was surprised when Bennett Cerf's business partner at Random House telegrammed, GERTRUDE LAWRENCE REFUSES TO SIGN. Years later, Gershwin learned that Lawrence's refusal was because Hildegarde's recording had been released prior to hers. A bemused Gershwin penned the following coda to "The Saga of Jenny":

Gertie made her mind up in '41
That because of Hildegarde she'd been undone.
She got even by the autographing she forebore:
So—no limited edition of the vocal score.[27]

Lawrence threw herself headlong into myriad war efforts, which at times threatened to derail the production. Her activities included attending a birthday gala for Bundles for Britain on February 12, speaking on a radio hookup for the American Theater's *Carnival for Britain* on February 21, sending a message to Adolf Hitler on the same day, attending a house-warming at the American Theatre Wing of the British Relief Fund's new workroom on February 25, taping a program about Cape Cod for British soldiers, speaking at a luncheon for the British War Relief Society on March 20, attending a dinner for Bundles for Britain on March 31, auctioning off Lord Nelson's portrait at Radio City Music Hall, enlisting British Merchant Marines to sell *Lady*'s souvenir playbill for British War Relief on April 3, and sponsoring an Easter egg roll for British refugee children with Mayor La Guardia on April 14. In addition, she was regularly photographed sewing, knitting, and ironing clothes destined for England, as well as getting friends to write checks for British relief.

Her schedule took its toll, and on Friday and Saturday, April 18 and 19, three performances of *Lady in the Dark* had to be canceled. Lawrence was suffering from bronchitis, and the *Daily Mirror* reported that Bert Lytell had to shake her before the Thursday performance because she broke down over the situation in Europe.[28] The lost performances cost about $11,000 of the weekly gross, which had been averaging between $31,500 and $32,000. Once recovered, Lawrence went right back to her benefit activities. Tongue in cheek, she called Victor Mature, who was recuperating from surgery, to inquire if she could auction off his appendix for British War Relief.[29]

Of all Lawrence's activities, the one most threatening to the future of *Lady in the Dark* was her plan to fly to England for war-relief activities during her contracted summer vacation. The *Times* leaked these plans on March 9. She claimed to have made reservations and would either drive an ambulance or a mobile canteen. On April 1 the *World-Telegram* reported that she had already booked passage on the transatlantic *Clipper*. Such reports made the show's investors very nervous. Moss Hart, Hassard Short, Richard Aldrich, and even Fanny Holtzmann tried to talk her out of going. Finally, around June 1, Lawrence made up her mind to stay in the United States and devote her summer to war-relief work there.

Sam Harris announced that *Lady in the Dark* would recess from June 15 to September 1. The press release read, "It has been felt necessary to take this unusual step to conserve Miss Lawrence's health and insure her continuance through next season of what is unquestionably one of the most tiring and arduous roles ever played by an actress anywhere."[30] The closing of a Broadway show with a healthy advance and sold-out houses elicited much tongue wagging from the press.

The last few weeks of the season were especially busy ones. Random House published the script of *Lady in the Dark*. The elegantly produced volume used the King James "Red Letter Edition" style to differentiate the spoken portions of the play (in black ink) from the sung dream sequences (in red ink). Hart dedicated the play "To L. S. K.," and it included an eight-page preface, signed by "Dr. Brooks." After much speculation, John Anderson of the *Journal-American* disclosed that Dr. Lawrence S. Kubie had written it.[31]

Kubie begins his preface by citing the cultural changes that occurred because of Freud and psychoanalysis. He draws a parallel between the transition from the perception of physical illness as "punishment visited by the gods" to its emancipation by scientific inquiry and the liberation of psychic pain from a moral issue to medical therapy. Kubie then voices his enthusiasm for *Lady in the Dark*: "And in the gay and tender play, perhaps for the first time on any stage, the struggle of a vigorous and gifted human spirit to overcome deep-seated, unconscious, self-destructive forces is portrayed accurately. This, then, is no ordinary play." Liza's symptoms of tension, anxiety, indecision, fatigue, depression, and fear are what the layman would call a nervous breakdown. Kubie believes that "from the technical psychiatric point of view the portrayal, both of the illness itself and of its evolution out of her normal life, is accurate in the subtlest details."[32] He regards her three suitors as "inert images" or dummies, each presenting different roles that correspond to various stages in her development. Kendall is the parental figure who ultimately cannot fulfill the role of spouse; Randy is a juvenile glamour-boy whose macho stance, once unmasked, reveals a dependent child; Charley is the mature man who refuses to play the role of subservient parent or submissive child. In the end, however, the struggle is not among the three suitors, but in the conflicting yearnings of Liza's nature.

Despite Kubie's belief that mental illness is now a scientific, rather than moral, issue, his analysis of *Lady in the Dark* is suffused with Judeo-Christian imagery. As expected, he traces Liza's problems as a woman of forty to when she was four, when her father compared her to her mother's legendary beauty. Her fate was sealed at age ten, when she felt no pain at her mother's death. The "moment of crucifixion" occurred when her father turned on her for posturing in her mother's blue cape instead of mourning her death. Liza's body then became shameful, and beauty is offered up only in "sacrificial expiation." To "atone for her guilt," Liza renounces her beauty and devotes herself instead to making other women beautiful.

Kubie concludes his preface by pointing out *Lady in the Dark*'s technical flaws in its portrayal of psychoanalysis. He feels that in telescoping the process Dr. Brooks's technique becomes too directly confrontational. Obviously the results are achieved too swiftly; however, he excuses Hart's dramatic license in condensing the process. The ultimate success of *Lady in the Dark*, according to Kubie, cannot be credited to Hart, Gershwin, or Weill, or even the production, but to the playgoer, "[who] has been awakened to a realization that subtle and powerful psychological forces play beneath the surface of his own life and the lives of those around him. This awakening cannot fail ultimately to have profound social and cultural significance."[33]

In addition to Kubie's preface, the Random House edition included a single production still of Gertrude Lawrence and a list of the original cast, scenes, and musical numbers. However, rather than transmitting the version of *Lady in the Dark* that was being performed at the Alvin, it published the play as Hart had originally written it. The various changes and excisions that were made during rehearsals and tryout were rarely incorporated. The edition reflected only major changes in the dream sequences, such as the dropped "It's Never Too Late to Mendelssohn" and the cut "Bats about You."

Simultaneously with the Random House release, a spring heat wave during the last week of May hurt Broadway business. Electric fans were installed backstage to keep Lawrence performing, and Weill was able to boast by midweek, "*Lady* is the only sell-out this week."[34] On June 4, *Variety* announced that the Drama Critics' Award for the best performance of the season would go to Paul Lukas for *Watch on the Rhine*, with Lawrence as the runner-up. The same day, the Fashion Academy presented Lawrence and Irene Sharaff with an award and cited *Lady in the Dark* as the "best dressed play" of the season. That citation was little comfort: it had been assumed that Lawrence would be a shoo-in for the Drama Critics' Award.

The next day *Lady in the Dark*'s producer, Sam Harris, died of pneumonia at the age of sixty-nine at the Ritz Tower Hotel. Born in 1872 and raised in poverty on the Lower East Side, Harris had teamed up with George M. Cohan in 1904 for *Little Johnny Jones*, and together they had produced a string of shows. After that partnership dissolved, Harris and Irving Berlin built the Music Box Theatre in 1921 to house Berlin's *Music Box Revues*. Harris was well respected as a producer and known to be trustworthy and honest, as well as a shrewd judge of plays. His funeral was held on June 6 at the Campbell Funeral Church at Madison and Eighty-first, while an estimated three thousand mourners gathered outside.[35]

Despite the tragedy, *Lady in the Dark* continued to play to packed houses. On the final Friday, June 13, Eleanor Roosevelt caught the show and wrote about it in her "My Day" column:

> It closed last night for the summer, but I imagine it will reopen it the autumn, for the house was packed and everyone seemed to enjoy it.
>
> Gertrude Lawrence [is] extremely good in this part. The play itself is entertaining and light enough, so what moral there is is sugar-coated and only presses itself home in the quiet hours after [the] play.[36]
>
> *Variety* reported on June 4 that Lawrence's weekly check was averaging slightly more than $4,300 on the average weekly gross of $31,500. This salary

was the highest paid to an actress since 1925 with Marilyn Miller in *Sunny*. In *Lady in the Dark*'s first season of nearly twenty-one weeks, it set a record for having standees at every performance. *Variety* reported that nearly eighty-five hundred people had seen *Lady in the Dark* on the hoof, at the reduced ticket rate of $2.20 ($1.65 at matinees).[37] Celebrities who saw the show that first season included Jack Benny, Eddie Cantor, Charlie Chaplin, Ina Claire, Greta Garbo, Lady Halifax, Helen Hayes, Mayor La Guardia, Ginger Rogers, Gladys Swarthout, and Loretta Young. A benefit performance was added on Sunday, June 15, for the Actors' Equity Fund, which brought the tally of performances for the first season to 162.

Behind the scenes Lawrence was creating havoc by complaining about the reopening date and "One Life to Live." As she explained, she wanted a first-act number with the effect of "The Saga of Jenny." Because composer and lyricist were on opposite coasts, Weill wrote to Gershwin, "The only way would be, in case you have an idea, that you would write the lyrics first."[38] Gershwin begged off, hoping Lawrence would forget about it over the summer. After the fall reopening had been announced for September 1, Lawrence wrote a terse note to Harris's office reminding them of a clause in her rider that gave her the option to reopen as late as September 15. To mollify her and to preserve the date, Hart, now acting as *Lady in the Dark*'s primary producer, allowed her to lay off the performances before Christmas and during Holy Week for the next season. Growing weary of her demands, Moss presented Gertie with a large wreath as she departed for the Cape. It was inscribed, "Rest in Peace!"[39]

Lady in the Dark announced that Victor Mature and Macdonald Carey would not be returning. Mature's reviews had never been particularly strong, and he wanted to return to Hollywood. Carey's, on the other hand, had been excellent; as a result, Paramount Pictures signed him to a deal. Bert Lytell added his name to the list of defectors because of his salary, which had begun at $250 a week and then had jumped to $550 with a run-of-show contract, was now voided because of the summer recess. Offered a role in a new show, Lytell jumped ship. The collaborators were not prepared for the devastating news when Danny Kaye signed for a new Cole Porter musical called *Let's Face It*. Things turned ugly, with Hart claiming that he had made Kaye a star, and Kaye retorting that his boost in salary from $250 to $300 "wasn't a bonus but an incentive to sign the contract."[40]

By the end of June, Willard Parker signed on to play Randy Curtis. The six-foot-four actor had been seen the previous season in Elmer Harris's play *Johnny Belinda*. For the part of Charley Johnson, Hart hired Walter Coy, whose credits with the Group Theatre included Maxwell Anderson's *Night over Taos* and Clifford Odets's *Waiting for Lefty*, *Till the Day I Die*, and

Paradise Lost. Paul McGrath, who had played opposite Lawrence in *Susan and God*, accepted the role of Kendall Nesbitt. On July 4 the *New York Times* reported that Rex O'Malley would take over Kaye's role. He was currently playing in *The Man Who Came to Dinner*.

That summer Lawrence busied herself with fundraising for the Gertrude Lawrence Chapter of the American Theatre Wing, a branch of the British War Relief Society. She also participated with Kaufman, Hart, and Harpo Marx in a production of *The Man Who Came to Dinner* at the Bucks County Playhouse. In addition, she appeared in a new John Van Druten play entitled *Behold We Live* at the Cape. By summer's end the *New York Telegraph* reported, "Lawrence is definitely not resting," and the *Boston Globe* predicted, only half in jest, that the residents of the Cape would be glad to see her leave so *they* could get some rest![41]

The Alvin box office had remained open two weeks past the June 15 closing, and it reopened on August 4. The following week, lines of ticket buyers once again formed, but the advance sale was a disappointing $10,473. To make matters worse, the summer layoff had cost $15,000. Hart began rehearsing the four new principals at the Music Box with Lawrence's stand-in, Ann Lee. Over at the Alvin, John Kennedy readied the turntables, lights, and props. One week later, Lawrence breezed into town and rehearsals began in earnest. By Thursday, Hart and O'Malley were clashing over his interpretation. Weill summarized the outcome in a letter to Gershwin: "Rex O'Malley was completely wrong. We tried everything to get him right, but he was just impossible. Finally, three days before the opening, we had to tell him that he couldn't do it."[42]

Hart chose Eric Brotherson to replace him. Newspapers reported that Hart had first seen him in Noël Coward's revue *Set to Music* and had "remembered the tall, good-looking actor and invited him to visit the Alvin Theatre to see the musical play whenever he had free time."[43] Although the aspiring actor went along with the publicity yarn and claimed he had seen *Lady in the Dark* fifty times, he had actually been a member of the Chorus for most of the first season.

To keep the fashions fresh, Hattie Carnegie rethought two of her previous ensembles and designed two new outfits. Liza's purple suit got a new weskit of "purple and wine paillettes" in a plaid design. The cape and headdress of the wedding gown remained the same, but the new dress featured "all over decoration of scintillate crystal bead" with a braided belt (Figure 41). One of Liza's two new outfits was a "striped satin dress of snuff brown and black." It probably replaced the black suit worn during the third and fourth scenes of Act I. Carnegie also redesigned the business suit that opened the show as a "Rio brown wool suit with a blue crêpe blouse print with large brown nut pattern [and] huge wooden nuts on the jacket" (Figure 42).[44] Although the lady still made her entrance in the dark, during the second season she sported a lighter shade.

Lawrence was not pleased with her new colleagues, and Weill went so far as to claim that she was working against them. Willard Parker remembered meeting her at the first full rehearsal while she was vocalizing. The actor called to her, "This is Parker," to which she replied, "Hi-ya Parker." However, when Hart tried to introduce Walter Coy, she said, "I'm sorry, I'm not meeting anyone today."[45] Brotherson estimated that she did not say more than three words to him before opening night. An extra benefit performance for the Stage Relief Fund was scheduled on Labor Day to give the actors practice before a live audience prior to the opening. For the Tuesday reopening, Hart invited the critics to review the show again.

The second season's opening was as much of an event as the first. Most of the "top hat and ermine audience present" were aware that Eric Brotherson had stepped into the role on three days' notice. The rookie remembered exiting the stage after his first scene and Lawrence clapping him on the back and exclaiming, "Good Boy!" "It set me up for the whole evening," enthused Brotherson.[46] At the conclusion, the audience called him back for an extra curtain call. The cast then formed a V on stage and sang the national anthem. This was no doubt an idea of Lawrence, who had spent the summer selling victory pins.

The new batch of reviews primarily addressed *Lady in the Dark*'s four replacements for the previous season's players, who were now, in critic John Anderson's terminology, AWOL (Amiss Without Lawrence).[47] The highest praise was reserved for Brotherson. Frank Farrell of the *World-Telegram* marveled that he "handled the toughest assignment of the season as if it were no task at all." Several critics believed that the new blond Randy Curtis was superior to Mature's, and Coy's Charley Johnson was not "quite so stubbornly aggressive as Macdonald Carey." Anderson pronounced McGrath "excellent in the part on which Mr. Lytell wasted his talents." With such strong replacements, Farrell concluded, "Every lady in the dark with a strange man has cause to be a little apprehensive, but for however long Gertrude Lawrence decides to grope around nightly in the psychiatric shadows . . . she need have no jitters over the four new men with whom she has surrounded her ingenious character portrayal of Liza Elliott." Anderson and John Mason Brown felt that the show seemed even longer than before, but both agreed that Weill's score "seems even better on re-hearing" and "deepens in its charm." Anderson, Brown, and Louis Kronenberger all voiced continuing reservations about the play: "fairly pretentious in its clinical clichés," "as Freud . . . a skip, if not a jump, ahead of Peter Rabbit," and "as fudge, and very slow-boiling fudge at that." All concurred, however, that Lawrence was "back in there pitching as hard as ever" despite "an entirely new infield." Sporting a summer tan, she was praised as the show's "best attraction," and "in the last analysis she is what matters most." Atkinson bestowed the highest accolade: "Sooner or later a stage-struck theatregoer has to reckon with Gertrude Lawrence, which is like gazing in rapture at a tornado."[48]

Nevertheless, Lawrence had not given up wanting a new opening number. Weill reported to Gershwin: "She keeps on kicking about 'One Life to Live' (which, by the way, gets a very good hand every night). She says it is just an ice-breaker and she has to work terribly hard to get anything out of it, and what she needs at this moment in the show is a funny song . . . because that would make the whole first act easier for her."[49] Because Gershwin was dragging his feet, Lawrence recommended that "Bats about You" be out-fitted with new lyrics and added to the show. In her opinion, the verse from "One Life to Live" could be retained, but its refrain needed to go. Weill relayed her ideas to Gershwin and added that both he and Hart thought a new song "would pep her up and give her some new fun."

Gershwin, unlike his colleagues, refused to appease her: "Of all the thank-less jobs in show business the worst is to be asked to write a new song for a hit which is in its second season. . . . If, as you say, the show makes too many demands on her physically, mightn't it be a good idea to lighten her burden somewhat and cut the number down to one chorus or even cut the whole number out. . . . Or, with my fingers crossed, I'm asking—are we that lucky that by this time she has forgotten about it or else is reconciled to it?"[50]

A month later Gershwin again wrote to Weill and cautiously suggested that his solution had worked: "The news is good, especially that item about Gertie seemingly having forgotten that she wanted a song to replace 'One Life to Live.'"[51] Like the proverbial elephant, however, Lawrence never forgot. A year and a half later, when *Lady in the Dark* played in Los Angeles, she snubbed Gershwin when he went backstage to congratulate her. Even more revealing of her unhappiness is a copy of the sheet music for "One Life to Live" that Lawrence inscribed to Gershwin's wife:

> To dear little Lee—
> Without whose help this
> song has been written fairly well.
> 　　　　　　Gertie[52]

Having lost its momentum, *Lady in the Dark* began the season slowly. But by the second week, business picked up, and Weill was able to report that there had been a line all day at the box office. When October turned the corner, *Lady in the Dark* regained its position as the top-grossing show on Broadway and once again played regularly to standees. Privately, the collaborators worried that *Let's Face It* might cut into *Lady's* sales, because it featured a patter number rather similar to "Tschaikowsky." Their fears were groundless. For the remainder of the fall, SRO audiences left people waiting in the lobby hoping to snag unclaimed tickets.

Lawrence's efforts for British War Relief continued unabated and kept her constantly in the news, which gave the show added publicity. In the beginning of October, *Lady in the Dark's* creative team provided the backbone for a pageant by Ben Hecht and Charles MacArthur. Sponsored by Fight for Freedom, Inc., a Broadway organization dedicated to fighting isolationism, *Fun to Be Free* played at Madison Square Garden. By the middle of the month, Lawrence was making headlines. She had refused a medal from the Finnish government in recognition of her efforts on that country's behalf. In her letter to Herbert Hoover, head of the Finnish Relief Fund, she wrote, "It makes me sad that I must refuse this offer made in the name of the Finnish people, but in reality made by a government which is now a vassal of Nazi Germany." In justifying her action, Lawrence quoted Churchill: "Any man or state that fights against Nazism will have our aid. Any man or state that marches with Hitler is our foe."[53]

Lawrence's growing prominence as a public figure is reflected in her inclusion as a speaker at a Town Hall Trustees Luncheon in honor of Eleanor Roosevelt. Among the six speakers for the November 6 event were the president's wife, who spoke on "The Basis of Morale in War and Peace"; Charles Poletti, lieutenant governor of New York, on "These Things Unite Us"; Mayor La Guardia on "Your Part in Civilian Defense Plants"; and Lawrence on "The Value of the Theatre in National Defense." Although the first six pages of her speech are now lost, her closing comments about the supreme sacrifice reveal that she was anything but a "girl of the moment" when it came to war relief.[54]

With the holiday season around the corner, Lawrence took it upon herself to write the *Times* with her latest idea:

> How saddening it is to realize that Christmas will soon be here again and that there will be no toys manufactured in England for home consumption for the first time in history. No dolls, no baby carriages, no roller skates, no sugar-cane umbrella sticks or any of the simplest things which delight

the heart of the poorest or sickest child. So from America we are sending "The Happiness Ship"—to take the place of Santa Claus—only where
he had his reindeer, our ship will have America's watchful convoys to escort her on her perilous journey. We want to send a ship such as only
children dream of—packed full of happy surprises—like the one I sing
about in my play:

> *My Ship has sails that are*
> *Made of silk;*
> *The decks are trimmed with gold,*
> *And of jam and spice*
> *There's a paradise*
> *In the hold!*

Please, once again, America, and your more fortunate children who are
now beginning to write their notes to Santa Claus—please send me a gift
for our happiness ship. Each gift should bear a label with the sender's
name and address on it so that the lucky little mite [on] the other end can
send you back words of a dream come true on Christmas, 1941. No toy need
cost more than one dollar, and can be sent to me at the Alvin Theatre.

God bless you all and grant you yet more safe Christmases in this vast
and bounteous land of the free.

Gertrude Lawrence
New York, Dec. 4, 1941[55]

The day after the *Times* published Lawrence's letter, 350 Japanese fighter
planes bombed Pearl Harbor, 2,388 Americans lost their lives, and the United
States plunged headlong into World War II. Less than twenty-four hours
later, the Alvin became the first theater to offer defense bonds and stamps at
the box office in lieu of change. By December 11, the Alvin's general manager
announced that $554 worth had been sold and that Lawrence herself would
begin staffing a window for an hour a day. So successful was the campaign
that they sold $1,000 worth in just two weeks.[56]

The theatrical community rallied to the American war effort. At a meeting
at the Hudson Theatre, nine hundred attended and decided to rename the
former American Theatre Wing of the Allied War Relief and British War
Relief the "American Theatre Wing War Service." Rachel Crothers was
elected its first president, and Lawrence spoke and made a presentation to Bert
Lytell on behalf of the British agencies. Later that week, the Alvin switched
the proceeds from the sale of *Lady in the Dark*'s souvenir playbill from British
War Relief to the American Naval Relief Fund. Before *Lady in the Dark* took
its Christmas holiday, the London columnist William Hickey gave Lawrence
one of a pair of Lucite rings made from the windshields of Nazi Stukas shot

down over Britain by the Royal Air Force. Its companion was presented to President Roosevelt.[57]

The tenor of *Lady in the Dark*'s playbills changed by month's end. In addition to a reminder that defense stamps were available at the box office, the playbill featured a full page of emergency instructions in case of air raid warnings while in the theater district. With strong allusions to Pearl Harbor, it cautioned patrons:

> We have learned of a new technique in the invasion of countries. There is no longer a "war zone." An entire country is subject to sudden, surprise attacks. Every civilian is exposed to danger. A vital part of our defense, therefore, is that civilians be trained to protect themselves and to know just what to do in the event of an attack from the air....
>
> ...The staff of this theatre has been trained to insure your safety. Should there be an air raid warning during the time that you are in the theatre, stay in your seats. This is most important. Information and instructions will be given you. Cooperate by keeping calm.[58]

On January 23, 1942, *Lady in the Dark* celebrated its first anniversary, even though it had not yet earned a full year's worth of performances. To mark the occasion, Lawrence gave away gifts at the end of each performance during the following week. The gifts were defense bonds, presented to audience members whose names had been selected by lot. So successful was the giveaway that in the following weeks she was besieged by companies asking her to continue the practice and distribute their products.

America's entrance into World War II profoundly affected the lives of its citizens, including those responsible for *Lady in the Dark*. Hart and Weill organized, produced, and wrote sketches for revues presented at defense plants, originally called the "Lunch Hour Follies." Because of round-the-clock production, the Follies gave performances at a given plant for each shift's lunch at 12:00 P.M., 8:00 P.M., and 4:00 A.M. In addition to being chair of the production committee, Weill composed several numbers for the shows. Hart and Weill also volunteered their time as "spotters," watching for enemy aircraft. The composer went so far as to register for the draft on February 14. Gershwin gives an idea of what life was like on the West Coast:

> Yes, it was quite exciting for a while—what with black-outs, sirens, last minute rushes to get black-out materials, search lights and soldiers appearing all over the place....
>
> ...The point is that although people are still going to movies, shows and concerts as formerly, night clubbing seems frivolous, to say the least.

All the women are studying and taking courses in first aid and airplane spotting and relief work. People think twice before undertaking any kind of long trip in their cars.[59]

Lawrence's husband, a member of the Naval Reserve, reported for active duty on the day of *Lady in the Dark*'s anniversary. Lawrence enrolled in the first Red Cross class of the American Theatre Wing War Service and gave blood on her day off. On February 13 she successfully passed her Red Cross exam and used it that evening when Audrey Costello, a member of the dance corps, fainted.[60] *Lady in the Dark* lost its first cast member to the armed forces when dancer Fred Hearn enlisted in the Army.[61]

Despite its efforts, the theatrical community soon found itself under attack. Controversy erupted in the House of Representatives over the deficiency appropriations bill and the Office of Civilian Defense (OCD). When it was discovered that the OCD had on its payroll performers such as screen actor Melvyn Douglas and dancer Mayris Chaney, all hell broke loose. Congressman Faddis from Pennsylvania testified, "This agency which the Congress has set up in an endeavor to protect the civilian components of this Nation in case of warfare is being prostituted to 'boondoggling' and to the interests of a class of the people of this Nation whose loyalty to the Nation is, indeed, in many cases questionable."[62] Unable to finish debate on the bill, the session continued on Lincoln's birthday.

Fueling the fire, the *Times* reported on Monday morning's front page that General Hershey, director of Selective Service System, had sent directions to California draft boards to grant draft deferments to actors, directors, producers, sound engineers, and other technicians in the motion picture industry. Representative Andresen from Minnesota demanded to know why the film industry should have received such prompt attention when a six-month-old draft deferment for farmers had not. Representative Culken from New York asked, "Does the gentleman think it is another case of glamour?" Andresen replied, "Undoubtedly. There may not be as much glamour in milking a cow as seeing a fan dancer, or some of these others who are engaged in movie activities, but when it comes to the safety and the welfare of the Nation and the success of the war, there is nothing that will compare with the need for an abundance of products from the farms."[63] With a vote of more than two-to-one in favor, the deficiency appropriations bill passed and went to the Senate with an amendment forbidding the OCD from supporting "physical fitness by dancers, fan dancing, street shows, theatrical performances, or other public entertainments."

The fallout included La Guardia's resignation as head of the OCD and the Screen Actors' Guild defending the appointment of Melvyn Douglas in a telegram read before the Senate. Equity's telegram, signed by Bert Lytell, expressed resentment over the "slurs cast upon us" and conversely claimed that "no single group in the country is doing more for its war effort at this time than the people of the theatre, screen, and radio."[64] The theater community launched an all-out counteroffensive. Brooks Atkinson wrote an extensive article about the American Theatre Wing, published on the front page of the *Times* arts section. He reminded readers and Congress that when six women founded the American Theatre Wing in 1940 (with Gertrude Lawrence as its first vice president) most Americans considered the war phony. Atkinson concluded that the American Theatre Wing was "abreast of its time today."[65] Nevertheless, the Senate passed the deficiency appropriation bill with the fan-dancing amendment.

Lady in the Dark's playbills addressed this controversy with two types of rebuttals. First, a series of advertisements featured quotations from drama critics on the importance of the theater during wartime, such as this one from the *Post*'s John Mason Brown: "We are the arsenal for more than the arms of democracy. We are the arsenal for democracy's values, too. This is why the theatre, and all the threatened decencies for which it stands, now takes their place among the most mobilizing causes which make this war ours."[66] Second, letters from Rachel Crothers, president of the American Theatre Wing, and Helen Menken, chair of the Radio Division, appeared in full-page ads. Under the banner "Curtain Up for Victory!," Menken's letter encouraged *Lady in the Dark*'s patrons, among other activities, to purchase copies of the book *America Goes to War* available at the concession stand.

Probably the best known of the Wing's activities was the Stage Door Canteen, which provided entertainment and "a warm human welcome from the heart of the theatre" for servicemen. Broadway personalities performed gratis and also helped out in the kitchen. Stage and radio actresses volunteered as waitresses, hostesses, and dancing partners. The Canteen had its unofficial opening on Monday, March 2, at 5:00 P.M. *Lady in the Dark*'s company performed from 6:00 to 7:00 before heading over to the Alvin. Lawrence's performance of "The Saga of Jenny" tore the place apart. Afterward, an RAF flyer rushed up, took her into his arms, and began to dance. An American sailor then cut in, and soon the star was besieged with partners. Not one to show any favoritism, Gertie began a conga line in what was described as a "snake-hip snake dance" with wild abandon.[67] Although Danny Kaye had been asked to be the Canteen's first master of ceremonies, he deferred, perhaps because of the bad feelings surrounding his departure, to Dan Harden, *Lady in the Dark*'s Ben Butler.[68]

The following week *Lady in the Dark*'s regularly scheduled Wednesday matinee was moved to Thursday because of Lawrence's participation in Tuesday night's Navy Relief Show at Madison Square Garden. That Thursday the Stage Door Canteen officially opened with an estimated one thousand to fifteen hundred servicemen in attendance. Brooks Atkinson reported, "Gertrude Lawrence and the *Lady in the Dark* company christened the canteen with an hour's performance of bits from the show, including the immortal 'Jenny,' which will probably turn out to be the theme song of the United States forces."[69] Atkinson's prediction would prove to be prophetic.

During the spring of 1942, Lawrence received many commendations for her ability to play Liza Elliott eight times a week and to devote herself so fully to the war effort. Even more miraculous was that she did not have to cancel any performances during the second season. By April she had reportedly sold $7,562 worth of war bonds and stamps at the Alvin's box office before matinees. The American Women's Voluntary Services recognized her as "the representative of the stage who had done the most for American Defense."[70] For Lawrence, one of her greatest honors during the war was when a C-46 transport and cargo plane based in Guam had "Lady in the Dark" painted in black and red letters on its nose.[71] A P-61 Black Widow, the only American aircraft nightfighter, also carried "Lady in the Dark" on its nose. It became the most famous P-61 of them all by scoring the last two kills of WWII (Figure 43).[72] Fittingly, Lawrence, who had worked tirelessly to end U.S. isolationism, saw the plane named after her show finally finish the war.

A couple of months into the new year, Broadway audiences began to fall off. As a result, on March 8 the Sam Harris office and Moss Hart posted *Lady in the Dark*'s closing notice. It stated that the show would close on April 25 after a run of 422 performances—six more than a typical year's run. There was to be a five-week tour before Lawrence's contracted season closing of June 1. Hart planned to open *Lady in the Dark* on April 27 for a two-week stint at the National Theater in Washington, DC, and then on May 11 for a three-week run at Philadelphia's Forrest Theatre. Ten days after the closing notice, the producers canceled the spring tour because of DC's child labor laws, which would have prevented the children in the cast from performing. In response to increased sales, the closing date was retracted. The producers announced that *Lady in the Dark* would run indefinitely or until Lawrence's summer vacation, and postponed any touring until the next season.

Variety reported on March 25 that *Lady in the Dark*'s profit so far that year had been approximately $35,000.[73] That month Saks Fifth Avenue released a Lady in the Dark perfume by Dorothy Gray with advertising copy that read, "gay, vivacious, versatile . . . a fragrance that's very dramatic, very feminine" (Figure 44). Photographers snapped Lawrence at the department store busily autographing the perfume's decorative box. To mark the occasion of *Lady in the Dark*'s 416th performance, the traditional performance indicating a full fifty-two weeks, the *Herald Tribune* published some statistics. During the past year, there had been six births in the company (three by dancers, two by Chorus members, and one by a stagehand) and five marriages (Virginia Peine's, Walter Coy's, Macdonald Carey's, Victor Mature's, and Evelyn Wyckoff's). With sixty revolutions of the four turntables per performance, 24,960 turns had been made. Dr. Brooks reportedly filled three pages of notes at each performance (one for each of Liza's sessions), which totaled 1,248 sheets. Donald Randolph, the actor playing Dr. Brooks, claimed to have saved each sheet and was planning on sending them to a psychiatrist for analysis. Lawrence had racked up 2,970 names in her dressing room guest book, and the "Press Department had turned down 9,280 requests for passes because of being sold out."[74]

On May 2 Weill wrote Gershwin that *Lady in the Dark* was still turning a profit. He expressed delight that "Jenny" was "being sung a lot in the army camps" and was "being used for all kinds of take-offs by the boys." He even tried to interest Gershwin in writing a war version of the piece called "The Saga of Adolf."[75] In its second season, *Lady in the Dark* played 300 performances, for a total run of 462.[76] During the final week it grossed $22,000 and on the final night, Saturday, May 30, 1942, had forty standees.[77] *Lady in the Dark* closed after a run of fifty-eight nonconsecutive weeks, of which thirty-two were at absolute capacity with standees.

On the night of the final performance, Hart spent the evening alone at Fairview Farm. He sent Lawrence a costly brooch—ironically, one of the "feminine adornments" she had had to forgo as the lady in the dark. Its accompanying card read, "Lord, this is nice of me!"[78]

6

Tour

Unlike today's tours of Broadway shows that headline lesser stars and often play concurrently with the New York production, musicals from *Lady in the Dark*'s era literally went on tour. That is, the set, properties, stars, and as many of the original cast and crew as possible traveled by train and recreated the show in other cities. Those audiences did not experience a version of the original with a simplified set and reduced forces, but almost exactly what had been seen on Broadway. The tour was thus an extension of the original production. Participation of the show's stars was critical for the success, or even the possibility, of a tour.

Planning for *Lady in the Dark*'s tour began in earnest during its second season. Weill wrote to Gershwin on November 13, 1941, "We intend to ask Gertie if she would give us at least a part of next season for a road tour."[1] In a follow-up telephone call, he expressed concern over potential competition from the Paramount film. Gershwin reassured him, "There is plenty of money around for top attractions and our show has been so publicized that it can't help being one of the two or three outstanding successes on the road next year. The movie I'm sure will not interfere with our show. It can only help it.... A good advertising campaign would soon make the $3.85 or $4.40 road audience aware that they'd be getting not only Gertrude Lawrence but also the original, unexpurgated play. I feel we would have a road season of not merely good business but of complete sell-outs."[2] Paramount did not release its version of *Lady in the Dark* until 1944 and consequently provided no competition—or boost—for the tour.

On March 9, 1942, Hart and Lawrence signed a letter of agreement for the coming season that gave her the possibility of laying off an entire week for both Christmas and Holy Week.[3] The original rider specified, "If the play goes on tour or is performed outside of the City of New York, the Manager will assume the salary and transportation of the Actor's maid and transportation, including private drawing room, whenever possible, for the Actor."[4] Publicly, it appeared that all was set for the tour; privately, Hart and Lawrence were going toe-to-toe. Exasperated, Weill wrote Lenya, on tour herself with Maxwell Anderson's play *Candle in the Wind*, "The fight between Moss's ego and Gertie's ego came to a clash and Moss wants to call off the road tour altogether just to punish Gertie. He is quite a problem boy now since he goes to the analyst twice a day. It is all about the transportation difficulties. Gertie wants to take the show to Chicago and stay there (which is the right thing to do) and Moss says she has no right to 'run the show.'"[5] Later that week, Weill took the star to lunch at Sardi's to smooth her ruffled feathers, and Gertie subsequently signed the contract.

Because of *Lady in the Dark*'s complicated setup, one-nighters and split weeks were impossible. Theaters in key cities qualified for inclusion solely because they possessed a stage large enough to accommodate the turntables. Transportation worries were very real: the war had caused a scarcity of baggage cars, and *Lady in the Dark* would require no fewer than seven. Lawrence's twenty-week contract, although it has not survived, covered an itinerary of eight cities: Philadelphia, Baltimore, Pittsburgh, Cleveland, Detroit, Cincinnati, St. Louis, and Chicago.

After *Lady in the Dark* closed in New York, Lawrence escaped to Dennis, Massachusetts, for the summer. Following the leads of Gershwin, Weill, and Hart, she and her husband pursued the American dream of owning a home. Located across from a cranberry bog on the Cape, the house was christened "The Berries." After purchasing their nine acres, Lawrence joined the Ocean Spray Cooperative and began harvesting. Working in the bog, she enticed friends and associates to lend a hand. "It's not in my legal retainer," demurred lawyer Fanny Holtzmann. Lawrence shot back, "It's part of your duty as a citizen to help the war effort."[6]

And help the war effort Gertie did. The summer of 1942 was a seemingly endless string of bazaars, lawn parties, clambakes, barn dances, teas, and auctions. All totaled, they netted $4,500 for the Gertrude Lawrence Chapter of the American Theatre Wing War Service. In addition to planting a victory garden, Lawrence starred in Noël Coward's *Fallen Angels* at the Cape. When asked by the *Boston Globe* for a rundown of her activities, Gertie banged out the following list on her portable typewriter:

I have joined the Red Cross Motor Corps as First Aid Nurse and driver, and my old station wagon now flies two large white flags with the scarlet emblem of mercy, and is equipped with stretchers for emergency calls. I have sung at Camp Edwards, at the Red Cross Hospital and at the outpost at Sagamore. During this concert an air raid warning was sounded which lasted for over half an hour. All the lights were extinguished, but we continued the concert by dancing in the dark to the light of the red glow from 300 cigarettes.... It is strange, how unity of purpose puts one on one's mettle and makes one realize the true values of the simple things which make up the art of living.[7]

For the tour, *Lady in the Dark* made a few cast changes. The continuing members included, in addition to Lawrence, Jeanne Shelby (playing Miss Bowers), Gedda Petry (Miss Foster), Margaret Dale (Maggie Grant), Eric Brotherson (Russell Paxton), and Willard Parker (Randy Curtis). Ann Lee, who had played Miss Stevens since the Boston tryout, stepped into the role of Alison Du Bois. Richard Hale took over as the new Dr. Brooks (Figure 42), Hugh Marlowe as Charley Johnson, and John Leslie as Kendall Nesbitt. In August the producers announced that, because of the war and the rising cost of living, Chorus members' weekly wage would increase from $40 to $55. Additional singers and dancers auditioned on August 10 at the Music Box Theatre.[8]

Rehearsals began in New York in September. On the 20th, workmen began to assemble the set and hang lights in Philadelphia. In addition to the fifteen company mechanics, forty local stagehands assisted the setup and four-week run. Tickets went on sale the following Monday. The cast left New York on the 24th and spent the remainder of the week in Philadelphia rehearsing. Weill's wife attended the dress rehearsal on Saturday and reported, "Gertie was in great form, overacting like a berserker, but still very amusing."[9] The following evening the cast gave a free preview performance for servicemen and their sweethearts.

The tour opened on Monday, September 28, with a full house. The four reviews published the following day could not have been better. (*Variety* dryly noted, "They were so enthusiastic they could have been written by Gertrude Lawrence and Moss Hart.")[10] The Philly critics all mentioned just how far *Lady in the Dark* had departed from the tried and true Broadway formula. Edwin H. Schloss of the *Record* called it "a musical of such style, imagination and adult sophistication that it makes the average run-of-the-footlights musical look like something dragged up from the bottom of the remnant counter in last year's bargain basement." The *News* critic marveled, "*Lady in the Dark* conforms to no rule, obeys no precedent and makes no obeisance to already perfected patterns."

With such reviews, the musical play grossed over $31,000 in its first week. Although very good, audiences were not at capacity in the eighteen-hundred-seat house, and some felt that the $3.50 top-ticket price was too high for Philadelphia. To help boost sales, the management of the Forrest Theatre placed a large poster in the lobby that read, "Miss Lawrence will *positively* appear at all performances: Evg's.—Wed. & Sat. Matinees." But during the third week, Lawrence confounded the Friday night audience by not taking her curtain calls. She had taken ill, and consequently both Saturday performances had to be canceled. In addition to playing Liza Elliott, she had been performing at Philadelphia's Stage Door Canteen and squeezing in extracurricular shows for the Merchant Marine. The producers considered insuring her with a Lloyds of London policy similar to the one that had covered the New York run, but then dropped the idea because of the cost.

After a weekend's rest, Lawrence regained her voice and was able to complete the fourth week. *Lady in the Dark*'s company left Philly in a happy mood: the thirty performances had grossed $119,400.[11] Giddy with the numbers, Gershwin wrote to Weill, "I'm tickled about the business *Lady in the Dark* is doing and so must you be. Guess we've got a hit in it. Maybe next year we'll see it in London. And the year after that we'll have it translated into Spanish and tour South America. Who knows?"[12] For the Baltimore stop, a publicity campaign in Washington, DC, urged residents to "come on over." The ploy worked, and the advance climbed to $35,000 the Friday before the scheduled opening.

And that's where the tour hit a snag. After a Saturday night closing in one city, the cast, crew, and baggage were to travel on Sunday. The setup in the new city would begin that evening for a planned Monday night opening. But in Philadelphia the crew had discovered that they would need more than twenty-four hours to set up. Consequently, the Baltimore opening had to be pushed back to Tuesday. To make up the lost performance and revenue, James F. Reilly, executive secretary of the League of New York Theatres, filed a request on behalf of *Lady in the Dark* to the Equity Council:

Where *Lady in the Dark* or any other play similarly situated is prevented from opening on Monday night, the following be permitted:

1. In cities where the attraction is booked for one week, the attraction be allowed to open on Tuesday night and play an additional matinee to make it possible to give eight performances during such week.
2. In cities where attraction is booked to play more than one week where Sunday performances are permitted, the attraction be allowed to play a Sunday night performance, which would fall between the first and second week of the engagement, and such Sunday night show to apply

to the first week of the engagement without any additional pay; it being understood that only seven performances shall be given during the first week and the Sunday show, if permitted, to apply to the first week shall constitute the eighth performance.

3. In cities where the attraction is booked for more than one week, and where Sunday performances are not permitted, then the same dispensation as outlined in paragraph 1 be permitted only during the first week of the engagement.[13]

Equity executive secretary Paul Dullzell replied to Reilly that his proposal had been accepted, with the condition that when Pullman sleepers (scarce because of the war) were unavailable for an overnight, the producers would compensate the actors the cost of the ticket. To save funds, *Lady in the Dark*'s company traveled during the day for each leg of the trip except the last.

To move a production as large as *Lady in the Dark* a total of twenty-one hundred miles during wartime presented difficulties and challenges. The cast numbered fifty-two; in addition, there were fifteen stagehands, a musical director, principal orchestral players, and other staff.[14] In addition to traveling during the day, a sign posted backstage reminded cast and crew to eat before boarding the train so that servicemen could have priority use of the dining cars.

With Monday night now free, Lawrence rounded up the cast to perform at Washington's Stage Door Canteen. Accompanied by three members of *Lady in the Dark*'s orchestra, they took the stage with Hugh Marlowe as master of ceremonies. The ninety-minute vaudeville show culminated with Lawrence bumping and grinding her way through "The Saga of Jenny" for 1,259 servicemen.[15] On the way back to Baltimore, Lawrence outlined another one of her benefit activities for reporters. At each tour stop, she was placing a barrel in the lobby where audience members could deposit items for servicemen. Lawrence herself then paid to have them sent to her mobile library and gift shop that toured military bases located on Cape Cod.

Lady in the Dark's opening the following evening concluded with an ovation for Lawrence that, according to the *Evening Sun*'s critic, was "of royal proportions." The three reviews published the following day were similarly laudatory.[16] The only letdowns, according to Gilbert Kanour of the *Evening Sun*, were Willard Parker, "a satisfactory caricature of a Hollywood Dream Prince," and John Leslie, "all right as the businessman who gets a divorce to marry Liza." By the end of the first week, *Lady in the Dark* had garnered a $30,000 gross with a top ticket price of $3.85 at Baltimore's nineteen-hundred-seat Ford's Theater.[17] After the second week's Thursday performance, Lawrence and the cast entertained two hundred merchant seamen and the soldier/sailor members of their gun crews. The appreciative crowd at the British Merchant Navy Club cried, "We want Gert." When the lady in question performed "Jenny," the men "let go with a roar."[18] On November 7, the curtain rang down on the engagement. The second week topped the first, with $32,000 in business, and most of the sixteen performances were SRO.

The company then traveled west to Pittsburgh. Chester Thompson, the tour's master carpenter, supervised each setup by fifty-five stagehands, which began with twenty-eight truckloads of machinery and scenery transported from the train station to the theater. At 7:00 on Sunday evening, eighteen stagehands began to assemble the turntables at the Nixon Theater. At 1:00 A.M. fifteen electricians arrived to hang the three hundred spotlights and wire them to three switchboards. By 7:00 on Monday morning the seven prop men supervised the assembly of the set and properties. The stage crew continued to work in shifts around the clock until Tuesday afternoon, when they ran a mechanical rehearsal prior to the opening.[19]

On Monday at Pittsburgh's William Penn Hotel, Lawrence gave her now customary press conference. Dressed in a two-piece purple wool suit with matching chapeau, she posed for photos. The dichotomy of her twin roles as glamorous stage actress and dedicated war-relief worker was nowhere more apparent than at these interviews. She explained that, as a lieutenant in the American Red Cross Motor Corps and a colonel in the American Ambulance Corps, she was making herself available to local chapters in each city. (In Baltimore she had helped set up an emergency canteen for Polish refugees.) When asked about future plans, she floated her idea of taking *Lady in the Dark* to London with Noël Coward as Dr. Brooks.[20]

More than at the previous stops, in Pittsburgh the critics gushed about Lawrence.[21] The *Sun-Telegraph* reviewer could not remember a "First Lady [who] toiled so magnificently through practically every second of a play lasting just minutes short of three hours." With his tongue planted firmly in his cheek, Kaspar Monahan of the *Press* suggested that Equity could take legal action against the star for playing a half dozen roles—and thereby keeping other actresses out of work. Despite these notices, Lawrence hit the ceiling when she heard that New York dailies had reported that the tour might have to be canceled because of her delicate health. She fired off a telegram that dispelled the rumor and quoted the *Post-Gazette* review from the previous day. It concluded, "With the boundless energy, the enthusiasm and the vitality the lady displayed last night at the Nixon, vitamins should take her."[22]

The next Monday Lawrence appeared with other entertainers in a pre-game show at the USO-Variety Club football game to benefit the proposed

Pittsburgh Canteen. Appearing before a crowd of nearly twenty-four thousand, Lawrence thanked the audience for "coming across for the boys who go across."[23] *Lady in the Dark* departed Pittsburgh on November 22 during a spell of Indian summer. The tally for the two-week run: eleven barrelfuls of donations for Lawrence and approximately $53,500 for the box office.[24]

Tickets had gone on sale for the Cleveland stopover only four days prior to the opening, but Milton Krantz, manager of the Hanna Theater, reported nearly $9,000 in advance mail orders. With such a buildup, the packed house and $3,684 one-night gross broke the opening-night record for the tour.[25] The following day the venerable *Plain Dealer* critic proclaimed *Lady in the Dark* "the best American musical show . . . since Jerome Kern's *Show Boat*."[26] *Lady in the Dark* closed its one-week run in Cleveland, which included a Friday matinee, with an estimated $28,300 gross.

With everyone else rushing to get *Lady in the Dark* ready for its Detroit opening, Lawrence stole a few hours to attend the opening of a new Red Cross Blood Donor Center. The Tuesday opening at the Cass Theatre went off without a hitch. Despite a set of positive reviews, *Lady in the Dark* concluded its first week in Detroit (with an added Sunday evening performance) with a disappointing $25,000 gross.[27] The next day Lawrence marked the first anniversary of Pearl Harbor by selling war bonds at Saks Fifth Avenue. Many of the Christmas shoppers did a double take when they recognized Gertie in her Red Cross emergency first aid uniform.[28]

Lady in the Dark's second week in Detroit matched the first, but ticket sales for the third and final week plunged to $19,250.[29] This proved to be the lowest return for the entire tour. A pragmatic Gershwin wrote to Weill, "I don't see that business has been bad at all unless the show is geared far higher than I imagined. Naturally we would like to see the show run as long as possible and I, for one, am willing to take a reasonable cut whenever necessary. If you and Moss and Gertie feel the same about it I'm sure management would feel encouraged to keep it running. I would far rather have a show running at 2%, say, than no show running at 3%."[30]

Lawrence exercised her option of laying off the week of Christmas and returned to New York. That Wednesday she met with Hart to discuss her idea of bringing *Lady in the Dark* back to New York after the tour. Hart agreed to scout out a suitable theater. The break also gave the crew time to move and set up. As a result, *Lady in the Dark* was able to open on Monday in Cincinnati, where tickets had gone on sale the previous week for a one-week engagement.

Lawrence arrived the day after Christmas and proceeded directly from Union Terminal to the Hotel Netherland Plaza for a press luncheon. Glancing over the menu, she expressed surprise that the three Bs—beef, bacon, and butter—were still available. After enjoying a lunch of boiled beef and cabbage, and polishing it off with a dish of chocolate ice cream, she made a request: "Please don't write that Miss Lawrence ate like a horse. I've had no breakfast, you know." As the American president of ENSA (Entertainments National Service Association, the British equivalent of the USO), Lawrence outlined her plan for returning British entertainers in the United States to England. Rising to leave, she added, "These luncheons are now almost my only period of relaxation."[31]

Despite positive reviews, attendance at the twenty-five-hundred-seat Taft Theater waned during the first half of the week because of rainy weather. Some of the musical play's franker passages disturbed conservative Cincinnati critics.[32] Howard W. Hess of the *Times-Star* felt that the "frequent cussing which peppered the performance was done in a devil-may-care manner." The *Enquirer*'s reviewer claimed that Lawrence's performance of the "saucy song and dance for the famous 'Saga of Jenny' makes Gypsy Rose Lee look like a tyro."

One of the tour's more humorous moments occurred in Cincinnati when Lawrence made herself available for local benefit work. At a quarter past noon on December 31, she was stationed to sell war stamps and bonds in the lobby of the Netherland Plaza:

> I was sitting at a table under a vast Christmas tree, wearing my Red Cross uniform and doing the best I could, and next to me was the chairman, a large florid lady elaborately dressed and blondly becurled. Suddenly a woman charged across the lobby, grabbed the chairman by the hand and gurgled effusively, "Oh! Miss Lawrence, I was at *Lady in the Dark* last night and I think you are simply marvelous." Apparently that so-called theatre aura is conspicuous by its absence when you are in uniform. (P.S.: In spite of everything, we sold a lot of bonds that day.)[33]

Both the weather and business picked up later in the week, and the show concluded its brief Cincinnati run with capacity houses and a $28,500 gross.[34]

The following day, the company traveled its longest leg to St. Louis. With a two-week engagement, *Lady in the Dark* opened on January 5, 1943, at the American Theater. Of the three reviews the show received, two were stellar and one panned everything except the show's indefatigable star.[35] Arthur Kuhl of the *Star-Times* described the analysis as "about as complex as a Mother Goose rhyme," the score as "undistinguished though pleasant," and the lyrics as having "little of [the] usual lustre of rhyme." Despite this chilly review and an actual blizzard, *Lady in the Dark* grossed approximately $50,000 with a $3.85 top.[36]

During the first week, the St. Louis Red Cross held a Friday afternoon meeting at the theater to award one-year service stripes. Among the two thousand volunteers recognized was Lawrence herself, who spoke on "What the Red Cross Means to Me." A subsequent newspaper photo essay high-lighted her dual roles.[37] Three frames featured Lawrence in her gowns from the show, with the fourth depicting "what Lawrence wears everyday." That Red Cross Uniform received, no doubt facetiously, a full-fledged fashion description: "plain suit of wool in khaki color. Jacket is tunic length, military collar and pockets trimmed with brass buttons." Like Liza Elliott, Lawrence now found herself in tailored suits during the day and in glamorous gowns at night.

On Thursday of the second week, Lawrence and ninety-six members of the company attended a special midnight performance aboard Capt. J. W. Menke's *Goldenrod Showboat*. The occasion was a farewell party for a cast member who had been drafted into the army. Lawrence recalled, "It was a gay evening especially for the children, who had their only late night during the tour, and they filled themselves with candy, root beer, and popcorn to their hearts' content. We loved the melodrama given by the floating theatre troupe."[38] During the tour, *Lady in the Dark* had to replace ten cast members who were called for duty. This problem became so acute during the next stop in Chicago that the *News* reported—only half in jest— that Chorus men were now hired not only for their voices, but also for their draft status.[39]

Despite the hefty sums of money the tour had taken in on its first seven stops, profits were slim. With 118 performances and a total gross of $402,795, the tour had turned a profit of only $13,000. Reasons included the high cost of transportation and setup, the weekly payroll of about $10,000, Lawrence's $2,000 weekly salary plus 15 percent of the gross exceeding $10,000, and the 13.5 percent of the weekly gross divided among Hart, Weill, Gershwin, and Short. As an example, with a gross of $50,580 in St. Louis, a profit of only $1.44 was realized for the first week after expenses and transportation, and $700 for the second week.[40]

Lawrence was the first cast member to arrive in Chicago because she took a plane in order to make a speech at 12:30 P.M. on Sunday. Arriving at the airport bundled in mink, she addressed an audience of five thousand hostesses who assisted in serving and entertaining servicemen at three local canteens. The remainder of the company arrived by train and began moving into the Civic Opera House. The immense size of the thirty-six-hundred-seat audi-torium proved a challenge. According to Ann Lee, "We were all screaming our lungs out to be heard, because nothing was miked in those days."

Lawrence joked, "We could comfortably have housed a cricket match and a baseball game, as well as *Lady in the Dark*."[41]

The opening was in part a benefit for the Margaret Etter Creche Day Nursery. Ticket revenue from the two thousand orchestra and box seats aided the city's oldest nursery, which was seeing increased demand because of mothers working in the war industry. The evening's festivities included a raffle of a Hattie Carnegie outfit and a $50 cash prize, both drawn by Lawrence at the end of the show. Donors and businesses made it possible for two hundred servicemen and women from nearby bases to attend. Braving the 10 degrees below zero temperature, patrons packed the Civic Opera House and warmly greeted *Lady in the Dark*. Afterward, the nursery's board threw a supper party for four hundred in Lawrence's honor at the Ambassador East Hotel.

Despite gremlins that caused the sets to bang together and the lighting to waver, *Lady in the Dark* received its best set of reviews in Chicago.[42] Ashton Stevens in the *Herald American* called Lawrence a genius who had "pulled off one of the greatest triumphs of her triumphal career." Cecil Smith of the *Daily Tribune* ranked the show "a high point in the history of the American musical stage." *Lady in the Dark*'s score received the most attention since the show's opening two years prior. In the *Sun*, Tracy York described it as "an integral and important part of the whole, not just a pleasant accompaniment to it, and gives one the impression that play and music were made together." Cecil Smith extolled the originality of *Lady in the Dark*'s form in a Sunday feature: "I should like to point out the shortsightedness of thinking of it merely as a brilliantly contrived vehicle for Gertrude Lawrence. She is wonderful, of course. So was Kirsten Flagstad wonderful in *Tristan and Isolde*, but nobody was ever tempted to think of *Tristan* as merely a vehicle for Flagstad."[43]

Lady in the Dark concluded its first week in Chicago with a Sunday evening performance and a whopping $43,000 gross. The amount topped not only other touring attractions, but everything playing on Broadway as well.[44] The following day Morris Jacobs, *Lady in the Dark*'s general manager, announced that the company would indeed return to New York for a reengagement. He offered possible opening dates of either February 21 or 28, depending on whether the Chicago run was extended. Two days later *Variety* reported that because of the overwhelming demand, *Lady in the Dark* would be held over a fifth week in the Windy City.[45]

Audiences built steadily through the fourth week, punctuated by Lawrence's social and war activities. The principals were guests of the Chicago Drama League at a breakfast, where the show's star received an honorary .

membership. On her first day off, Lawrence gave a tea at the Seneca Hotel for 150 midshipmen from the Naval Midshipmen's School at Northwestern University. The next Sunday, members of the cast appeared at the Chicago Service Men's Center No. 2. Lawrence capped the evening with her notorious "Jenny" for a crowd of three thousand.[46]

In his season wrap-up, New York drama critic Burns Mantle underscored just what a gamble the Civic Opera House had been: "Dire pictures were painted of the bleakness of a comparative handful of auditors sprinkled among thousands of vacant seats, with the production invisible and inaudible on a stage gauged for *Aïda* and *Turandot*. Even Miss Lawrence's management had serious doubts."[47] So serious were the doubts that there had been a contingency plan to go to Boston. After the announcement was made that from Chicago the show would return to New York, the *Christian Science Monitor* reported that the prospects of a Boston stop had been dashed.

During the forty-performance Chicago run, *Lady in the Dark* racked up weekly box-office totals of $43,793, $49,295, $50,526, $52,486, and $49,823. The near quarter-million-dollar total shattered records—not only for the Civic Opera House, but also for the city at large. The concluding performance marked the end of a tour that had a total of 158 performances and a profit of $59,000—$46,000 of which had been earned on the shores of Lake Michigan.[48]

Reflecting on the previous five months, Lawrence mused, "While traveling around the country with a production the size of *Lady in the Dark* is not without its problems in wartime, it is also a lot of fun. It is very seldom that one feels as a star is supposed to feel. I don't know just what I mean by that, but I guess it's a little important, a little pampered and, to use that generally disliked but still overworked adjective, even a little glamorous."[49] In an interview with the *Herald Tribune*, she reported, "Doing war work with people in the cities we've played in has been a wonderful experience for me. I know I have friends in all those places, and now I realize that you're not a star until you get that feeling for the road—that sense of belonging to it. Stars don't shine merely over Broadway you know."[50]

The box office at New York's Broadway Theatre opened on February 22 with reduced prices of $2.75 top for all evening performances except Saturdays, when the price rose to $3.30 (the top for *Lady in the Dark* at the Alvin had been $4.40). Matinee prices dropped from the original $2.75 to $2.20. The week between the Chicago closing and the New York opening allowed the cast a brief respite and the crew time to touch up the sets.

Lady in the Dark's new digs were considerably more spacious than they had been at the Alvin. Located a block north at Broadway and Fifty-third, the Broadway had led a checkered life. B. S. Moss had opened it as a motion-picture theater in 1924 with a Douglas Fairbanks movie. In 1930 Moss changed its name from the Colony to the Broadway and began exclusively hosting live theater. The first tenant was Cole Porter's *The New Yorkers*. Although a hit, it had to do big business, because the Broadway was New York's largest theater. Other shows struggled to fill the 1,752 seats, and by the mid-1930s Moss changed it back to a cinema. In 1942, however, the theater once again reverted to live attractions.[51]

On February 27 a long line formed at the box office, telephones rang off the hook, and by the time the curtain rose on *Lady in the Dark*, the theater was filled to the gills. Lawrence's fans greeted her enthusiastically. During the second act, they applauded before "The Saga of Jenny" and refused to let the show continue after her performance. Despite *Lady in the Dark*'s triumphant return (as it was advertised), critics could not agree whether it was "as good as it ever was" (the *Sun*'s Ward Morehouse) or "not the delight that it once was" (the *Herald Tribune*'s Howard Barnes). Lewis Nichols at the *Times* claimed that *Lady in the Dark* would run "until the next century or the end of the world, whichever is sooner."[52]

Lawrence lost no time in throwing herself into war-relief activities. The Wednesday before the opening, Sol Lesser had filmed her sequences for the upcoming movie *Stage Door Canteen*. Distributed by United Artists, the film included Lawrence singing "We Meet in the Funniest Places." The day after *Lady in the Dark*'s opening she participated in a Red Cross benefit where actors and actresses posed for sculptors and painters. In a twist of life imitating art (in this case, *Lady in the Dark*'s first dream sequence), Lawrence's portrait was not glamorous: "While Gertrude Lawrence posed for Dana Gibson, one old lady turned to another and said, 'A most unattractive costume for poor Gertrude, isn't it?' Evidently Miss Lawrence heard the remark because she gazed in their direction and appraised them for a moment, then brushed a speck from her left shoulder of her Volunteer Red Cross Uniform insignia. She resumed her original pose as she raised her chin—a little higher than before."[53] Two days later she performed for the first anniversary of the Stage Door Canteen, and soon she resumed performing there on alternate Sundays. Although she introduced her "Funniest Places" song, the men insisted on "Jenny" instead.

After *Lady in the Dark*'s performance on March 15, Lawrence participated in "The Red Cross at War," a rally and pageant at Madison Square Garden. Featured speakers included Eleanor Roosevelt, Princess Martha of Norway, and Mme. Chiang Kai-shek. The pageant, which demonstrated how the Red Cross assisted men in uniform, featured a script by Moss Hart. Lawrence essayed the pageant's principal women's roles. Unfortunately, she contracted a cold during the rally, and all but one of *Lady in the Dark*'s remaining performances that week had to be canceled.

On the same day as the rally, the *Times* reported that Edwin Lester, founding general manager of the Los Angeles Civic Light Opera Association, had offered to bring *Lady in the Dark* west. He proposed that it wind up its reengagement on May 15 and then play four weeks in San Francisco and two in Los Angeles. A partnership between the cities had been necessary to raise the $112,000 that he was guaranteeing the producers.[54] That week, while the theater was dark, the management negotiated with an ailing Lawrence for a West Coast tour, which would extend past her contracted summer layoff. On March 20, the producers finalized plans to take the show to California in late May and announced *Lady in the Dark*'s closing date. Such an announcement only two and a half weeks after a reopening was highly unusual, especially because *Lady in the Dark* had been playing to near capacity.

Fearful that Lawrence's health would cause further cancellations, the producers took out another policy with Lloyds of London. Always unpredictable, Lawrence did not miss any more performances, but kept herself immersed in benefit activities. She even mounted her own campaign, called "British Blood for American Forces." It urged British subjects in the United States to donate blood on May 24, Empire Day and the birthday anniversary of Queen Victoria. On May 15, *Lady in the Dark* closed its return engagement with a total of eighty-three performances. Although the show had a respectable $26,000 average weekly gross and some weeks had even topped $27,000, it turned little profit. Operating costs and royalties were about all that could be supported by bargain ticket prices.

For the West Coast tour, Lawrence signed a new Equity contract that dropped her weekly pay from $2,000 to $250, but now guaranteed her 35 percent of the net profits in addition to the 10 percent of the management's 30 percent she had been receiving before. The remaining 35 percent of the profits were divided among Hart, Weill, Gershwin, and Short.[55]

Unlike the previous tour, *Lady in the Dark* traveled to California with its full complement of stagehands. George Stanton, eastern agent of the New York Central line, masterminded the schedule. He staggered the company's departure in three groups, the first leaving the day after the New York closing, followed by the second and third on Monday and Tuesday. Once in Chicago, the company reunited, joined Lawrence, and traveled on to California in six different trains. The Chorus rebelled when they heard that Standard Pullman Sleepers were unavailable. The tourist Pullmans they were given did not cool tempers, because the cars had neither drawing rooms nor compartments. Although they were given the $6.05 difference between the two fares and $3.00 a day for meals, the three-day trip from Chicago to San Francisco was grueling. All told, the cost of transporting the

101-member company and seven baggage cars of properties was $20,000, which was borne by the two opera associations.[56]

Onboard, Lawrence read a flock of scripts for the next season. Among the projects offered to her was S. J. Perelman and Weill's "One Man's Venus" (which would later go to Mary Martin as *One Touch of Venus*), a dramatization of Francis Hackett's biographical protrait of Anne Boleyn, Rose Franken's new play "Beyond the Farthest Star," a musical version of *Rain* with Somerset Maugham adapting his own book and Rudolph Friml contributing the score (this went first to Ethel Merman and then to June Havoc as *Sadie Thompson*), and Richard Rodgers and Oscar Hammerstein II's proposed adaptation of Sheridan's *School for Scandal*. Lawrence informed all parties that she would not commit to anything before the following spring because she was set to return to Britain for ENSA duty.[57]

Toward the end of the journey, Lawrence jotted a postcard to the *New York Sun* reviewer: "Just passing Reno.... Wonderful trip. Everybody still aboard—we think. Look for a great season in Coast cities.... Come and meet us in Los Angeles."[58] Upon arriving on Friday morning, Lawrence was greeted by San Francisco Mayor Rossi, who presented her with a corsage. The next day she donated a pint for "British Blood," because the official day for the drive conflicted with *Lady in the Dark*'s opening. She excitedly wrote her husband, "Were you up in time to hear the broadcast? It was for the Red Cross blood bank. I see a possible 10,000 pints or more, plus my own measly one. I gave on Saturday, and I feel wonderful, though at the time I was terrified that I would not be able to fill the bottle. But it came out beautifully, a deep, dark American Beauty rose."[59] Proud of her campaign that resulted in fifteen thousand pints, Lawrence kept the blood-donation card in her wallet for the rest of her life.

The same day, the stage crew began to ready the theater for *Lady in the Dark*'s opening. The Light Opera season had begun with Cheryl Crawford's revival of *Porgy and Bess* and was slated to conclude with Rudolf Friml's operetta *The Firefly*. The financial arrangement for *Lady in the Dark* stipulated that the show would receive the first $18,000, the house the next $10,000, with the show and theater management splitting 70–30 takings over $28,000.[60]

The Curran Theatre's capacity crowd gave both Lawrence and Margaret Dale entrance applause. The crowd roared after the leading lady's sexy and lowdown rendition of "Jenny."[61] By Saturday, the box office had taken in nearly $32,500, which broke the house record for a weekly gross.[62] Lawrence appeared at the local Stage Door Canteen on Sunday and began her set accompanied by some of *Lady in the Dark*'s cast members. Afterward she relaxed in her suite at the Hotel Mark Hopkins and dashed off a note to the critic of the *New York Sun*: "This wonderful San Francisco is completely transformed since I was here last, when all was dead, locked in dock strikes. Now the city is a thriving mass of war workers, men and women, and Treasure Island, which was like a miracle at night during the Fair days of three years ago, is now entirely occupied by the Navy for all purposes.... In all its years San Francisco has probably never been more stirring and exciting.... And the Stage Door Canteen here is terrific!"[63]

Also in town was Moss Hart, who was touring Army Air Corps installations and taking notes for his new play. Lawrence lent him her hotel suite for an impromptu press conference. Hart gabbed on about Fairview Farm: "300 acres planted with alfalfa, corn and kindred crops, some 300 hogs, a kennel of sheep dogs and a house built in 1710." He then turned his attention to the type of analysis portrayed in *Lady in the Dark*. Impressed, the reporter from the *Oakland Tribune* wrote, "He is deadly serious about the virtues of psychoanalysis and not only can but does talk at some length and with great show of learning on the subject."[64]

Lady in the Dark's business built, and the second week concluded with a $33,000 gross. Soon offers began pouring in to extend the tour. Seattle and Portland proposed hosting it under the same guarantees covering the California bookings. The Curran offered to bring *Lady in the Dark* back after its Los Angeles engagement. Because both weeks in Los Angeles were already sold out, the Light Opera Association offered to extend the engagement by an extra week. After considering all the offers, Lawrence gave in to playing an additional week in Los Angeles. The final two weeks in San Francisco quickly sold out, and each took in an estimated $35,000.[65]

Lady in the Dark's L.A. opening was scheduled for June 22. As on the previous tour, the stage crew required two days for the move and setup. On Monday Lawrence was the guest of honor at a welcoming luncheon thrown by the Light Opera Association. The leading lady explained to those assembled that this would be *Lady in the Dark*'s last stop. Freed from her obligations, she would finally be able to take out an entertainment unit to soldiers on foreign duty. A columnist for the *Los Angeles Times* complained that Lawrence was becoming a civic institution and wished she would go back "to just being Lawrence."[66]

Variety reported that *Lady in the Dark*'s capacity audience at Philharmonic Auditorium contained "more than a scattering from the cinema's upper strata." Although the crowd stopped the show cold and demanded an encore after "The Saga of Jenny," none was forthcoming. Some of the show's more adult turns bothered Edwin Schallert of the *Los Angeles Times*. He warned Southern Californians, "Get prepared for some slightly shocking and risqué moments, for *Lady in the Dark* doesn't spare a few lusty, vigorous and ribald references when the occasion arises." Virginia Wright, one of the few women to review the show, made an insightful observation concerning *Lady in the Dark*'s subtext: "What psychoanalysis does for Liza is to convince her she should be less concerned with business and more interested in a cocky young advertising man. What psychoanalysis does for the *Lady* is to launch it into a wonderful spectacle of the subconscious."[67]

Lawrence spent her forty-fifth birthday performing a condensed version of *Lady in the Dark* for servicemen. In response to Ed Sullivan's birthday wish, she wired, THANKS FOR THE MEMORY IN YOUR SUNDAY COLUMN. I SPENT MY BIRTHDAY...WITH 1,500 OF OUR BOYS. STOP. WE CUT A CAKE AND MADE A WISH FOR THE INDEPENDENCE FOR WHICH WE'RE FIGHTING; NOT FOR THE INDEPENDENCE WE HAD ALL BEGUN TO TAKE FOR GRANTED. AFFECTIONATELY, G.L.[68]

During the final week, the backstage was awash with agents cutting deals. Metro signed both Hugh Marlowe and Walter Stane (a member of the dance corps); Columbia chose Willard Parker; and Universal snatched up half the dancers and all the circus costumes for *Ali Baba and the 40 Thieves*. Andrew Stone successfully convinced Lawrence to play Sarah Bernhardt on a new radio series for Revlon in the fall.[69] That Saturday *Lady in the Dark* completed its sold-out run with a $130,000 gross; the final week had topped each of the first two at approximately $45,000. For the first time in its six-year history, the Civic Opera Association had shown a profit.[70]

Lady in the Dark then disbanded, having played a gambler's dream of 777 performances: 16 during its Boston tryout, 462 at the Alvin Theatre, 160 during the eight-city tour, 83 at the Broadway Theatre, and 56 during the West Coast engagement. Only five of the principals, all actresses, played the entire run: Gertrude Lawrence, Margaret Dale, Jeanne Shelby, Ann Lee, and Gedda Petry. *Lady in the Dark*'s gross during its two seasons in New York had been $1,833,975.75; during the third season it reached $964,068.76. With the $285,000 Paramount deal, the grand total amounted to $3,083,044.51.[71] In spite of the insurance policies, Gertie had canceled only eleven performances because of ill health: three the first season and eight during the third (two in Philadelphia and six in New York).

Lawrence remained in L.A. a few days to confer with Louis Verneuil, author of *The Fabulous Life of Sarah Bernhardt*, about the possibility of a film based on the life of that actress. As she explained, "Everything that I have done on the stage has been transformed into a picture with some other star, so on this occasion I hope to do the picture first."[72] On July 13 she boarded the train for New York. After changing trains in Chicago on the 16th, she arrived in New York over the weekend. Unlike virtually all of her other activities during the past three years, this event was covered by a lone reporter.

7

Cultural Context

The context in which *Lady in the Dark* found itself by tour's end had drastically changed from the time of the show's genesis. World War II profoundly altered the lives of Americans, the reception of psychoanalysis, and the American musical theater. Marriage rates soared; unemployment plummeted. With men shipping off to war, women took their place in the workforce. Gender roles changed. Leisure and fashion were rethought. The freedom of the individual versus community responsibility was the topic of the hour. War bonds replaced savings bonds, ration stamps joined postage stamps, and victory gardens supplanted flower gardens. The social climate of 1943 was so far removed from that of 1940 that *Lady in the Dark* went from up-to-the-minute to out-of-date.

Nowhere is this degree of cultural shift more obvious than in a pair of *Playbill* cigarette advertisements, one from *Lady in the Dark*'s first season, the other from its third. The 1941 "Camel portrait" features Mrs. John Hyland Hemingway of New York. Photographed in a dinner dress by a famous American designer, Mrs. Hemingway's outfit is described as "a softly draped crêpe of Sahara beige and red, belted in leather." The rest of the ad reads: "'Like most women,' says Mrs. Hemingway, 'I love beautiful clothes. But my every-day interests are in the house...having a few friends in for dinner, planning the meals, doing the marketing.' In her spare time, Mrs. Hemingway does welfare work...enjoys fox-hunting...reads a great deal. 'Wherever I am, I usually have a package of Camels handy. Camel is the grandest-tasting cigarette...and so much milder!'"[1]

The 1943 "Camel portrait" depicts a nameless young man in the U.S. Air Force, standing in for American troops at home and abroad: "They've got what it takes! They know their engines . . . their machine guns—these men in the Air Force ground crews have what it takes 'to keep 'em flying.' His name can't be revealed, but you may remember him—the young mechanic who could always get your car started, somehow. He's still in overalls . . . still smokes Camels (they're the favorite of *all* the services) . . . only now he's grooming B-17E's instead of delux '43s."[2]

Lady in the Dark aged quickly because it tried to be so modern. Contemporary references littered its script and libretto, and the stage crew updated the mock-up covers of *Allure* every two weeks to keep pace with changing hemlines. *Lady in the Dark* was on the cutting edge of 1941 and sought to address delayed marriage, women in the workplace, and appropriate gender roles for men and women. With a cast of urban sophisticates and a New York setting, it exemplified a 1930s musical. Its dialogue was clipped and urbane, the repartee of café society. When *Lady in the Dark* opened, its foremost competition on the Great White Way was the equally adult *Pal Joey.* When it closed, its rival was the homespun *Oklahoma!* Broadway had indeed changed.

The reception of psychoanalysis took a turn as well. Regarded as exotic in the late 1930s, it was practiced by only the wealthiest. Daily treatment carried an annual price tag of $2,600 to $2,750 and lasted two years or so. (The median annual income in 1941 was just $2,000.) Most Americans associated psychoanalysis with "cultural modernism," which included relaxed sexual mores and left-of-center politics.[3] After Pearl Harbor, however, psychiatrists were drawn into the armed forces. Faced with the psychological trauma of American servicemen, they began to apply their theories to the common man. The war gave psychiatry legitimacy and a scientific toehold. By the time *Lady in the Dark* reached Detroit, one reviewer observed that the behavioral science had "invaded every corner, from the nursery to the draft boards."[4]

That *Lady in the Dark* found itself out of step with the very subjects it sought to address does not diminish the musical play's accomplishment. Rather, the shift in context brings into relief just how forward thinking the show had been. In hindsight, it is easy to trivialize *Lady in the Dark* as thoroughly Freudian or merely a lavish vehicle for Gertrude Lawrence. It is much more difficult to pinpoint that historical moment to which it spoke. For example, at the play's end Liza's willingness to share editorial responsibility with Charley and her offer to step aside and let him run the magazine strikes us today as sexist. But in what context was the ending originally understood? By mapping the various seismic shifts the United States underwent, both social and theatrical, one comes to appreciate *Lady in the Dark* as not just a topical show, but a progenitor of the concept musical.

Social Context

At first blush *Lady in the Dark*'s plot appears to reflect the war years, which saw many American women join the workforce. However, its portrayal of an unmarried, middle-aged working woman comes out of the Great Depression. That economic crisis had caused many women to seek employment. Most jobs available to them were low-paying ones in light manufacturing, service positions, or clerical work. Single women who took these jobs most often chose to live with their parents to conserve finances. Although many of these women felt a sense of obligation to help their parents financially, they also enjoyed some limited economic independence. By 1940 nearly 30 percent of all American women were employed.[5]

During the Depression, men were reluctant to marry if they believed they would be unable to provide for their family. Eking out a living took precedence over starting a family. As a result, the marriage rate fell to an all-time low in the early 1930s, and the national birthrate dropped from 25.1 per one thousand population in 1925 to 18.4 in 1936.[6] The concern over delayed marriage grew to such an extent that a 1937 Roper poll showed that one third of Americans favored government subsidies to assist young couples in marrying. The lingering effects of the Depression were felt as late as 1941, when 40 percent of all American families were still living below the poverty level.[7]

Although such economic hardship theoretically made it possible for both husbands and wives to work, the U.S. government, labor, business, and even Hollywood promoted women returning to the home after marriage and allowing husbands to be the sole breadwinners. Section 213 of the 1932 Economy Act required that when personnel reductions took place in the executive branch, married persons were to be the first discharged if their spouse was also a government employee. In the first year alone, 1,505 married persons (75 percent women) lost their jobs.[8] Eight states passed laws excluding married women from state employment. And by 1940 the proportion of communities that would hire a married woman as a teacher fell to 13 percent.[9]

Hollywood explored the dire consequences of married women working in such films as *Blonde Venus*, *Weekend Marriage*, *Female*, and *Housewife*.[10] In *Weekend Marriage*, Loretta Young tricks Norman Foster into marrying her by claiming to have another proposal, but then insists on continuing to work. The film documents the havoc this causes their marriage (an unmade bed, dirty laundry, eating dinner out of a can). Young arrives home one evening to find that her husband has ended up in jail for drunken and disorderly conduct. She bails him out, but he has met another woman in jail. Young subsequently meets another man while on assignment in St. Louis, but is called back to her husband, now on his deathbed. The attending doctor drives home Hollywood's message to the working wife:

> Let me give you a little advice. One way or another, a man will find a woman to look out for him not only when he's sick, but when he's well. That's something you so-called modern girls never seem to count on. You talk about freedom because you think it's something that men have and cherish. But they don't. They hate it. They get along best when they're not free. It's human nature. That's all. They need old-fashioned women looking after their health, nagging them into caution, feeding them properly and giving them families to live for. A great many of these women are just as well fitted as you are for business. But they don't want it. They put their talents to work instead in what people today think is a narrow sphere. Well, I don't think it's narrow. I think it's the most important sphere of all. Not much recognition in it, perhaps, no spectacular publicity, but it's built up nations before now and it will build them up again.[11]

After this, Young lies to her husband, telling him she has been fired from her job. When he asks, "What are you going to do?," she picks up an apron and proclaims, "Be a wife."

Society labeled women who tried to combine being a wife with a career greedy and selfish because they were potentially taking jobs from unemployed men. (In reality, most pink-collar jobs had little appeal for men.) Widespread was the belief that a career woman with an unemployed husband would undermine his power and authority over the family.[12] For example, a 1936 Gallup poll reported that 82 percent of the respondents agreed that wives with employed husbands should not work outside the home. By 1939 nearly 90 percent of the men polled held that women should not hold a job after marriage.[13] Similarly, a *Ladies' Home Journal* poll found that 90 percent of women believed that a wife should give up employment if her husband requested her to do so. As a consequence, by 1940 only 15 percent of married women were working outside the home.[14]

In *Lady in the Dark*, Liza has delayed marriage to pursue a career in journalism. In fact, all of the female members of *Allure*'s staff (receptionist, secretary, fashion editor, and columnist) are referred to as "Miss." Charley's harassing remarks, as offensive as they are today, when understood in terms of 1930s rhetoric, result from his emasculation at the hands of a female superior in the workplace. He calls her "Boss Lady" and taunts, "You married that desk long ago." Although Liza and Charley appear at first to be simply editor and advertising manager, his romantic designs conflict with prevailing notions of working women and marriage. This explains why, at the end of the play, Liza offers to step aside and allow Charley to be both boss and husband.

Pearl Harbor effectively ended the Depression. Almost overnight the unemployment rate of 14 percent dropped to nil. The lives of Americans, marriage rates, and gender roles all drastically changed. Many men enlisted or were drafted into the armed forces and shipped off to Europe, Africa, and Asia. The most significant openings for women were factory jobs, especially those in industries that were producing defense materials, such as ordnance plants, shipyards, and airplane factories. Women were also afforded their first opportunity to serve as members of the armed forces; 140,000 joined the Women's Army Auxiliary Corps (WAAC), 100,000 the Navy's WAVES, 23,000 the Marine Corps Women's Reserve, and 13,000 the women's reserve of the Coast Guard.[15] By 1945 the female labor force had increased 60 percent, and three quarters of these new workers were married.[16]

Like the Depression, WWII dramatically affected marriage and the national birthrate. Whereas in 1936 82 percent of Americans did not believe wives should work outside the home, six years later only 13 percent were still opposed.[17] By war's end 25 percent of married women were working. With unemployment nonexistent, marriage and birthrate trends of the early 1930s reversed. Over one million more families were started between 1940 and 1943 than could have been predicted during peacetime, and between 1940 and 1945 the birthrate rose from 19.4 to 24.5 per one thousand population. Americans rushed headlong into marriage and parenthood, even as the war separated husbands from wives.[18]

Hollywood portrayed women during WWII as both independent heroines and devoted girlfriends and wives. Films featuring women in the military included *So Proudly We Hail*, *Here Come the Waves*, and *Keep Your Powder Dry*. Women war workers appeared in such films as *Swing Shift Maisie*, *Government Girl*, *Meet the People*, and *Ladies Courageous*. Other films portrayed women as comrades, able to help one another in the absence of men; these include *Mrs. Miniver*, *Tender Comrade*, and *Since You Went Away*. All these movies helped give American women new images of themselves during wartime.

These very same films, however, advised women to return to the role of housewife after the war was over. In *Tender Comrade*, a series of flashbacks shows the relationship of one of the women and her husband, played by

Ginger Rogers and Robert Ryan. At the height of their squabbles over his working overtime, Rogers says, "You want money? Okay, I'll go out and get a job. Either you give up this night work and spend your evenings with me, or I'll go out and get myself a job."[19] Ryan acquiesces. Clearly her threat lay beyond the acceptable peacetime role for a married woman. In *This Is the Army*, the war year's most popular film, an army nurse wants a soldier, played by Ronald Reagan, to marry her. At the end of the film, they wed before he leaves to fight on foreign shores while she keeps the home fires burning.[20]

By its third season, *Lady in the Dark*, with a staff of single women postponing marriage in favor of careers, no longer fit the national profile. In Detroit a critic complained, "The author asks you seriously to regard the mental miseries of his heroine and this, let's say it, is hard to do with thousands dying on a dozen battlefields. These are not the days when one worries greatly over the nervous troubles of somebody safe and snug and with a fine job. The whole idea of *Lady in the Dark* seems paltry in the exact degree in which you are supposed to take it seriously. When a gasoline tank is a more appropriate place for a tempest than a tea-pot is nowadays."[21]

For a time Gertrude Lawrence's war-relief work helped bridge the world within the show and a world at war, but even she began to doubt the show's relevance. When asked by a Cincinnati reporter about her plans to take *Lady in the Dark* to London, she faltered, "I am not sure that English audiences at this time are prepared to be interested in a lady's inhibitions. They might say, 'A good day on the land is all she needs.' "[22]

Wartime opportunities for women also challenged traditional gender roles. A 1943 *Woman's Home Companion* assured readers that Rosie-the-Riveters could still be glamorous: "American women are learning how to put planes and tanks together, how to read blueprints, how to weld and rivet and make the great machinery of war production hum under skillful eyes and hands. But they're also learning how to look smart in overalls and how to be glamorous after work. They are learning to fulfill both the useful and the beautiful ideal."[23] Similarly, a wartime pamphlet warned working women not to lose their "femininity" while enjoying newfound freedoms.[24] Army publicity claimed that WAACs were "just as feminine as before they enlisted" and were, in fact, developing "new poise and charm."[25] When asked about her own fashion sense during wartime, Lawrence shared a pet peeve: "Women who appear in restaurants and nightclubs in uniform": "Do you think a man likes to dance with someone who looks like his major?...I don't! It just doesn't look right to see women in uniform at night...in the daytime, fine! I'm all for it, but at night men still want to see women looking sweet and feminine."[26]

Lady in the Dark's use of fashion to parallel psychological states went from remarkable to commonplace. The drama is predicated on the idea that the reason Liza dresses austerely and skips jewelry and makeup is her fear of competing as a woman. The suits she wears to the office and the gowns she dreams about mirror her journey from depression to mental health. In wartime, American women wore military uniforms and factory overalls during the day, but also appeared in dresses during their off-hours. Liza's alternation of clothing, unusual for 1941, became a reality for millions of women during the war.

Lady in the Dark's playbills reveal some of the tensions created by women's changing roles during the war. For example, a Chesterfield cigarette ad from 1942 featured Adrienne Ames, supervisor of canteen supplies for Bundles for Bluejackets, in full uniform, enjoying a cigarette. The Camel ad from the same issue, however, featured "Fashions for your off-duty hours" by designer Vera Maxwell. A perfume ad targeted women involved in the war effort: "You lead the conga line at USO dances. You organize bond drives, scrap drives, charity drives. Your whole set follows your lead! Your perfume is, obviously, Varva's 'Follow Me'... the fragrance that beckons, leads, lasts!"[27]

The war changed men's roles as well. They found themselves living, working, and fighting in all-male environments. The Navy and Army instituted buddy systems for some units, in which pairs of men were responsible for each other's welfare. In New York enlisted men banded together to perform Irving Berlin's all-male revue *This Is the Army* and impersonated actresses during the celebrated "I Left My Heart at the Stage Door Canteen." *Theatre Arts* magazine pictured two "female impersonators extraordinary" from the show. They were Private Alan Manson (decked out as the first lady of the Stage Door Canteen, Jane Cowl) and Corporal Nelson Barclift, who had originated the role of Tom in *Lady in the Dark* (Figures 45 and 46).[28]

Altered gender roles certainly had a bearing on how audiences read the character of Russell Paxton. Although *Allure*'s flamboyant staff photographer appears to be a gay stereotype today, the role drew on the prevailing male "invert" profile. Two influential and independent studies from the late 1930s closely linked gender with sexual orientation. George W. Henry, in a preliminary report on a study of one hundred male and female homosexuals in 1937, concluded that significant deviations from established gender roles were directly linked to the development of overt homosexuality.[29]

A year prior, Lewis M. Terman and Catharine Cox Miles developed gender norms for men and women through their Attitude-Interest Analysis

Test.[30] To validate it, they compared scores gathered from "normal" test groups with those of male and female homosexuals. They in turn defined two categories of homosexuals based on sexual practices. "Invert," or passive, homosexuals were classified as "true" homosexuals because of their gender-role deviation, whereas "pervert," or active, homosexuals were considered to be experimenting with "new types of sexual gratification." In other words, true homosexuality manifested itself in gender-role inversion.

Russell's effeminate manner, loquaciousness, and attention to clothing conform to Terman and Miles's description of the invert or passive male homosexual. In one scene Russell even reclines with a lady's evening cape thrown over him and a woman's hat over his face. The character's cross-gender identification was underscored in a letter from Gershwin to Weill concerning Danny Kaye's replacement: "Regarding Rex O'Malley I'm inclined to agree with you that his performance may be criticised. Obviously he is too lady-like for the lady-like character and may make the character far too realistic."[31]

Homosexual characters were certainly nothing new on Broadway: audiences back in 1896 had seen two women passionately hug and kiss on stage (one of them under a magic spell). During the following intermission ushers reportedly offered ice water to audience members on the verge of fainting.[32] Lesbians, however, proved to be more palatable than gay men. In 1927 the first play to introduce such characters was shut out of New York. *Variety* described Mae West's *The Drag* in its Bridgeport tryout as "a dramatization of a wild party given by a rich pervert and bedizened men friends." Seventy-six producers met to oppose bringing *The Drag* to town. New York legislators went a step further by amending the penal code to prohibit plays "depicting or dealing with, the subject of sex degeneracy, or sex perversion." Section 1140A of the criminal code warned theater-owners that playhouses could be padlocked for a year if they rented to a producer of a show that "would tend to the corruption of youth or others."[33]

Although homosexual characters continued to appear in plays, New York drama critics during the 1930s carefully avoided references to them, which would have alerted law enforcement. Once a show was successful, however, critics were less tight-lipped. In response, State Senator John J. Dunnigan authored a bill in 1937 proposing to make the commissioner of licenses a political appointee. Such a change would have made the commissioner as powerful on Broadway as the Lord Chamberlain's Office was in the West End. Gathering sixty-three thousand signatures, the theater community successfully petitioned Governor Herbert Lehman to veto the bill.[34] Nevertheless, the state penal code still prohibited "the subject of sex degeneracy or sex perversion" on stage.

Of the nine metropolitan reviews that appeared the day after *Lady in the Dark* opened, six were mum about Russell Paxton. One reviewer obliquely referred to the character as the "not-all-there-photographer." Two reviewers went somewhat further, albeit cautiously. One described Danny Kaye as "immensely amusing, less in the somewhat lavender business of a style photographer than in his hilarious doings in the circus fantasy." Another praised him for managing to make "a swishy magazine photographer...both bearable and funny." He added, "I should say that his chief virtue is that he indicates to you pretty clearly that he is only acting."[35] Such a comment attempted to distance Kaye's portrayal from the actual gay men who had appeared in Mae West's *The Drag* and *Pleasure Man* (the latter was shut down *during* its second performance).

Once *Lady in the Dark* was a smash, however, the very same critics were more forthcoming. The reviews for the second season referred to the character as "the precious Russell Paxton," "the swishing Russell Paxton," "the ebullient photographer," "the giddy, sissy photographer," "the daffodil photographer," "a not-so-masculine magazine fritillary," and "the photographer who would wince if Flit were mentioned."[36]

After Pearl Harbor, Russell's character gained an added dimension in light of "Momism." Philip Wylie, in his 1942 best seller, *Generation of Vipers*, claimed the condition resulted from wives who, absent their husbands, smothered their children with affection and protection.[37] The fear was that these women would render their sons weak and potential homosexuals. Wylie claimed that Momism could potentially cripple the United States, making it vulnerable to enemy takeover. In *Lady in the Dark*'s second act, Russell calls Alison a "stinking blinking ruddy bloody bitch!" Charley rejoins, "I always thought you were fond of your mother, Russell."

Today the use of cross-gender identification to signal sexual orientation (in Russell's case) or neurosis (in Liza's) appears primitive. Lawrence Kubie's theory of "The Drive to Become Both Sexes," however, comprehensively lays out the use of gender inversion, or dysphoria, in *Lady in the Dark*. First presented as a paper before the American Psychoanalytic Association in 1954, the article did not see print until a year after Kubie's death in 1974. In the article, he admitted his reluctance to publish it: "I realize that to emphasize this concept brings me into conflict with artists and indeed with almost all creative people in the world, although more in the arts and letters than in the sciences. Time and again it has blocked me from carrying this project through to completion, but now I feel that it can no longer be postponed."[38]

In Hart's play, Liza is identified in masculine terms, from those severely tailored suits to her "man's desk." Charley reinforces the portrayal by calling her "Sir." When leaving for *Town and Country*, he tells her, "If we ever need a good man over there, I'll make you an offer." Liza's masculine business persona contrasts with her feminine dream self. According to Kubie, "The unconscious drive is *not* to give up the gender to which one was born but to supplement or complement it by developing side by side with it the opposite gender." Liza's opposing identities are delineated by sleeping and waking states, which, according to Kubie, is typical. He notes that the outward signs of the drive can be found in occupational choices and "acted out and lived out through clothes."[39] In Liza's case, she is the editor of a successful women's fashion magazine who dresses the part only in her dreams.

Kubie describes how the drive is rooted in critical childhood events that may prevent a child from "emulating either parent wholeheartedly." As the audience observes in Liza's final session, when she was four her father told her that she would never be a beauty like her mother. Kubie addresses what he feels are the most characteristic manifestations of the drive. The first describes Liza's relationship with Kendall: "an angry and perpetual search for a parental figure who is an idealized father and mother combined, to replace one who has 'failed.'" For Liza, her success as *Allure*'s editor has not produced fulfillment but instead has put her into a double bind. Kubie explains: "These men and women could not accept success either in their professional lives or in their love lives because to them success meant either, 'Now you are a man and cannot be a woman' or 'Now you are a woman and can never be a man.' Each step in the process was punctuated by rage, panic, and depression."[40]

In the penultimate section of his article, Kubie takes a "Detour into Biography and Fiction" for illustrations of the drive, but conspicuously avoids references to *Lady in the Dark*. Instead, he refers to the show only in the scientific portion of the article. This reinforces his claim from the Random House preface published some thirty years earlier, that "as a case history [*Lady in the Dark*] is wholly accurate." Among the case histories discussed in "The Drive to Become Both Sexes," a possible model for Liza Elliott might be found in Kubie's first paper for the American Psychoanalytic Association in 1932. "Transvestitism in a Teen-Age Girl" documented his analysis of a fifteen-year-old girl who wore riding breeches and boots during the day but formal ball gowns at night. Because the girl's family ended the analysis prematurely, Kubie never published the paper.[41] But the daytime masculine persona alternating with a nighttime feminine one parallels Hart's lady in the dark.

Nevertheless, some of Hart's associates regarded *Lady in the Dark* as autobiographical. Irene Sharaff, who had been the costumer for five of Hart's shows, told Weill that the playwright could only write about himself. In a subsequent letter to Lenya, Weill wholeheartedly agreed. Producer Billy Rose even referred to Hart as "poor little Laddy in the Dark."[42] Obviously there are parallels: Liza and her creator are at the height of their careers and about the same age. Each success plunges them into depression instead of fulfillment. Both suffer from insomnia. But how does Liza, a woman choosing among three men, stand in for the bachelor playwright who created her? The answer can again be found in Kubie's theory.

Unquestionably Liza possesses the drive to become both sexes (remember Whipple's interview with Kubie, where "Dr. K." refers to her "bi-sexual disposition"). Her struggle, according to Kubie, is not in choosing among the three suitors, but rather in those "conflicting yearnings of her own nature."[43] He traced how neurotic tendencies developed in childhood (as dramatized at the end of Hart's play) continue into adulthood: "Whenever anyone works under the whiplash of unsolved unconscious conflicts, whether he is painting a picture, writing a play, pursuing a scientific discovery, or making a million dollars, the individual is prone to work with desperation. If there is a failure, he blames unhappiness on his failure. But, to his amazement and dismay, he discovers that depression may follow success no less than failure. Basically this is because success also leaves his deeper problems unsolved."[44]

Kubie linked the drive to become both sexes with gender identity, although he admitted that it manifested itself differently in men and women: "Girls and women are actively encouraged to be male as well as female: in dress, activities, occupations, hobbies, interests, speech, and manner." Conversely, "The drive is almost wholly repressed in men except for some overt homosexuals, transvestites, and 'hippies.'"[45] Hart's play includes male and female manifestations of the drive through the characters of Russell and Liza. Although they do not possess the same sexual orientation, their opposing identities (an "effeminate" man and a "mannish" woman) set Kubie's theory in bold relief.

Hart's biographer suggests that Hart began psychoanalysis because of questions concerning his own sexual identity. Homosexuality in the 1940s was classified as a mental illness, and Kubie counseled a number of patients (including Vladimir Horowitz and Tennessee Williams) whom he attempted to "cure."[46] Although Hart's self-portrayal in *Lady in the Dark* is probably not restricted solely to the title character, Danny Kaye vividly remembered that the closed dress rehearsal when Hart played Liza was "the greatest performance, I think, ever done on the New York stage."[47] Perhaps the combination of Russell and Liza is like the god Janus: Russell looks back at the unrepressed and evidently unhappy life that Hart was attempting to leave behind, while Liza looks forward to the life that could begin anew once the repressed drive has been brought to light.

Theatrical Context

Lady in the Dark came at the end of a bleak period for Broadway. The 1920s had introduced a series of outstanding composers and lyricists: the Gershwin brothers, Rodgers and Hart, Oscar Hammerstein II, Cole Porter, Vincent Youmans, and DeSylva, Brown, and Henderson. Along with Jerome Kern and Irving Berlin, these men created what were usually light frothy musicals or operettas that matched the giddy and euphoric age. The stock market crash resulted in real competition from film musicals, as Hollywood lured away many of the most talented creative teams. Despite the serious and experimental nature of some 1930s musicals, the economic realities of the Depression had a profound and lasting effect on Broadway.

The 1940–1941 season was rich with evergreen dramas and comedies. *Tobacco Road*, *Life with Father*, and *The Man Who Came to Dinner* were all still running when the season began. (*Tobacco Road*, which opened in 1933, would close that year with a record number of performances for a straight play: 3,182.)[48] The hit straight plays of that season included *My Sister Eileen*, *Arsenic and Old Lace*, *The Corn Is Green*, and *Claudia*. Most tended to be lightweight in an effort to boost morale.[49] The ravages of the Depression and competition from Hollywood were still apparent, as fewer than a hundred new musicals and plays opened that season. (Before the crash, there had typically been 250 or more per season.) Of the twelve musicals that debuted, half were revues. Only three of the book musicals were bona fide hits. Cole Porter's *Panama Hattie* became the first book show since the onset of the Depression to run more than five hundred performances. This slim excuse for a musical could not have prepared audiences for the openings less than a month apart of two daring and innovative shows: *Pal Joey* and *Lady in the Dark*.

Rodgers and Hart's *Pal Joey*, which opened on Christmas 1940, is *Lady in the Dark*'s tougher, poorer cousin. The similarities between the shows are striking. Both involve a past-their-prime married partner having an affair with the title character. The mature lovers, Vera Simpson and Kendall Nesbitt, respectively, each establish their younger flames, Joey Evans and Liza Elliott, in business. Although *Pal Joey* portrays the underside of the city and *Lady in the Dark* its upper crust, both were shot through with topical references. The two numbers that were most up to date, "Zip" and "Hux-ley," were both sung by a character in some state of undress:

> Zip! Walter Lippmann wasn't brilliant today.
> Zip! Will Saroyan ever write a great play?

Zip! I was reading Schopenhauer last night.
    Zip! And I think Schopenhauer was right.
            ("Zip" from *Pal Joey*)
Epstein says you simply have to pose for him.
    Here's the key to the Island of Tobago.
Du Pont wants you wearing the new hose for him.
    Can you christen a battleship in San Diego?
            ("Huxley" from *Lady in the Dark*)

Young, naïve love interests complicate both plots, but in neither Vera's nor Kendall's case does the love triangle resolve favorably. At the final curtain of *Pal Joey*, the title character, a gigolo, fails to change his destructive behavior by literally singing the same song to another girl. At *Lady in the Dark*'s curtain, Liza nearly makes the same mistake by choosing the wrong man. However, through psychoanalysis she has been able to see the negative pattern in her relationships. Liza finds her way out of the darkness—a darkness that Joey cannot escape.

Critics recognized the common themes of these two musicals, which attempted in different ways to reformulate the function of music and drama. Brooks Atkinson noted that both were moving in the direction of "a drama in which the music and the splendors of the production rise spontaneously out of the heart of the drama."[50] Sidney Whipple made a similar observation, but pointed out an important difference: "Its [*Lady in the Dark*'s] book, like that of *Pal Joey*, is a piece of realism and not merely happy make-believe, despite the fact that at least two-thirds of it is sheer fantasy."[51] Critics and audiences found Joey's harshness and the show's bleak conclusion difficult to stomach. (Atkinson asked, "Can you draw sweet water from a foul well?")[52] Both presented possibilities and directions for the American musical theater, but neither inspired an immediate successor.

Instead, they were joined the next season by entertainment designed to keep the public's mind off the war. A revue, farce, and failed operetta, and vaudeville shows accounted for half the season's musical openings. Midway through the 1941–1942 season, most critics had pronounced the year the worst in Broadway history.

The *successful* straight plays were, without exception, light entertainment. At least four tried to interest audiences in topical stories about the war. The most popular of these was *The Wookey*, set in the London Blitz with actual sound effects recorded by the BBC. After the realities of war had been brought home that December, *The Wookey* fizzled—who wanted to pay for a ticket to see the war reenacted? Instead, audiences clamored for comedies such as *Blithe Spirit*, *Junior Miss*, and *Spring Again*. Thrillers, such as *Angel Street* and *Uncle Harry*, were also high up on the list. At season's end, the New York Drama Critics' Circle could not find one play worthy of an award. It was obvious that playgoers were paying only for escapist fare.

Lady in the Dark would seem to fit that bill, and indeed it flourished in the half season after Pearl Harbor. But it began to find itself out of step during the 1942–1943 season. That is when the theater began in earnest to reflect the war experience. Writers experimented by combining topical plots with patriotic themes. A number of plays about the war opened that season, but most were not hits.[53] The season concluded with a single performance of *The Army Play-by-Play*, which featured five one-act plays from an enlisted men's contest.

Three comedies that all ran simultaneously with *Lady in the Dark*'s re-engagement dealt with the war obliquely by setting their plots on U.S. soil. *Doughgirls* was a romp about three women who share a hotel suite in wartime Washington, DC. It hit pay dirt with the winning combination of topicality and escapist fare and ran up 671 performances. *Janie* had its young heroine throwing a party for Pvt. Dick Lawrence and his friends from a nearby camp. The comedy started slowly but went on to play 642 performances. *Three's a Family*, which concerned pregnant wartime mothers who share a small apartment, played 497 performances.

Two war-related dramas were also highly successful. *Tomorrow the World*, which chalked up 500 performances, was about a boy raised by the Nazis who had killed his father. The boy comes to the United States, where he tries to spy for the Germans, but his American relatives enable him to see the error of his ways. *The Eve of St. Mark*, at 307 performances, told the story of an upstate New York family whose oldest son enlisted in the Army. The play follows his relationship with a neighbor girl he met on his day off. The climax of the play occurs in a cave in the Philippines, where he and his comrades attempt to defend an island from the Japanese. At play's end, he is missing in action and his two brothers have now enlisted.

Musicals also proved to be a successful medium for combining topical plots with patriotic themes. The season's first big hit was Irving Berlin's all-soldier revue *This Is the Army*. An updating of the WWI show *Yip Yip Yaphank*, the new revue featured Berlin himself reprising "Oh, How I Hate to Get Up in the Morning." Intended as a benefit for the Army Emergency Relief Fund, the show played only twelve weeks before touring, but every performance sold out with standees.[54] Of the five new book musicals that season, only two were hits. *Something for the Boys* reunited Ethel Merman with a Cole Porter score. The book involves three cousins who inherit a

Texas ranch, which is subsequently appropriated by a nearby army base. The topical setting, with Merman belting out Porter's tunes, enabled *Something for the Boys* to run for more than a year.

A *New York Times* article reported that in the eighteen months since Pearl Harbor, thirty plays with war themes had hit the boards. However, only eight of these were successes, of which five dated from the 1942–1943 season. Broadway was learning slowly by trial and error: if a show was too opulent and escapist, it was out of sync with the times. Those were precisely the charges leveled against *Lady in the Dark* while on tour. On the other hand, if a show was too realistic and dramatic in its portrayal of war, it failed as entertainment.

In the *Times* article, Helen Hayes described the additional problem of satisfying the actors: "I couldn't personally be interested in doing pure escapist plays now. I can't tell you why. I can see the tremendously important place of escapist entertainment for men and women who work so hard these days, particularly at wartime jobs. But I personally can't ignore the agony of the war even for three hours of performance an evening—I couldn't." Shepard Traube, a producer and director, concluded, "We must find out what we are going to die for or not die for, and state or restate that cogently in the theatre."[55]

Americans affirmed what they were willing to defend with the season's second successful book musical: *Oklahoma!* Richard Rodgers and Oscar Hammerstein II's historic show opened on March 31. Five days later its ads appeared in *Lady in the Dark*'s playbill. Advertised as "The Theatre Guild's New Musical Play," the artwork showed a cowgirl throwing a lasso around the work's title surrounded by musical notes and stars. *Oklahoma!* ran long after *Lady in the Dark* closed, racking up an unprecedented 2,248 performances. The statistics are staggering: by 1948, 8 million people had seen *Oklahoma!*, more than 500,000 cast albums had been sold, 2 million copies of its sheet music had been purchased, it had grossed $7 million in New York alone, and it had earned $1 million each for Rodgers and Hammerstein.[56]

Unlike 1930s musicals that had urban settings, *Oklahoma!* celebrated America's heartland and frontier. Rodgers and Hammerstein set the pastoral tone of the work in the opening moments of the show. From offstage Curly sings a song celebrating the bright, golden haze of the land and the resources of the American landscape. "Oh, What a Beautiful Mornin'" is a veritable hymn to America's spacious skies and fruited plains. Whereas *Lady in the Dark* chronicles urban sophisticates, each idiosyncratic, *Oklahoma!* recounts a tight-knit community of like-minded people.[57] Aunt Eller refers to them as "territory folks." Emblematic of their values are the two props specified for the opening: a brass-banded butter churn and a quilt on the clothesline. The churn alludes to the hard physical labor of America's pioneers, and the quilt to the collaborative effort of a quilting bee.

Lady in the Dark and other 1930s musicals depicted modern America and contained topical references (Cole Porter's "You're the Top" is a virtual litany of them). Conversely, the dramatization of Oklahoma represents a simple life practically devoid of the modern, except as portrayed in the show's third song, "Kansas City." It metaphorically distances the territory community from the evils of the big city. Will Parker tells the residents about women stripping in a burlesque hall and the syncopated music of "colored fellers." The implication is that such people are not part of Oklahoma's landscape and do not belong there.

Oklahoma! would appear to have nothing to do with World War II, but it had everything to do with the United States in 1943. The show drew on American archetypes: the frontier, a land to be settled through common ideals; the folk, a community of citizens who uphold justice; the hero, who fights hard and wins the girl; and the future, full of endless and bountiful possibilities. *Oklahoma!* articulated what Americans were willing to go to war to defend: that sense of community, those common ideals, and the hope of a bright tomorrow.

Oklahoma! also caught the wave of America's optimism about the future. In January 1943, a National Opinion Research Center poll showed that a majority of Americans felt that the country had entered the final throes of the war: 42.1 percent predicted that Mussolini could be stopped in six months, 47.6 percent that Hitler would be defeated in 1943, and 35 percent that in one additional year Japan would be brought to its knees.[58] In addition, domestic conditions were improving: for the first time since 1929, the commodity price index topped 100. At the end of *Oklahoma!*, the imminence of statehood stood in for the bright future of a postwar America.

By the summer of 1943, *Lady in the Dark*'s run was finished. Although it could have continued its West Coast tour, Lawrence was ready to call it quits. She wanted to devote herself fully to the war effort. In 1944 the Gertrude Lawrence Unit of ENSA toured England, France, and Belgium. Two months after D-Day, her unit was one of the very first to play in France. Lawrence wrote her account of the tour for an autobiography, which was published the next year as *A Star Danced*. She followed that up with a USO tour of Pacific naval bases. Tour directors and chaplains, however, banned her performance of "The Saga of Jenny." Demands from servicemen finally enabled her to sing it, but without the bumps or grinds. The troops rebelled. Finally the Pentagon issued the following directive: "Miss Lawrence may do the bumps, *provided she does them sideways*."[59]

Back in the States, *Oklahoma!*'s brand of American folklore caught on, and the only book musicals to play more than a hundred performances during the 1944–1945 season all dealt with Americana: *Bloomer Girl*, *On the Town*, *Up in Central Park*, and *Carousel*. A revue called *Swing Out Sweet Land* billed itself as a "Salute to American Folk and Popular Music" and celebrated the country's musical heritage. The America of all these shows is that of Norman Rockwell and Carl Sandburg.

Because of the direction the American musical theater took during the late 1940s, *Oklahoma!* has often been hailed as the first modern musical. It consequently has overshadowed the experimental musicals of the 1930s, shows such as *Of Thee I Sing*, *Porgy and Bess*, *The Cradle Will Rock*, *Pal Joey*, and *Lady in the Dark*. Broadway criticism has a tendency to equate the success of a show with its artistic merit, the assumption being that the shows that run the longest must therefore be the most innovative and influential. However, many of the claims made about *Oklahoma!* do not hold up under scrutiny.

Some have claimed that Rodgers and Hammerstein were the first to dispense with an opening production number or Chorus line. Certainly the opening moments of *Oklahoma!* are striking: Aunt Eller alone on stage churning butter and Curly singing from the wings. However, the innovation had been Lynn Riggs's, whose 1931 play, *Green Grow the Lilacs*, on which the musical is based, commenced with Curly singing offstage a folksong that begins, "As I walked out one bright sunny morning." Not only did *Lady in the Dark* do away with an opening production number, but it also dispensed with the overture. When the music finally did start after pages of dialogue, a single clarinet played two notes to initiate humming.

Probably the most often repeated claim is that *Oklahoma!* was the first "integrated musical," in that all of the elements of the production—script, songs, lyrics, and dances—are fused into a continuous whole with songs growing out of character and plot, without any extraneous specialty numbers. Rodgers accomplished this musically by limiting the number of songs and repeating them often. "Oh, What a Beautiful Mornin'" is heard three times in the first scene alone. "The Surrey with the Fringe on Top" is reprised twice by Curly himself. Nearly every first-act number is repeated at least twice before they are all heard again during the ballet. By reprising numbers immediately and having the orchestra play them as underscoring, Rodgers gave the impression of a continuously unfolding story.[60]

Some of what has been attributed to *Oklahoma!* can actually be traced to *Lady in the Dark*. Its dream sequences are integral to the show; without them the musical play collapses. Dr. Brooks's discussions with Liza following each of the sequences make no sense without first having experienced the dream. Remove *Oklahoma!*'s score and one is, for all intents and purposes, back to *Green Grow the Lilacs*, a play that is understandable with or without its folk songs. Unlike *Oklahoma!*'s dream ballet, which was appended to the first act, *Lady in the Dark*'s dream sequences are integral to the plot and advance the drama. After dreaming about the consequences of accepting Kendall's marriage proposal, Liza is able to decline his offer the next day and go out with Randy instead.

Hammerstein originally wanted *Oklahoma!*'s dream ballet to center around a circus, in which Curly would be cast as the ringmaster and Laurey as a bareback rider; echoes of the *Circus Dream* are obvious. Agnes De Mille convinced the creators to allow her to explore the consequences of Laurey accompanying Jud to the box social. Like *Lady in the Dark*'s dream sequences two years earlier, it provided the audience with a window into the heroine's dream world. Although the ballet foreshadowed the end of the show, it did not advance the story.

Oklahoma!'s musical director jettisoned the practice of having the Chorus sing only the melody. Instead, he incorporated part-singing in the operetta tradition (note that Weill had the Chorus sing "Girl of the Moment" in six-part harmony). Rather than a presentational style of performance, where the actor or actress sings directly to the audience (such as Lawrence's rendition of "The Saga of Jenny"), most numbers in *Oklahoma!* were staged with one character singing to another. The director, Rouben Mamoulian, recalled, "For the last two weeks before we opened *Oklahoma!* on Broadway, no one even spoke to me. Rodgers thought I was destroying his music. He couldn't accept the singers having their backs to the audience. Everyone wanted me to restage it as an ordinary musical comedy. I refused, and they didn't even invite me to the opening night party."[61]

Oklahoma!'s innovation was neither integration, Laurey's dream ballet, the Chorus's multipart singing, nor even the director's innovative staging. Rather, Rodgers and Hammerstein's real accomplishment was to reinvent operetta. In keeping with most examples of the genre, it has a sentimental, romantic, and relatively serious story. As a result, gone are the specialty numbers (like "Tschaikowsky"), the cynical edge, up-to-the-minute dance idioms and orchestrations, and the laugh lines of 1930s musical comedy. Instead, there was an emphasis on earnest, lyric singing from the principals. A nostalgic look back at America's heartland replaced the foreign, exotic setting of most operettas. Rather than dukes, princes, and kings, *Oklahoma!* celebrated territory folk. The spoken Okie dialect, stylized backdrops inspired from the paintings of Thomas Hart Benton and Grant Wood, and period costumes worked together to create the Western motif. Classifying *Oklahoma!* as an operetta is in keeping with the original production's critical reception. In the *Times*, Lewis Nichols concluded, "In addition to being a musical play, *Oklahoma!* could be called a folk operetta."[62]

Lady in the Dark and *Oklahoma!* are diametrically opposed in subject matter, form, and style. Hart and Weill intentionally separated the music from the drama, whereas Rodgers and Hammerstein attempted to integrate them. *Lady in the Dark* portrayed a businesswoman undergoing psychoanalysis; *Oklahoma!* mythologized the American heartland at the turn of the century. With its urban setting, *Lady in the Dark* was contemporary and modern; with a rural setting, *Oklahoma!* looked back to a bygone era. *Lady in the Dark* dispensed with the typical musical comedy plot (boy meets girl) for a Freudian allegory; *Oklahoma!* revived the typical operetta formula with its two love triangles.[63] The divergent style of the works can be distilled from two American rituals: the community box social at noon for *Oklahoma!* and the cocktail verandah party at 10:00 P.M., as drama critic Harold Clurman so aptly characterized the milieu of *Lady in the Dark*.[64]

Despite these fundamental differences, there are a few parallels. For example, both were subtitled "musical plays." For Hart and Weill, this captured the work's hybrid form and parodying of operetta. For Rodgers and Hammerstein, the term was a serious throwback to romantic operetta (Lorenz Hart even predicted after *Oklahoma!*'s opening-night party, "The thing will run longer than [Romberg's] *Blossom Time*").[65] In addition, both works invoke the metaphor of light. For *Lady in the Dark*, light represents mental health at the end of a psychological journey. In *Oklahoma!* sunshine represents the lifeblood of a community tied to the land. Both are about beginnings: Liza in the last scene finally understands her past and is poised to begin a new life; *Oklahoma!* is about the beginning of a new day, a new marriage, and a new state. The two works are bookends, but bookends facing in opposite directions. *Lady in the Dark* represents a daring re-evaluation of the function of music and drama—the last of the 1930s most experimental musicals. *Oklahoma!* proved to be a blueprint for how to meld music and drama—the first of many 1940s "integrated" musicals.

Just as Rodgers and Hammerstein set out to replicate the formula of *Oklahoma!*, Hart, Weill, and Gershwin actively pursued ideas to capitalize on *Lady in the Dark*. During the first season, Weill had written to Gershwin, "Moss insists that we shouldn't do just another musical comedy, but something on the line or let's say in the form of *Lady*—and, as you know, that is very hard to find. . . . We both feel that it would be very important to continue the form [of] *Lady* as soon as possible with another show, because otherwise it would be an isolated experiment."[66] At one point Weill and Hart were actively brainstorming three times a week, with Weill relaying their ideas to Gershwin. However, the three could never agree on the same idea. After Pearl Harbor, Gershwin suggested suspending their effort: "I feel about this period exactly as I did ten years ago when we were in the midst of the worst depression the country had ever known and at the same time George and I had the biggest hit we had ever had—*Of Thee I Sing*. I felt then that it was a tough period for any new show unless it was so extraordinary that it could overcome the prevailing gloom.... It's ten years later now and there's a war instead of an economic depression and we have a hit. Let's not do anything unless we feel it's something that *has* to be done."[67]

As a consequence, Hart went off to write and direct and Army Air Corps play, *Winged Victory*, which followed three young men from Mapleton, Ohio, from their enlistment through combat.[68] With a company of 300 servicemen, fifteen wives of soldiers, and twenty-four professional actresses, *Winged Victory* played the entire season for 212 performances. Modeled on the success of *This Is the Army*, *Winged Victory* reportedly earned more than $10 million for the Army.

Simultaneously, Weill embarked on a musical adaptation of F. Anstey's novella *The Tinted Venus*. Originally intended to be, in Weill's words, an "'opéra comique' on the Offenbach line," *One Touch of Venus* turned out to be almost a regulation musical comedy.[69] With its lighthearted plot and unabashed love story, it came as close to Cole Porter in its style and subject as Weill was capable ("Speak Low" even recalled Porter's beguines). Agnes De Mille's two ballets (one of the dream variety) capitalized on her success with *Oklahoma!* With Mary Martin in the title role, *One Touch of Venus* played 567 performances before heading out on tour.

Weill and Gershwin collaborated on the score to the film *Where Do We Go from Here?* It featured Fred MacMurray doing his bit for the war by collecting scrap metal and washing dishes at a USO canteen. While scavenging, he discovers a lamp that contains a genie. MacMurray uses one of his three wishes to get into combat, but ends up in Washington's army at Valley Forge. The second wish lands him in the Navy, but this time on Columbus's ship about to discover America. The third wish is the charm, and he finds himself in the modern-day army. The fantasy segments of *Where Do We Go from Here?* provided Weill and Gershwin the chance to write extended musical sequences modeled on the dreams of *Lady in the Dark*.

Weill's desire to compose an operetta in the European tradition came to pass with *The Firebrand of Florence*. Based on a 1924 play, the story concerned the escapades of Benvenuto Cellini. At the Boston tryout, George S. Kaufman attempted to play doctor, but to no avail. The production was leaden, and *Song of Norway*, an operetta presented earlier that season, had already captured the best vocalists and audience. *The Firebrand of Florence* closed after a mere forty-three performances. It marked the last collaboration of Weill and Gershwin and dashed their hopes of recapturing their previous success.

Moss Hart's next effort, *Christopher Blake*, followed the decision of a twelve-year-old boy who must choose whether he will live with his mother or his father following their divorce. A series of dream sequences depicts the boy's unconscious. Essentially a "Child in the Dark," *Christopher Blake* owed more to *Lady in the Dark* than just its revolving turntable. But without music to articulate the unconscious, the play died.

Because Hart, Weill, and Gershwin never collaborated again, *Lady in the Dark* remains, as Weill feared, an isolated experiment. He liked to think of it as a stepping-stone to his "American opera," *Street Scene*: "When I arrived in this country, in 1935, another dream began to get hold of me: the dream of an American opera.... In the different Broadway shows which I wrote during the following years I tried to make music an integral part of the plays; especially in *Lady in the Dark*, with its three little one-act operas, I continued the story in musical fantasies when the realistic story stopped."[70] Weill's observation that music played an integral part of *Lady in the Dark* is indisputable. The change of ink color in the Random House edition signified music's integral, but separate, function.

On Broadway, music typically functions in one of two realms. The first, referred to as either diegetic music or a "prop song," is when the situation demands or occasions singing.[71] Examples include Magnolia in *Show Boat* performing "After the Ball" or Adelaide in *Guys and Dolls* leading "A Bushel and a Peck." In both instances, it is clear that the characters and also those around them on stage know that they are singing. The songs, like props, form part of the scenery. The second realm is when music expresses a character's emotional state and for which the audience must suspend disbelief. Song is accepted here as either heightened speech or an internal monologue. Examples of nondiegetic music include Laurey warning Curly that "People Will Say We're in Love" in *Oklahoma!* or Tony excitedly repeating Maria's name in *West Side Story*. There is no rational reason why these characters should be singing and no indication that they realize that they have broken into song.

In *Lady in the Dark*, "My Ship" is a good example of diegetic music. In Liza's first appointment with Dr. Brooks, he asks her to hum its melody. In the concluding scene, Liza and Charley are aware that they are singing (Liza: "Why—do *you* know that song too?" Charley: "Yeah—haven't heard it since I was a kid, though."). Maggie watches *and* listens in amazement as the curtain descends.

But what about *Lady in the Dark*'s dream sequences? With the exception of "Mapleton High Choral" and "The Princess of Pure Delight," they are neither diegetic nor nondiegetic. It is not that Randy, upon seeing Liza at *Allure*, launches into "This Is New." Rather, Liza dreams about an encounter with Randy that is fantasy projection. It is not Randy singing, but a figment of him in her dream state. In film criticism, the term "metadiegetic" is employed for music that has first appeared diegetically but reappears nondiegetically and is understood to be running through the mind of one of the characters. Yet *Lady in the Dark*'s dream sequences are not metadiegetic because they represent the unconscious of one of the characters, not her conscious self. With three exceptions, this is not music that Liza has heard before. Instead, most of *Lady in the Dark*'s music occupies a conceptual realm.

The term "concept musical" may have outlived its novelty but is still often invoked for two types of shows. The first might be likened to director's theater, where the director-author decides what the work is to be about and then attempts to have it reflected in all aspects of the production.[72] An example is *Fiddler on the Roof*. The story was culled primarily from four of Sholom Aleichem's eight stories about Tevye the Dairyman. Boris Aronson, however, took the central concept from Marc Chagall's painting *The Green Violinist*. For the artist, who included rooftop violinists in other paintings, the fiddler represented the central figure in the life-cycle events of an Eastern European village. His appearance at births, weddings, and funerals made him the symbol of *Fiddler on the Roof*. The musical is about tradition, and that concept is distilled in the figure of the fiddler on the roof. All the production's elements were unified by this concept.

The second type of concept musical abandons a linear plot in favor of a series of vignettes unified by theme. This type of musical is heavily indebted to the revue, where the various sketches are all held together by some overriding theme. But the revue and the concept musical diverge, because the latter aims to be a serious evening in the theater. An example of this type is *Company*. It originated as a collection of eleven one-act plays by George Furth, which examined aspects of relationships between couples, not all of them married. For the musical, Furth revised three of the plays and added two others. The stories concern five couples and the havoc that urban living is wreaking on their relationships. What holds the show together is the character Bobby, who interacts with his friends. His birthday parties are employed as a framework to tie the vignettes together. Each couple tries to explain to Bobby the joys of marriage, but none of them makes a compelling case.

Both types of concept musical can be traced to Kurt Weill and Alan Jay Lerner's *Love Life*, subtitled "A Vaudeville," from 1948. The book scenes record the changing economic effects on Sam and Susan Cooper's marriage: from the transition of an agrarian to an industrial economy, through the halcyon days of the 1920s, to the postwar period. The intervening vaudeville acts comment on the book scenes and prevent the audience from becoming emotionally involved with the Coopers. The black barbershop quartet's number "Economics" sums up the show's central concept. With its scenes of the Coopers' marriage in different historical periods in a series of vignettes, *Love Life* prefigures the second type of concept musical. The intervening vaudeville acts adumbrate the use of comment songs in *Company* as well as the Kit Kat Club numbers in *Cabaret*. The overriding concept of economics' effect on the institution of marriage foreshadows the first type of concept musical.[73]

What has not been previously recognized is the debt that *Love Life* owes to *Lady in the Dark*. First, the leading role of Susan Cooper had been intended for Gertrude Lawrence. Second, the suffragette number, "Women's Club Blues," which begins all buttoned up but ends down and dirty attempted to recreate the effect of "The Saga of Jenny." Third, Weill patterned the twenty-five-minute finale, which has the Coopers and the vaudevillians join together for an "Illusion Minstrel Show," directly on the first incarnation of the *Circus Dream*. For *Love Life*'s minstrel show, a magician reappears as the interlocutor, and Weill reworked Maggie's and Alison's roles into the fortune-telling sisters, the Misses Horoscope and Mysticism.

Eschewing any subplot or secondary love interest, *Lady in the Dark* is actually the progenitor of the first type of concept musical. The relationship between the book scenes and dream sequences was dictated by the topic of psychoanalysis. The costume designs of tailored monochrome suits and colorful ball gowns were motivated by her drive to become both sexes. A woman choosing among three men representing the roles of father, lover, and husband is a Freudian conceit. The turntables and plastic furnishings attempted to capture the cinematic quality of dreams. All of the elements of the production reflected the central concept of psychoanalysis. Freud, metaphorically and physically (through his signed photograph in Dr. Brooks's vestibule), hovered over the proceedings.

Looking backward to social norms of the 1930s and forward to the concept musical of the post–Rodgers and Hammerstein era, virtually every aspect of *Lady in the Dark* depicted its moment of composition. However dated it seems now, the show nonetheless packed a wallop in its time. The radical reassessment of music's function stands up there with the most progressive of all works for the American musical theater. For the first time, the distinctions between diegetic and nondiegetic had been superseded. Music was freed to occupy a conceptual realm in *Lady in the Dark*. Despite the musical play's revolutionary form and the subsequent efforts of its creators, it was in many ways unrepeatable. In the final analysis, *Lady in the Dark* remains a "girl of the moment."

8

Revivals

In his book *The American Musical Theater*, Lehman Engel described *Lady in the Dark* as a show that "will come back again and again."[1] Although not a staple of stock and amateur companies, *Lady in the Dark* has periodically resurfaced in the decades following the original production. The 1940s featured the much anticipated Paramount film starring Ginger Rogers as well as two radio adaptations. The 1950s saw a television special starring Ann Sothern, the first German production, and a radio broadcast with Judy Garland. The 1960s began with a recording by Risë Stevens and concluded with a benefit concert with Angela Lansbury. In between, Julie Andrews starred as Lawrence in the biopic *Star!* The 1970s witnessed a second German production. The 1980s saw a British production at the Nottingham Playhouse, a third German *Lady in the Dark*, and an Edinburgh Festival performance. The 1990s were a busy decade, with a New York *Encores!* presentation, Japanese and Italian productions, and the London premiere at the Royal National Theatre and subsequent cast recording.

Despite the various performance media, none of the revivals has topped the original. Few have aimed as high, and none, save the two films, has had a comparable budget. Some that were financially successful, such as the Paramount film, are artistically a disaster. Those that capture some of the magic, such as Lawrence's radio broadcast and *Star!*, are by necessity incomplete. Recent revivals have usually made the fatal mistake of reinstating cut portions of the script and score. With a running time of over three hours, the result is deadly. But then again, less is not always more. *Lady in the Dark* is a big show that depends on theatrical values. Producing it on a shoestring is unsatisfactory, as recent concert performances and chamber productions have demonstrated.

Nevertheless, *Lady in the Dark*'s revivals shed light on the work itself and the adaptation process. Through revisiting them, one discovers which parts of the show might still be viable. Can the very long first act, with both the *Glamour* and *Wedding Dreams*, be shortened to a manageable ninety minutes? With only one dream sequence, can the second act's relationship between spoken dialogue and music be better balanced? How can Charley's remarks push Liza to the edge without being grounds for sexual harassment? How might the ending be rethought so that Liza need not sacrifice her career for a relationship? By surveying the revivals, one glimpses what *Lady in the Dark*'s future might hold.

The Paramount Film Starring Ginger Rogers

In 1941 Paramount Pictures bid what was then the highest amount ever paid for the screen rights of a literary work, $285,000. Both Weill and Gershwin hoped that Paramount would use their musical score. Gershwin took advantage of a call from B. G. DeSylva, the executive producer, to promote the incomplete "Hollywood Dream." Not only did DeSylva forget about it, but so did Weill when the studio requested his musical score: "John Bryant called me and said the coast had requested to ask if I would let them have my original orchester-score [*sic*] (which, I think, is a unique case in the history of Hollywood's musical departments.) They also asked if there was any additional material in the show which is not contained in the printed [piano-vocal] score. There isn't, as far as I remember."[2] Less than a month later, Gershwin relayed the bad news:

> We were a little premature in thinking that Paramount would use our score exclusively. It seems "This Is New" wasn't the tempo that was right . . . and they have been marketing around for a new song. Arthur Schwartz had a song with [Howard] Dietz that Paramount wanted but evidently they asked for too much money because I now hear that Burke–Van Hueston [Johnny Burke and Jimmy Van Heusen] are going to write the song. Also [Johnny] Mercer and [Harold] Arlen had been approached. Also [Jerome] Kern, who, I understand, asked for 10 grand. Paramount called me the other day telling me the Rockefeller-S.A. [South America] Good Will group objected strongly to the 4th stanza of "Jenny" (about the Latins) and would I be so kind as to favor them with a new stanza which of course I didn't have to do—but I did.[3]

Although Burke and Van Heusen did compose "Suddenly It's Spring" to replace "This Is New," neither the original fourth stanza of "Jenny" nor Gershwin's substitute were used.

When the press announced that Ginger Rogers would play Liza Elliott, Lawrence expressed disappointment: "I have nothing in the world against Ginger Rogers or her ability, but I feel like a mother who is kissing her favorite child goodbye. I want to say, 'Miss Rogers, take good care of Liza. I love her so much. Do be good to her.'"[4] Rogers felt differently: "The press razzed me unmercifully for running away with someone else's role.... The studio, not I, bypassed Miss Lawrence. Was I supposed to turn the role down?"[5] Truth be told, Rogers had lobbied for the role as part of a three-picture deal with Paramount. The other principals included Ray Milland (Charley), Warner Baxter (Kendall), Jon Hall (Randy), Barry Sullivan (Dr. Brooks), and Mischa Auer (Russell).

The studio enlisted Frances Goodrich and Albert Hackett to write the screenplay. However, Mitchell Leisen, who was approached to direct the picture, rejected their adaptation:

> Buddy DeSylva called me and said that he had never expected to have to make it, but part of his three picture deal with Ginger Rogers was that she play this part, and for God's sake, would I please agree to do it. I said I would not shoot the Hackett script. He said, "I don't give a damn what you shoot. Just say you'll make the picture."
>
> So I went to Moss Hart and got his original prompt copy, and I came back to California and wrote the script of *Lady in the Dark*.... The Hacketts got credit but their script was thrown in the wastebasket.[6]

Leisen's screenplay opens in a general physician's office. After Liza's checkup, Dr. Carleton recommends that she see a psychoanalyst. Liza is next seen arriving at the offices of *Allure*. A number of conversations introduce Alison (played by Phyllis Brooks), Miss Foster (Catherine Craig), Russell, and Maggie (Mary Philips). Charley presents his idea of the circus cover and, after feeling the lapel of Liza's jacket, remarks that they must go to the same tailor. This prompts Liza to hurl a paperweight at him. Charley then discusses Liza's "big executive pose" with Maggie. This concludes the introduction, and we next see Liza in Dr. Brooks's office, corresponding to the first scene of the stage play.

From here the screenplay, like Hart's script, alternates scenes in Dr. Brooks's and Liza's offices. Save for small changes, the only significant addition is a new scene. It occurs after Liza leaves for dinner with Randy. Whereas in the theater, audience members had to learn from Alison what transpired, the screenplay takes us to a posh nightclub (Figure 47). We see Randy expressing interest in Liza and her reaction to his advances. Charley and *his* date interrupt their romantic interlude. He informs Liza that in an evening gown she looks like a woman and admits that he is after her job. Insulted, Liza abruptly ends the evening. Charley's snide comment exemplifies how Leisen ratcheted up the gender stereotypes.

Leisen, who began his career as a costume designer for Cecil B. De Mille, color-coded each of the dream sequences: the first, "glamorous blue"; the second, rose colored for Randy and Liza's scene, turning to gold for the wedding; and the third, "gaudy red and green hues." Setting and costume designer Raoul Pene du Bois chose to have each dream fade in from blue mist, which would then chromatically progress from primary shades to more violent hues.[7]

For the costumes, Leisen wanted to pull out all the stops: "When I came back from New York, I had made deals with all the different couturiers to have each one dress a different character. [Paramount's] Y. Frank Freeman then told me he had signed Valentina up and she was going to come out here for one day and design all the clothes. I said, 'That's great. Everybody will look the same.'" Instead the three designers who contributed most to the picture were Raoul Pene du Bois, Edith Head, and Leisen himself. Head recalled, "Mitch did more of it than either Raoul or I did, but he insisted that I take sole credit for the street clothes, which was extremely generous of him since many of them were his."[8] Leisen had Liza's business suits made at his own tailor shop, ensuring that they would be suitably masculine.

For the circus sequence, Leisen designed the most expensive costume ever made for a Hollywood film up to that time. The outfit was made of real mink, except for a jeweled and beaded bodice. When opened, the long skirt revealed a lining of red and gold glass beads. The lining was so heavy that Rogers could not dance in it, so a redesigned dress substituted sequins (Figure 48). Rogers still found the dress difficult: "There are two weights of mink, male and female; female is more prized because it is lighter. Naturally, my dress was constructed of the male skins and must have weighed fifteen pounds. Heavy or no, the dress was truly spectacular and, according to the public relations department at Paramount, cost $30,000."[9]

The film began a projected three-month shoot on December 9, 1942. Almost immediately, Rogers and Leisen clashed. According to Rogers, "Mitch's interest was in the window draperies and the sets, not in the people and their emotions."[10] According to Leisen, for a story about psychoanalysis, Rogers, a cheerful and well-adjusted Christian Scientist, "didn't know what the hell she was talking about." The director recalled his frustration: "She was always late coming to the set. The day we did the 'Suddenly It's Spring' number, she arrived on the set at half past three in the afternoon. I had 165 electricians waiting all day. I told DeSylva, 'I'm not going to be a policeman;

if you don't like it, you talk to her.'"[11] Once filming began, Rogers and specialty dancer and choreographer Don Loper found themselves in a sea of fog: "For over two and half hours I worked on the dream dance. To keep the dry ice from melting too rapidly, all the outside doors were shut. Inside, I was groping through the fog and inhaling the overwhelming dry ice. It was like swimming underwater on one breath" (Figure 49).[12] The dry ice saturated Rogers's dress, causing the material to become wet and heavy and making it almost impossible for her to dance. "Between takes we had sixteen wardrobe girls with ironing boards all around her trying to dry it out so she could go on and do another take," Leisen remembered.[13]

The complexity of the shoot was heightened by the relatively new color technology. Leisen described the process: "It was very difficult working with Technicolor because you didn't get color rushes and you never knew what the colors would be. They sent three frames of each take in color and that was projected along the side while the film ran in black and white. We cut it in black and white and then Technicolor made the first color answer print. The color would be way off and then you'd start fighting them, sending the scene back over and over until they finally balanced it in the printing."[14] Leisen and associate producer Richard Blumenthal spared no expense for special color effects, even renting lights from other studios for the opening shot of the *Circus Dream*, which progressed from blue to green to gold, and finally contained all three.[15]

Because of the film's complexity, two extra assistant directors were required. Leisen passed over his longtime assistant, Chico Day, for the more important of the two positions, and instead gave it to a friend of his partner, Billy Daniels. Havoc ensued among Leisen's staff. His decision had upset the seniority ranking of the unit, and to punish him, the staff became as uncooperative as possible. So tense were working conditions that when Leisen's secretary smiled at him one day on the set, he looked over his shoulder to see whom she might be addressing.[16]

Rogers's personal life further complicated matters. The previous September on a USO tour of military bases, she had met Marine Private First Class John Calvin Briggs II. Since then their relationship had gotten serious, and one month into the shoot, she announced her engagement. Leisen was less than enthusiastic:

We were doing the scenes on the couch and she blew take after take until I thought I'd go out of my mind. Finally she said, "I'm sorry. I just can't keep my mind on this because I'm getting married tomorrow." Mr. De-Sylva let her go off and get married in the middle of the picture and the entire company just sat there for two weeks. He said, "You can shoot around her." I said, "No we can't. She's been late every day and we've shot up every scene she's not in." She came back and gave us two weeks at the end of the picture free. She would have been sued if she hadn't.[17]

For the climactic musical number, Rogers and Leisen butted heads one last time. He wanted "Jenny" to be sexy, the way Lawrence was performing it. Rogers balked, telling him that it would hurt her girl-next-door image. They proceeded to shoot the number, each attempting to outwit the other. "When we came in for the closer shots," Leisen remembered, "she kept covering her legs up with the skirt. So I moved the camera way back, but put a long lens on so we got a full figure of her showing the legs."[18] Unbeknown to him, Rogers's stiletto heels were catching in the hemp rug on the floor, and the static electricity from closing the mink dress was giving her shocks.

Although budgeted at $2.3 million, *Lady in the Dark* climbed to $2.6 million by the end of the shoot on March 20. This gave the film the dubious distinction of being the most expensive picture made since *Gone With the Wind*. Contractually Paramount could have released *Lady in the Dark* while the stage tour was winding down; however, the film lay on the shelf for well over a year. Concerned with the exorbitant price tag, Paramount was quick to publicize that the rights had been purchased and the production planned prior to America's involvement in WWII. The studio was so jittery about the film's topic that the publicity campaign excluded all references to its subject matter. The advertisement ran with the banner, "The Girl of the Moment... with the Loves of the Year... in the Picture of a Lifetime." Small inset pictures featured the star alone ("Ginger Rogers: A Minx in Mink with a Yen for Men") and with each of her suitors (Figure 50). From the sales pitch, no one would have guessed that the picture had anything to do with psychoanalysis.

Lady in the Dark was first shown on February 9, 1944, at the Paramount Hollywood Theater. Critics were divided. Those from the *Hollywood Reporter*, *Variety*, and *Daily Variety* all gave it an enthusiastic thumbs up.[19] The first critic wrote, it is "not enough to say it is one of the most beautiful pictures ever made," but "possibly THE most beautiful." All three critics roundly praised the film's physical production, especially the Technicolor achievement. Ginger Rogers's portrayal of Liza Elliott was similarly commended: *Daily Variety* claimed that her performance was "second to none she has ever done," and the *Hollywood Reporter* called it her "greatest performance."

Writing for newspapers outside the entertainment industry, Dorothy Manners, Edwin Schallert, and David Hanna had less flattering things to say.[20] Manners delivered the backhanded compliment, "Ginger . . . wears her gowns marvelously"; Schallert reported, "Technicolor photography is not too kind to Ginger Rogers" in this, her first color feature; and Hanna decided that Rogers was "no longer a beauty" and her dance with Don Loper was "decidedly second rate." He concluded, "The picture's impressive production stature neither awes the spectator into liking it nor camouflages the fact that its story is old hat."

The next day, *Lady in the Dark* also opened at L.A.'s Downtown Paramount. Despite the mixed reviews, both venues reported breaking box-office records for an opening day, Hollywood by 40 percent and Los Angeles by 48 percent. For East Coast promotion, Paramount sponsored live trailers in the form of fashion shows featuring costumes from the film. In New York, the studio recruited five hundred women from various branches of the U.S. Armed Forces to watch the parade. Despite the opulence of the fashions on the runway, the attendees were all dressed in uniform.[21] Hoping to cash in, Saks reintroduced *Lady in the Dark* perfume with a new sales pitch, "A subtle moving fragrance that makes an enchantress of any woman, even an executive . . . for the important spring evenings ahead."

In New York, *Lady in the Dark* opened at the Paramount Theatre in Times Square.[22] The following day the *New York Times* reported that approximately twenty-three thousand people had paid about $22,000 to see it for "the biggest opening day in the history of the theatre."[23] By the end of the week, *Lady in the Dark* had broken the record set by *Star Spangled Rhythm* with Benny Goodman and Frank Sinatra the previous year, by grossing $123,000. As part of the publicity, a "distinguished psychiatrist . . . with degrees from two universities" analyzed the film for *Coronet* magazine. The text, accompanied by stills from the film, bears the unmistakable thumbprint of Lawrence Kubie and reveals his continued involvement in promoting *Lady in the Dark*.[24]

One inexplicable omission in the film was that "My Ship" was never sung. A bemused Gershwin jotted off a note to Weill: "I attach a small clipping from the *Citizen News*. This item has appeared in other papers here also. I take it to mean that there must have been many inquiries about what the hell Liza was humming all through the film. At Arthur Schwartz's party the other night I asked Ginger Rogers about the song. She said she had made a charming rendition and had no idea why it had been cut. She suggested that I call Mitch [Leisen]. I told her I didn't know Mitch and that anyway from a box office viewpoint it didn't matter anyway."[25] Leisen in turn claimed that the decision to cut "My Ship" had been DeSylva's, not his:

> We had made a live recording of Ginger singing it right on the set, and she sang it *a cappella* in the park with the boy as the band played "Ain't She Sweet" in the gymnasium dance. But Buddy just put his foot down. He couldn't stand Kurt Weill and he couldn't stand that song. Having been a songwriter himself, he was adamant about it. It was vital to the story, the one spot where she remembers the lyrics finally, after being haunted by the tune through the whole story. The whole picture hung on that song. I said, "You'll take it out over my dead body," but I was overruled.[26]

After the film's general release on August 21, it racked up $4.3 million, making it the fourth-largest grossing film of 1944. Yet despite its box-office success, the film is a major disappointment. Paramount did not use most of Weill's score; instead, numbers by Johnny Burke and Jimmy Van Heusen, Clifford Grey and Victor Schertzinger, and Robert Emmett Dolan were interpolated. Leisen, who had never directed a musical, tried to turn it into a psychological drama. Despite DeSylva's discomfort with the idea that Liza is suffering from an Electra complex (harboring unconscious sexual desire for her father), Leisen won out, with the play portion of *Lady in the Dark* surviving mostly intact.

As a result, the dream sequences had to be sacrificed. The nearly twenty-five-minute *Glamour Dream* was hacked down to less than five; the *Wedding Dream* suffered a similar fate. Only the *Circus Dream* survived relatively unscathed. Throughout the film many of the musical numbers were robbed of their context. On stage, "This Is New" signified the budding relationship between Randy and Liza. In the film, the principals never sing the replacement song, and Ginger Rogers dances with a character who is never identified, as Randy looks on. In the original, each of the sequences built to a musical climax; in the film, they all fade innocuously back into Dr. Brooks's office.

What had been literate in *Lady in the Dark* was dumbed down for the film. Leisen's screenplay preserved Liza's question about Dr. Brooks "getting into his beard," but the missing Viennese accent loses the allusion to Freud. Instead of letting the viewer discover Kendall's role, Dr. Brooks says flatly, "Isn't it because your affection for Kendall Nesbitt is based on the fact that he resembles your father? That you have, in fact, transferred your love for your father to him?" Because most of the music consists of instrumental arrangements by Robert Russell Bennett, virtually all of Gershwin's lyrics were cut.[27]

The film includes some moments that defy explanation. Dr. Brooks's opening line, "You're not yourself, Miss Elliott," makes no sense as they are meeting one another for the first time. *Allure*'s female staff members all wear hats and carry purses while going about the office, giving the impression that the scenes were shot outdoors. Another anachronistic moment occurs when Rogers struggles to put on the mink dress. Instead of half-sobbing a phrase of "My Ship," she says matter-of-factly, "I'm going out, Maggie. I'm going to spend the evening with Mr. Curtis. You can get the magazine to press. I'm going out." So much for a woman on the verge of a nervous breakdown!

The film does have a few interesting moments. The credit sequence cleverly mimics the format of a fashion magazine. The opening shot is equally arresting: Rogers's head in a tight close-up lit in silhouette with one eye illuminated by Dr. Carleton's instrument. Rogers gives her portrayal of Liza Elliott gravitas, which underscores the work's dramatic pretensions, and Ray Milland softens some of Charley Johnson's harder edges. For the snippets of "My Ship," Bennett's orchestration employs the Theremin, an early electronic instrument. The film and its 350 specially designed costumes look every bit the nearly $3 million that it cost.

Lady in the Dark received Academy Award nominations in color cinematography, art direction (color), and scoring of a musical picture. However, it failed to pick up a single Oscar.[28] The film also proved to be a bad omen for both Rogers and Leisen. Paramount did not exercise its option for a third picture with Rogers despite doubling its investment. Although she commanded a record salary the next year for MGM's remake of *Grand Hotel*, her career had peaked. Similarly, *Lady in the Dark* was Leisen's highest grossing film, but it contained the first signs of his decline as a director: a tendency to let the visual overwhelm the dramatic.[29]

Ginger Rogers's *Lux Radio Theatre* Broadcast

A year after the film's release, Rogers, who had hawked Lux Toilet Soap in the pages of *Photoplay* since 1935, appeared in *Lux Radio Theatre*'s one-hour adaptation. Joining Rogers from the film was Ray Milland. The other principal roles were filled by Carlton KaDell (Randy), Herb Rawlinson (Kendall), and Howard McNear (Dr. Brooks). Lionel Barrymore stepped in as guest "producer" (actually, host).

Typical for *Lux* adaptations, Sanford Barnett broke Paramount's screenplay into three acts. He divided each act into a number of small scenes, which effectively kept the drama moving. Because of airwave restrictions, some of *Lady in the Dark*'s adult themes had to be sanitized. Kendall and Liza no longer live together, and their relationship is nonphysical. Barnett excised all of the swearing, and even the word "sex" had to go (Charley's line became "Rage is a pretty good substitute for love"). The script omitted all of the music except "My Ship." A bit of a bridal march initiates the *Wedding Dream* and a snatch of a circus march sets the tone for the *Circus Dream*. Typical for radio drama, musical bridges tied the scenes together. Musical Director Louis Silvers employed these to convey a change in place or time, and generally they reflect the mood of the previous scene. As an example, a "scary" musical bridge concludes with a stereotypical diminished-seventh chord after Charley says, "What's wrong, Boss Lady, can't take it?"

Sound effects were an important part of radio drama, and Charles Forsyth was a master at creating them. For *Lady in the Dark*, he used the sound of a typewriter to suggest when an office door at *Allure* was open or had just been opened. With the sound of a shutting door and the typewriter ceasing, we know that the characters are alone. When Kendall takes Liza out onto the terrace to inform her of his divorce, street noise tells us that they are outside. As the volume increases, we know that they have moved to the far edge for a private moment. Forsyth, who joined *Lux* with its first Hollywood broadcast in 1936 and stayed until its last in 1955, was capable of providing approximately sixty-five thousand different sound effects.[30]

What tended to set *Lux* apart from its competitors was preparation. Director Fred MacKaye rehearsed each scene so that the dialogue, special effects, and musical bridges flowed. He spent upward of thirty hours preparing the one-hour broadcast. A typical week went something like this:

> Thursday: Sound rehearsal with sound effects artist Charlie Forsyth, engineer Ed Whittaker, and director Fred MacKaye, lasting approximately two hours. Friday: Two hours' rehearsal with the supporting cast (and stand-ins for the stars), followed by a two-and-a-half-hour rehearsal with the full cast (including stars). Saturday was a day off. Sunday: Rehearsal beginning at 10:30 A.M. and lasting two hours; lunch break at 12:30, during which the orchestra rehearsed; and after lunch, a one-hour dress rehearsal, which was recorded by a studio on Hollywood Boulevard. As soon as the dress rehearsal was completed, a messenger rushed over with the record, which was then played back for the director and cast.... Monday: Cast and crew arrived at 3:30 P.M. and rehearsed until 5:00, when there was an hour break before 6:00 [PST] airtime.[31]

As a result, *Lux*'s payroll could reach $20,000 per episode. The listening audience was reportedly more than thirty million.

Lux broadcast *Lady in the Dark* on January 29, 1945, from Hollywood's Vine Street Theatre, and CBS carried it on the airwaves. Hours before a typical broadcast, a line of fans would stretch from the theater. Tickets were free, and *Lux* regularly had to turn away hundreds of people. The cast members were all formally dressed and seated on stage. The spoken introduction always worked in a plug for the sponsor. In this case, the combination of "dark" and "lux" proved irresistible: "Now, of course, the meaning of tonight's title, *Lady in the Dark*, is a lady who's in the dark about herself. And not a lady in the dark about Lux Toilet Soap. Although they may be one in the same thing. A lady who isn't sure of her appearance may prefer a dim light, while a woman with a captivating, smooth complexion wouldn't choose to stay in darkness very long. Now if you recall your Latin you'll remember the word 'lux' means light, so if by any chance you are a lady in the dark yourself, perhaps, the easiest solution to your problem is Lux Toilet Soap."

Barrymore informs us that Liza is late to the office because of her appointment with Dr. Harris. Liza's entrance exemplifies Barnett's mastery at condensing a screenplay:

Miss Foster:	Good morning, Miss Elliott.
Liza:	Hello, Foster.
Miss Foster:	Oh, Dr. Harris just phoned.
Liza:	But I just left Dr. Harris.
Miss Foster:	But he said you forgot to take Dr. Brooks's address, and you were to see him.
Liza:	Dr. Brooks is a psychoanalyst! I refuse to see him; I told Dr. Harris that. It's perfectly ridiculous. All right let's get to work.
Miss Foster:	Yes, Miss Elliott.

In just seven lines, the listener learns why Liza is late for work, where she has been, and her resistance to psychoanalysis.

After the introductory scenes, the remainder of the radio play follows the outline of the film. Here, however, Rogers sings a full rendition of "My Ship." Unlike most actresses who step out of character for the number, she continues using her high school voice, even ad-libbing a girlish "la, dee, dee." Rogers's performance here is much more convincing than in the Paramount film. One gets the distinct impression that given what amounted to a second chance at *Lady in the Dark*, she tried to redeem herself. Due to broadcast's success, *Lux* choose to encore *Lady in the Dark* nine years later.

Stock and Amateur Productions

The Dramatists Play Service initially controlled the rights for amateur productions of *Lady in the Dark*. The collaborators and the Play Service's president, Howard Lindsay, signed the agreement on March 9, 1942, the day after the Sam Harris office had posted *Lady in the Dark*'s first closing notice.[32] The agreement gave the Play Service the sole right to lease the musical play for amateur production in the English language. During this period, the Sam H. Harris and Company licensed stock, or professional, productions.

During Weill's only trip back to Europe in 1947, he negotiated possible productions for *Lady in the Dark* in Paris and London. While waiting for a flight in Geneva, he wrote a pessimistic note to his wife regarding his experience: "You can imagine what a rush those few days in Paris were. I did more in those 3 days than a Frenchman does in 3 years.... And I had negotiations for 'Lady' and Street Scene. [Ernst Josef] Aufricht's friends are awfully nice, Blanquet especially, and I will give them the rights although I am pretty sure that neither they nor anybody else will do anything in Paris. It is absolutely the atmosphere of a Balkan town, deeply corrupt and defeatist. One feels every minute what Hitler has done to a people that was weak and that went into all the pitfalls of an enemy occupation."[33] After visiting his parents and brother Nathan in Palestine, Weill planned to check the French translation in Paris on his way back to the United States. Despite these plans, a contract is all that survives.

Among the actresses who portrayed Liza Elliott on the straw-hat circuit was Kitty Carlisle, who had married Hart in 1946. Six years later, she played *Lady in the Dark* at the Westport Country Playhouse, the Cape Playhouse, which Lawrence's husband was still previously managing, and the Bucks County Playhouse, located near Fairview Farm, where much of *Lady in the Dark* had been written. She recalled her preparation for the role: "[Moss] coached me in every scene, he chose costumes and went to fittings, and he even prevailed on Gertie, who was then in *The King and I*, to take time out to teach me her routine for 'Jenny.'"[34] The *Boston Post*'s Elliot Norton reported, "Kitty Carlisle...plays Liza Elliott...with direct simplicity and sings the songs in fine voice. She is lovely to look at and immensely appealing, which is fine from all points of view, including the sentimental."[35] That fall Moss and Kitty sailed for London, but were unsuccessful in finding a producer to mount the show.[36]

Sometime prior to Hart's death in 1961, the Dramatists Play Service exercised its right to publish its own edition of *Lady in the Dark*. This new edition omitted Kubie's preface, Hart's dedication of the work to him, and the "Red Letter Edition" style. The Play Service decided to reprint, with some minor editing, the Random House script, rather than what had been performed on stage. This proved to be a mistake. Directors were not afforded Hart's expertise in cutting his own play down to a manageable size. The unavailability of a script that transmits the stage version has hampered all subsequent stage productions, both stock and amateur.

Theatre Guild of the Air Broadcast Featuring Gertrude Lawrence

The Theatre Guild of the Air presented *Lady in the Dark* on October 19, 1947, and invited Gertrude Lawrence to recreate her title role. Although the Guild had also announced Bert Lytell, Macdonald Carey was the only other cast member from the original production to join Lawrence. Stepping into the other principal roles were Arthur Vinton (Kendall), James Monks (Randy), and Hume Cronyn (Dr. Brooks). The musical numbers included "Oh Fabulous One in Your Ivory Tower," "One Life to Live," "Girl of the Moment," "It Looks Like Liza," "The Saga of Jenny," and "My Ship." James Gould, writing for the *New York Times*, commended the Guild for broadcasting it live: "The broadcast originated from the Opera House in Boston instead of the usual radio studio, with Gertrude Lawrence and her supporting cast working on the stage itself and a full audience out front. The result from the listener's standpoint was a play that sounded as if it came from a playhouse and not from a padded cell." Unlike the *Lux* broadcast, *Lady in the Dark*'s more risqué moments were not censored. Gould wrote, "In particular, her robust and broad interpretation of 'The Saga of Jenny' was a rare kilocycle treat, thanks to the fact that neither the Guild nor the ABC network got squeamish over the meaningful lyrics."[37]

This adaptation boiled the work down to its essential ingredients: Liza's sessions with Dr. Brooks, her dreams, and her relationships with Kendall, Randy, and Charley. Russell's role was curtailed, with most of his entrances eliminated. Gone are the minor characters at *Allure*; one hardly misses them here, which points to how the play could be shortened today. Virtually all of the banter between the remaining staff members was also eliminated, which keeps the story focused on Liza. The shortened opening session in Dr. Brooks's office suggests that by the late 1940s psychoanalysis no longer required a lengthy explanation. A young Hume Cronyn makes Dr. Brooks particularly sympathetic with a reassuring bedside manner.

Although no substitute for a cast recording, this adaptation (now available on CD) enables one to experience Lawrence in the title role.[38] When she speaks, there is a faint British accent, clipped delivery, and occasional bleating quality. When agitated, the accent comes to the fore and haughtiness takes over. Her singing voice has a songbird quality with a fast vibrato and a tendency to be slightly under pitch. Her histrionics are apparent during "The Saga of Jenny" and in a series of nuzzling sounds in her final scene with Charley. To everything she does, there is star quality, yet her talent is elusive. She herself even admitted, "I must have been a lucky star. I've never been a great dancer, but I'm light on my feet, and I've never been a great singer, but I know how to put over a song."[39]

Although Lawrence's involvement in *Love Life* had fallen through by the time of the broadcast, she wrote Weill two days later, "How very sweet of you to wire me. I am so glad that you were pleased with the LADY IN THE DARK Broadcast. Of course I had hoped you would be listening and now I hear that Moss was too, and that he got a kick out of it; in fact *everybody* got very sentimental about the whole evening and as you can imagine I was overcome with nostalgia. 'The greatest musical of all time' must have been remarked a thousand times during rehearsals and after the broadcast."[40]

This note appears to have been their last correspondence. Two and a half years later, Weill died of cardiac arrest at age fifty while working on a musical based on the *Adventures of Huckleberry Finn*. Two and a half years after that, Lawrence died at age fifty-four of liver cancer while starring in *The King and I*. At her funeral, Oscar Hammerstein II eulogized Lawrence as "a true star of the theatre" who possessed "a kind of glow...mystic and intangible...a magic light. I think it had something to do with a warm love for the world, and an eagerness to have the world love her."[41] That evening at 8:30, theaters on Broadway and in the West End stood dark for two minutes.

Judy Garland's *Lux Radio Theatre* Broadcast

If anyone was born to star in *Lady in the Dark*, it was Judy Garland. Like Liza, Judy grew up a daddy's girl with a love-hate relationship with her mother. By the time she was two-and-a-half, "Baby" joined her two sisters in a vaudeville act. When her father died, the thirteen-year-old Judy lost the person who loved her most. Her rising success at MGM was hindered by the presence of Metro beauties such as Hedy Lamarr and Lana Turner. The studio's father figure, Louis B. Mayer, called Judy not "my little ugly duckling," but "my little hunchback."[42] Lana Turner married heartthrob Artie Shaw, much the way Barbara, the most beautiful girl, steals Ben away from Liza. Garland's serious relationships followed *Lady in the Dark*'s plot lines to a tee: there was a string of May-December romances and marriages with Spencer Tracy, Johnny Mercer, David Rose, and Vincente Minnelli. In between were dashing movie stars, such as Tyrone Power, Tom Drake, and Yul Brynner. Garland's Charley Johnson was either Joe Mankiewicz (the man who got away) or Sid Luft (the one who should have).

Garland knew firsthand the torments of a troubled psyche: she reportedly looked in the mirror and saw nothing but ugliness and doubted that she possessed any real talent.[43] In 1943 she began seeing Ernst Simmel, one-time president of the Berlin Psychoanalytic Society, for daily sessions. Though initially taken with the experience, she eventually lost interest. In 1946 she suffered a mental breakdown and spent time in clinics in Beverly Hills and Stockbridge, Massachusetts, before returning briefly to Simmel. The roller coaster of her career and dependencies reached its nadir in 1950, when she was effectively locked out of Hollywood's studio system.

Garland then turned to a concert career and had a comeback in London, New York, Los Angeles, and San Francisco prior to her portrayal of Liza Elliott.[44] By June 1952 she again had a movie contract. After daughter Lorna's birth in November, a postpartum depression ensued. It briefly abated, but then resumed when news of her estranged mother's death reached her in New York. Six weeks after that, she appeared in *Lux*'s encore presentation of *Lady in the Dark*.[45] Joining her that evening were John Lund (Charley), Stephen Dunne (Randy), Joe Kearns (Russell), and Herb Butterfield (Dr. Brooks). Two veterans from the 1945 broadcast recreated the roles of Foster (Doris Singleton) and Maggie (Verna Felton).

Lux's script was shortened to make room for additional music. In the *Glamour Dream*, a male Chorus performed "Girl of the Moment" as underscoring, while Garland sang a few measures of the verse to "One Life to Live." She also added a full refrain of "This Is New" to the *Wedding Dream*. Rudy Schrager's musical bridges are not as artful as Louis Silvers's had been. Although Schrager dipped into Weill's score for several of them, they appear less perfectly matched to the scenes they follow.

The February 16, 1953, broadcast began with producer Irving Cummings introducing the stars. Reflecting Garland's troubled status, John Lund commanded top billing. The first scene in Dr. Brooks's office, however, demonstrates Garland's dramatic genius. She appears to be holding herself together, but a fragile emotional state underneath keeps peaking through. As Garland begins to recount the *Glamour Dream*, she becomes animated and gets carried away by its grandiosity. Even the doctor's probing questions cannot stop her, and we suddenly hear a different person. It is Liza, the glamorous woman. After the dream, however, all life is drained out of Garland's voice and depression returns. The effect is psychologically chilling.

Garland was able to bring the same theatricality to her singing, which provided an added dimension to *Lady in the Dark*. After recounting the incident of putting on her mother's blue gown, Garland begins to cry. She pulls herself together, and her voice loses years as she tells about Ben and the graduation dance. Before they enter the gymnasium, she sings "My Ship." Her soulful voice with its signature warm, viola-like vibrato and open-throated delivery is tinged with yearning. She sings it with the voice of a woman but the innocence of a child. Her palpable heartache captures the song's pathos and the play's drama.

Despite Garland's triumph, the broadcast ended on a sour note. As was *Lux*'s custom, the producer returned to chat with the stars. The banter typically included something about their current films and a preview of next week's radio program. With no film in release, Garland was forced to discuss Paramount's *The Stars Are Singing*. Her voice dripping with disdain, Garland ad-libbed, "I hear Rosemary Clooney is simply wonderful in it." Garland's life was indeed one for the couch, and associates did not shy away from giving their own analyses. The *Saturday Evening Post* even interviewed one of Garland's psychiatrists about her condition. For Judy, he claimed, "we would need a word that means a personality that's split at least five ways."[46] Such a life gave Garland an insight into *Lady in the Dark* that no actress before or since has possessed.

Television Special Starring Ann Sothern

The NBC production of *Lady in the Dark* exploited the new medium of color television. During the 1950s, advertisers sponsored specials in what was termed "compatible color." This meant that those households without an RCA Compatible Color System could still receive the transmission on a black-and-white set. Such telecasts employed the Kinescope process, in essence, "a motion picture camera filming a small television screen and recording the sound on an optical track. Although color film was available, the Technicolor process was too unwieldy and costly to warrant its use and the Eastman mono-pack was not sufficiently developed." The Kinescopes were technically advanced for their day, but the sound and picture are inferior by current standards, so they are rarely rebroadcast.[47]

Under Oldsmobile's sponsorship, Max Liebman produced and directed a series of musicals, which featured *Lady in the Dark* on September 25, 1954. Broadcast before a live audience, it opened with the host, Lee Bowman, dressed in a tuxedo as if he were attending the theater. With playbill in hand, he strolls through a mock lobby and passes posters of *Lady in the Dark*'s Broadway reengagement, the Paramount film, and that evening's "color spectacular." Bowman greets "patrons," as the camera pans to various Oldsmobiles pulling up to the "theater." The lights dim, and, over an abbreviated overture, the credits roll.

Billy Friedberg's and Max Liebman's ninety-minute adaptation substantially shortened the stage play. Dr. Brooks and Liza's opening discussion, for example, is a mere three sentences. Shepperd Strudwick as the psychiatrist says to Ann Sothern, already on the couch, "I know you don't believe in psychoanalysis, Miss Elliott. Nevertheless, it can help you, if you give it a chance. So why don't you relax and tell me your dream?" Although remarkably efficient, the dialogue fails to set up the importance of the childhood song "My Ship."

Friedberg's script attempted to bring *Lady in the Dark* into the new decade. Maggie's line about Schiaparelli's designing at Wuthering Heights was updated to Christian Dior's. Liza's office, rather than masculine and Georgian, was decorated with swagged floral draperies and French provincial furniture. In a similar vein, Irwin Kostal's jazzy arrangements of the score are very 1950s.

The use of a body double enabled Sothern to make what were supposed to be split-second costume changes. These were not entirely successful in the live broadcast: one can hear Sothern's running, as well as squeaks and groans from the moving sets. Strudwick's portrayal of Dr. Brooks is on the overbearing side, and he and Sothern occasionally step on each other's lines. However, there is an electricity in their interchanges, which had been lacking in the Paramount film. Sothern's anger boils and then rises to the surface as she hastily cancels the analysis. With her arched eyebrows, her portrayal recalls Lawrence's.

The choreography in the telecast is first-rate. "Girl of the Moment" is what one hoped to have seen from Ginger Rogers. For the *Wedding Dream*, a pas de deux between a woman pictured outside a church (Bambi Linn) and a man (choreographer Rod Alexander) occurs. The dancing is superb, but it is not at all clear *who* these dancers are supposed to be or represent. The most likely candidates would be Liza and Kendall, yet Liza's dream of marrying Kendall is intended to be a nightmare, not the loveliness that the ballet projects. Worse yet, the couple dances to an orchestrated version of "My Ship," but that song should appear in its entirety only at the end of the play.

Of the three sequences, the *Circus Dream* is the most complete, save for "Dance of the Tumblers." It is hardly missed because a tumbling sequence accompanies "The Greatest Show on Earth." Because of television restrictions, the word "mistress" had to be expurgated from "The Best Years of His Life" (it is less clear why "mish mash" was changed to "mish mosh"). As the ringmaster, Carleton Carpenter performs a lightning fast, perfectly enunciated "Tschaikowsky," which takes the studio audience by surprise. Sothern then sings five of the six stanzas to "The Saga of Jenny" (omitting the one about the "Good Neighbor Policy"). She sashays through her rendition and earns a hearty round of applause.

As in the Paramount film, the high school flashback becomes a major dance number. Liza and Ben's conversation is heard over "Oh, Fabulous One in Your Ivory Tower" in waltz tempo. The underscoring both helps to increase the amount of music in this scene and to provide a cyclic link with the first sequence. Like Lawrence, Sothern is great at affecting a schoolgirl quality, but her rendition of "My Ship" breaks mood and character. With eyes half shut, she gives a rhythmically free performance in the manner of a cabaret chanteuse. One could barely imagine an eighteen-year-old Liza singing in such a sultry manner.

The reviews published the next day were mixed.[48] John Crosby, writing for the *New York Herald Tribune*, felt that Liebman had given *Lady in the Dark* "color with an opulence and imagination and taste that have never been equaled on color TV." The *New York Sun*'s Harriet Van Horne seconded, "Never has so much grandeur been seen in so many colors." The *New York Times* reviewer went even further and suggested that Liebman's "skilled application of the rainbow hues" should convince manufacturers to "turn out color sets on a mass basis." Despite high marks for production, the first reviewer deemed "Carleton Carpenter as the fey photographer . . . no Danny Kaye" and "Victor Mature . . . a lot more convincing [as the] cowboy star than Robert Fortier." The second blasted the adaptation ("If adapters Billy Friedberg and Max Liebman managed to cut the heart out of Moss Hart's play, Miss Sothern went a step further and removed the mind") and Sothern's singing ("Her voice is a curious blend of chocolate sauce and broken glass. It's at once too sweet and too grating"). Only the *Times* reviewer gave *Lady in the Dark* an unqualified rave.

The cast subsequently recorded an album in New York's Webster Hall, which featured most of the numbers from the telecast. The ballet scoring of "My Ship" was moved to the end of the recording, and Sothern sang a brief reprise to conclude. In general, the numbers correspond to the way they were performed on the telecast, except the recording (now available on CD) reinstates the choral repetition and descant to "The Best Years of His Life." In 1997 David Cunard produced a compact disc of the telecast for American Entertainment Industries. Rather than remastering the original RCA cast album, he derived his version from the optical sound-track of the Kinescope. This recording is much more complete, including the two interpolated numbers ("Hobo Dance" and "Two-Step") and the flash-back scenes. As a bonus, Lawrence's 1941 sides for RCA Victor are included, as well as three of the numbers from the 1947 *Theatre Guild of the Air* broadcast.

The Risë Stevens Album

In 1963 Columbia Records produced a studio album of *Lady in the Dark* with Risë Stevens, who had just completed twenty-three years at the Met. Lehman Engel, who would predict *Lady in the Dark*'s longevity, conducted. John Reardon, whose Met debut was still a couple of years in the future, took the part of Randy. From the musical comedy side, Adolph Green played Russell. For the other roles, Kenneth Bridges played Charley, Roger White had the role of Kendall, and Stephanie Augustine reprised her portrayal of Miss Foster from the television special. The recording took place at CBS's Thir-tieth Street Studios in New York on January 23 and May 22.

Engel had to make a number of cuts to fit *Lady in the Dark* onto a single long-playing record. The *Glamour Dream* suffered ten different excisions; the *Wedding Dream* went through a similar trimming. The *Circus Dream*, however, remained almost intact, but "Dance of the Tumblers" had to be dropped. Adolph Green sang "Tschaikowsky" twice, in the manner of Danny Kaye's nightclub act. Despite such changes, *Lady in the Dark* was available for the first time in a form resembling a cast album. The recording has much to offer: tempos are relaxed, rhythms are crisp, and the music dances off the page. Stevens's best cut on the album is "My Ship": she controls her vibrato, and the recording captures the otherworldly quality that she was after. Green's account of "Tschaikowsky" gives it just the type of Borscht Belt reading it so clearly deserves.

Columbia released the stereo recording that fall. The album cover pic-tured Stevens in a pink office setting, completely contrary to the drama's blue associations. The idea for the cover, according to Stevens, was her own: "The glamorous setup for the cover was prepared by the director of the photo session. I took several gowns of my own. Once there, I said to myself, 'Now wait a minute, I think I am going to put on this gown and drape a large scarf around me, and do a caricature of this person as I see her.' So I posed; and to my very great surprise, of all the photographs that were taken, that was the one chosen."[49]

The recording has a couple of regrettable moments. A reverb unit is used for the beginning of the *Glamour* and *Wedding Dreams*, and the album concludes with a schmaltzy coda to "My Ship" that someone (undoubtedly Engel) concocted. The recording was rereleased by CBS in 1973 and was also included in the Time-Life Records *American Musicals* series in 1982. Sony Classical digitally remastered it for release in 1997 on compact disc. The CD includes eleven photographs from the recording sessions, as well as an interview with Risë Stevens. For bonus tracks, Danny Kaye's six sides for Columbia from 1941 are included.

Stock Rights Renegotiated

In early 1965, Gershwin and the heirs of Weill's and Hart's estates entered into an agreement with the Tams-Witmark Music Library for stock rights.[50] In preparation for licensing, Tams produced an updated version of the script and arranged for a new full score and set of orchestral parts. In the process, many of the original orchestral parts were dismembered. Those deemed unusable were recopied, and in some instances, the originals were discarded. Weill's orchestrations now became the de facto sole property of the licensing agency.

Tams tried to bring the script into the 1960s. An "Eisenhower button" substituted for a "Willkie button," sessions with Dr. Brooks increased from $20 to $30, and so on. In addition, the Tams editor rewrote Liza's part to make her character less abrasive, rearranged entrances and exits of characters within a scene, and added numerous phrases so that the characters are more civil to one another. Some of *Lady in the Dark*'s colorful language was censored and almost all of Alison's astrological references were removed. (This was shortsighted: three years later *Hair* and the Age of Aquarius came to Broadway.) All of these changes—almost three hundred in number—produced a kinder, gentler *Lady in the Dark*. However, some of them seriously weaken the drama. At the moment of psychoanalytic transference, Liza cancels her sessions but then turns to *thank* Dr. Brooks!

Despite all of the effort that Tams put into its new property, *Lady in the Dark* received few stock performances after 1965. Without a major Broadway revival, the property languished.

Julie Andrews and 20th Century Fox's *Star!*

If Judy Garland was meant to play Liza Elliott, then Julie Andrews was born to play Gertrude Lawrence. Both had a mother in show business and had gotten their start as child actors in vaudeville and pantomime. In addition, both had married their first husband in England, and each had a daughter there. They were both fêted as the toast of Broadway in their American debuts. After settling in the United States, both married American producers and played the role of Eliza Doolittle, Gertie in a revival of Shaw's *Pygmalion* and Julie in Lerner and Loewe's *My Fair Lady*. Andrews herself admitted the similarities: "We both whistled a lot and we both were always lapsing into bits of cockney. She had a habit of singing a high note to relieve the tension. I do the same thing, sing as loud and high as I can. . . . [We both had] an absolute fear of any kind of commitment [and were] always putting on an act. She would play at being a mother one minute, a gardener the next, a shopper the next. I'm rather like that."[51]

William Fairchild's screenplay for *Star!* follows Lawrence's rags-to-riches story from her childhood days in Clapham, England, through her *Lady in the Dark* success, with "The Saga of Jenny" serving as the film's climax. Fairchild went so far as to graft the plot of *Lady in the Dark* onto Lawrence's life. She becomes the character of Liza Elliott, unable to make up her mind about which of three men she wants after her first marriage. The role of Sir Anthony Spencer (modeled on the real-life Captain Philip Astley) functions as the Kendall Nesbitt figure. Wealthy and from a different class, he proposes marriage, but she is unable to accept. The role of actor Charles Fraser (modeled on Bert Taylor, the scion of a wealthy American family) serves as a young, dashing Randy Curtis. Finally, Richard Aldrich (Lawrence's second husband) fulfills the Charley Johnson role.

The grafting of *Lady in the Dark*'s plot onto Lawrence's biography became doubly reflexive with Julie Andrews playing the role of Gertrude Lawrence. During the filming of *The Sound of Music*, Andrews herself had consulted a psychiatrist: "I needed some answers. I had been going toward it for some time, asking about it. I thought it would be pleasant to try one day, for a lot of reasons—all of them obvious. One day I just did it. I rang up everybody I knew who had a psychiatrist and asked who would be good." As she explained, "I have enormous phobias about singing, stemming from the Broadway days when I was trotted out every night and was pretty much mixed up." Andrews continued, "I am able to see both sides of anything to such an extent that it is terribly hard for me to make a decision or do anything involving a drastic change."[52] And so, the actress who had difficulty making up her mind (and consulted a psychiatrist) played the role of another actress—who herself had played a woman who had difficulty making up her mind (and consulted a psychiatrist)—in a film about that actress not being able to make up her mind!

Aspects of *Lady in the Dark*'s elaborate production were repeated with *Star!* Designer Donald Brooks turned out a total of ninety-four separate outfits for Andrews, costing $350,000. (Andrews signed for the picture in 1963 for a paltry $225,000, with no percentage of the profits.) In exchange for a cameo location in the film, Cartier's loaned more than $3 million worth of diamonds, rubies, and other jewels. "I had never felt so glamorous before in all my life," recalled Andrews.[53] So that she could age from sixteen to forty-two, Andrews wore thirty-six different sets of makeup and twenty different wigs. The shoot included twenty different sites in London and fourteen in New York, in addition to specialty shots at the Cape Playhouse and a villa in the south of France. The film set a record for the number of sets assembled for one movie (185) and employed between nine and ten thousand extras. Andrews kept a file entitled "Impressions of Gertrude Lawrence—Confidential" to help her stay in character. Of the 1,400 separate camera setups, Andrews appeared in 1,372. There were only a handful of times during the five-month shoot when she was not required. Reminiscent of Lawrence's regime at Doctor's Hospital, a physician arrived daily on the set to give Andrews a shot of vitamin B. With the grueling schedule, Andrews confessed, "Sometimes I'd get muddled—where did Gertrude leave off and where did I begin?"[54]

Most of the music in *Star!* was confined to diegetic stage performances. Of the twenty-four musical numbers, Andrews performed in twenty-one of them. Michael Kidd staged them, including such Lawrence staples as "Burlington Bertie from Bow," "Parisian Pierrot," and "Limehouse Blues." Kidd choreographed "The Saga of Jenny" with acrobatic stunts, which Andrews herself perfected. The song took weeks of rehearsal, two weeks to film, but lasted just over six minutes in the film.

Star! owes even more to *Lady in the Dark* than its plot, climactic musical number, and denouement. From the beginning, the subtext of psychoanalysis is hard to miss. The film begins with a medley overture of songs, as if we are in a theater. A curtain parts to reveal a scrim on which are the titles of Lawrence's shows. Then the film cuts to a black-and-white credit sequence with a copyright date of 1940. The sixteen-millimeter documentary about Lawrence called *Star!* is filled with scratchy newsreel footage. Suddenly, the film switches back to seventy-millimeter color as the middle-aged Lawrence yells to stop the projector. It turns out we have been in the screening room previewing a documentary about her life and career:

> *Director:*   Miss Lawrence, I need your o.k. to show this picture.
> *Lawrence:*   Mm. You need it to use that title song, too, darling.

Director:	ow, don't be awkward...
Lawrence:	I am never awkward. I just hate being rushed into decisions.
Director:	Well, are we right? That you want to be *lots* of different people?
Lawrence:	Well, as an actress I did, yes.
Director:	As a person?
Lawrence:	Now look here, Jerry Paul. I get analyzed on stage every night in *Lady in the Dark*. Don't you go probing my psyche. I'll say your film's lousy and you died broke.
Director:	Now, don't be afraid to tell me what you really think.
Lawrence:	Now, darling, I've never been afraid of telling a man that in my entire life.

The directors' purpose (both the fictitious director's and Robert Wise's) is precisely that: to probe Gertrude Lawrence's psyche. With the directors in the role of Dr. Brooks, Lawrence assumes the role of patient. We are meeting her at middle age, and the movie traces the root of her problem back to childhood and chronicles the ways it has played out across her adult life. Through the interchange between the fictitious director and Lawrence, we learn that the problem manifests itself in a difficulty making decisions and a tendency to be many different people.

The film cuts next to Lawrence's disastrous vaudeville debut in Brixton at age sixteen with the number "Picadilly" performed with her father and his female companion. (In a neat parallel, Andrews also played Brixton as a teenager, but with her mother and stepfather.) After Lawrence saves the act, her father proposes a toast: "Wherever my little Gertie goes, she'll always find herself." This becomes the psychoanalytic leitmotif equivalent to "My Ship." *Star!*'s lavish production numbers have much the same effect as the dream sequences do in *Lady in the Dark*: we leave spoken dialogue, the stage blossoms, and music takes over. Instead of a sliding portal, the change is often signaled by black-and-white sixteen millimeter expanding to full-screen color.

In the first half of the film, Lawrence rejects both the father figure of Sir Anthony Spencer (played by Michael Craig) and the young American actor named Charles Fraser (Robert Reed). After *Star!*'s intermission and musical entr'acte, the stage is set for Lawrence to encounter her third suitor. At the cast party for *Private Lives*, she meets Richard Aldrich (Richard Crenna), a banker from Boston. He attempts to get Lawrence's opinion about a new play at his Cape Playhouse, but the actress is disinterested. Later she is recovering from her hangover in Noël Coward's apartment when he returns to apologize. (Coward is played by Daniel Massey, Coward's actual godson.)

This scene precipitates the transference situation. By calling her bluff and pointing out her fear of intimacy, Aldrich becomes the storm center of intense emotions. After he leaves, she breaks down. Nondiegetic music based on the first four notes of "My Ship" intensifies the scene.

The scene cuts to Cartier's in New York; "My Ship" plays in the background as Larwrence impulsively buys jewelry. She says to herself, "Completely alone, huh?" and chooses a bauble. She continues to think out loud in a series of non sequiturs, while being trailed by three salesmen (stand-ins for the men in her life?):

Salesman: Good morning, Miss Lawrence. Miss Lawrence?
Lawrence: He's absolutely and utterly impossible. Whereas, I am completely reasonable and logical.
Salesman: Miss Lawrence!
Lawrence: I'm sick? Indeed! Poppycock!
Salesman: Of course!
Lawrence: I am not unsure of myself. I know exactly what I want. *(Pause)* How do I get to Cape Cod?

Once there, Lawrence is confounded when Aldrich asks her to wait until he finishes a letter. Their power struggle has begun.

On the spur of the moment, Lawrence agrees to star in a new play at the Cape Playhouse. During rehearsals for *Skylark*, she attempts to draw Aldrich, as the producer, into a disagreement with the director. He rebuffs her attempt to get the upper hand: "I suggest you get on with the rehearsal and stop wasting everybody's time with cheap jokes, Miss Lawrence." Like Charley Johnson, he refuses to play her game. Aldrich later calls to invite her to dinner. She refuses and tells him off. Undaunted, he proposes marriage.

The black-and-white documentary suggests that there are problems with Lawrence's new show. Reporters try to get a response as she enters the Alvin for *Lady in the Dark*'s rehearsals. The screen widens to color. Aldrich and Coward observe from the back of the theater as Lawrence runs through "My Ship." When she gets to the final phrase, the camera cuts between close-ups of Lawrence and Aldrich. Just as this number brought Liza and Charley together in the actual play, it now draws Lawrence and Aldrich together. The actor playing Moss Hart asks her to run through "Jenny." She sings a bit of the first stanza, but then breaks off: "Oh God. It's no good. The lyrics are terrible. The music's lousy. The production's hopeless, and that swing is a bloody abomination." Outside the theater, Aldrich whisks her off to the Cotton Club accompanied by Coward. As the three take their seats, she continues to rant: "I know you're trying to take my mind off it, but it's no use. It won't work. You don't begin to understand. Neither of you understands. I'm the one who has to be up there on that stage. Me! I've got to face an audience and sing a song and I just don't know . . . how." In the pause she has observed the black dancers presumably bumping and grinding their way through a blues number. Racial politics aside (white actors dipping into black culture to access their sexuality), Coward remarks to Aldrich, "You're a very clever man." Lawrence, awestruck, says to Aldrich, "Oh, you bastard" and embraces him. She has been able to make up her mind—about both her performance and the man she will marry.

"The Saga of Jenny" begins in black and white, but when Andrews leaps off the swing, slides down a rope, and bursts through a hoop, the film switches to color. Accompanied by midgets, tumblers, acrobats, lion tamers, and clowns, she sings five of the six stanzas. As the number concludes, the curtains close, and the opening-night audience, back in black and white, rises to its feet. (As we know, Gertie's improvised bumps and grinds occurred at the Boston tryout, not opening night. The Cotton Club inspiration is Hollywood fiction.) The narrator tells us that a few days later Aldrich and Lawrence married (that really happened the summer before). They are shown leaving the wedding in a car. The screen widens into color, and the film cuts to the screening room, where it began. Lawrence tells the director, "Whatever else I've said, forget it. Don't change a thing. Leave it just the way it is. (*Pause*) Just the way it was."

The black-and-white film rewinds and we find ourselves in the car in color. Lawrence is unsure of herself:

Lawrence: Richard, I shouldn't have done it.
Aldrich: What?
Lawrence: Married you.

Suffering from a psychological relapse, Lawrence is again acting and replaying a scene from her first marriage. Aldrich plays along:

Aldrich: Don't worry. Divorce is quite simple in America.
Lawrence: Oh, cripes! You don't mean that, do you, about divorce?
Aldrich: I mean everything I say.
Lawrence: Well, I don't. I just think I do at the time.
Aldrich: Good.
Lawrence: Your trouble is that you've got no sense of . . .

Aldrich: Humor.

Lawrence: Worse—no sense of occasion. You should know that when a lady has just been married, she's in a highly emotional state and treat her accordingly.

Aldrich: Accordingly? *(He leans over and kisses her on the cheek)*

Lawrence: Don't imagine you can get around me by just being nice. I may not be as clever as you, but I haven't been an actress for nothing. I know an awful lot more about life and men than most people. And I know the only things that matter are understanding and happiness and being absolutely genuine all the bloody time!

As in *Lady in the Dark* when Liza is able to remember all the words to "My Ship," Lawrence here is no longer acting, but knows what she wants. The father's role was significant in both cases. By the end of Liza's journey, the song that her father insisted she sing at bedtime has brought healing and "her own true love." Lawrence's father, who deserted the family, tells her, "Wherever my little Gertie goes, she'll always find herself." At the end of the film, Lawrence has indeed found herself and *her* own true love.

The world premiere screening of the nearly three-hour *Star!* occurred at the Dominion Theatre in London on July 18, 1968. A cocktail party thrown by Noël Coward in his suite at the Savoy Hotel for friends of Lawrence preceded the glittering affair. The one person missing was Julie Andrews, who was in Brussels with her next picture. This turned into a fiasco: the media portrayed Andrews as ungrateful to the public who had supported her, and Fox's executives were furious at Paramount and Blake Edwards for not allowing her to attend.

The London reviews were more positive than those that appeared after the film opened in New York on October 22. The *New York Times* gave it a paltry 250-word review, the ultimate insult given the scope and cost of the picture.[55] *Star!* limped along until March, when Fox withdrew the film. After shortening it to 165 minutes, it was rereleased. The tide of public opinion had turned against Julie Andrews, and in road-show cities audiences still avoided *Star!* Despite seven Academy Award nominations, the film failed to earn a single Oscar. In a final desperate move, Fox shortened it to two hours and retitled it *Those Were the Happy Times*. It was re-rereleased that October with a poster that recalled *The Sound of Music*. All the efforts proved fruitless. At $12 million, *Star!* was the most expensive Hollywood flop until *Heaven's Gate* in 1981.[56]

Andrews's interest in *Lady in the Dark*, however, had evidently been piqued. Not only had she sung "My Ship" and "The Saga of Jenny," but she had virtually played the role of Liza Elliott. Rumors abounded that she was interested in reviving the show. Even twenty years later a studio recording was reputedly scheduled in England. In listing the projects she was currently mulling over, a production in England and/or the United States was supposedly on the drawing boards.[57] Unfortunately, neither came to pass. *Star!* was as close as Julie Andrews ever got to *Lady in the Dark*, which, in hindsight, was pretty close.

A Benefit Concert with Angela Lansbury

On November 9, 1969, a benefit concert for The Foundation for International Child Health entitled *The Music of Kurt Weill* was held at Lincoln Center. The concert featured Elizabeth Carron, Nancy Dussault, Jack Gilford, Richard Kiley, Danny Meehan, Mabel Mercer, Gary Oakes, Robert Ryan, and Lotte Lenya singing selections from Weill's songbook. After intermission, *Lady in the Dark* was performed in a concert version with a narration written by Roderick Cook and delivered by Douglas Fairbanks Jr. (Ironically, the young actor and Lawrence had enjoyed a tempestuous affair in London during the early 1930s.) Angela Lansbury, who had established herself as one of Broadway's leading ladies after her two-year triumph in *Mame*, led the performance.

Don Pippin, who had served as musical director for *Mame* and the flop follow-up *Dear World*, conducted. The audience stopped the *Glamour Dream* cold with entrance applause for Lansbury. So long was the ovation that it nearly capsized the beginning of "The World's Inamorata." *Lady in the Dark* had once again found a star bright enough for its title role.

Robert Mackintosh, who had designed Lansbury's costumes for *Mame*, fashioned her gowns for the evening. For the onstage dream projections, Lansbury modeled Pauline Trigere's current collection. Cook had fashioned his witty narration of *Lady in the Dark* in rhymed couplets, and Fairbanks delivered them with a droll sense of humor.

Lady in the Dark was reduced to fifty-five minutes, using many of the same cuts as the 1963 studio album ("The Princess of Pure Delight" was skipped here). An updated libretto had Liza posing for the new *five*-cent stamp. However, the updates were inconsistent, with the "Good Neighbor Policy" stanza retained for "The Saga of Jenny." Gershwin's lyrics for "Jenny" got the better of the leading lady (at one point Lansbury began one stanza but concluded with another), but the number still stopped the show. It is clear from the ovation at evening's end that Lansbury could have headlined a first-class revival of *Lady in the Dark*.

German Productions

Although rumors abounded that Angela Lansbury or Julie Andrews might star in a revival, nothing happened. Although the 1970s did not see an American revival, one did occur in Germany. *Lady in the Dark* has been produced there three times, each under a different title and translation. In 1951 Maria Teichs translated it as *Das verlorene Lied* ("The Lost Song"). The U.S. Office of Military Government for Germany, Education and Cultural Relations Division, Theater and Music Section printed the translation.[58] *Lady in the Dark* opened at the State Theater's Blauer Saal in Kassel in May 1951, with Vera Solvotti-Stroem playing Liza Elliott.

Marianne Schubart and Karl Vibach translated *Lady in the Dark* anew as *Die Dame im Dunkel* for performances by the Lübeck Theater during its 1976–1977 season. The production starred Nadja Tiller. The most recent German production occurred in 1983 at the City Theater in Freiburg. The translation, which preserved the original English title, was not credited, but the playbill cited director Markus Weber for additional text. The production included the overture, which was here played before the first act and accompanied by a children's ballet. The Freiburg *Lady in the Dark* opened on March 24, 1983, and starred Susanne Peter as the German Liza Elliott, "Norma Herrenberg."

Musical Comedy Tonight Starring Danny Kaye and Lynn Redgrave

In 1979 Sylvia Fine convinced Prudential Life Insurance Company to underwrite the taping of three musical comedy lectures she had given at Yale. Although students had originally performed for those lectures, Broadway performers took the honors for the PBS special. The sequel series, produced on February 11, 1981, included *Lady in the Dark*. The segment featured Danny Kaye reprising his role as Russell Paxton with Lynn Redgrave as Liza Elliott and Richard Crenna as Charley Johnson (Crenna had played Richard Aldrich in *Star!*). Taped before a live audience in Los Angeles, *Lady in the Dark* was reduced to two scenes: Liza's office and an abbreviated *Circus Dream*. Musical numbers included "The Best Years of His Life," "Tschaikowsky," and "The Saga of Jenny."

Lynn Redgrave gamely sang four out of six stanzas of "Jenny," although she was clearly upstaged by Kaye (he even joined her for a reprise of the coda). During the sequence, he sang "Tschaikowsky" only once; however, after the segment he joined Fine at the piano to sing it again to break his "last world record." Having performed the number for forty years and overrehearsed the same anecdotes, Kaye's performance was affected: every physical tick overplayed, each mannerism exaggerated. His biographer captured it best: "In playing the introductory scene to 'Tschaikowksy,' he had a grotesque take on the effeminate character. By current standards, this parody of stereotypical homosexual mannerisms was not only inane but tasteless and unpleasant. As played by a mincing, aging Danny Kaye, it was nasty. When he finished this business and finally got around to singing 'Tschaikowsky,' he made its bravura as lifeless as his dyed hair, as mean as his dead eyes."[59] The one glimpse of spontaneity was when Kaye recounted *Lady in the Dark*'s opening night in Boston. He wistfully remarked, "It was the most proudest moment of my life."

Nottingham Playhouse Production with Celeste Holm

Lady in the Dark finally reached Great Britain with a production at the Nottingham Playhouse. Although only a regional theater production, it was viewed as a tryout that might transfer to the West End. Making her British debut was Celeste Holm, who had gotten her break decades earlier as Ado Annie in *Oklahoma!* and went on to star in *Bloomer Girl*. During *The King and I*, she had taken over while Lawrence was on her summer vacation.

As would be typical with first-class productions, the director, Crispin Thomas, attempted to rethink the original. Thomas persuaded Kitty Carlisle Hart, Lotte Lenya, and Ira Gershwin to give him permission to do so. This included trying to complete the "Hollywood Dream," although that did not prove feasible. Thomas broke the second dream sequence in two. The first half was retitled *High School Dream* (with the songs "Mapleton High Choral," "This Is New," and "It's Never Too Late to Mendelssohn"), and the second *Wedding Dream* (with the numbers "The Princess of Pure Delight" and the finale, titled here "Wedding Nightmare"). Given the limited budget, the Nottingham Playhouse reduced the cast to seventeen adults (the models and office boys doubled as the Chorus) and six children, and the orchestra to nine players.

The British *Lady in the Dark* opened on December 9, 1981. The playhouse went so far as to use the original *Playbill* cover but substituted Holm's photograph for Lawrence's. The reviews, however, were mixed.[60] Writing for *Opera*, Charles Osborne praised Holm's performance: "She has a gentle charm and an impressively natural way with dialogue, and she put her songs across with superb professionalism." But Marian Bryson complained in

Stage, "Not a real musical, not entirely a play with music, it is neither old enough to be a period piece nor familiar enough to warrant a send-up." In the year the megamusical *Cats* descended on the West End, *Lady in the Dark* seemed tame by comparison. In a regional production with reduced forces, the show failed to create the necessary spectacle.

Edinburgh International Festival Concert Performance

In the mid-1980s, the creators' heirs requested that Tams-Witmark return Weill's orchestral score and what remained of the parts. Conductor John Mauceri then set out under a National Endowment for the Humanities grant to restore the score. This involved reinstating those sections that Hart, Short, Weill, and Gershwin had discarded, cut, or changed during its genesis and tryout. Under Mauceri's supervision, a new orchestral score was prepared, which incorporated everything possible; even passages that Weill had never orchestrated were included. This "complete" *Lady in the Dark* debuted at the 1988 Edinburgh International Festival. With a condensed book, the overture and three dream sequences shared a program with works by Richard Strauss and Arnold Schoenberg.

As performed by the Scottish Opera Chorus and Orchestra with Patricia Hodge in the title role, *Lady in the Dark* was bursting at the seams. The musical score had been expanded to a size that exceeded even the original Boston tryout. Such concert programming tried to suggest that *Lady in the Dark* could stand on its own in a symphonic setting, but the orchestral reading weighed it down. Instead of the rumba, bolero, and circus march giving the score a light dance feel, it had lugubrious quality.

In his program note, Mauceri claimed that *Lady in the Dark* could "finally be heard as the composer envisioned it," but such a reconstruction ignored the working methods of Broadway.[61] Unlike the Strauss and Schoenberg works, *Lady in the Dark* had been created in a collaborative process. Weill and Gershwin in their earliest correspondence agreed to overwrite and expected the work to be molded through rehearsals and tryout. Only when *Lady in the Dark* opened on Broadway had it found its final form. Small wonder then that the Edinburgh concert resulted in "a procession of early departures by people who could have had no idea that the concert would go on so long."[62]

The 1990s and Beyond

Before Lotte Lenya's death in 1981, she bequeathed her rights in Weill's works to the Kurt Weill Foundation for Music, which she had established in 1962 primarily as a tax shelter. The Foundation subsequently faced the prospect of untangling contracts for the composer's works. The licensing situation with *Lady in the Dark* resulted in a Catch-22, which was hampering its revival. The Dramatists Play Service was still licensing amateur rights but could supply only a script and piano-vocal score. High school, college, and community productions were prevented access to *Lady in the Dark*'s orchestrations, as those were available only to professional companies from Tams-Witmark.

On the Foundation's initiative, the heirs decided to transfer *Lady in the Dark*'s stock *and* amateur rights to The Rodgers and Hammerstein Theatre Library. So-called first-class productions were not included in the agreement and must still be negotiated with the heirs. With these licensing agreements, the logistics of producing *Lady in the Dark* were finally sorted out nearly fifty years after it was first performed. This paved the way for a number of revivals beginning in the late 1980s. Many of these have been amateur performances by colleges, conservatories, and community theater groups. Professional and first-class productions have included an *Encores!* Concert Performance at New York's City Center (1994) with Christine Ebersole, a Japanese production (1996) with Mira Anju, the London premiere by the Royal National Theatre (1997) and subsequent London cast recording (1998) with Maria Friedman, a production at the Hal Prince Theatre in Philadelphia (2001) with Andrea Marcovicci, and an Italian production (2001) with Raina Kabaivanska.

These have explored various solutions to the problems of reviving *Lady in the Dark* for contemporary audiences. Dr. Brooks's pronouncements about Liza "withdrawing as a woman" and her lack of "feminine adornments" are hopelessly dated after the multiple waves of feminism. Much of Kubie's brand of Freudian analysis is downright sexist today. The Philadelphia production cast a woman in the role of Dr. Brooks, which changed the dynamics. Reframing the sessions under the guise of seeing a sympathetic therapist rather than an overbearing psychoanalyst makes the subtext of *Lady in the Dark* more palatable. In any case, judicious cutting of Dr. Brooks's part is necessary. Charley Johnson's barbs ("having magazines instead of babies," etc.) are also no longer tenable; audiences for the *Encores!* performances laughed and then booed. By eliminating most of these lines, Charley can still chafe under an indecisive boss without having to sexually harass her. Completely updating *Lady in the Dark* is impossible, because its plot, dialogue, and lyrics all reflect the year 1940. The best solution has been to keep it loosely as a period piece, without being slavish to the original. Because the dialogue for the *Allure* staff was a send-up of *Vogue*, Diana Vreeland, and contemporary fashion, these scenes have lost their relevance and are overripe for trimming.

Almost all of the recent productions have omitted Liza's line about "stepping aside" and letting Charley run the magazine himself. In London, director Francesca Zambello's decision to have Liza walk away from Charley and into the light metaphorically resolved the drama without having Liza sacrifice her career for romance. That production also demonstrated how well an abstract set can work. Designer Adrianne Lobel used a series of movable sails inspired by the Lyonel Feininger painting *Yachts*. They finally coalesced into a seascape for "My Ship."

What continues to hamper revivals are the rental materials. What played on Broadway in 1941 was nearly thirty minutes shorter than these, and even then some critics found it too long. Without major production values, the dream sequences are overlong. As a partial solution, the New York *Encores!* performance enlisted acrobats for "Dance of the Tumblers" to enliven the *Circus Dream*. But unless there is something spectacular to accompany the dances, it would be better to omit them. Weill himself recognized this and wrote possible cuts into his orchestral score, which continue to be overlooked.

Although Hart, Gershwin, and Weill collaborated and compromised, their estates now have vested interests in protecting their individual contributions. Consequently, only a director for a first-class production would have the freedom necessary to return *Lady in the Dark* to a performable state. As has been repeatedly demonstrated, restoring and preserving every scrap of dialogue and shred of music is not the solution. Like other Broadway shows with title characters, such as *Gypsy*, *Hello Dolly!*, and *The Producers*, this show needs a major star at the helm—one with the radiance of a Gertie Lawrence, Judy Garland, or Julie Andrews. A Broadway revival of *Lady in the Dark* may always be just over the next horizon, but as the decades have proven, her ship will return again and again.

Epilogue

So let our imagination drift back to that day in 1943, that day in July when we spot a celebrity on the platform in LaSalle Street Station. Why my friend and I are there, we cannot remember, but that chance encounter remains in my dreams. Although busy with her luggage, the flash of blue, the coordination of her suit and suitcase draw our eyes to her. She is in her mid-forties and moves like an actress, every movement seemingly choreographed and blocked. We edge on over, as does another woman, who begins to talk to her. It couldn't be. But it is—Gertrude Lawrence. Thrilled by our discovery, we try not to call attention to ourselves but get close enough to observe what is happening. She looks around, desperate for a red cap to help her with her luggage. With the war, there is a shortage of them, most are overseas fighting. She commandeers a cart and begins stacking her luggage. What a trooper! Can you believe it? Gertrude Lawrence is hoisting her own bags!

She takes a moment to straighten her blouse and check to see if a small pin is still in place. Smiling, she begins talking to the woman. Must be a reporter. Next she is lifting her skirt to show something on one of her legs. She laughs, takes the woman's arm, and whispers something in her ear. Gertie's ash blond hair seems to shimmer in the light, caught in a permanent silver spotlight. She leans back on one heel, tosses her head back, laughing. Glancing at her watch, she excuses herself and then hurries away. Dumbfounded, we didn't think of asking for an autograph. How will anyone believe us? It wasn't really Gertrude Lawrence, they'll say. She's out West. We decide to approach the woman still standing beside the stack of luggage.

Turns out she is a reporter (what did I tell you?). Her name is Adeline Fitzgerald and she writes the weekly column "These Charming People" for the *Herald American*. We ask, "Was that who we thought it was?" She smiles at our naïveté. "Yes, that was Miss Lawrence herself, disembarking the train." "Where was she going?" "Where did she leave from?" "What are her plans?" The questions tumble out at such a rate that Miss Fitzgerald bursts out laughing. "This is what I know," she says. Before she can tell us, I offer to buy her a soda pop. As we turn, I steal a look at the large wool suitcase. There on the tag is Gertie's name. I pinch myself with delight at our good fortune.

Now seated, Miss Fitzgerald opens her small notebook and begins to compose her story. Miss Lawrence was indeed returning from Los Angeles, where *Lady in the Dark* had enjoyed a three-week run. Before she gets too much farther into her story, we share our experiences of seeing the show. How we couldn't take our eyes off her. All of her crazy antics—"she even ate the flowers off her desk during one scene," I offer. Miss Fitzgerald continues (indicating, so it seems, that she must have somewhere else to go). Miss Lawrence is heading for the Cape to meet her husband. "Richard Aldrich," my friend injects. "Lieutenant Commander Richard Aldrich," Miss Fitzgerald corrects. "Funny," I remark, "how the manager of the Cape Playhouse ends up a commander in the Navy." We all know that during these times, anything is possible.

Miss Fitzgerald recalls how momentous these past few years have been for Miss Lawrence. Getting married three years ago on her birthday, performing *Lady in the Dark*, all of her benefit work. "Did you see her pin?" she asks. "A Red Cross Pin—she told me she even gave blood during the stop in San Francisco." Silence. I imagine Gertie's blood being administered to some dying soldier on a war-torn battlefield. Miss Fitzgerald has nearly finished her malted milk. We had better talk fast. "Where was she going?" "To New York, to meet her husband." "Her new radio show sounds interesting," my friend volunteers. The aura of Gertrude Lawrence's presence is beginning to fade. The bill is paid. We shake Miss Fitzgerald's hand and thank her for her time. "We must buy Wednesday's paper," I remember saying.

Walking out of the shop, we tip our hats to two women approaching. My friend absentmindedly says, "Blue." "Blue what?" "Blue, didn't you notice," he punches my arm. "She was wearing blue. Her suitcases were blue." I am lost. "Remember the play! The first dream . . . the one with the feather dress." "Yes, yes, of course! The *Glamour Dream*" I shout. "It is all about blue," my friend, says. "She couldn't wear blue because of what her mother told her when she was a little girl! And look how she was dressed—all in blue." Silence hits us like a ton of bricks. It's as if the scene we have just witnessed is out of the end of the play. My friend gets in the last word: "And she is going to meet her husband, just as Liza ends up with what's-his-name at the end of the show."

We check the board: our train leaves in five minutes. We look at each other, back to the board, and both realize we can catch a later train and maybe spot Gertrude Lawrence on the platform. Without a moment to lose we begin running, wildly, to the stairs. What luck! What good fortune! We search madly, eventually splitting up and then meeting back at the loco-motive to compare notes. She is gone, probably already aboard. Disappointed and tired, we head for our train. We try to remember everything the re-porter told us, but it is all now hopelessly jumbled. We wonder when we'll see her in a play again. "If 'Myth Lawrence' plays again on tour," we should go. "Yes," I say. "Most definitely—it's a deal."

I have a difficult time sleeping. I keep seeing her there in the blue suit with the flowing blouse, her blond hair, the big blue suitcase, and the ring of malted milk on the table. On Wednesday I run to the corner to buy the *Herald American.* I drop sections of the paper, looking for Miss Fitzgerald's column. There it is! I sit down and read it quickly. A small article, but proof that we were there. I call my friend. He forgot to pick up the paper. I read the article, slowly this time. Together, we bask in the moment. Placing the receiver back on the cradle, I read the story one more time before reaching for the scissors:

> Getting off the next train from the west was Gertrude Lawrence, bound for Cape Cod and six weeks' rest. Immediately after Labor Day she begins a new radio program. The absence of red caps at the station didn't bother Miss Lawrence, who simply piled everything, including her handsome blue wool Chesterfield, on top of a baggage truck and trusted to the rail-road to produce it at the *Century* an hour later. With a pale blue gabardine suit she wore a tailored blouse of mimosa crêpe, fastened at the neck with her Red Cross pin. The deep golden tan of her bare legs didn't come out of a bottle, she announced proudly. She got it the hard way, out in the Cal-ifornia sun. The polish on her long tapering nails was colorless and she wore no hat on her short silver blond hair.... With *Lady in the Dark* now a happy memory, she was just a navy wife, hurrying to the Grand Central station in New York to meet her husband, Lieut. Comdr. Richard Aldrich.[1]
>
> —*Chicago Herald American*, July 21, 1943

Notes

Prologue

1. Kurt Weill, "Two Dreams-Come-True," undated (c. 1945), unpublished, and unpaginated essay, WLA (it was subsequently used as the basis for the liner notes to the cast recording of *Street Scene*, Columbia Special Products COL 4139); undated (c. July–August 1940) typescript letter from Moss Hart to Katharine Cornell, WLRC (for archival sigla, see Selected Bibliography and Discography); Deena Rosenberg, *Fascinating Rhythm: The Collaboration of George and Ira Gershwin* (New York: Dutton, 1991; reprint, Ann Arbor: University of Michigan Press, 1997), 376.

2. Brooks Atkinson, "Struck by Stage Lightning: Comments on the Theatre Wonders of *Lady in the Dark* with Special Reference to Kurt Weill and Gertrude Lawrence," *New York Times*, September 7, 1941.

3. Alvin Theatre souvenir program, quoted in William C. Young, *Documents of American Theater History*, vol. 2, *Famous American Playhouses, 1900–1971* (Chicago: American Library Association, 1973; reprint, 1986), 79.

4. "Builders Take Over the Alvin Theatre: Control of West 52d Street Playhouse Passes from Aarons and Freedley," *New York Times*, May 16, 1932.

1. Opening Night

1. Ira Wolfert, "Miss Lawrence—Lady in a Hit," *San Francisco Chronicle*, February 2, 1941.

2. Information about opening night from Mary Braggiotti, "Feast of Fashions Seen at *Lady in the Dark* Premiere," *New York Post*, January 24, 1941; Nell Gwynne, "Audience on Parade," *Playbill*, February 3, 1941; Dorothy Kilgallen, "The Voice of Broadway: Miss Midnight's Diary: Or, Sneezing through the

Silken Saloons," *New York Journal-American*, January 25, 1941; Robert Rice, "Broadway Report: *Lady in the Dark* Is in the Money," *PM*, January 26, 1941; "The Skirt," "Of People and Places," *Variety*, January 29, 1941; Ed Sullivan, "Little Old New York," *Daily News*, January 25, 1941; Dixie Tighe, " 'Trip,' Says *Vogue* Editor of Stage Counterpart," *New York Post*, January 24, 1941.

3. Weill's telegrams, WLA. Hart's letter to Lawrence reprinted in John Peter Toohey, "And All for One: *Lady in the Dark*," *New York Herald Tribune*, December 7, 1941.

4. Descriptions of costumes from "Fashions Brilliant with Color Worn in *Lady in the Dark*," *Madisonville* (KY) *Messenger*, January 28, 1941; Joan Gardner, "Stage Star Gives 'One-Man' Style Review in New Play," *Miami News*, February 9, 1941; Jacque J. Lansdale, "To Whom It May Concern," *Dallas News*, February 23, 1941.

5. There are three published scripts of *Lady in the Dark*: Moss Hart, Ira Gershwin, and Kurt Weill, *Lady in the Dark* (New York: Random House, 1941; reprint, Cleveland: World Publishing, 1944); Moss Hart, Ira Gershwin, and Kurt Weill, *Lady in the Dark*, acting ed. (New York: Dramatists Play Service, n.d.); Moss Hart, Ira Gershwin, and Kurt Weill, *Lady in the Dark*, in *Great Musicals of the American Theatre*, ed. Stanley Richards (Radnor, PA: Chilton, 1976), 2: 55–123. However, all of them transmit a version of the preproduction script. All quotes from the opening-night performance are from the script belonging to second assistant stage manager Frank Spencer, typed by the Rialto Service Bureau with penciled changes and stage directions.

6. Timing, stage movement, and blocking from Harry Horner, "Twenty Minutes of the Show," *Christian Science Monitor*, February 28, 1941; FS.

7. Chorus member Davis Cunningham sang this section. He also played the small role of Jack, one of Liza's high school classmates, in the final scene.

8. Descriptions of the properties from Harry Horner, "Of Those Four Revolving Stages," *New York Times*, April 6, 1941; Harry Horner, "Designer in Action," *Theatre Arts* 25 (1941): 265–75; [Harry Horner], "Sam H. Harris Presents Gertrude Lawrence in *Lady in the Dark*," *Modern Plastics* 18 (April 1941): 34, 35, 90, 92.

9. Gershwin borrowed the first tercet of Robert Herrick's "Upon Julia's Clothes":

When as in silks my Julia goes,
Then, then (me thinks) how sweetly flowes
That liquefaction of her clothes.

Next, when I cast mine eyes and see
That brave Vibration each way free;
O how that glittering taketh me!

Robert Herrick, *The Complete Poetry of Robert Herrick*, ed. J. Max Patrick, *Hesperides: Or, The Works Both Humane and Divine* (New York: Doubleday,

1963; reprint, New York: Norton, 1968), 344. Regarding Gershwin's rhyme of "glamorous" with "Hammacher Schlammorous," Hammacher Schlemmer is a New York store that during the time of *Lady in the Dark* specialized in innovative household products, the very antithesis of glamour. Thomas D. Fuller, "A Concordance to *Lady in the Dark*," 4, WLRC.

10. Frank Spencer, interview by author, April 9, 1994.

11. Igor Stravinsky and Robert Craft, *Expositions and Developments* (London: Faber and Faber, 1962; reprint, 1981), 66.

12. Sometime during *Lady in the Dark*'s run and because of a postage-rate increase, Liza began posing for the new *three*-cent stamp, FS.

13. "Things Too Little, Too Big—or Too Last-Minute—To Go Elsewhere—But We Thought You'd Like to Know Them," *Vogue*, February 15, 1941.

14. Landsdale, "To Whom It May Concern."

15. The bass soloist was Harold Simmons.

16. Helen Ormsbee, "Making the Magic of *Lady in the Dark*," *New York Herald Tribune*, May 18, 1941.

17. Wolfert, "Miss Lawrence—Lady in a Hit."

18. Kilgallen, "The Voice of Broadway: Miss Midnight's Diary."

19. Alice Hughes, "Today's Woman: Shop Talk and Style Chatter about Women at Work, at Play, at Home and at Leisure," *New York Post*, January 27, 1941.

20. The voices from the Chorus were Larry Siegle, Davis Cunningham, and Hazel Edwards, respectively.

21. The voices were Hazel Edwards and Larry Siegle.

22. The critic for the *Daily News Record* (NY) concurred, comparing it to Stravinsky's *Petrouchka* and Rimsky-Korsakov's *Snow Maiden*. Thomas R. Dash, "Blend Dream and Reality into Miracle of Theatre," *Daily News Record*, January 31, 1941.

23. *Pittsburgh Post-Gazette*, January 9, 1941. An article published eight months later revealed that the critics who traveled to Boston for the tryout were Brooks Atkinson, Robert Coleman, and Richard Watts Jr. "Drama Desk: Lawrence Play Is Pet of Broadway Critics," *New York Journal-American*, September 7, 1941.

24. Helen Ormsbee, "One More Hit for Miss Lawrence," *New York Herald Tribune*, February 9, 1941.

25. John Anderson, "*Lady in the Dark* Premiere at Alvin: Gertrude Lawrence Stars in Lavish Musical Play about a Fashion Editor and Her Complexes," *New York Journal-American*, January 24, 1941; Brooks Atkinson, "The Play in Review: Gertrude Lawrence Appears in Moss Hart's Musical Drama, *Lady in the Dark*, with a Score by Kurt Weill and Lyrics by Ira Gershwin," *New York Times*, January 24, 1941; John Mason Brown, "Gertrude Lawrence Seen in *Lady in the Dark*," *New York Post*, January 24, 1941; Robert Coleman, "Miss Lawrence Proves Artistry Again in Lavish Musical," *Daily Mirror*, January 24, 1941; Louis Kronenberger, "*Lady in the Dark* Gets the Nod from Mr. K.," *PM*, January 24, 1941; Richard Lockridge, "The New Play: *Lady in the Dark*, with Gertrude

Lawrence, Opens at the Alvin," *New York Sun*, January 24, 1941; Burns Mantle, "*Lady in the Dark*: Evening of Dreams for Gertrude Lawrence," *Daily News*, January 24, 1941; Richard Watts Jr., "The Theaters: Dreaming *Lady*," *New York Herald Tribune*, January 24, 1941; Sidney B. Whipple, "*Lady in the Dark*: Triumph for Gertrude Lawrence," *New York World-Telegram*, January 24, 1941.

26. Edward Jablonski, *Gershwin* (New York: Doubleday, 1987; reprint, Boston: Northeastern University Press, 1990), 334.

27. Weill described the property to *New York Post* columnist Leonard Lyons as follows:

> Before I came to this country I lived for two years outside of Paris in a lovely old stonehouse, with beautiful trees and a long stone wall all around the place and a brook in back.... Well, about 3 or 4 years ago I went to see Maxwell Anderson ... just next to his estate I saw a lovely old stonehouse, with beautiful trees and a long stone wall all around the place and a brook in back.... Even if it would have been for sale, I couldn't have bought it because I had no money. But things changed, thanks to Dr. Freud and a certain *Lady in the Dark*—and yesterday I signed contracts which make me owner of the house, the trees ... the brook and the stone wall.

Typescript letter dated April 5, 1941, from Kurt Weill to Leonard Lyons. On May 5, 2005, Smythe auctioned three letters from Kurt Weill to Leonard Lyons. The quotation is from the auction catalogue.

28. Kitty Carlisle Hart, *Kitty: An Autobiography* (New York: Doubleday, 1988; reprint, New York: St. Martin's Press, 1989), 128.

2. Genesis

1. Benjamin Welles, "Lyricist of 'The Saga of Jenny' et al.: A History of the Life and Some of the Works of Ira Gershwin," *New York Times*, May 25, 1941.

2. Transcription of an oral history interview with Ira Gershwin from the 33 1/3 rpm record *A Living Liner: Recollections of Kurt Weill*, RCA Victor LL-201 (SRLM-8309) originally included with the Morton Gould recording *The Two Worlds of Kurt Weill*, RCA Victor LSC-2863, WLRC.

3. Mario R. Mercado, "I Remember: A Podium with a View—Recollections by Maurice Abravanel," *Kurt Weill Newsletter* 5, no. 1 (1987): 8.

4. For more on this production, see Kim H. Kowalke, "*The Threepenny Opera* in America," in *Kurt Weill: The Threepenny Opera*, ed. Stephen Hinton, Cambridge Opera Handbooks (Cambridge, UK: Cambridge University Press, 1990), 80–86.

5. For more about the Group Theatre, see Harold Clurman, *The Fervent Years: The Story of the Group Theatre and the Thirties* (New York: Knopf, 1945; reprint, New York: Da Capo Press, 1983); Wendy Smith, *Real Life Drama: The Group Theatre and America, 1931–1940* (New York: Knopf, 1990; reprint, New York: Grove Weidenfeld, 1992).

6. Kurt Weill, "What Is Musical Theatre?," undated and unpublished essay, WLA.

7. The film was eventually made under the title *Blockade*. For an inventory of the music Weill composed for this project, see David Drew, *Kurt Weill: A Handbook* (Berkeley: University of California Press, 1987), 282–86.

8. Quoted in Cheryl Crawford, *One Naked Individual: My Fifty Years in the Theatre* (Indianapolis: Bobbs-Merrill, 1977), 99.

9. For more about the Federal Theatre Project, see John O'Connor and Lorraine Brown, eds., *The Federal Theatre Project: "Free, Adult, Uncensored"* (London: Eyre Methuen, 1980; reprint, 1986).

10. For differing accounts of this work, see Ronald Sanders, *The Days Grow Short: The Life and Music of Kurt Weill* (New York: Holt, Rinehart, and Winston, 1980; reprint, Los Angeles: Silman-James Press, 1991), 264–65; Drew, *Kurt Weill: A Handbook*, 294–96.

11. For an inventory of Weill's music for this project, see Drew, *Kurt Weill: A Handbook*, 297–300.

12. For a history of the Playwrights' Producing Company, see John F. Wharton, *Life among the Playwrights: Being Mostly the Story of the Playwrights' Producing Company, Inc.* (New York: Quadrangle/New York Times Book Co., 1974).

13. For an exegesis of the politics of *Knickerbocker Holiday*, see Maxwell Anderson, "The Politics of *Knickerbocker Holiday*," in *Off Broadway: Essays about the Theater* (New York: William Sloane, 1947; reprint, New York: Da Capo Press, 1971), 81–86.

14. Weill and Anderson salvaged some of their adaptation of *Aeneas Africanus* for *Lost in the Stars*.

15. For more about *Railroads on Parade*, see Larry Zim, Mel Lerner, and Herbert Rolfes, *The World of Tomorrow: The 1939 New York World's Fair* (New York: Harper & Row, 1988), 100–105. Weill later traversed American history in *Love Life*, where the institution of marriage replaces the railroad as the operative mechanism. For *Street Scene*, Weill set a portion of Walt Whitman's poem inspired by the lilacs heaped on Lincoln's casket as it made its trip by rail to the cemetery, an event dramatized in *Railroads on Parade*.

16. William G. King, "Composer for the Theater—Kurt Weill Talks about 'Practical Music,'" *New York Sun*, February 3, 1940.

17. Moss Hart, foreword to *Lady in the Dark*, by Kurt Weill and Ira Gershwin, vocal score, ed. Albert Sirmay (New York: Chappell Music Company, 1941), n.p.

18. Robert Kimball and Alfred Simon, *The Gershwins* (New York: Atheneum, 1973), 235.

19. Welles, "Lyricist of 'The Saga of Jenny' et al."

20. Moss Hart, *Act One: An Autobiography* (New York: Random House, 1959; reprint, 2002).

21. Malcolm Goldstein, *George S. Kaufman: His Life, His Theater* (New York: Oxford University Press, 1979), 185.

22. Ibid., 270.

23. Ibid., 287.

24. John Peter Toohey, "Regarding Those Who Would Rather Be Right," *New York Times*, November 7, 1937.

25. Although Moss Hart did not regularly date his correspondence to Dore Schary, his discussions of production dates make it possible to approximate the period of the letters.

26. Undated (c. 1937–1938) typescript letter from Moss Hart to Dore Schary, DSP; undated (c. 1937–1938) typescript letter from Moss Hart to Dore Schary, DSP; undated (c. January 1–10, 1938) typescript letter from Moss Hart to Dore Schary, DSP.

27. Undated (c. August 21–28, 1938) typescript and manuscript letter from Moss Hart to Dore Schary, DSP.

28. Undated (c. December 1938) typescript letter from Moss Hart to Dore Schary, DSP.

29. Moss Hart, "The Saga of Gertie: The Author of *Lady in the Dark* Tells How He Found a Star," *New York Times*, March 2, 1941.

30. [Moss Hart], "The How and Why of *Lady in the Dark*," *Lady in the Dark* Souvenir Playbills, n.d.

31. Hart, foreword to *Lady in the Dark*.

32. [Hart], "The How and Why of *Lady in the Dark*."

33. "Hart Writes Play; Has No Co-Author," *New York Times*, January 11, 1940.

34. "Rialto Gossip: Notes on Plays and Playwrights, Also the Producers and Their Plans," *New York Times*, February 18, 1940.

35. "Moss Hart Play Will Have Songs," *New York Times*, February 24, 1940.

36. "News of the Stage," *New York Times*, February 26, 1940.

37. Carlisle Hart, *Kitty*, 117. According to New York City telephone directories, Kubie's office prior to 1940 was at 34 East Seventy-fifth; in 1940 it moved to 7 1/2 East Eighty-first. Prior to 1937, Hart saw psychoanalyst Dr. Gregory Zilboorg in New York and Dr. Ernst Simmel in Los Angeles. Steven Bach, *Dazzler: The Life and Times of Moss Hart* (New York: Knopf, 2001; reprint, Cambridge: Da Capo Press, 2002), 115–16, 144.

38. Robert Rice, "Rice and Old Shoes," *PM*, February 3, 1941.

39. Edward Glover, "In Honor of Lawrence Kubie," *Journal of Nervous and Mental Disease* 149, no. 1 (1969): 5–18.

40. Lawrence S. Kubie, *Practical Aspects of Psychoanalysis: A Handbook for Prospective Patients and Their Advisors* (New York: Norton, 1936), vii.

41. Quoted in Peter Gay, *Freud: A Life for Our Time* (New York: Norton, 1988; reprint, 1998), 491–92.

42. Sigmund Freud, "The Theme of the Three Caskets," in *The Standard Edition of the Complete Psychological Works of Sigmund Freud*, ed. and trans. James Strachey, vol. 12, *The Case of Schreber, Papers on Technique, and Other Works* (London: Hogarth Press and the Institute of Psycho-Analysis, 1958), 291–301.

43. Quoted in George Brandes, *William Shakespeare* (New York: Macmillan, 1931), 159.

44. Hart's typescripts of "I Am Listening" are bound as volume 40 of his personal library, MH-KCP.

45. Undated (c. May 5–15, 1940) typescript letter from Moss Hart to Dore Schary, DSP.

46. " 'Stage' to Portray Freud," *New York Times*, March 22, 1940; "Gossip of the Rialto," *New York Times*, March 24, 1940; "Screen News Here and in Hollywood," *New York Times*, February 26, 1940; "By Way of Report," *New York Times*, March 3, 1940; "Screen News Here and in Hollywood," *New York Times*, March 13, 1940; "Items in the News," *New York Times*, March 17, 1940. None of these projects came to fruition.

47. Typescript letter dated March 18, 1940, from Ira Gershwin to Kurt Weill, WLA.

48. Ira Gershwin, *Lyrics on Several Occasions: A Selection of Stage & Screen Lyrics Written for Sundry Situations; and Now Arranged in Arbitrary Categories. To Which Have Been Added Many Informative Annotations & Disquisitions on Their Why & Wherefore, Their Whom-for, Their How; and Matters Associative* (New York: Knopf, 1959; reprint, New York: Limelight, 1997), xi.

49. Typescript letter dated March 18, 1940, from Ira Gershwin to Kurt Weill, WLA.

50. Kurt Weill, "Dreams are, at the moment . . . ," undated and unpublished typescript, WLA.

51. New York City telephone directories from the years 1939 and 1940 do not list an actual restaurant named Le Coq d'Or.

52. Richard Taruskin, *"The Golden Cockerel,"* in *The New Grove Dictionary of Opera*, ed. Stanley Sadie (London: Macmillan, 1992), 2: 474–76.

53. Kubie, *Practical Aspects of Psychoanalysis*, 90.

54. *British Medical Journal*, Supplement, Appendix 2 (June 29, 1929): 266, quoted in ibid., 18–19.

55. Kubie, *Practical Aspects of Psychoanalysis*, 50, 51.

56. Ibid., 149, 141, 53.

57. Eugene B. Brody, "Lawrence S. Kubie's Psychoanalysis," in Lawrence S. Kubie, *Symbol and Neurosis: Selected Papers of Lawrence S. Kubie*, ed. Herbert J. Schlesinger, Psychological Issues, No. 44 (New York: International Universities Press, 1978), 1. In 1934 Kubie published analyses of two literary works: "The Literature of Horror: William Faulkner's *Sanctuary*," *Saturday Review of Literature* 11 (1934): 218, 224–226; and *"God's Little Acre*: An Analysis," *Saturday Review of Literature* 11 (1934): 305–306, 312.

58. Kubie, *Practical Aspects of Psychoanalysis*, xiv.

59. Gershwin, *Lyrics on Several Occasions*, 208.

60. Gershwin, *A Living Liner*.

61. Undated (c. May 5–15, 1940) typescript letter from Moss Hart to Dore Schary, DSP.

62. Richard Kislan, *The Musical: A Look at the American Musical Theater*, rev. and exp. ed. (New York: Applause Books, 1995), 228.

63. Gershwin, *Lyrics on Several Occasions*, 201. A year later Hart gave one of the sheepdog's offspring to Weill, which he and Lenya named "Wooly" after Alexander Woollcott. Bill Blowitz, "Biography of Kurt Weill," unpublished biography dated April 20, 1945, WLA.

64. Goldstein, *George S. Kaufman*, 333–34. Kaufman and Hart's *George Washington Slept Here* played 173 performances, but *The White-Haired Boy*'s director, George Abbott, withdrew it after a one-week tryout in Boston.

65. Moss Hart, "Dream Two" and "Dream Three," GC.

66. This "Unforgettable" has no relation to the song by the same name made famous by Nat "King" Cole.

67. Gershwin, *Lyrics on Several Occasions*, 201–202.

68. Typescript letter dated September 2, 1940, from Kurt Weill to Ira Gershwin, GC.

69. Ira Gershwin, typescript of Third Dream "Minstrel," GC.

70. Ira Gershwin's annotation dated September 1967 for "Manuscripts of the 3 Dreams," GC.

71. The exotic personae of Maggie and Alison prefigure the fortune-telling sisters in *Love Life*'s Minstrel Show, the Misses Horoscope and Mysticism.

72. Moss Hart, "Dream Four," quoted in Ira Gershwin, *The Complete Lyrics of Ira Gershwin*, ed. Robert Kimball (New York: Knopf, 1993; reprint, New York: Da Capo Press, 1998), 302.

73. Undated (c. August 1940) typescript letter from Moss Hart to Dore Schary, DSP.

74. Manuscript letter dated August 22, 1940, from Benjamin Britten to Elizabeth Mayer, transcribed as letter 283 in Donald Mitchell and Philip Reed, eds., *Letters from a Life: The Selected Letters and Diaries of Benjamin Britten 1913–1976, vol. 2, 1939–1945* (Berkeley: University of California Press, 1991), 845–47. Britten and Pears stayed at the Owl's Head Inn August 10–26, 1940. Donald Mitchell and John Evans, *Benjamin Britten: Pictures from a Life 1913–1976* (New York: Scribner's, 1978), 133.

75. Manuscript letter dated August 26, 1940, from Ira Gershwin to Kurt Weill, WLA. Coincidentally, "Lady in the Dark" is also the name of a dance tune in John and Henry Playford's *The English Dancing Master*, published in numerous editions in the late seventeenth and early eighteenth centuries.

76. Typescript letter dated September 14, 1940, from Kurt Weill to Ira Gershwin, GC.

77. No musical sketches for "Tschaikowsky" survive. Maurice Abravanel believed that Sylvia Fine actually composed this song. The critic for New York's *Daily News* at the beginning of *Lady in the Dark*'s second season concurred:

> Take, as you will have to, the case of Danny Kaye and the chief comedy
> rôle in *Lady in the Dark*. Danny, in the original production, was, next to

the star, the entertainment's chief attraction. He had come up slowly from summer stock and winter nightclubs. His wife had written several clever patter songs for him, and he was ready for a major Broadway assignment.

To help him, Kurt Weill, composer, and Ira Gershwin, lyricist, of *Lady in the Dark*, copied one of Miss Fine's patter songs, replacing the twisted names of Russian ballet dancers with those of Russian composers, calling it "Tschaikowsky," and spotting it in a fantastic circus scene in the play.

Burns Mantle, "'Lady in Dark' Has Undergone Cast Changes," *Chicago Daily Tribune*, September 14, 1941.

78. The exchange took place at a production meeting at Sam H. Harris's office on August 27, 1940, and is recounted in the typescript letter dated September 2, 1940, from Kurt Weill to Ira Gershwin, GC.

3. Musical Score

1. Weill, "Two Dreams-Come-True."

2. Bertolt Brecht, "A Short Organum for the Theatre," trans. John Willett, in *Brecht on Theatre: The Development of an Aesthetic* (New York: Hill and Wang, 1964; reprint, 1992), quoted in Kim H. Kowalke, *Kurt Weill in Europe*, Studies in Musicology, No. 14 (Ann Arbor, MI: UMI Research Press, 1979), 117. Geoffrey Block believes that *gestus* enabled Weill to borrow from his European works for those he composed in the United States. Geoffrey Block, *Enchanted Evenings: The Broadway Musical from Show Boat to Sondheim* (New York: Oxford University Press, 1997; reprint, 2003), 144–46.

3. Ira Gershwin had previously used this lyric in *Oh, Kay!*

4. Tom Parkinson, "Circus Music," in *The New Grove Dictionary of American Music*, ed. H. Wiley Hitchcock and Stanley Sadie (London: Macmillan, 1986), 1: 447–48.

5. That two of the three dances were Latin is no surprise: bandleaders Don Azpiazú (who made the rumba popular) and Xavier Cugat introduced Latin dances during the 1930s. Barry Kernfeld, "Latin Jazz," in *The New Grove Dictionary of American Music*, 3: 16. In 1939–1940, a Latin wave was sweeping the country, making its way into numerous Broadway numbers, including "The South American Way" from *The Streets of Paris*, "The Mexiconga" from *George White Scandals of 1939–1940*, "Soused American Way" from *The Straw Hat Review*, "All Dressed Up (Spic and Spanish)" and "She Could Shake the Maracas" from *Too Many Girls*, "Katie Went to Haiti" from *DuBarry Was a Lady*, "I Want My Mama" from *Earl Carroll Vanities*, "Latins Know How" from *Louisiana Purchase*, and "The Rhumba Jumps" from *Walk with Music*.

6. Gershwin's September 1967 annotation for his worksheets to "The Princess of Pure Delight" included the following: "For a time, Weill and I had 'Bolero' as a working title, because he felt he would orchestrate most of this dream in that rhythm," GC.

7. Weill's teacher at the Berlin Hochschule für Musik, Engelbert Humperdinck, invented *Sprechstimme*, or *Sprechgesang*, for his opera *Königskinder* (1897). Weill adopted his teacher's notation for *Sprechstimme*. Paul Griffiths, "Sprechgesang," in *The New Grove Dictionary of Music*, 2nd ed., ed. Stanley Sadie (London: Macmillan, 2001), 24: 223.

8. J. Bradford Robinson maintains that Weill's first attempt at composing in American popular song form was "Johnny's Song" from *Johnny Johnson*. The song's refrain has a form of AABACA and was marketed under the title "To Love You and to Lose You." J. Bradford Robinson, "Learning the Ropes: Kurt Weill and the American Theater Song," *Kurt Weill Newsletter* 15, no. 2 (1997): 3–7.

9. Gershwin, *Lyrics on Several Occasions*, 202.

10. Ibid., 187. As a young man, Gershwin created his pseudonym by taking the given names of his youngest brother, Arthur, and sister, Frances, to avoid unfavorable comparison with his famous brother, George.

11. Gershwin neglected to count this name when he published his memoir and claimed that there were forty-nine, an error that has made its way into many other sources. Gershwin, *Lyrics on Several Occasions*, 186–89.

12. Gershwin and Weill revised the "Song of the Zodiac" for part of "You Have to Do What You Do Do" for their next collaboration, *The Firebrand of Florence*. The song as it existed in *Lady in the Dark* is lost.

13. Typescript letter dated November 14, 1949, from Kurt Weill to Olin Downes, WLA.

14. David Drew, "Motifs, Tags, and Related Matters," in *Kurt Weill: The Threepenny Opera*, ed. Hinton, 149–60. Drew's term for this motive is the "*Moritat*-motif."

15. Robert C. Bagar, "Kurt Weill Has Secured Niche of His Own at 35: He's Visiting in the Interest of His Incidental Music to *The Eternal Road*—Explains Role of Jazz," *New York World-Telegram*, December 21, 1935.

16. I am grateful to David Shildkret for first alerting me to this nursery rhyme. It may be found in the following collections: Iona Opie and Peter Opie, comps., *The Oxford Nursery Rhyme Book* (New York: Oxford University Press, 1955; reprint, 1997), 200; Iona Opie and Peter Opie, eds., *The Oxford Dictionary of Nursery Rhymes* (New York: Oxford University Press, 1951; reprint, 1995), 381–82; William S. Baring-Gould and Ceil Baring-Gould, *The Annotated Mother Goose: Nursery Rhymes Old and New* (New York: Bramhall House, 1962; reprint, 1970), 163. The captain in the poem may refer to Sir Francis Drake, who, along with Sir Walter Raleigh, was responsible for introducing several "comfits" into Elizabethan society, including potatoes, tobacco, plums, cherries, apricots, grapes, and gooseberries.

17. Discussed in bruce d. mcclung, "*Psicosi per musica*: Re-examining *Lady in the Dark*," in *A Stranger Here Myself: Kurt Weill Studien*, ed. Kim H. Kowalke and Horst Edler, Haskala wissenschaftliche Abhandlungen, No. 8 (Hildesheim, Germany: Georg Olms Verlag, 1993), 250–59; and analyzed in bruce d. mcclung,

"American Dreams: Analyzing Moss Hart, Ira Gershwin, and Kurt Weill's *Lady in the Dark*" (PhD diss., University of Rochester, 1994), 372–426.

18. "The two elements are linked together in such a way that either triad can serve as the local representative of the tonic complex. Within that complex itself, however, one of the two elements is at any moment in the primary position while the other remains subordinate to it." Robert Bailey, "An Analytical Study of the Sketches and Drafts," in Richard Wagner, *Prelude and Transfiguration from Tristan und Isolde*, ed. Robert Bailey, Norton Critical Scores (New York: Norton, 1985), 122.

19. Typescript letter dated July 24, 1948, from Kurt Weill to Irving Sablosky, WLA. Robert Bailey makes the same point: "The function of this major triad with added 6th should not be confused with the function of the added-6th chord in twentieth-century popular music, which acts as a decorated triad (a triad with an extra nontriadic note). The actual notes of the two chords are the same, but this double-triadic sonority functions here [in Wagner's Prelude and Transfiguration from *Tristan and Isolde*] as the harmonic representative of the double-tonic complex at work throughout the structure." "An Analytical Study," 122.

20. Frank Spencer's assistant stage manager's script uses "Childhood Dream" for a handwritten tab, and it was also used as a heading in the published piano-vocal score. However, the term never appeared in any of *Lady in the Dark*'s playbills. On *Lady in the Dark*'s official time sheet, the flashbacks were simply designated "4th Dream," MCNY.

21. In this regard, Weill's experience with *Lady in the Dark* was exceptional. During the Boston tryout of Weill's next show, *One Touch of Venus*, he described orchestrating its score: "It's hard work.... You sleep about two hours a night for the four weeks that it takes, but it's fun. Not until the rehearsals get under way can you start your orchestrating since until you know who the singers are going to be you can't tell what key to put each number in." Warren Storey Smith, "Music of Kurt Weill Called Unusual: Composer, Who Contributed the Score to the Current Musical Comedy, *One Touch of Venus*, Is a Refugee with Fine Record of Achievement," *Boston Post*, September 26, 1943.

22. These drinking songs may have been in some way a response to Prohibition and were probably made all the more exciting because of it. Richard Traubner, *Operetta: A Theatrical History*, rev. ed. (New York: Routledge, 2003), 385.

23. In retrospect, the term "operetta" has come to be applied to all national schools of late nineteenth-century and early twentieth-century light comic opera.

24. Richard Traubner and David Drew have both observed that *Lady in the Dark*'s dream sequences are organized in the manner of extended operetta finales, although neither explored the possible antecedents. Traubner, *Operetta: A Theatrical History*, 318; Drew, *Kurt Weill: A Handbook*, 315.

25. In American operetta the male romantic lead was usually cast as a baritone; in Europe such a role had been for a tenor.

26. Rosenberg, *Fascinating Rhythm*, 378. Ira had previously spoofed *Trial by Jury* in *Of Thee I Sing*.

27. Traubner, *Operetta: A Theatrical History*, 155.

28. Morris Stonzek, comments made on November 4, 1983, "I Remember... Recollections of Weill and Lenya by Their Associates," International Kurt Weill Conference and Festival, Yale University, tape recording, WLRC.

29. Weill included another early electronic keyboard instrument in his orchestrations during this period. The Novachord, which was produced from 1939 to c. 1943, is included in his orchestration of *Railroads on Parade* and the incidental music for Sidney Howard's *Madame, Will You Walk?* He also composed a Novachord solo for Elmer Rice's *Two on an Island*.

30. Hugh Davies, "Hammond Organ," in *The New Grove Dictionary of Musical Instruments*, ed. Stanely Sadie (London: Macmillan, 1984), 2: 120–22. The overtone series activated by the drawbars is not the natural one. Save for the octaves, all the overtones are slightly tempered, and the seventh is omitted altogether.

31. Kurt Weill, "Broadway and the Musical Theatre," *Composer's News-Record*, May 1947.

32. Maurice Abravanel, telephone interview by author, October 4, 1991.

33. Kurt Weill, "Score for a Play," *New York Times*, January 5, 1947.

4. Tryout

1. Moss Hart, "Life with Gertie: In Which Some Light Is Thrown on *Lady in the Dark*," MH-KCP. When the essay was published in the *New York Times*, this passage was altered to give the impression that in Philadelphia Hart and Cornell together decided that the role was "now a little out of her province." Hart, "The Saga of Gertie."

2. Hart later parodied McClintic's volatile nature with the character of Carleton Fitzgerald in his play *Light Up the Sky*.

3. Moss Hart, "One World—One Trip—One Play," undated and unpublished typescript, MH-KCP.

4. Richard Stoddard Aldrich, *Gertrude Lawrence as Mrs. A: An Intimate Biography of the Great Star* (New York: Greystone Press, 1954; reprint, New York: Greenwood Press, 1969), 66; Charles Gentry, "Lawrence, Lady of Energy," *Detroit Evening News*, December 1, 1942.

5. Hart, "Life with Gertie," 4.

6. Aldrich, *Gertrude Lawrence as Mrs. A*, 73.

7. Hart, "Life with Gertie," 5.

8. "Gossip of the Rialto," *New York Times*, May 5, 1940. In his essay Hart claims that Cornell was out of New York State at this time. As evinced by Coward's travel itinerary, his autobiography, the report of the SS *Washington*'s arrival, and the schedule of Cornell's *No Time for Comedy* tour, Cornell was in New York at the time of Hart's meeting with Coward.

9. Hart, "Life with Gertie," 6.

10. Ibid., 6–7.

11. Noël Coward, *Future Indefinite* (London: William Heinemann, 1954; reprint, New York: Da Capo Press, 1980), 126.

12. Hart, "Life with Gertie," 7.

13. Ibid., 8–9.

14. Ibid., 11.

15. Ibid., 12.

16. Ibid., 13.

17. Hart's biographer claims that Lawrence's contract was not signed until July 1941, "six months after *Lady in the Dark* opened." Bach, *Dazzler*, 222. This, however, was a renegotiated contract. The original one and the signed rider are both dated June 21, 1940, GLP.

18. Lawrence's contracts for *Lady in the Dark*, GLP. At this time Actors' Equity contractually defined Broadway seasons as "the period between the first day of September and the following first day of June."

19. Hart, "Life with Gertie," 8. The previous season, Holtzmann had secured Lawrence 25 percent of the sale of the screen rights for *Skylark*, despite the Dramatists Guild's basic agreement of 60 percent for the playwright and 40 percent for the producer. "News of the Stage," *New York Times*, April 16, 1940.

20. Undated (c. July–August 1940) typescript letter from Moss Hart to Katharine Cornell, WLRC.

21. Martin Gottfried, *Nobody's Fool: The Lives of Danny Kaye* (New York: Simon & Schuster, 1994), 24–27.

22. Ibid., 47–54.

23. Moss Hart, "Thirty-five Years of Broadway Musicals," interview by Brooks Atkinson, broadcast June 17, 1960, on WQXR, New York, MH-KCP.

24. Typed annotation by Harry Horner accompanying an early script of *Lady in the Dark*, BRTC; Horner, "Of Those Four Revolving Stages." Horner had also designed the scenery and costumes for Weill's pageant *Railroads on Parade*.

25. Harry Horner, "Designer in Action," *Theatre Arts* 25 (1941): 268.

26. Ibid., 273–74.

27. Horner, "Of Those Four Revolving Stages."

28. "He Made the Stage a Moving Thing," *New York Sun*, March 28, 1941; Horner, "Of Those Four Revolving Stages."

29. Ibid.

30. [Horner], "Sam H. Harris Presents Gertrude Lawrence in *Lady in the Dark*."

31. For an overview of Sharaff's career, see Irene Sharaff, *Broadway and Hollywood: Costumes Designed by Irene Sharaff* (New York: Van Nostrand Reinhold, 1976).

32. Bernadine Morris, "Museum Celebrates the Flair That Was Vreeland," *New York Times*, December 7, 1993. For an overview of Vreeland's contributions to fashion, see Amy Fine Collins, "The Cult of Diana," *Vanity Fair* 56 (November 1993): 174–83, 188–90; Eleanor Dwight, *Diana Vreeland* (New York: HarperCollins, 2002). In addition to the character of Alison Du Bois being based on Vreeland, fashion editor for *Harper's Bazaar*, *Lady in the Dark* had another

connection with the magazine. Its staff photographer, Louise Dahl-Wolfe, created an original *Lady in the Dark* montage, which was featured in the January 1941 issue and is reproduced for this book's cover.

33. Alice Hughes, "Today's Woman: Star of *Lady in the Dark* Steals Play from Celanese Creative Fabrics Showing," *New York Post*, February 19, 1941.

34. "Fashions Brilliant with Color Worn in *Lady in the Dark.*"

35. Typescript letter dated September 14, 1940, from Kurt Weill to Ira Gershwin, GC.

36. Macdonald Carey, *The Days of My Life* (New York: St. Martin's Press, 1991), 75.

37. Typescript letter dated August 24, 1940, from Kurt Weill to Gertrude Lawrence, WLRC; typescript letter dated September 14, 1940, from Gertrude Lawrence to Kurt Weill, WLA.

38. Typescript letter dated October 7, 1940, from Kurt Weill to Gertrude Lawrence. This letter was offered for sale by James Lowe Autographs of New York. The quotation comes from a 1992 Lowe catalogue.

39. Ibid.

40. Gershwin, *Lyrics on Several Occasions*, 144. Victor Mature signed on November 12 for *Lady in the Dark*. "Mature Will Act in Hart's Musical," *New York Times*, November 13, 1940.

41. Lehman Engel, "Kurt Weill and I," undated (c. 1970s) and unpublished typescript essay, KWP.

42. Lehman Engel, *This Bright Day: An Autobiography* (New York: Macmillan, 1974), 95.

43. Manfred Hecht, telephone interview by author, September 16, 1993.

44. Hart, "Life with Gertie," 14. When the essay was published, the section concerning John Golden was suppressed.

45. Ibid., 16–17.

46. Hart, *Act One*, 311–12.

47. Hart, "Life with Gertie," 17–18.

48. Atkinson, "Thirty-five Years of Broadway Musicals."

49. Helen Ormsbee, "One More Hit for Miss Lawrence."

50. Maurice Abravanel, telephone interview by author, February 13, 1992.

51. Ann Lee, telephone interview by author, March 31, 1994; Fred Hearn, telephone interview by author, January 20, 1994.

52. Atkinson, "Thirty-five Years of Broadway Musicals."

53. Coincidentally, one of the Russian composers' names was Dimitri Tiomkin, who had brought his first wife, Albertina Rasch, to the United States in 1929.

54. "Gertrude Lawrence Styles," *New York Post*, January 16, 1941.

55. Spencer, telephone interview.

56. "Designer in Action," 274. The property master was Sam Roseman.

57. Although the portable dressing room appears on Horner's ground plan (Figure 29), this drawing was made for *Theatre Arts* magazine after *Lady in the Dark* had opened in New York.

58. Ormsbee, "Making the Magic of *Lady in the Dark*."

59. Hecht, telephone interview.

60. "Unsuspected Duet During *Lady in the Dark*," *New York Herald Tribune*, February 16, 1941.

61. Goldstein, *George S. Kaufman*, 342–43.

62. Aldrich, *Gertrude Lawrence as Mrs. A*, 111, 112.

63. Gershwin, *Lyrics on Several Occasions*, 209.

64. Atkinson, "Thirty-five Years of Broadway Musicals."

65. Peggy Doyle, "Gertrude Lawrence's Most Difficult Role," *Boston American*, December 30, 1940.

66. Abravanel, telephone interview by author, October 4, 1991.

67. Carey, *The Days of My Life*, 88.

68. Atkinson, "Thirty-five Years of Broadway Musicals."

69. Gershwin, *Lyrics on Several Occasions*, 209.

70. Abravanel, telephone interview by author, October 4, 1991. Other first-hand accounts are in Aldrich, *Gertrude Lawrence as Mrs. A*, 112–13; Gershwin, *Lyrics on Several Occasions*, 208–209; Atkinson, "Thirty-five Years of Broadway Musicals." Gershwin, unaware of Abravanel's excision of the score, believed that the brief section after "Tschaikowsky" was not heard because of applause.

71. Helen Eager, "'Lady in Dark' at Colonial," *Boston Traveler*, December 31, 1940; Elinor Hughes, "Gertrude Lawrence in Hart-Weill-Gershwin Musical," *Boston Herald*, December 31, 1940; John K. Hutchens, "Musical Dream: Gertrude Lawrence at the Colonial in Moss Hart's *Lady in the Dark*," *Boston Evening Transcript*, December 31, 1940; Elliot Norton, "Unusual Show at Colonial: *Lady in the Dark* Is Great Spectacle for Theatregoers," *Boston Post*, December 31, 1940; L. A. Sloper, "Gertrude Lawrence Starred in Hart-Weill Show: *Lady in the Dark* Combines Fantasy with Musical Comedy," *Christian Science Monitor*, December 31, 1940; "Two New Plays: Colonial Theatre, *Lady in the Dark*," *Boston Globe*, December 31, 1940.

72. Eager, "'Lady in Dark' at Colonial"; Leo Gaffney, "*Lady in the Dark* Sheds Light," *Green Magazine*, January 3, 1941.

73. Ormsbee, "One More Hit for Miss Lawrence."

74. Dan Harden, telephone interview by author, September 21, 1993.

75. Gershwin, *Lyrics on Several Occasions*, 144.

76. Priscilla T. Campbell, "This Week," *Worcester* (MA) *Gazette & Post*, January 4, 1941; "Stars at Benefit Greek Ball Tonight," *Boston Traveler*, January 3, 1941; "Of *Lady in the Dark*," *Boston Post*, January 12, 1941.

77. "Gertie's *Lady* $26,000 Boston," *Variety*, January 8, 1941.

78. Maurice Abravanel, interview by author, Rochester, New York, January 31, 1991. Years later in London, when Gertrude Lawrence and Danny Kaye appeared on the Bebe Daniels–Ben Lyons broadcast *High Gang*, Gertie took a turn at reeling off "Tschaikowsky" and allowed Danny to top *her* performance by bumping and grinding his way through "The Saga of Jenny." Aldrich, *Gertrude Lawrence as Mrs. A*, 114.

79. *Daily News*, January 9, 1941.

80. John R. Stingo, "Thespians Tall Tattle," *New York Enquirer*, February 26, 1941.

81. "Lawrence SRO $27,000 in Hub," *Variety*, January 15, 1941.

82. Toohey, "And All for One: *Lady in the Dark*."

83. Leonard Lyons, "Broadway Medley: Gertrude Lawrence in Intricate Play," *Boston American*, January 20, 1941.

84. Ormsbee, "One More HIt for Miss Lawrence."

5. Broadway Run

1. "Prosperity Notes," *New York Herald Tribune*, January 27, 1941; "Two Songs Interrupt Show," *New York Times*, January 1, 1941; Rice, "*Lady in the Dark* Is in the Money"; Arthur Pollock, "How to Write a Hit Play Like *Lady in the Dark*," *Brooklyn Eagle*, January 28, 1941; "News and Comment of Stage and Screen," *Pittsburgh* (MA) *Sentinel*, February 1, 1941; Wilbur Morse Jr., "Manhattan Memo," *Your Charm*, April 1941.

2. Claude A. La Belle, "From an Aisle Seat," *California News*, February 28, 1941. The $32,100 figure did not take into account standees.

3. Although originally budgeted at $100,000, by opening night *Lady in the Dark* had cost about $125,000. This figure was widely cited, but the actual amount was $127,715. Stingo, "Thespians Tall Tattle."

4. Ormsbee, "One More Hit for Miss Lawrence."

5. "Harris, Shumlin Insures Stars against Illness," *Variety*, February 12, 1941.

6. "Manhattan Memo."

7. Warner Brothers had previously paid that amount for Kaufman and Hart's *The Man Who Came to Dinner*. "Para 'Shelves' *Lady in the Dark:* Production of $283,000 Play Put Off until B'way Road Runs Are Ended," *New York Telegraph*, February 12, 1941.

8. Although the figure of $283,000 was widely reported by the press, the letter of agreement for the motion picture rights put the actual amount at $285,000. Typescript letter dated February 20, 1941, from Moss Hart, Kurt Weill, and Ira Gershwin to Sidney Fleischer, Esq., GC. Weill's attorney's records confirm this amount, ZP.

9. Ibid.

10. *Women's Wear Daily*, February 11, 1941; "Purple Hat Group of Wearable Brims Shown by Maker," *Women's Wear Daily*, February 18, 1941; "New Sheers for This Summer's Draped Afternoon and Dinner Gowns," *Women's Wear Daily*, February 19, 1941; "Celanese Offers Creative Fabrics," *New York Journal of Commerce*, February 20, 1941.

11. "Sponsors Group of Enka Rayon Dresses," *Women's Wear Daily*, February 26, 1941.

12. Sidney Whipple, "Diagnosis of Liza Authentic," *New York World-Telegram*, February 21, 1941.

13. Vesta Kelling, " 'Gertie' Lawrence Loves Her Work: Current Hit Is *Lady in the Dark*," *Boston Traveler*, March 12, 1941. When the letter was quoted in Philadelphia, the third and fourth sentences were deleted. Arthur Bronson, "Gertrude Lawrence Keeps Fingers Crossed," *Philadelphia Record*, September 27, 1942. The letter was quoted in its entirety in Chicago. "Liza Wins Praise of Psychiatrist," *Chicago Sun*, February 15, 1943.

14. This Associated Press interview was distributed by the news agency and appeared in Herman Allen, "*Lady in the Dark* Moves in Circles to Straighten the Heroine's Kinks," *Montgomery* (AL) *Advertiser*, March 30, 1941; *Columbia* (SC) *State*, April 6, 1941; *Columbus* (GA) *Ledger-Enquirer*, April 13, 1941.

15. *New York World-Telegram*, February 14, 1941.

16. A photo essay of the session, "How a Record Is Made," was published in the *Norwalk* (CT) *Hour*, March 31, 1941.

17. Typescript letter dated March 8, 1941, from Kurt Weill to Ira Gershwin, GC.

18. Typescript letter dated April 11, 1941, from Kurt Weill to Ira Gershwin, GC.

19. Russell Sanjek, *American Popular Music and Its Business: The First Four Hundred Years*, vol. 3, *From 1900 to 1984* (New York: Oxford University Press, 1988), 182.

20. Typescript annotation dated July 14, 1967, by Ira Gershwin to accompany typescript letter dated February 20, 1941, from Kurt Weill to Ira Gershwin, GC.

21. Typescript letter dated April 11, 1941, from Kurt Weill to Ira Gershwin, GC.

22. At the end of the number, the choral interjections are given to the vocalist.

23. Typescript letter dated February 20, 1941, from Kurt Weill to Ira Gershwin, GC. Weill used the term "piano score" for what was then marketed as a "vocal score" and today would be called a "piano-vocal score."

24. Typescript annotation dated July 17, 1967, by Ira Gershwin to accompany typescript letter dated March 8, 1941, from Kurt Weill to Ira Gershwin, GC.

25. Virgil Thomson, "Plays with Music," *New York Herald Tribune*, February 23, 1941; Samuel L. M. Barlow, "In the Theatre," *Modern Music* 18 (March–April 1941): 192. For an examination of Thomson's and Barlow's critiques, see mcclung, "*Psicosi per musica*."

26. Typescript letter dated March 8, 1941, from Kurt Weill to Ira Gershwin, GC.

27. Haskel Frankel, "Theatregoers' Scrapbook: Everyone—Except the Lady in the Dark," *Playbill* (April 1972): 31. In 1988 "The Saga of Jenny" was again outfitted with new words, this time by Stephen Sondheim, for Leonard Bernstein's seventieth birthday concert at Tanglewood. Sondheim called his parody "The Saga of Lenny."

28. Walter Winchell, "Walter Winchell on Broadway," *Daily Mirror*, April 21, 1941.

29. "Gert Lawrence's Illness Darkens *Lady* for 3 Shows; No Ins. Payoff," *Variety*, April 23, 1941; Leonard Lyons, "The Lyons Den," *New York Post*, April 19, 1941. For the weeks of April 14, April 28, and May 5, Edward Trevor played the role of Randy Curtis.

30. "Gertrude Lawrence to Vacation," *New York Sun*, April 30, 1941.

31. John Anderson, "Play Preface Yields 'What Doctor Orders': Foreword to *Lady in the Dark* Signed 'Dr. Brooks' Provides Excellent Argument for Staff Itself," *New York Journal-American*, May 27, 1941.

32. "Dr. Brooks" [Lawrence S. Kubie], preface to *Lady in the Dark* by Hart, Gershwin, and Weill, viii.

33. Ibid., xiv.

34. Typescript letter dated May 28, 1941, from Kurt Weill to Ira Gershwin, GC.

35. "Sam H. Harris, 69, Dies of Pneumonia," *New York World-Telegram*, June 3, 1941; "High, Low Pack Rites for Harris," *Daily Mirror*, June 7, 1941.

36. Eleanor Roosevelt, "My Day," *New York World-Telegram*, June 16, 1941.

37. "Gertie Lawrence's $4,300 Wkly.: Best on B'way since Marilyn Miller in *Sunny*," *Variety*, June 4, 1941; "*Lady* Taking Vacation after Setting Unusual Record: 8,500 Standees," *Variety*, June 11, 1941.

38. Typescript letter dated May 28, 1941, from Kurt Weill to Ira Gershwin, GC.

39. Helen Eager, "Gertrude Lawrence Begins Her 'Rest' at Dennis," *Boston Traveler*, June 19, 1941.

40. Wood Soanes, "Curtain Calls: Battle Is Raging on Broadway: Moss Hart Is Peeved at Danny Kaye, and Also Doesn't Like Freedley," *Oakland Tribune*, July 15, 1941.

41. "No Rest for . . . Gertrude Lawrence," *New York Telegraph*, August 20, 1941; "Gertrude Lawrence 'Rested' During Her Vacation at Dennis," *Boston Globe*, August 17, 1941.

42. Typescript letter dated September 9, 1941, from Kurt Weill to Ira Gershwin, GC. In the BRTC there are three publicity photographs of Rex O'Malley. In the WCFTR, there is a publicity still with all four new men (Walter Coy, Paul McGrath, Rex O'Malley, and Willard Parker) in their circus costumes.

43. "Moss Hart Remembers," *Toledo Blade*, September 15, 1941; "Three Rehearsals Serve Eric: He's Seen Comedy 50 Times," *New York Herald Tribune*, September 21, 1941.

44. Jean Pearson, "Star Wears Carnegie's Ensemble: Purple Jacket Outfit Has Smart Waist of Paillettes," *Detroit Free Press*, September 6, 1941; "New Illumination for the Lady in the Dark," *New York World-Telegram*, September 2, 1941.

45. Earl Wilson, "Gertie's Wonderful, Understand? Terrific!: Miss Lawrence's 4 New Leading Men Think She's Pretty Swell," *New York Post*, September 28, 1941.

46. Ibid.

47. John Anderson, "Gertrude Lawrence, 'Lady in Dark' Return: New Supporting Players Aid Star as Splendiferous Musical Reopens," *New York Journal-American*, September 3, 1941; Brooks Atkinson, "The Play: Gertrude Lawrence Reopens in Moss Hart's *Lady in the Dark* with Four New Members in the Cast," *New York Times*, September 3, 1941; John Mason Brown, "Miss Lawrence Reopens *Lady in the Dark*," *New York Post*, September 3, 1941; Robert Coleman, "'Lady in Dark' Back with a Splash," *Daily Mirror*, September 4, 1941; Frank Farrell, "*Lady in the Dark* Returns: Four New Men in Cast with Gertrude Lawrence," *New York World-Telegram*, September 3, 1941; Louis Kronenberger, "We've Met the *Lady* Before Somewhere," *PM*, September 3, 1941; Richard Lockridge, "The New Play: *Lady in the Dark*, with Miss Lawrence, Reopens at the Alvin," *New York Sun*, September 3, 1941; Burns Mantle, "*Lady in the Dark* and *Pal Joey* Doing Well with New Help," *Daily News*, September 3, 1941.

48. Atkinson, "Struck by Stage Lightning."

49. Typescript letter dated September 9, 1941, from Kurt Weill to Ira Gershwin, GC.

50. Typescript letter dated September 29, 1941, from Ira Gershwin to Kurt Weill, WLA.

51. Typescript letter dated October 22, 1941, from Ira Gershwin to Kurt Weill, WLA.

52. Gershwin, *Lyrics on Several Occasions*, 220; "One Life to Live" with Lawrence's inscription, MCNY.

53. "Finnish Medal Rejected by Gertrude Lawrence: She Says Nation She Helped in '39–'40 Is Nazi 'Vassal' Now," *New York Herald Tribune*, October 16, 1941; "Gertrude Lawrence Refuses Medal, Calls Finland 'Vassal,'" *New York World-Telegram*, October 15, 1941.

54. A program from the event and the last page of Lawrence's speech, GLS.

55. Gertrude Lawrence, letter to the editor, *New York Times*, December 6, 1941.

56. "Alvin Theatre Selling Defense Bonds," *Daily News*, December 11, 1941; "The News in a Note Shell...," *Washington* (DC) *Times-Herald*, December 27, 1941.

57. "Stage Fold Pledge $75,000 for War Aid: Theatre Wing Reorganized for Defense," *New York Times*, December 16, 1941; John Anderson, "Theatre Organizes for Its War Effort," *New York Journal-American*, December 16, 1941; *New York Telegraph*, December 19, 1941; Leonard Lyons, "The Lyons Den," *New York Post*, December 23, 1941.

58. "This Is for You...," *Playbill*, December 29, 1941, 5.

59. Typescript letter dated January 15, 1942, from Ira Gershwin to Kurt Weill, WLA.

60. George Ross, "So This Is Broadway," *New York World-Telegram*, February 27, 1942. Gertrude Lawrence received a card certifying that she passed the American National Red Cross Standard Course in First Aid on February 13, 1942. Gertrude Lawrence's wallet, GLP. Lawrence went on to pass the Advanced Course on March 17, 1942.

61. Hearn, telephone interview.

62. Congress, House of Representatives, Congressman Faddis of Pennsylvania speaking on the Deficiency Appropriations Bill HR 6548, 77th Cong., 2d Sess., *Congressional Record* (February 6, 1942), vol. 88, pt. 1, 1097.

63. Congress, House of Representatives, Congressman Andresen of Minnesota speaking on the Deficiency Appropriations Bill HR 6548, 77th Cong., 2d Sess., *Congressional Record* (February 9, 1942), vol. 88, pt. 1, 1143.

64. W. H. Lawrence, "La Guardia Resigns as Defense Head—Landis Gets Post," *New York Times*, February 11, 1942.

65. Brooks Atkinson, "American Theatre Wing," *New York Times*, February 15, 1942.

66. John Mason Brown, "Drama Critic of the World-Telegram [*recte Post*] Says," *Playbill*, April 6, 1942, 19.

67. "Theatre Wing's Canteen B'way's 1st Winter Hit; Show Biz Hosts Mob of U.S., Allied Servicemen," *Variety*, March 4, 1942.

68. Harden, telephone interview.

69. Brooks Atkinson, "Curtain's Up at the Stage Door Canteen," *New York Times*, March 13, 1942.

70. Talbot Lake, "Gert Lawrence Plays Biggest Role of Life," *Wheeling* (WV) *News Register*, April 12, 1942.

71. Aldrich, *Gertrude Lawrence as Mrs. A*, 212.

72. Larry Davis and Dave Menard, *P-61 Black Widow in Action*, Aircraft No. 106 (Carrollton, TX: Squadron/Signal Publications, 1990), 27; Warren Thompson, *P-61 Black Widow Units of World War 2*, Osprey Combat Aircraft, ed. Tony Homes, No. 8 (Elms Court, UK: Osprey Publishing, 1998), 95. The plane's nose art was painted by LeRoy F. Miozzi.

73. "*Lady* to Continue Indef on Broadway," *Variety*, March 25, 1942.

74. "Play Statistics Add 3 Months to Actors' Year," *New York Herald Tribune*, April 26, 1942.

75. Typescript letter dated May 2, 1942, from Kurt Weill to Ira Gershwin, GC. In 1990 Sotheby's of London auctioned off an autograph manuscript of "The Saga of Jenny" signed, "This ms. of 'Jenny' was written for the benefit of the Treasury Department. Kurt Weill March 1943." Because the manuscript contains only the first stanza and is missing the verse, perhaps it was intended to be outfitted with other lyrics.

76. Although this figure was widely reported in the press, when Burns Mantle published *The Best Plays of 1941–1942*, he mistakenly put the second season at 305, for a total run of 467 performances. This error has subsequently found itself into virtually all reference books on the American musical theater. It appears that

Mantle forgot about the Christmas layoff, which resulted in four lost performances, and assumed that *Lady in the Dark* had played a full thirty-eight weeks during the second season (for 304 performances). The phantom 305th performance can be traced to the preview in September. Stage Relief Fund benefits were typically held on Sunday evenings so that performers from other shows could attend. *Lady in the Dark*'s benefit was held on Labor Day (Monday) for regular patrons, which made it the first of eight performances for the first week, rather than an additional ninth performance.

77. "Gertrude Lawrence Will Operate Dennis Strawhat," *Variety*, June 3, 1942.

78. George Ross, "So This Is Broadway," *New York World-Telegram*, June 16, 1942.

6. Tour

1. Typescript letter dated November 13, 1941, from Kurt Weill to Ira Gershwin, GC.

2. Typescript letter dated January 15, 1942, from Ira Gershwin to Kurt Weill, WLA.

3. Typescript letter of agreement dated March 9, 1942, between Moss Hart and Gertrude Lawrence, GLP.

4. Section F of the corrected rider attached to and forming part of the Actors' Equity Association Agreement dated June 21, 1940, between Sam H. Harris and Gertrude Lawrence, GLP.

5. Manuscript letter dated May 20, 1942, from Kurt Weill to Lotte Lenya, WLA.

6. Aldrich, *Gertrude Lawrence as Mrs. A*, 164.

7. Dorothy Kilgallen, "Gertrude Lawrence Says," *Boston Globe*, August 5, 1942.

8. "Chorus Pay Increase on Road," *New York Herald Tribune*, August 9, 1942.

9. Manuscript letter dated September 28, 1942, from Lotte Lenya to Kurt Weill, WLA.

10. *Variety*, October 7, 1942; Sidney Gathrid, "*Lady in the Dark*," *Philadelphia News*, September 29, 1942; Linton Martin, "*Lady in the Dark* Opens at Forrest," *Philadelphia Inquirer*, September 29, 1942; Edwin H. Schloss, "*Lady in the Dark* Opens at Forrest," *Philadelphia Record*, September 29, 1942; Robert Sensenderfer, "Gertrude Lawrence in *Lady in the Dark*: A Musical Play about Psychiatry," *Philadelphia Bulletin*, September 29, 1942.

11. "Many See Gertrude Lawrence," *New York Times*, October 26, 1942. A revised amount of $119,673 was reported at the conclusion of the tour. "Gossip of the Rialto: News of the Doings of Those Who Make the Times Square Theatre Hum," *New York Times*, February 28, 1943.

12. Manuscript letter dated October 24, 1942, from Ira Gershwin to Kurt Weill, WLA.

13. "Big Productions on Tour May Have Problems," *Equity*, November 1942.

14. Maurice Abravanel confirmed that principals of the orchestra toured with the show, and the other members were hired from the local musicians' union. This is borne out by some of the orchestral parts that contain signatures of musicians with addresses corresponding to the tour's stops.

15. Bernie Harrison, "Gertrude Lawrence Jokes with Service Men: *Lady in the Dark* Unit Appears at Canteen," *Washington Times-Herald*, October 27, 1942.

16. Norman Clark, "'Lady in Dark' Brings Its Charm to Ford's Stage," *Baltimore News-Post*, October 28, 1942; Gilbert Kanour, "Miss Lawrence Scores Hit as 'Lady in Dark,' Now at Ford's," *Baltimore Evening Sun*, October 28, 1942; Donald Kirkley, "*Lady in the Dark*: Gertrude Lawrence Star of Musical Play Opening Two-Week Engagement at Ford's," *Baltimore Sun*, October 28, 1942.

17. "Lawrence—*Dark* Smash 30G, Balto," *Variety*, November 4, 1942.

18. "Actress Sings with Seamen: 200 Britons and U.S. Gun Crews Greet Miss Lawrence," *Baltimore Evening Sun*, November 6, 1942.

19. Kaspar Monahan, "Show Stops: Army of Back-Stage Workers Toil for *Lady in the Dark*," *Pittsburgh Press*, November 4, 1942.

20. Frances C. Walker, "Gertrude Lawrence Plays Favorite Role in Defense Service," *Pittsburgh Post-Gazette*, November 10, 1942; Kaspar Monahan, "Show Stops: Miss Lawrence, 'Lady Bountiful' to the Servicemen 'Down East,' Hopes to Do Her Play with All-Star Cast for Charity in London," *Pittsburgh Press*, November 10, 1942.

21. Harold V. Cohen, "*Lady in the Dark* Is Gertie: Miss Lawrence Brings a Lush Play with Music to the Nixon," *Pittsburgh Post-Gazette*, November 11, 1942; Karl Krug, "Miss Lawrence Superb in *Lady in the Dark*, Fine Musical in Nixon," *Pittsburgh Sun-Telegraph*, November 11, 1942; Kaspar Monahan, "Gertrude Lawrence Sparkles at Nixon: Gifted Actress Gives Amazing Displayal of Her Many Talents in Musical Play, *Lady in the Dark*—Production Is Stunning," *Pittsburgh Press*, November 11, 1942.

22. Lawrence's telegram was cited in *Daily Mirror*, November 12, 1942; *Washington Times-Herald*, November 12, 1942; *New York Herald Tribune*, November 13, 1942; "'Feel Fine,' Gert Tells Off N.Y. Columnists for False 'Illness' Report," *Variety*, November 18, 1942; *Wilmington* (DE) *Star*, December 6, 1942; and *Minneapolis Tribune*, January 3, 1943. Lawrence also disputed the rumor in an article she wrote for the *New York Times* after the tour had concluded. Gertrude Lawrence, "Touring the Provinces: Miss Lawrence Has Fun as She Gads about Wartime America," *New York Times*, March 7, 1943.

23. "Canteen Benefit Was Not All Football," *Pittsburgh Post-Gazette*, November 16, 1942.

24. Lucille Schulberg, "A Brief Moment with 'Gertie' Reveals Stage Star's War Work," *Pittsburgh Carnegie Tartan*, November 24, 1942; "*Lady* Pulls $53,000 in Two Pitt Weeks," *Variety*, November 25, 1942. *Variety*'s headline is misleading as

the article gives the box-office gross for the individual weeks at $25,000 and $28,500.

25. "Start Advance Sale for *Lady in the Dark*," *Cleveland Press*, October 20, 1942; "*Lady in the Dark* Gets Large Advance Sale," *Cleveland Press*, November 5, 1942; "Premiere Tonight for 'Big Doorstep,'" *New York Times*, November 26, 1942.

26. William F. McDermott, "Gertrude Lawrence Fine in Musical: Show Is One of Best of Its Kind," *Cleveland Plain Dealer*, November 25, 1942. Other Cleveland reviews include Peter Bellamy, "The Play—Gertrude Lawrence Shows Herself the Queen of Them All in the Hanna's Flamingly Colorful *Lady in the Dark*: The Play Is a Triumph for Its Star and Entertainment," *Cleveland News*, November 25, 1942; Omar Ranney, "Star Shines in *Lady in the Dark*: Gertrude Lawrence Gives Hanna Its Best of Season," *Cleveland Press*, November 25, 1942.

27. Charles Gentry, "Gertrude Lawrence Goes Neurotic: You'll Enjoy It," *Detroit Evening News*, December 2, 1942; Len G. Shaw, "Miss Lawrence Scores with *Lady* at the Cass," *Detroit Free Press*, December 2, 1942; Russell McLauchlin, "The New Play," *Detroit News*, December 2, 1942.

28. "Lawrence 25G in Strong Det.," *Variety*, December 9, 1942; "Pearl Harbor Day Sale: Star Has Busy Time with War Bonds," *Detroit News*, December 8, 1942.

29. "*Lady* Winds Up 3 Wks in Det. with 72 1/2 G," *Variety*, December 23, 1941; "Auditing Department," *New York Times*, August 1, 1943.

30. Typescript letter dated December 15, 1942, from Ira Gershwin to Kurt Weill, WLA. Both Weill and Gershwin received 3 percent of all gross weekly box-office receipts when the gross amounted to $17,000 or more. If the gross fell to less than $17,000, they received 2.5 percent each.

31. Edward Carberry, "Pretty Lady in the Dark: Gertrude Lawrence Helps Cheer Our Boys in Camp: Actress Finds War 'Near and Urgent' Sign Others to Aid British USO Units," *Cincinnati Post*, December 27, 1942.

32. Edward Carberry, "*Lady in the Dark* Opens at the Taft," *Cincinnati Post*, December 29, 1942; Howard W. Hess, "Gertrude Lawrence Scores in *Lady in the Dark* at Taft," *Cincinnati Times-Star*, December 29, 1942; E. B. Radcliffe, "Out in Front: *Lady in the Dark*—Taft," *Cincinnati Enquirer*, December 29, 1942.

33. Lawrence, "Touring the Provinces."

34. "*Lady* Won $28,500," *Variety*, January 6, 1943.

35. Arthur Kuhl, "'Lady in Dark' Scales Heights, Thanks to Gertrude Lawrence," *St. Louis Star-Times*, January 6, 1943; Colvin McPherson, "*Lady in the Dark*: A Fascinating Show, Gertrude Lawrence Gives Magnificent Performance in Musical Play at American," *St. Louis Post-Dispatch*, January 6, 1943; Herbert L. Monk, "*Lady in the Dark* One of Season's Outstanding Plays," *St. Louis Globe-Democrat*, January 6, 1943.

36. "*Lady* Wow $52,000 in 16 Shows, St. Loo," *Variety*, January 20, 1943.

37. "Hattie Carnegie Designed Them for Gertrude Lawrence," *St. Louis Globe-Democrat*, December 25, 1942.

38. Lawrence, "Touring the Provinces."

39. Adeline Fitzgerald, "Monday Memos: Almost Among the Missing," *Chicago Herald American*, February 1, 1943.

40. The *New York Times* reported the following gross amounts for the first seven stops of the tour: Philadelphia, $119,673 (30 performances); Baltimore, $60,784 (16); Pittsburgh, $50,067 (16); Cleveland, $28,321 (8); Detroit, $67,090 (24); Cincinnati, $26,280 (8); and St. Louis, $50,580 (16). "Gossip of the Rialto: News of the Doings of Those Who Make the Times Square Theatre Hum." A profit of $13,000 was reported by *Variety*. "*Lady* Profits Neg Up to Chi," *Variety*, January 27, 1943.

41. Lee, telephone interview; Lawrence, "Touring the Provinces."

42. William Leonard, "On the Aisle: *Lady in the Dark* Has Everything—Including That Great Performer, Gertrude Lawrence," *Chicago Journal of Commerce*, January 20, 1943; Lloyd Lewis, "*Lady in the Dark* Smash Hit with Miss Lawrence," *Chicago Daily News*, January 20, 1943; Robert Pollack, "'Lady in Dark' a Blend of Matchless Theater," *Chicago Daily Times*, January 20, 1943; Cecil Smith, "'Lady in Dark' Is High Mark in Musical Show," *Chicago Daily Tribune*, January 20, 1943; Ashton Stevens, "Can't Help It; She's a Genius," *Chicago Herald American*, January 20, 1943; Tracy York, "*Lady in the Dark* Superb, Gertrude Lawrence Ditto: Critic Raves about Play at Civic Opera and Winds Up Talking to Himself," *Chicago Sun*, January 20, 1943.

43. Cecil Smith, "Future of American Opera Seen in Theater Music: Opportunities for New Ideas Cited by Critic," *Chicago Daily Tribune*, February 14, 1943.

44. "*Lady* 43G, Chi, Leads Nation," *Variety*, January 27, 1943. At the conclusion of the run, *Variety* revised the first week's earnings to $43,793. "Inside Stuff—Legit," *Variety*, March 3, 1943.

45. "*Lady in the Dark* Plans," *New York Times*, January 26, 1943.

46. "Drama League Fetes Cast of 'Lady in Dark,'" *Chicago Herald Tribune*, January 27, 1943; "Actress to Attend Matinee Breakfast," *Chicago Sun*, February 1, 1943; "Special Show, for 'Lady in Dark,'" *Chicago Herald American*, February 6, 1943.

47. Burns Mantle, ed., *The Best Plays of 1942–1943 and the Year Book of the Drama in America* (New York: Dodd, Mead, 1943; reprint, 1968), 14.

48. "Inside Stuff—Legit."

49. Lawrence, "Touring the Provinces."

50. Helen Ormsbee, "Lieut. Lawrence Finds the Time to Appear in *Lady in the Dark*," *New York Herald Tribune*, March 7, 1943.

51. Mary C. Henderson, *The City and the Theatre: The History of New York Playhouses, A 250 Year Journey from Bowling Green to Times Square*, rev. and exp. ed. (New York: Back Stage Books, 2004), 343.

52. Howard Barnes, "The Theaters: The Lady Returns," *New York Herald Tribune*, March 1, 1943; Robert Coleman, "Mr. Coleman's Verdict: *Lady in the*

Dark Lights Broadway," *Daily Mirror*, March 1, 1943; Burns Mantle, "*Lady in the Dark* Takes Over B'way Theatre for Spring Run," *Daily News*, March 1, 1943; Ward Morehouse, "The New Play: Gertrude Lawrence Is Back in *Lady in the Dark*, Opening at Broadway," *New York Sun*, March 1, 1943; Lewis Nichols, "The Play: Gertrude Lawrence Gets Warm Reception on Return Here in *Lady in the Dark*, Now Running at Popular Prices," *New York Times*, March 1, 1943; Burton Rascoe, "Theater: Miss Lawrence Returns with *Lady in the Dark*," *New York World-Telegram*, March 1, 1943; Wilella Waldorf, "Two on the Aisle: Gertrude Lawrence Returns to Broadway in *Lady in the Dark*," *New York Post*, March 1, 1943.

53. *Waterbury* (CT) *Democrat*, March 2, 1943.

54. Burt A. Folkart, "Edwin Lester, Civic Light Opera Founder, Dies," *Los Angeles Times*, December 15, 1990. The affiliation between the San Francisco and Los Angeles companies that began with *Lady in the Dark* was still ongoing in 1990.

55. Lawrence's signed Equity contract, typescript confirmation letter dated May 15, 1943, from Moss Hart to Gertrude Lawrence, and the rider attached to the contract initialed by Hart and Lawrence, GLP.

56. "'Lady in Dark' Trip to the Coast Beset by Wartime Travel Curbs," *Variety*, May 19, 1943.

57. Radie Harris, "New York Runaround," *Variety*, May 26, 1943. Neither the dramatization of Francis Hackett's biographical portrait of Anne Boleyn nor Rodgers and Hammerstein's adaptation of Sheridan's *School for Scandal* came to fruition. As it turned out, Lawrence's ENSA tour did not commence until May 1944.

58. Ward Morehouse, "Broadway after Dark," *New York Sun*, May 25, 1943.

59. Aldrich, *Gertrude Lawrence as Mrs. A*, 170.

60. "*Lady* Failed to Profit in N.Y. Repeat Despite 26G Avge.: Costs High," *Variety*, May 23, 1943.

61. Fred Johnson, "*Lady in the Dark* Wins Gertrude Lawrence Cheer: Light Opera Season's Peak Attraction," *San Francisco Call Bulletin*, May 25, 1943; Alexander Fried, "Lawrence Magnificent in Romance at Curran," *San Francisco Chronicle*, May 26, 1943.

62. "*Lady*'s 32 1/2G Sets S.F. House Mark," *New York Sun*, June 4, 1943.

63. Ward Morehouse, "Broadway after Dark," *New York Sun*, June 4, 1943.

64. Wood Soanes, "Curtain Calls: Author Entertains Critics Here: Moss Hart's Tales Range from 'Cabbages and Kings' to Dogs with Eczema," *Oakland Tribune*, June 15, 1943.

65. "End of Record *Lady* Run in Frisco to Beat Opening," *Variety*, June 7, 1943.

66. "Hundred in One," *Los Angeles Times*, June 24, 1943.

67. "Play Review: *Lady in the Dark*," *Variety*, July 1943; Harrison Carroll, "'Lady in Dark' Spectacular Musical: Has Everything," *Los Angeles Herald*, June 23, 1943; Florence Lawrence, "'Lady in Dark' on Stage at Philharmonic," *Los Angeles Examiner*, June 23, 1943; Richard D. Saunders, "*Lady in the Dark* Opens L.A. Run," *Hollywood Citizen News*, June 23, 1943; Edwin Schallert, "Musical

Play Victory for Noted Star," *Los Angeles Times*, June 23, 1943; Virginia Wright, "Picturized Review," *Los Angeles News*, June 23, 1943.

68. Hedda Hopper, "Hollywood," *Daily News*, June 29, 1943; Ed Sullivan, "Little Old New York," *Daily News*, July 8, 1943.

69. That fall Lawrence hosted a twenty-six week series for Revlon called "Gertrude Lawrence's Guest House."

70. "*Lady*'s 130G, L.A.; Doughgirls' 9G," *Variety*, July 14, 1943; "*Lady* Wow $42,000 in L.A. Third; Doughgirls' 13 1/2G," *Variety*, July 7, 1943.

71. "Auditing Department."

72. "E. S." [Edwin Schallert], "Saga of Liza Elliott Now Drawing Near Close," *Los Angeles Times*, June 9, 1943. The film project about Sarah Bernhardt never materialized.

7. Cultural Context

1. *The Playbill*, June 2, 1941, 18–19.

2. *The Playbill*, May 9, 1943, 10–11.

3. Nathan G. Hale, *The Rise and Crisis of Psychoanalysis in the United States: Freud and the Americans, 1917–1985* (New York: Oxford University Press, 1995; reprint, Bridgewater, NJ: Replica Books, 2000), 118, 101.

4. Gentry, "Gertrude Lawrence Goes Neurotic."

5. Elaine Tyler May, *Homeward Bound: American Families in the Cold War Era*, rev. and updated ed. (New York: Basic Books, 1999), 42.

6. United States Bureau of the Census, *Historical Statistics of the United States: Colonial Times to 1970*, Bicentennial ed., pt. 1 (Washington, DC: Government Printing Office, 1975), 49.

7. May, *Homeward Bound*, 32–33.

8. Lois Scharf, *To Work and to Wed: Female Employment, Feminism, and the Great Depression*, Contributions in Women's Studies, No. 15 (Westport, CT: Greenwood Press, 1980; reprint, 1985), 46, 48.

9. Ibid., 79.

10. Jeanine Basinger, *A Woman's View: How Hollywood Spoke to Women 1930–1960* (New York: Knopf, 1993; reprint, Hanover, NH: Wesleyan University Press, 1995), 357–79.

11. Quoted in ibid., 363.

12. Mirra Komarovsky, *The Unemployed Man and His Family: The Effect of Unemployment upon the Status of the Man in Fifty-nine Families* (New York: Dryden Press, 1940; reprint, Walnut Creek, CA: Alta Mira Press, 2004).

13. Susan M. Hartmann, *The Home Front and Beyond: American Women in the 1940s*, American Women in the Twentieth Century, ed. Barbara Haber (Boston: Twayne Publishers, 1982; reprint, 1995), 17; Glen Elder, Jr., *Children of the Great Depression: Social Change in Life Experience* (Chicago: University of Chicago Press, 1974), 202.

14. May, *Homeward Bound,* 56, 48.

15. Hartmann, *The Home Front and Beyond*, 31–32.

16. May, *Homeward Bound*, 50.

17. Peter Filene, *Him/Her/Self: Sex Roles in Modern America*, 2nd ed. (Baltimore: Johns Hopkins University Press, 1986), 163.

18. May, *Homeward Bound*, 50.

19. Basinger, *A Woman's View*, 197.

20. May, *Homeward Bound*, 51–52.

21. McLaughlin, "The New Play."

22. Carberry, "Pretty Lady in the Dark."

23. Virginia Bennett Moore, "Begrimed—Bewitching or Both," *Woman's Home Companion*, October 1943, 80.

24. "Boy Meets Girl in Wartime," pamphlet A496, 1943, American Social Hygiene Association, quoted in May, *Homeward Bound*, 59.

25. Quoted in Hartmann, *The Home Front and Beyond*, 42.

26. "Simple Lines, Solid Colors Star's Choice: Gertrude Lawrence Likes 'Comfortable' Clothes above All," *Camden* (NJ) *Courier-Post*, May 3, 1943.

27. *The Playbill*, March 14, 1943, 3.

28. *"This Is the Army," Theatre Arts* 27 (1943): 164.

29. George W. Henry, "Psychogenic Factors in Overt Homosexuality," *American Journal of Psychiatry* 93 (1937): 889–908. The Committee for the Study of Sex Variants, a privately funded corporation established in 1935, sponsored Henry's study, and Eugene Kahn, a Yale professor of psychiatry, headed its Executive Committee. The final results of Henry's project were published in two volumes. George W. Henry, *Sex Variants: A Study of Homosexual Patterns*, 2 vols. (New York: P. B. Hoeber, 1941; reprint, 1959).

30. Lewis M. Terman and Catharine Cox Miles, *Sex and Personality: Studies in Masculinity and Femininity* (New York: McGraw-Hill, 1936; reprint, New York: Russell & Russell, 1968). For more about Henry's article and Terman and Miles's book, see Henry L. Minton, "Femininity in Men and Masculinity in Women: American Psychiatry and Psychology Portray Homosexuality in the 1930's," *Journal of Homosexuality* 13 (1986): 1–21.

31. Typescript letter dated August 23, 1941, from Ira Gershwin to Kurt Weill, WLA.

32. Kaier Curtin, *"We Can Always Call Them Bulgarians": The Emergence of Lesbians and Gay Men on the American Stage* (Boston: Alyson Publications, 1987), 1.

33. Ibid., 69–70, 100. The Wales Law, named after the legislator who introduced the bill, was dubbed the Wales Padlock Law.

34. Ibid., 210.

35. Coleman, "Miss Lawrence Proves Artistry Again in Lavish Musical"; Anderson, *"Lady in the Dark* Premiere at Alvin"; Watts, "The Theaters: Dreaming *Lady*."

36. Mantle, *"Lady in the Dark* and *Pal Joey* Doing Well with New Help"; Lockridge, "The New Play: *Lady in the Dark*, with Miss Lawrence, Reopens at the Alvin"; Atkinson, "The Play: Gertrude Lawrence Reopens in Moss Hart's

Lady in the Dark with Four New Members in the Cast"; Farrell, *"Lady in the Dark Returns"*; Coleman, " 'Lady in Dark' Back with a Splash"; Anderson, "Gertrude Lawrence, 'Lady in Dark' Return"; Brown, "Miss Lawrence Reopens *Lady in the Dark.*" In 1940s slang "flit" could mean either an effeminate man or a male homosexual. Lester V. Berrey and Melvin Van Den Bark, *The American Thesaurus of Slang: A Complete Reference Book of Colloquial Speech* (New York: Thomas Y. Crowell, 1943), 372, 473.

37. Philip Wylie, *Generation of Vipers* (New York: Rinehart, 1942).

38. Lawrence S. Kubie, "The Drive to Become Both Sexes," *Psychoanalytic Quarterly* 43 (1974): 349–426; reprinted in Kubie, *Symbol and Neurosis*, 191–263 (page citations are to the reprint edition); ibid., 200–201.

39. Ibid., 198, 252.

40. Ibid., 214, 217, 240.

41. Ibid., 196, 198, 235.

42. Manuscript letter dated September 25, 1941, from Kurt Weill to Lotte Lenya, WLA; quoted in Bach, *Dazzler*, 291.

43. "Dr. Brooks" [Kubie], preface to *Lady in the Dark*, x.

44. Lawrence S. Kubie, "Some Unsolved Problems of the Scientific Career, Part I," *American Scientist* 41 (1953): 599.

45. Kubie, "The Drive to Become Both Sexes," 253.

46. Bach, *Dazzler*, 156, 214.

47. Quoted in ibid., 228; Ethan Mordden reads Liza's relationships with Randy and Charley as a "gay coming-out parable." Ethan Mordden, *Beautiful Mornin': The Broadway Musical in the 1940s* (New York: Oxford University Press, 1999), 60–61. One can sample a taste of Hart's portrayal of Liza Elliott in the recording *Moss Hart Speaking on and Reading from* The Man Who Came to Dinner *and* Lady in the Dark, Spoken Arts 725.

48. *Life with Father*, however, would go on to surpass it with 3,224 performances, a record yet to be broken.

49. Burns Mantle, ed., *The Best Plays of 1940–1941 and The Year Book of the Drama in America* (New York: Dodd, Mead, 1941; reprint, 1969), 3.

50. Atkinson, "The Play in Review: Gertrude Lawrence Appears in Moss Hart's Musical Drama, *Lady in the Dark.*"

51. Whipple, *"Lady in the Dark:* Triumph for Gertrude Lawrence."

52. Brooks Atkinson, "The Play: Christmas Night Adds *Pal Joey* and *Meet the People* to Musical Stage," *New York Times*, December 26, 1940.

53. These included *Broken Journey, The Morning Star, Vickie, Yankee Point, Winter Soldiers, Lifeline, Flare Path, Proof through the Night, The Russian People, The Barber Had Two Sons, Counterattack, Ask My Friend Sandy, This Rock, Men in Shadow,* and *Sons and Soldiers.*

54. This revue was the basis of the 1943 film with the same title starring Ronald Reagan.

55. Martha Dreiblatt, "Words on the Theatre and War: Some Producers and Others Discuss a Problem," *New York Times*, May 16, 1943.

56. Timothy P. Donovan, "Oh, What a Beautiful Mornin': The Musical, *Oklahoma!* and the Popular Mind in 1943," *Journal of Popular Culture* 8 (1974): 477–78.

57. *Oklahoma!*'s working title, "Away We Go," also stressed community.

58. Mabel Rugg, comp., "Public Opinion Polls," *Public Opinion Quarterly* 7 (1943): 329.

59. Quoted in Aldrich, *Gertrude Lawrence as Mrs. A*, 212–13.

60. Joseph P. Swain, *The Broadway Musical: A Critical and Musical Survey*, 2nd ed. (Lanham, MD: Scarecrow Press, 2002), 103–105.

61. Aljean Harmetz, *The Making of "The Wizard of Oz"* (New York: Bantam Doubleday, 1977), 68, quoted in William G. Hyland, *Richard Rodgers* (New Haven: Yale University Press, 1998), 146.

62. Lewis Nichols, "*Oklahoma!*: A Musical Hailed as Delightful, Based on *Green Grow the Lilacs*, Opens Here at the St. James Theatre," *New York Times*, April 1, 1943.

63. The six principal characters in Rodgers and Hammerstein's musical plays are as vocally interchangeable as they are in Gilbert and Sullivan's operettas.

64. Harold Clurman, "*Lost in the Stars* of Broadway," in *The Collected Works of Harold Clurman: Six Decades of Commentary on Theatre, Dance, Music, Film, Arts and Letters*, ed. Marjorie Loggia and Glenn Young (New York: Applause Books, 1994), 227.

65. Traubner, *Operetta: A Theatrical History*, 402. So prevalent were *Blossom Time*'s road shows, which toured for over twenty-five years in ever cheaper productions, that "'a road company for *Blossom Time*' became synonymous with the shabbiest theatrical commercialism." Gerald Bordman, *American Musical Theatre: A Chronicle*, 3rd ed. (New York: Oxford University Press, 2001), 412.

66. Typescript letter dated April 11, 1941, from Kurt Weill to Ira Gershwin, GC.

67. Typescript letter dated January 15, 1942, from Ira Gershwin to Kurt Weill, WLA.

68. Mapleton, Ohio, is a leitmotif that runs through Moss Hart's plays, including *The American Way*, *Lady in the Dark*, *Winged Victory*, and *Christopher Blake*. Although there is actually a Mapleton, Ohio, Hart based his fictional town on Rutland, Vermont. Bach, *Dazzler*, 183–84.

69. Typescript letter dated November 13, 1941, from Kurt Weill to Ira Gershwin, GC.

70. Weill, "Two Dreams-Come-True."

71. Swain, *The Broadway Musical*, 51–52.

72. Stephen Banfield, *Sondheim's Broadway Musicals*, Michigan American Music Series, ed. Richard Crawford (Ann Arbor: University of Michigan Press, 1993), 147–48.

73. Kim H. Kowalke, "'I Hate Brecht!': Sondheim, *Love Life*, and the Concept Musical," paper presented at the 1998 annual meeting of the American Musicological Society, Boston.

8. Revivals

1. Lehman Engel, *The American Musical Theater*, rev. ed. (New York: Macmillan, 1975), 61.

2. Manuscript letter dated November 24, 1942, from Kurt Weill to Ira Gershwin, GC.

3. Typescript letter dated December 15, 1942, from Ira Gershwin to Kurt Weill, WLA. Gershwin's revised fourth stanza is preserved in his worksheets, GC:

Liza

Jenny made her mind up at thirty-nine
That to be an artist's model would be divine.
Though she never posed for portrait there were dozens of men
At each exhibition whispering, "That lady is Jen!"

Jury

    Poor Jenny!
    Bright as a penny!
Her equal would be hard to find.

Liza

    From Troy to Tallahassee
    They recognized her chassis—
But she would make up her mind.

4. Wauhillau La Hay, "Actress Loves and Loses All Favorite Roles to Films: Gertrude Lawrence Yearns to Do Movie Lead of *Lady in the Dark*, but So Did Ginger Rogers," *Chicago Sun*, February 2, 1943.

5. Ginger Rogers, *Ginger: My Story* (New York: Harper Collins, 1991), 252–53. One of Rogers's previous films, *Carefree*, had her falling in love with a psychiatrist (played by Fred Astaire), and in another as the love object of three suitors, *Tom, Dick, and Harry*.

6. David Chierichetti, *Mitchell Leisen: Hollywood Director* (Los Angeles: Photoventures Press, 1995), 182.

7. Philip Schurer, "This Town Called Hollywood," *Chicago Herald Tribune*, January 3, 1943.

8. Chierichetti, *Mitchell Leisen*, 188, 189.

9. Rogers, *Ginger*, 255. Rogers wears both of the dresses in the film and reported that the studio donated one of them to the Smithsonian Institution.

10. Ibid., 253.

11. Chierichetti, *Mitchell Leisen*, 183.

12. Rogers, *Ginger*, 254–55.

13. Chierichetti, *Mitchell Leisen*, 185.

14. Ibid., 177.

15. "Unlike Movies Tax Skill," *Rochester* (NY) *Democrat & Chronicle*, May 9, 1943.

16. Chierichetti, *Mitchell Leisen*, 176.

17. Ibid., 183–84.

18. Ibid., 186.

19. *"Lady in the Dark* Opulent Feast: Magnificent Prod. Marked with Leisen Talent; Blumenthal, Rogers, Milland Hit," *Hollywood Reporter*, February 10, 1944; "Trade Showing: *Lady in the Dark,"* *Daily Variety*, February 10, 1944; *"Lady in the Dark,"* *Variety*, February 16, 1944. The reviewer from *Variety* saw the film in a New York preview on February 3, 1944.

20. Dorothy Manners, "Screen's *Lady in the Dark* Cost 2 Million—Worth It," February 10, 1944; Edwin Schallert, "'Lady in Dark' Glamour Victory," *Los Angeles Times*, February 10, 1944; David Hanna, "Film Review: *Lady in the Dark,"* n.d.

21. "Fashion Shows Used to Promote 'Lady in Dark,'" *Motion Picture Herald*, February 19, 1944.

22. The film was accompanied by a live stage show, which featured Xavier Cugat and his orchestra, Walter "Dare" Wahl ("Acrobatic Star of *Star Spangled Rhythm*"), and the satirist Dean Murphy from the *Ziegfeld Follies*.

23. "Screen News Here and in Hollywood," *New York Times*, February 23, 1944.

24. *"Lady in the Dark,"* *Coronet* (March 1944): 100–116. A few years later, Kubie went so far as to make several recommendations to Hollywood regarding films with psychoanalytic themes. In an article for *Hollywood Quarterly*, he recommended first that a foundation endowed by the film industry be set up to study the influence of films on American culture and the use of the medium in education. His second recommendation was that a board of psychiatrists advise filmmakers on the technical accuracy of films with psychoanalytic subjects. Lawrence S. Kubie, "Psychiatry and the Films," *Hollywood Quarterly* 2 (1947): 113–17. For a discussion of how psychiatry is portrayed in the film version of *Lady in the Dark*, see Glen O. Gabbard and Krin Gabbard, *Psychiatry and the Cinema*, 2nd ed. (Washington, DC: American Psychiatric Press, 1999), 7–15.

25. Typescript letter dated March 8, 1944, from Ira Gershwin to Kurt Weill, WLA.

26. Chierichetti, *Mitchell Leisen*, 187.

27. Seven years after scoring the Paramount film, Robert Russell Bennett arranged a medley of *Lady in the Dark*'s score for summer concerts at the Hollywood Bowl and Lewisohn Stadium. The fifteen-minute symphonic treatment of *Lady in the Dark* presents most of the numbers from the score in the order they appear in the show. Unlike Weill's orchestration, which has a light, dance feel, Bennett's is heavily scored. Such treatment did not please all the critics, many of whom remember the original production (one critic complained, "The overbearing orchestration could not seem less related to the seldom heard and intriguing score of the Broadway musical"). Bennett's *Lady in the Dark: Symphonic Nocturne* is available on the 2005 recording *Kurt Weill: Symphonies*

Nos. 1 and 2, Bournemouth Symphony Orchestra, Marin Alsop, conductor, Naxos 8.557481.

28. The winners in those areas were Joseph LaShelle for *Laura* (20th Century Fox), Wiard Ihnen and Thomas Little for *Wilson* (20th Century Fox), and Carmen Dragon and Morris Stoloff for *Cover Girl* (Columbia), respectively.

29. Chierichetti, *Mitchell Leisen*, 177.

30. Connie Billips and Arthur Pierce, *Lux Presents Hollywood: A Show-by-Show History of the Lux Radio Theatre and the Lux Video Theatre, 1934–1957* (Jefferson, NC: McFarland, 1995), 63.

31. Ibid., 7, 37.

32. Photocopy of Dramatists Play Service contract, WLRC. Members of the Dramatists Guild established the Dramatists Play Service in 1936.

33. Manuscript letter dated May 17, 1947, from Kurt Weill to Lotte Lenya, WLA.

34. Carlisle Hart, *Kitty*, 158.

35. Quoted in ibid., 158–59.

36. Bach, *Dazzler*, 304.

37. Jack Gould, "Programs in Review," *New York Times*, October 26, 1947.

38. When American Entertainment Industries released a monaural recording of the radio broadcast in 1984, the jacket falsely advertised, "The Stars of the Original Broadway Cast." Nowhere does the documentation for the LP (or for the 1993 rerelease on compact disc, AEI-CD 003) reveal that the recording is actually a radio play or the date of broadcast. The unsigned essay about the conception of the musical play contains some errors, but does include a fine synopsis of Lawrence's career.

39. Interview with Williams Hawkins, *New York World-Telegram*, quoted in unsigned essay, "Gertrude Lawrence in *Lady in the Dark*," American Entertainment Industries AEI 1146.

40. Typescript letter dated October 21, 1947, from Gertrude Lawrence to Kurt Weill, WLA.

41. "5,000 Jam Streets at Lawrence Rites: 1,800 Others Fill Auditorium of Fifth Avenue Presbyterian for Actress' Funeral Service," *New York Times*, September 10, 1952.

42. Gerald Clarke, *Get Happy: The Life of Judy Garland* (New York: Random House, 2000), 82.

43. Ibid., 183.

44. Ironically, the venues in California had been the last two tour stops for *Lady in the Dark* nine years earlier.

45. Judy Garland had previously been heard in broadcasts of *Strike Up the Band*, *A Star Is Born*, *Meet Me in St. Louis*, and *The Wizard of Oz*.

46. Cameron Shipp, "The Star Who Thinks Nobody Loves Her," *Saturday Evening Post*, April 2, 1955, quoted in Clarke, *Get Happy*, 337.

47. David Cunard, liner notes for *Lady in the Dark: Starring Ann Sothern*, American Entertainment Industries AEI-CD 041.

48. V. A., "Television: Liebman Bounces Back, Offers Exciting *Lady in the Dark* in Color, N.B.C. 'Spectacular' Stars Ann Sothern," *New York Times*, September 27, 1954; John Crosby, "Lady in Color," *New York Herald Tribune*, September 27, 1954; Harriet Van Horne, "*Lady in the Dark*: A 23-Carat Dazzler," *New York Sun*, September 27, 1954. Paul McGrath, who had played the role of Kendall Nesbitt during *Lady in the Dark*'s second season, reprised his role for the television special.

49. Interview of Risë Stevens by Mario Mercado, liner notes to *Kurt Weill's Lady in the Dark*, Masterworks Heritage Vocal Series, Sony Classical MHK 62869.

50. Copies of the proposed Tams-Witmark contract with a typescript letter dated January 25, 1965, from Louis H. Aborn (president of Tams-Witmark Music Library, Inc.) to Irving Cohen, Esq., and the signed contract of March 25, 1965, WLRC.

51. Robert Windeler, *Julie Andrews: A Biography* (New York: St. Martin's Press, 1983; reprint, 1986), 166.

52. Robert Windeler, *Julie Andrews: A Biography* (New York: Putnam, 1970), 207, 208, 209.

53. Julie Andrews, "Special Introduction," *Star!*, VHS, directed by Robert Wise (Beverly Hills: Fox Video, 1993).

54. Windeler, *Julie Andrews* (1983 ed.), 160, 162, 164, 165.

55. Les Spindle, *Julie Andrews: A Bio-Bibliography*, Bio-Bibliographies in the Performing Arts, ed. James Robert Parish, No. 6 (New York: Greenwood Press, 1989), 15.

56. Robert Windeler, *Julie Andrews: A Life on Stage and Screen* (Secaucus, NJ: Carol Publishing Group, 1997), 147.

57. Spindle, *Julie Andrews*, 17, 133.

58. *Das Verlorene Lied*, WLRC. It is stamped "OMGUS [Office of Military Government, United States] 9–732 L&P Mar. 49 1M."

59. Gottfried, *Nobody's Fool*, 324.

60. Marian Bryson, "Dated European Stage Premiere," *Stage*, December 27, 1981; Charles Osborne, "*Lady in the Dark*," *Opera* 33 (April 1982): 429–30.

61. John Mauceri, "Programme Notes," *Edinburgh International Festival 1988*, program for August 31, 1988.

62. Gerald Larner, "Weill's Lyrical, Lilting *Lady*," *Guardian*, September 2, 1988.

Epilogue

1. Adeline Fitzgerald, "These Charming People," *Chicago Herald American*, July 21, 1943.

Selected Bibliography and Discography

This bibliography is not a complete accounting of every work and source I consulted. Rather, it indicates the range of sources and readings on which I have based my research. The discography includes only the most important recordings of *Lady in the Dark*. I have not endeavored to include instrumental arrangements or vocal renditions of individual numbers, save for those made by original cast members. Nor have I included subsequent compilation albums by these artists that contain songs from *Lady in the Dark*.

Primary Sources

Archival Sources

BRTC	Billy Rose Theatre Collection, The New York Public Library for the Performing Arts
DSP	Dore Shary Papers, State Historical Society of Wisconsin
FS	Frank Spencer Production Script
GC	Gershwin Collection, Library of Congress
GLP	Gertrude Lawrence Papers, Museum of the City of New York
GLS	Gertrude Lawrence Scrapbooks, The New York Public Library for the Performing Arts
HCP	Hattie Carnegie Papers, Museum of the City of New York
HH	Harry Horner Production Script, Billy Rose Theatre Collection
KWP	Kurt Weill Papers, Museum of the City of New York
MCNY	Museum of the City of New York
MH-KCP	Moss Hart–Kitty Carlisle Papers, State Historical Society of Wisconsin
WCFTR	Wisconsin Center for Film and Theater Research, State Historical Society of Wisconsin

WLA   Weill/Lenya Archive, The Beinecke Rare Book Library, Yale University
WLRC   Weill-Lenya Research Center, New York
ZP   Zelenko Papers, Weill-Lenya Research Center, New York

Oral History Interviews with Cast and Crew

Abravanel, Maurice. Interview by author, January 31, 1991. Rochester, NY. Tape recording.

———. Telephone interview by author, February 13, 1992. Tape recording.

———. Telephone interview by author, October 4, 1991. Tape recording.

Elliott, Rose Marie. Telephone interview by author, November 2, 1993. Tape recording.

Gershwin, Ira. *A Living Liner: Recollections of Kurt Weill*, RCA Victor LL-201 (SRLM-8309), originally included with the Morton Gould recording *The Two Worlds of Kurt Weill*, RCA Victor LSC-2863, WLRC.

Harden, Dan. Telephone interview by author, September 21, 1993. Tape recording.

Hart, Moss. "Thirty-five Years of Broadway Musicals." Interview by Brooks Atkinson. Broadcast June 17, 1960, on WQXR, New York, MH-KCP.

Hearn, Fred. Telephone interview by author, January 20, 1994. Tape recording.

Hecht, Manfred. Telephone interview by author, September 16, 1993. Tape recording.

Lee, Ann. Telephone interview by author, March 31, 1994. Tape recording.

Marel, William. Telephone interview by author, September 8, 1993. Tape recording.

Nicholas, Carl. Telephone interview by author, September 7, 1993. Tape recording.

Perrone, Fred, and Christine Horn. Telephone interview by author, January 13, 1994. Tape recording.

Spencer, Frank. Telephone interview by author, April 9, 1994. Tape recording.

Stonzek, Morris. "I Remember...Recollections of Weill and Lenya by Their Associates." International Kurt Weill Conference and Festival, Yale University, November 4, 1983. Tape recording, WLRC.

Playbills

Playbill (1). Colonial Theatre, Boston, BRTC.
Playbills (58). Alvin Theatre, New York, BRTC.
Playbill (1). Forrest Theatre, Philadelphia, BRTC.
Playbill (1). Nixon Theater, Pittsburgh, BRTC.
Playbill (1). Cass Theatre, Detroit, BRTC.
Playbill (1). American Theater, St. Louis, BRTC.
Playbills (12). Broadway Theatre, New York, BRTC.
Playbill (1). Curran Theatre, San Francisco, BRTC.
Playbill (1). Philharmonic Auditorium, Los Angeles, BRTC.

1941 Souvenir Playbill, BRTC.
1941–1942 Souvenir Playbill, BRTC.
1942–1943 Souvenir Playbill, BRTC.

Newspapers and Periodicals

Baltimore Evening Sun: October 28, November 6, 1942.
Baltimore News-Post: October 28, 1942.
Baltimore Sun: October 28, 1942.
Boston American: December 30, 1940; January 20, 1941.
Boston Evening Transcript: December 31, 1940.
Boston Globe: December 31, 1940; August 17, 1941; August 5, 1942.
Boston Herald: December 31, 1940; January 4, 1941.
Boston Post: December 31, 1940; January 12, 1941; September 26, 1943.
Boston Traveler: December 31, 1940; January 3, March 12, June 19, 1941.
Brooklyn Eagle: January 28, 1941.
California News: February 28, 1941.
Camden (NJ) *Courier-Post*: May 3, 1943.
Chicago Daily News: January 20, 1943.
Chicago Daily Times: January 20, 1943.
Chicago Daily Tribune: September 14, 1941; January 20, February 14, 1943.
Chicago Herald American: February 1, February 6, 1943.
Chicago Herald Tribune: January 3, January 20, January 27, 1943.
Chicago Journal of Commerce: January 20, 1943.
Chicago Sun: January 20, February 1, February 2, February 15, 1943.
Christian Science Monitor: December 31, 1940.
Cincinnati Enquirer: December 29, 1942.
Cincinnati Post: December 27, December 29, 1942.
Cincinnati Times-Star: December 29, 1942.
Cleveland News: November 25, 1942.
Cleveland Plain Dealer: November 25, 1942.
Cleveland Press: October 20, November 5, November 25, 1942.
Columbus (GA) *Ledger-Enquirer*: April 13, 1941.
Columbia (SC) *State*: April 6, 1941.
Coronet: March 1944.
Dallas News: February 23, 1941.
Daily Mirror (New York): January 24, February 24, April 21, June 7, September 4, 1941; November 12, 1942; March 1, 1943.
Daily News (New York): January 9, January 24, January 25, September 3, December 11, 1941; March 1, June 29, July 8, 1943.
Daily News Record (New York): January 31, 1941.
Daily Variety: February 10, 1944.
Detroit Evening News: December 1, December 2, 1942.
Detroit Free Press: September 6, 1941; December 2, 1942.
Detroit News: December 1, December 2, December 8, 1942.

Equity: November 1942.

Green Magazine (Boston): January 3, 1941.

Guardian (London): September 2, 1988.

Hollywood Citizen News: January 23, 1941.

Hollywood Reporter: February 10, 1944.

Los Angeles Examiner: June 23, 1943.

Los Angeles Herald: June 23, 1943.

Los Angeles News: June 23, 1943.

Los Angeles Times: June 9, June 23, June 24, 1943; February 10, 1944.

Madisonville (KY) *Messenger*: January 28, 1941.

Miami News: February 9, 1941.

Minneapolis Tribune: January 3, 1943.

Montgomery (AL) *Advertiser*: March 30, 1941.

Motion Picture Herald: February 19, 1944.

New York Enquirer: February 26, 1941.

New York Herald Tribune: January 24, January 27, February 9, February 16, February 23, May 18, September 7, September 21, October 16, December 7, 1941; April 26, August 9, November 13, 1942; March 1, March 7, 1943; September 27, 1954.

New York Journal-American: January 24, January 25, May 27, September 3, September 7, December 16, 1941.

New York Journal of Commerce: February 20, 1941.

New York Post: January 16, January 24, January 27, February 19, April 21, September 3, September 28, December 23, 1941; March 1, 1943.

New York Sun: February 3, 1940; January 24, February 3, March 28, April 30, September 3, 1941; March 1, May 25, June 4, 1943; September 27, 1954.

New York Telegraph: February 12, August 20, December 19, 1941.

New York Times: May 16, 1932; November 7, 1937; January 11, February 18, February 24, February 26, March 3, March 13, March 17, March, 22, March 24, April 16, May 5, November 13, December 26, 1940; January 1, January 24, May 25, September 3, September 7, December 16, 1941; February 11, March 13, October 26, November 26, December 27, 1942; January 26, February 28, March 1, April 1, May 16, August 1, 1943; January 23, February 23, 1944; October 26, 1947; September 10, September 27, 1954.

New York World-Telegram: December 21, 1935; January 24, February 14, February 21, June 3, June 16, September 2, September 3, October 15, 1941; February 27, June 16, 1942; March 1, 1943.

Norwalk (CT) *Hour*: March 31, 1941.

Oakland Tribune: July 15, 1941; June 15, 1943.

Opera: April 1982.

Philadelphia Bulletin: September 29, 1942.

Philadelphia Inquirer: September 29, 1942.

Philadelphia News: September 29, 1942.

Philadelphia Record: September 27, September 29, 1942.

Pittsburgh (MA) *Sentinel*: February 1, 1941.

Pittsburgh Carnegie Tartan: November 24, 1942.

Pittsburgh Post-Gazette: January 9, 1941; November 10, November 11, November 16, 1942.

Pittsburgh Press: November 4, November 10, November 11, 1942.

Pittsburgh Sun-Telegraph: November 11, 1942.

Playbill: February 3, June 2, December 29, 1941; April 6, 1942; March 14, May 9, 1943.

PM (New York): January 24, January 26, February 3, September 3, 1941.

Rochester (NY) *Democrat & Chronicle*: May 9, 1943.

St. Louis Globe-Democrat: December 25, 1942; January 6, 1943.

St. Louis Post-Dispatch: January 6, 1943.

St. Louis Star-Times: January 6, 1943.

San Francisco Call Bulletin: May 25, 1943.

San Francisco Chronicle: February 2, 1941; May 26, 1943.

Stage: December 27, 1981.

Toledo Blade: September 15, 1941.

Variety: January 8, January 15, January 29, February 12, April 23, June 4, June 11, 1941; March 4, March 25, June 3, October 7, November 4, November 18, November 25, December 9, December 23, 1942; January 6, January 20, January 27, March 3, May 23, May 26, June 7, July 7, July 14, 1943; February 16, 1944.

Vogue: February 15, 1941.

Washington (DC) *Times-Herald*: December 27, 1941; October 27, November 12, 1942.

Waterbury (CT) *Democrat*: March 2, 1943.

Wheeling (WV) *News Register*: April 12, 1942.

Wilmington (DE) *Star*: December 6, 1942.

Woman's Home Companion: October 1943.

Women's Wear Daily: February 11, February 18, February 19, February 20, February 26, 1941.

Worcester (MA) *Gazette & Post*: January 4, 1941.

Your Charm: April 1941.

Works by Cast and Crew

"Brooks, Dr." [Lawrence S. Kubie]. Preface to *Lady in the Dark*, by Moss Hart, Ira Gershwin, and Kurt Weill. New York: Random House, 1941. Reprint, Cleveland: NY: World Publishing, 1944.

Hart, Moss. Foreword to *Lady in the Dark*, vocal score, by Kurt Weill and Ira Gershwin. Edited by Albert Sirmay. New York: Chappell Music Company, 1941.

———. "The How and Why of *Lady in the Dark*." *Lady in the Dark* Souvenir Playbills, BRTC.

———. "Life with Gertie: In Which Some Light Is Thrown on *Lady in the Dark*," MH-KCP.

——. "One World—One Trip—One Play," MH-KCP.

——. "The Saga of Gertie: The Author of *Lady in the Dark* Tells How He Found a Star." *New York Times*, March 2, 1941.

Horner, Harry. "Designer in Action." *Theatre Arts* 25 (1941): 265–75.

[——]. "Sam H. Harris Presents Gertrude Lawrence in *Lady in the Dark*." *Modern Plastics* 18 (April 1941): 34, 35, 90, 92.

——. "Of Those Four Revolving Stages," *New York Times*, April 6, 1941.

——. "Twenty Minutes of the Show." *Christian Science Monitor*, February 28, 1941.

Lawrence, Gertrude. Letter to the editor. *New York Times*, December 6, 1941.

——. "Touring the Provinces: Miss Lawrence Has Fun as She Gads about Wartime America." *New York Times*, March 7, 1943.

Sharaff, Irene. "*Lady in the Dark*." *Theatre Arts* 25 (1941): 166.

Weill, Kurt. "Broadway and the Musical Theatre." *Composer's News-Record*, May 1947.

——. "Dreams are, at the moment…," WLA.

——. "Score for a Play." *New York Times*, January 5, 1947.

——. "Two Dreams-Come-True," WLA.

——. "What Is Musical Theatre?," WLA.

Published/Rental Scripts

Hart, Moss, Ira Gershwin, and Kurt Weill. *Lady in the Dark*. New York: Random House, 1941. Reprint, Cleveland, NY: World Publishing, 1944.

——. *Lady in the Dark*. Acting ed. New York: Dramatists Play Service, n.d.

——. *Lady in the Dark*. New York: Tams-Witmark, [1965].

——. *Lady in the Dark*. In *Great Musicals of the American Theatre*, edited by Stanley Richards, 2: 55–123. Radnor, PA: Chilton, 1976.

Published Music

Weill, Kurt, and Ira Gershwin. "Girl of the Moment." Sheet music. New York: Chappell, 1941.

——. "Jenny." Sheet music. New York: Chappell, 1941.

——. *Lady in the Dark*. Vocal score. Edited by Albert Sirmay. New York: Chappell Music Co., 1941.

——. "My Ship." Sheet music. New York: Chappell, 1941.

——. "One Life to Live." Sheet music. New York: Chappell, 1941.

——. "The Princess of Pure Delight." Sheet music. New York: Chappell, 1941.

——. "This Is New." Sheet music. New York: Chappell, 1941.

——. "Tschaikowsky (and Other Russians)." Sheet music. New York: Chappell, 1941.

Secondary Sources

Memoirs and Published Correspondence

Carey, Macdonald. *The Days of My Life*. New York: St. Martin's Press, 1991.

Carlisle Hart, Kitty. *Kitty: An Autobiography*. New York: Doubleday, 1988. Reprint, New York: St. Martin's Press 1989.

Clurman, Harold. *The Fervent Years: The Story of the Group Theatre and the Thirties*. New York: Knopf, 1945. Reprint, New York: Da Capo Press, 1983.

Coward, Noël. *Future Indefinite*. London: William Heinemann, 1954. Reprint, New York: Da Capo Press, 1980.

Crawford, Cheryl. *One Naked Individual: My Fifty Years in the Theatre*. Indianapolis: Bobbs-Merrill, 1977.

Engel, Lehman. *This Bright Day: An Autobiography*. New York: Macmillan, 1974.

Gershwin, Ira. *Lyrics on Several Occasions: A Selection of Stage & Screen Lyrics Written for Sundry Situations; and Now Arranged in Arbitrary Categories. To Which Have Been Added Many Informative Annotations & Disquisitions on Their Why & Wherefore, Their Whom-for, Their How; and Matters Associative*. New York: Knopf, 1959. Reprint, New York: Limelight, 1997.

———. "Which Came First?" *Saturday Review*, August 29, 1959, 31–33, 45.

Hart, Moss. *Act One: An Autobiography*. New York: Random House, 1959. Reprint, 2002.

Lawrence, Gertrude. *A Star Danced*. Garden City, NY: Doubleday, Doran, 1945.

Rogers, Ginger. *Ginger: My Story*. New York: Harper Collins, 1991.

Schary, Dore. *Heyday: An Autobiography*. Boston: Little, Brown, 1979. Reprint, New York: Berkley Books, 1981.

Sharaff, Irene. *Broadway and Hollywood: Costumes Designed by Irene Sharaff*. New York: Van Nostrand Reinhold, 1976.

Weill, Kurt, and Lotte Lenya. *Speak Low (When You Speak Love): The Letters of Kurt Weill and Lotte Lenya*. Edited and translated by Lys Symonette and Kim H. Kowalke. Berkeley: University of California Press, 1996.

Wharton, John F. *Life among the Playwrights: Being Mostly the Story of the Playwright's Producing Company, Inc*. New York: Quadrangle/New York Times Book Co., 1974.

Lady in the Dark

Fuller, Thomas D. "A Concordance to *Lady in the Dark*," WLRC.

———. "I *Love* Russian Composers!," WLRC.

mcclung, bruce d. "American Dreams: Analyzing Moss Hart, Ira Gershwin, and Kurt Weill's *Lady in the Dark*." PhD diss., University of Rochester, 1994.

———. "Art Imitating Life Imitating Art: *Lady in the Dark*, Gertrude Lawrence, and *Star!*" *Kurt Weill Newsletter* 19, no. 2 (2001): 4–7, 12.

———. "Life after George: The Genesis of *Lady in the Dark*'s *Circus Dream*." *Kurt Weill Newsletter* 14, no. 2 (1996): 4–8.

————. "*Psicosi per musica*: Re-examining *Lady in the Dark*." In *A Stranger Here Myself: Kurt Weill Studien*, edited by Kim H. Kowalke and Horst Edler, 235–65. Haskala wissenschaftliche Abhandlungen, No. 8. Hildesheim, Germany: Georg Olms Verlag, 1993.

mcclung, bruce, Joanna Lee, and Kim Kowalke, eds. *Lady in the Dark: A Sourcebook*. 2nd ed. New York: Kurt Weill Foundation for Music, 1997.

New York Theaters

Henderson, Mary C. *The City and the Theatre: The History of New York Playhouses, A 250 Year Journey from Bowling Green to Times Square*. Revised and expanded ed. New York: Back Stage Books, 2004.

Morrison, William. *Broadway Theatres: History and Architecture*. Mineola, NY: Dover, 1999.

Young, William C. *Documents of American Theater History*. Vol. 2, *Famous American Playhouses, 1900–1971*. Chicago: American Library Association, 1973. Reprint, 1986.

American Theater

Alpert, Hollis. *The Life and Times of Porgy and Bess: The Story of an American Classic*. New York: Knopf, 1990.

Anderson, Maxwell. *Off Broadway: Essays about the Theater*. New York: William Sloane, 1947. Reprint, New York: Da Capo Press, 1971.

Atkinson, Brooks. *Broadway*. Revised ed. New York: Macmillan, 1974. New York: Limelight Editions, 1985.

————. *Broadway Scrapbook*. New York: Theatre Arts, 1947. Reprint, Westport, CT: Greenwood Press, 1970.

Banfield, Stephen. *Sondheim's Broadway Musicals*. Michigan American Music Series, edited by Richard Crawford. Ann Arbor: University of Michigan Press, 1993.

Block, Geoffrey. *Enchanted Evenings: The Broadway Musical from Show Boat to Sondheim*. New York: Oxford University Press, 1997. Reprint, 2003.

Bordman, Gerald. *American Musical Comedy: From Adonis to Dreamgirls*. New York: Oxford University Press, 1982. Reprint, Bridgewater, NJ: Replica Books, 2000.

————. *American Musical Theatre: A Chronicle*. 3rd ed. New York: Oxford University Press, 2001.

————. *American Operetta: From H.M.S. Pinafore to Sweeney Todd*. New York: Oxford University Press, 1981.

Clurman, Harold. *The Collected Works of Harold Clurman: Six Decades of Commentary on Theatre, Dance, Music, Film, Arts and Letters*. Edited by Marjorie Loggia and Glenn Young. New York: Applause Books, 1994.

Curtin, Kaier. *"We Can Always Call Them Bulgarians": The Emergence of Lesbians and Gay Men on the American Stage*. Boston: Alyson Publications, 1987.

Donovan, Timothy P. "Oh, What a Beautiful Mornin': The Musical, *Oklahoma!* and the Popular Mind in 1943." *Journal of Popular Culture* 8 (1974): 477–88.

Engel, Lehman. *The American Musical Theater*. Revised ed. New York: Macmillan, 1975.

Everett, William, and Paul Laird, eds. *The Cambridge Companion to the Musical*. Cambridge, UK: Cambridge University Press, 2002.

Ewen, David. *The Story of America's Musical Theater*. Revised ed. New York: Chilton, 1968.

Green, Stanley. *Broadway Musicals Show by Show*. 5th ed. Revised by Kay Green. New York: Hal Leonard, 2001.

———. *The World of Musical Comedy: The Story of the American Musical Stage as Told through the Careers of Its Foremost Composers and Lyricists*. 4th ed., revised and enlarged. New York: Da Capo Press, 1984.

Guernsey, Otis L., Jr. *Broadway Song and Story: Playwrights/Lyricists/Composers Discuss Their Hits*. New York: Dodd, Mead, 1985.

Hasbany, Richard. "Bromidic Parables: The American Musical Theatre During the Second World War." *Journal of Popular Culture* 6 (1973): 642–65.

Hyland, William G. *Richard Rodgers*. New Haven: Yale University Press, 1998.

Jones, John Bush. *Our Musicals, Ourselves: A Social History of the American Musical Theatre*. Hanover, NH: Brandeis University Press, University Press of New England, 2003.

Kislan, Richard. *The Musical: A Look at the American Musical Theater*. Revised and expanded ed. New York: Applause Books, 1995.

Kowalke, Kim H. "'I Hate Brecht!': Sondheim, *Love Life*, and the Concept Musical." Paper presented at the 1998 annual meeting of the American Musicological Society, Boston.

Kreuger, Miles. *Show Boat: The Story of a Classic American Musical*. New York: Oxford University Press, 1977. Reprint, New York: Applause Books, 1995.

Laufe, Abe. *Broadway's Greatest Musicals*. Revised ed. New York: Funk & Wagnalls, 1977.

Loney, Glenn, ed. *Musical Theatre in America: Papers and Proceedings of the Conference on the Musical Theatre in America*. Westport, CT: Greenwood Press, 1984.

Mantle, Burns, ed. *The Best Plays of 1940–1941 and the Year Book of the Drama in America*. New York: Dodd, Mead, 1941. Reprint, 1969.

———, ed. *The Best Plays of 1941–1942 and the Year Book of the Drama in America*. New York: Dodd, Mead, 1942. Reprint, 1969.

———, ed. *The Best Plays of 1942–1943 and the Year Book of the Drama in America*. New York: Dodd, Mead, 1943. Reprint, 1968.

Mates, Julian. *America's Musical Stage: Two Hundred Years of Musical Theatre*. Westport, CT: Greenwood Press, 1985. Reprint, New York: Praeger, 1987.

Mordden, Ethan. *Beautiful Mornin': The Broadway Musical in the 1940s*. New York: Oxford University Press, 1999.

————. *Better Foot Forward: The History of American Musical Theatre*. New York: Grossman, 1976.

————. *Broadway Babies: The People Who Made the American Musical*. New York: Oxford University Press, 1983. Reprint, 1988.

O'Connor, John, and Lorraine Brown, eds. *The Federal Theatre Project: "Free, Adult, Uncensored."* London: Eyre Methuen, 1980. Reprint, 1986.

Smith, Cecil, and Glenn Litton. *Musical Comedy in America*. 2nd ed. New York: Routledge, 1991.

Smith, Wendy. *Real Life Drama: The Group Theatre and America, 1931–1940*. New York: Knopf, 1990. Reprint, New York: Grove Weidenfeld, 1992.

Swain, Joseph P. *The Broadway Musical: A Critical and Musical Survey*. 2nd ed. Lanham, MD: Scarecrow Press, 2002.

Traubner, Richard. *Operetta: A Theatrical History*. Revised ed. New York: Routledge, 2003.

Tumbusch, Tom. *The Theatre Student: Guide to Broadway Musical Theatre*. Revised ed. New York: Rosen, 1983.

Wilder, Alec. *American Popular Song: The Great Innovators, 1900–1950*. Edited by James Maher. New York: Oxford University Press, 1990.

Wilk, Max. *OK! The Story of Oklahoma!* 2nd ed. New York: Grove Press, 2002.

Moss Hart

Aronson, Steven M. L. "Broadway Legends: Moss Hart, the Playwright's Fairview Farm in Pennsylvania." *Architectural Digest*, November 1995, 170–73, 265–66.

Atkinson, Brooks, Bennett Cerf, Edna Ferber, Alan J. Lerner, Howard Lindsay, and Dore Schary. *A Memorial Tribute to Moss Hart*. New York: Random House, 1962.

Bach, Steven. *Dazzler: The Life and Times of Moss Hart*. New York: Knopf, 2001. Reprint, Cambridge: Da Capo Press, 2002.

Farmer, Patrick Alan. "Moss Hart: American Playwright/Director." PhD diss., Kent State University, 1980.

Gilder, Rosamond. "The Fabulous Hart." *Theatre Arts* 28 (1944): 92–98.

Goldstein, Malcolm. *George S. Kaufman: His Life, His Theater*. New York: Oxford University Press, 1979.

Pollack, Rhoda-Gale. *George S. Kaufman*. Boston: Twayne, 1988.

Kurt Weill

Citron, Atay. "Pageantry and Theatre in the Service of Jewish Nationalism in the United States: 1933–1946." PhD diss., New York University, 1989.

Cook, Susan C. *Opera for a New Republic: The "Zeitopern" of Krenek, Weill, and Hindemith*. Studies in Musicology, No. 96. Ann Arbor, MI: UMI Research Press, 1988.

Drew, David. *Kurt Weill: A Handbook.* Berkeley: University of California Press, 1987.

———. "Motifs, Tags, and Related Matters." In *Kurt Weill: The Threepenny Opera*, edited by Stephen Hinton, 149–60. Cambridge Opera Handbooks. Cambridge, UK: Cambridge University Press, 1990.

Farneth, David, Elmar Juchem, and Dave Stein. *Kurt Weill: A Life in Pictures and Documents.* Woodstock, NY: Overlook Press, 2000.

Graziano, John. "Musical Dialects in *Down in the Valley.*" In *A New Orpheus: Essays on Kurt Weill*, edited by Kim H. Kowalke, 297–319. New Haven: Yale University Press, 1986. Reprint, 1990.

Hirsch, Foster. *Kurt Weill on Stage: From Berlin to Broadway.* New York: Knopf, 2002. Reprint, New York: Limelight Editions, 2003.

Kilroy, David Michael. "Kurt Weill on Broadway: The Postwar Years (1945–1950)." PhD diss., Harvard University, 1992.

Kowalke, Kim H. *Kurt Weill in Europe.* Studies in Musicology, No. 14. Ann Arbor, MI: UMI Research Press, 1979.

———. "The Threepenny Opera in America." In *Kurt Weill: The Threepenny Opera*, edited by Stephen Hinton, 78–119. Cambridge Opera Handbooks. Cambridge, UK: Cambridge University Press, 1990.

Robinson, J. Bradford. "Learning the Ropes: Kurt Weill and the American Theater Song." *Kurt Weill Newsletter* 15, no. 2 (1997): 3–7.

Sanders, Ronald. *The Days Grow Short: The Life and Music of Kurt Weill.* New York: Holt, Rinehart, and Winston, 1980. Reprint, Los Angeles: Silman-James Press, 1991.

Scott, Matthew. "Weill in America: The Problem of Revival." In *A New Orpheus: Essays on Kurt Weill*, edited by Kim H. Kowalke, 285–95. New Haven: Yale University Press, 1986. Reprint, 1990.

Spoto, Donald. *Lenya: A Life.* Boston: Little, Brown, 1989. Reprint, New York: Ballantine Books, 1990.

Stempel, Larry. "*Street Scene* and the Enigma of Broadway Opera." In *A New Orpheus: Essays on Kurt Weill*, edited by Kim H. Kowalke, 321–34. New Haven: Yale University Press, 1986. Reprint, 1990.

Thornhill, William R. "Kurt Weill's *Street Scene.*" PhD diss., University of North Carolina, Chapel Hill, 1990.

Willard, Charles. "Life's 'Progress': *Love Life* Revisited." *Kurt Weill Newsletter* 2, no. 2 (1984): 4–5, 8.

Ira Gershwin

Furia, Philip. *Ira Gershwin: The Art of the Lyricist.* New York: Oxford University Press, 1996. Reprint, 1997.

Gershwin, Ira. *The Complete Lyrics of Ira Gershwin.* Edited by Robert Kimball. New York: Knopf, 1993. Reprint, New York: Da Capo Press, 1998.

Jablonski, Edward. *Gershwin.* New York: Doubleday, 1987. Reprint, Boston: Northeastern University Press, 1990.

Jablonski, Edward, and Lawrence D. Stewart. *The Gershwin Years*. New York: Doubleday, 1973. Reprint, New York: Da Capo Press, 1996.

Kimball, Robert, and Alfred Simon. *The Gershwins*. New York: Atheneum, 1973.

Rosenberg, Deena. *Fascinating Rhythm: The Collaboration of George and Ira Gershwin*. New York: Dutton, 1991. Reprint, Ann Arbor: University of Michigan Press, 1997.

Cast, Crew, and Close Associates

Aldrich, Richard Stoddard. *Gertrude Lawrence as Mrs. A: An Intimate Biography of the Great Star*. New York: Greystone Press, 1954. Reprint, New York: Greenwood Press, 1969.

Berkman, Ted. *The Lady and the Law: The Remarkable Life of Fanny Holtzmann*. Boston: Little, Brown, 1976. Reprint, Carpinteria, CA: Manifest, 1999.

Coward, Noël. *Future Indefinite*. London: William Heinemann, 1954. Reprint, New York: Da Capo Press, 1980.

———. *The Noël Coward Diaries*. Edited by Graham Payn and Sheridan Morley. Boston: Little, Brown, 1982. Reprint, London: Phoenix, 2000.

Dwight, Eleanor. *Diana Vreeland*. New York: HarperCollins, 2002.

Fine Collins, Amy. "The Cult of Diana." *Vanity Fair* 56 (November 1993): 174–83, 188–90.

Gottfried, Martin. *Nobody's Fool: The Lives of Danny Kaye*. New York: Simon & Schuster, 1994.

Mercado, Mario R. "I Remember: A Podium with a View—Recollections by Maurice Abravanel." *Kurt Weill Newsletter* 5, no. 1 (1987): 6–8.

Morley, Sheridan. *Gertrude Lawrence*. New York: McGraw-Hill, 1981.

Sharaff, Irene. *Broadway and Hollywood: Costumes Designed by Irene Sharaff*. New York: Van Nostrand Reinhold, 1976.

Vreeland, Diana. *D. V.* Edited by George Plimpton and Christopher Hemphill. New York: Knopf, 1984. Reprint, Cambridge: Da Capo Press, 2003.

Sigmund Freud, Lawrence S. Kubie, and Psychoanalysis

Brody, Eugene B. "Lawrence S. Kubie's Psychoanalysis." In Lawrence S. Kubie, *Symbol and Neurosis: Selected Papers of Lawrence S. Kubie*, edited by Herbert J. Schlesinger, 1–40. Psychological Issues, No. 44. New York: International Universities Press, 1978.

Freud, Sigmund. *The Standard Edition of the Complete Psychological Works of Sigmund Freud*. Edited and translated by James Strachey. Vol 4: *The Interpretation of Dreams* (First Part); Vol. 5: *The Interpretation of Dreams* (Second Part) and *On Dreams*; Vol. 12: *The Case of Schreber, Papers on Technique, and Other Works*. London: Hogarth Press and The Institute of Psycho-analysis, 1958.

Gabbard, Glen O., and Krin Gabbard. *Psychiatry and the Cinema*. 2nd ed. Washington, DC: American Psychiatric Press, 1999.

Gay, Peter. *Freud: A Life for Our Time*. New York: Norton, 1988. Reprint, 1998.

Glover, Edward. "In Honor of Lawrence Kubie." *Journal of Nervous and Mental Disease* 149, no. 1 (1969): 5–18.

Hale, Nathan G., Jr. *Freud and the Americans: The Beginnings of Psychoanalysis in the United States, 1876–1917*. New York: Oxford University Press, 1971. Reprint, 1995.

———. *The Rise and Crisis of Psychoanalysis in the United States: Freud and the Americans, 1917–1985*. New York: Oxford University Press, 1995.

Kubie, Lawrence S. "The Drive to Become Both Sexes." *Psychoanalytic Quarterly* 43 (1974): 349–426. Reprinted in Lawrence S. Kubie, *Symbol and Neurosis: Selected Papers of Lawrence S. Kubie*, edited by Herbert J. Schlesinger, 191–263. Psychological Issues, No. 44. New York: International Universities Press, 1978.

———. *Neurotic Distortion of the Creative Process*. Porter Lectures, No. 22. Lawrence: University of Kansas Press, 1958. Reprint, New York: Noonday Press, 1975.

———. *Practical Aspects of Psychoanalysis: A Handbook for Prospective Patients and Their Advisors*. New York: Norton, 1936.

———. "Psychiatry and the Films." *Hollywood Quarterly* 2 (1947): 113–17.

———. "Some Unsolved Problems of the Scientific Career, Part I." *American Scientist* 41 (1953): 596–613.

Pumpian-Mindlin, Eugene, Ernest R. Hilgard, and Lawrence S. Kubie. *Psychoanalysis as Science: The Hixon Lectures on the Scientific Status of Psychoanalysis*. Stanford: Stanford University Press, 1952. Reprint, Westport, CT: Greenwood Press, 1970.

Schneider, Irving. "Images of the Mind: Psychiatry in the Commercial Film." *American Journal of Psychiatry* 134 (1977): 613–20.

Sievers, W. David. *Freud on Broadway: A History of Psychoanalysis and the American Drama*. New York: Hermitage House, 1955. Reprint, New York: Cooper Square, 1970.

Silverman, Kaja. *The Acoustic Mirror: The Female Voice in Psychoanalysis and Cinema*. Theories of Representation and Difference, edited by Teresa de Lauretis. Bloomington: Indiana University Press, 1988.

Zilboorg, Gregory. *Sigmund Freud: His Exploration of the Mind of Man*. New York: Scribner, 1951. Reprint, Clifton, NJ: A. M. Kelley, 1973.

Revivals

Billips, Connie, and Arthur Pierce. *Lux Presents Hollywood: A Show-by-Show History of the Lux Radio Theatre and the Lux Video Theatre, 1934–1957*. Jefferson, NC: McFarland, 1995.

Chierichetti, David. *Mitchell Leisen: Hollywood Director*. Los Angeles: Photoventures Press, 1995.

Clarke, Gerald. *Get Happy: The Life of Judy Garland*. New York: Random House, 2000.

Dickens, Homer. *The Films of Ginger Rogers.* Secaucus, NJ: Citadel Press, 1975.

Halliwell, Leslie. *Mountain of Dreams: The Golden Years of Paramount Pictures.* New York: Stonehill, 1976.

Morley, Sheridan. *Shall We Dance: The Life of Ginger Rogers.* New York: St. Martin's Press, 1995.

Spindle, Les. *Julie Andrews: A Bio-Bibliography.* Bio-Bibliographies in the Performing Arts, edited by James Robert Parish, No. 6. New York: Greenwood Press, 1989.

Windeler, Robert. *Julie Andrews: A Biography.* New York: Putnam, 1970.

———. *Julie Andrews: A Biography.* New York: St. Martin's Press, 1983. Reprint, 1986.

———. *Julie Andrews: A Life on Stage and Screen.* Secaucus, NJ: Birch Lane Press, 1997.

American Social History

Basinger, Jeanine. *A Woman's View: How Hollywood Spoke to Women, 1930–1960.* New York: Knopf, 1993. Reprint, Hanover, NH: Wesleyan University Press, 1995.

Chafe, William. *The Unfinished Journey: America since World War II.* 5th ed. New York: Oxford University Press, 2003.

Elder, Glen H., Jr. *Children of the Great Depression: Social Change in Life Experience.* 25th Anniversary ed. Boulder, CO: Westview Press, 1999.

Filene, Peter. *Him/Her/Self: Sex Roles in Modern America.* 2nd ed. Baltimore: Johns Hopkins University Press, 1986.

Hartmann, Susan M. *The Home Front and Beyond: American Women in the 1940s.* American Women in the Twentieth Century, edited by Barbara Haber. Boston: Twayne Publishers, 1982. Reprint, 1995.

Henry, George W. "Psychogenic Factors in Overt Homosexuality." *American Journal of Psychiatry* 93 (1937): 889–908.

———. *Sex Variants: A Study of Homosexual Patterns.* 2 vols. New York: Hoeber, 1941. Reprint, 1959.

Komarovsky, Mirra. *The Unemployed Man and His Family: The Effect of Unemployment upon the Status of the Man in Fifty-nine Families.* New York: Dryden Press, 1940. Reprint, Walnut Creek, CA: AltaMira Press, 2004.

May, Elaine Tyler. *Homeward Bound: American Families in the Cold War Era.* Revised and updated ed. New York: Basic Books, 1999.

Millett, Kate. *Sexual Politics.* Garden City, NY: Doubleday, 1970. Reprint, Urbana: University of Illinois Press, 2000.

Minton, Henry L. "Femininity in Men and Masculinity in Women: American Psychiatry and Psychology Portray Homosexuality in the 1930's." *Journal of Homosexuality* 13 (1986): 1–21.

Sanjek, Russell. *American Popular Music and Its Business: The First Four Hundred Years.* Vol. 3, *From 1900 to 1984.* New York: Oxford University Press, 1988.

Sanjek, Russell, and David Sanjek. *American Popular Music Business in the 20th Century*. New York: Oxford University Press, 1991. Reprint, Bridgewater, NJ: Replica Books, 2000.

Scharf, Lois. *To Work and to Wed: Female Employment, Feminism, and the Great Depression*. Contributions in Women's Studies, No. 15. Westport, CT: Greenwood Press, 1980. Reprint, 1985.

Terman, Lewis M., and Catharine Cox Miles. *Sex and Personality: Studies in Masculinity and Femininity*. New York: McGraw-Hill, 1936. Reprint, New York: Russell & Russell, 1968.

Wylie, Philip. *Generation of Vipers*. New York: Rinehart, 1942. Reprint, Normal, IL: Dalkey Archive Press, 1996.

Wyman, David S. *The Abandonment of the Jews: America and the Holocaust, 1941– 1945*. New York: Pantheon, 1984. Reprint, New York: New Press, 1998.

Zim, Larry, Mel Lerner, and Herbert Rolfes. *The World of Tomorrow: The 1939 New York World's Fair*. New York: Harper & Row, 1988.

Discography

1941   Hildegarde, *Lady in the Dark*. Decca 208 [78 rpm].
          Musical selections: "The Saga of Jenny," "This Is New," "Girl of the Moment," "My Ship," "One Life to Live."
          With Robert Hannon.
          Conducted by Harry Sosnik.
          CD edition: Dutton Vocalion CDEA 6078, 2002.
          CD edition ("The Saga of Jenny" only): Prism Platinum PLATCD 999, 2003.

1941   Gertrude Lawrence, *Lady in the Dark*. Victor P-60 [78 rpm].
          Musical selections: "My Ship," "Jenny," "This Is New," "One Life to Live," "Oh, Fabulous One," "Huxley," "Girl of the Moment," "The Princess of Pure Delight."
          Male Quartet: Gordon Gifford, T. Davis Cunningham, Len Frank, William Marel.
          Conducted by Leonard Joy. Musical arrangements by Sidney Green.
          Rereleased: RCA 10″ LRT-7001, with *Nymph Errant*, 1954; RCA Victor LPV 503, with *Down in the Valley*, 1964.
          CD edition (save for "Girl of the Moment" and "Oh, Fabulous One"): AEI-CD 041, 1997
          CD edition: Prism Platinum PLATCD 999, 2003.
          CD edition: Pearl GEM 0208, 2004.

1941   Danny Kaye, *Lady in the Dark*. Columbia 36163, 36042, 36025 [78 rpm].
          Musical selections: "It's Never Too Late to Mendelssohn," "One Life to Live," "The Princess of Pure Delight," "My Ship," "Jenny," "The Trial of Liza Elliott/Tschaikowsky."

Conducted by Maurice Abravanel.

Rereleased: Columbia on LP-107, LP-527, and CL-6249.

CD edition: Sony Classical MHK 62869, 1997.

CD edition: Prism Platinum PLATCD 999, 2003.

1954   Ann Sothern, *Max Liebman Presents Ann Southern in a Musical Play: Lady in the Dark*. RCA Victor LM-1882 [33 1/3 rpm].

Musical selections: "Oh, Fabulous One," "One Life to Live," "Girl of the Moment," "What Is Liza Really Like," "This Is New," "The Greatest Show on Earth," "The Trial of Liza Elliott," "Tschaikowsky," "The Saga of Jenny," "Make Up Your Mind," "My Ship," "Ballet," "Finale."

With Carleton Carpenter, James Daly, Shepperd Strudwick.

Music adapted by Clay Warnick and Mel Pahl. Orchestrations by Irwin Kostal.

Conducted by Charles Sanford.

CD edition: Sepia Records 1052, 2005.

1956   Moss Hart, *Moss Hart Speaking on and Reading from* The Man Who Came to Dinner *and* Lady in the Dark. Distinguished Playwright Series. Spoken Arts 725 [33 1/3 rpm].

Spoken selection: Act I, Scene 1.

Rereleased in the c. 1980–1986 compilation *The Sound of Modern Drama* on Spoken Arts PCC 22 [6 cassettes].

1963   Risë Stevens, *Kurt Weill's Lady in the Dark*. Columbia Masterworks OL 5990 [33 1/3 rpm].

Musical selections: *Glamour Dream*: "Oh Fabulous One," "Huxley," "One Life to Live," "Girl of the Moment"; *Wedding Dream*: "Mapleton High Chorale," "This Is New," "The Princess of Pure Delight"; *Circus Dream*: "The Greatest Show on Earth," "The Best Years of His Life," "Tschaikowsky," "The Saga of Jenny"; *Childhood Dream*: "My Ship."

With Adolph Green and John Reardon.

Conducted by Lehman Engel.

Reissued in 1973 on Columbia COS 2390 [33 1/3 rpm] and BT 2390 [cassette].

Rereleased in 1982 as part of the Time-Life boxed set *American Musicals: Kurt Weill, One Touch of Venus, Lady in the Dark, The Threepenny Opera*, Time Life Records STL-AM10.

CD edition: Sony Classical MHK 62869, 1997.

n.d.   Ginger Rogers, *Ginger Rogers*. Curtain Calls CC 100/21 [33 1/3 rpm].

Musical selections: "Girl of the Moment," "The Greatest Show on Earth," "The Saga of Jenny," "My Ship."

n.d.   Judy Garland, *Lady in the Dark*. Command Performance Records LP-10 [33 1/3 rpm].

Release of 1953 *Lux Radio Theatre* broadcast with Judy Garland and John Lund.

Musical selections: "Girl of the Moment," "One Life to Live," "This is New," "My Ship."

Conductor: Rudy Schrager.

1984   Gertrude Lawrence, *Lady in the Dark*. AEI Records 1146 [33 1/3 rpm].

Release of 1947 *Theatre Guild of the Air* broadcast with Gertrude Lawrence and Macdonald Carey.

Musical selections: "Oh, Fabulous One in Your Ivory Tower," "One Life to Live," "Girl of the Moment," "It Looks Like Liza," "The Saga of Jenny," "My Ship" (Liza), "My Ship" (Liza and Charley).

CD edition: AEI-CD 003, 1993.

1997   Ann Sothern, *Lady in the Dark*. AEI-CD 041 [CD].

Musical selections: *Glamour Dream*: "Introduction," "Oh, Fabulous One," "Hobo Dance," "One Life to Live," "Girl of the Moment," "It Looks Like Liza"; *Wedding Dream*: "Wedding Dream Ballet," "The Mapleton High Chorale," "This Is New," "The Woman at the Altar"; *Circus Dream*: "Scene," "The Greatest Show on Earth," "Transition," "The Best Years of His Life," "Tschaikowsky," "Jenny," "Finaletto"; *Childhood Dream*: "Scene," "Two-Step," "Scene," "My Ship"; *Conclusion*: "My Ship."

Bonus tracks from 1941 Gertrude Lawrence, *Lady in the Dark*, P-60 and 1984 Gertrude Lawrence, *Lady in the Dark*, AEI 1146.

Note: this release is not a reissue of the 1954 cast recording of the NBC televised *Color Spectacular*. Rather, it was edited from the original optical soundtrack of the original Kinescope.

1998   Original London Cast Recording, *The Royal National Theatre Production of Lady in the Dark*. Jay Productions CDJAY 1278 [CD].

Musical selections: "Oh, Fabulous One," "Huxley," "One Life to Live," "Girl of the Moment," "Liza, Liza," "Mapleton High Chorale," "This Is New," "The Princess of Pure Delight," "The Woman at the Altar," "Overture," "The Greatest Show on Earth," "Dance of the Tumblers," "The Best Years of His Life," "Tschaikowsky," "The Saga of Jenny," "My Ship," "Exit Music."

Maria Friedman with James Dreyfus and Steven Edward Moore.

Conducted by Mark W. Dorrell

Index

© Al Hirschfeld/Margo Feiden Galleries Ltd., New York. www.alhirschfeld.com.
Courtesy and permission of Al Hirschfeld/Margo Feiden Galleries Ltd., New York.